Simon and Swerdlik do an excellent job of paying homage to past theoretical and practical supervision models and crafting these into their own easily digestible framework that is definitively "school psychological" in aim and scope. The use of case scenarios aids in demonstrating application of techniques and the use of reflection questions and other activities allows for consolidation of concepts. This text will be invaluable to field supervisors of both practicum and internship students at either level of school psychology training. It should also serve as a primary text in classroom-based pedagogy within school psychology graduate training programs.

—**Greg R. Machek**, Ph.D., Associate Professor of School Psychology, University of Montana, USA

SUPERVI
PSYCHO___.

Supervision is a core professional competency requiring specific training for the benefit of supervisees, clients, and the profession. *Supervision in School Psychology: The Developmental, Ecological, Problem-solving Model* examines specific factors that contribute to successful supervision in school psychology, including the integration of a developmental process of training, the ecological contexts that impact practice, and evidence-based problem-solving strategies. Written for graduate students, researchers, and professionals in the field of school psychology, this book provides thorough, specific, and immediately applicable methods and principles for supervisory practice. Featuring a diverse set of pedagogical tools, *Supervision in School Psychology* is an important resource for navigating the distinct challenges specific to the demanding and diverse core competencies associated with supervision in school-based settings.

Dennis J. Simon, Ph.D., is a licensed clinical and school psychologist with over three decades of experience supervising interns, professionals, and psychological services. He was Director of NSSEO Timber Ridge Therapeutic Day School, a zero-reject public school program serving the Chicago area. He has been Lecturer in School Psychology, Clinical Psychology, and Teacher Education Programs at Loyola University of Chicago, USA.

Mark E. Swerdlik, Ph.D., ABPP, NCSP, is Professor of Psychology, Coordinator of the Specialist and Doctoral Degree Programs in School Psychology, University Supervisor of Internship Training, and Clinical Supervisor in the Psychological Services Center at Illinois State University, USA. He is Co-chair of the NASP Graduate Education Committee, past Chair of the Council of the Directors of School Psychology Programs, and has been a leader in program initiatives for training intern supervisors in Illinois.

CONSULTATION, SUPERVISION, AND PROFESSIONAL LEARNING IN SCHOOL PSYCHOLOGY
Series Editor: Daniel S. Newman

CONSULTATION AND INTERVENTION IN SCHOOL PSYCHOLOGY
Series Editor: Sylvia Rosenfield

SUPERVISION IN SCHOOL PSYCHOLOGY

The Developmental, Ecological, Problem-solving Model

Dennis J. Simon and Mark E. Swerdlik

Routledge
Taylor & Francis Group

NEW YORK AND LONDON

First published 2017
by Routledge
711 Third Avenue, New York, NY 10017

and by Routledge
2 Park Square, Milton Park, Abingdon, Oxon, OX14 4RN

Routledge is an imprint of the Taylor & Francis Group, an informa business

© 2017 Taylor & Francis

The right of Dennis J. Simon and Mark E. Swerdlik to be identified as authors
of this work has been asserted by them in accordance with sections 77 and 78
of the Copyright, Designs and Patents Act 1988.

Library of Congress Cataloging in Publication Data
A catalog record for this book has been requested

ISBN: 978-1-138-12152-2 (hbk)
ISBN: 978-1-138-12153-9 (pbk)
ISBN: 978-1-315-65056-2 (ebk)

Typeset in Bembo
by Out of House Publishing

Supervision is a commitment to the next generation of professionals and clients. We dedicate this text to our families. We remember our parents' commitment to our development; and as we watch our grandchildren grow, we are moved by the quality and commitment of our children to their children and to their own chosen professions.

CONTENTS

PREFACE

When we ask psychology graduates to share the most important influences on their professional development, they invariably highlight their internship experience and the critical contributions of their clinical supervisors. Decades after our own training, we each maintain contact with the important supervisors and mentors who shaped our early career development. When the supervisory relationship is effective, clinical supervision has a lasting impact on the supervisee's professional development and positively impacts the quality of services delivered to children and families for years to come. The skilled practice of supervision is one of the most important and far reaching professional contributions we make in our careers.

Supervision as Quality Control for the Profession

For preservice preparation, clinical supervision integrates classroom preparation and field experience to ensure that the next generation of psychologists is prepared to practice competently. Initial professional competencies are solidified and deepened when early career psychologists receive routine clinical supervision. The nature of psychological practice is rapidly evolving across all disciplines. Innovations like integrated healthcare in clinical settings and multitier systems of support in school settings require psychologists to adopt new roles, acquire additional skill sets, and collaborate in new ways with other professionals. In schools in particular, psychology has expanded practice activity to focus on promotion of social-emotional health, early intervention, and integrated intervention plans that address both individual and systemic issues. This evolution of psychological service delivery requires veteran credentialed psychologists to engage in continual professional development. Clinical supervision supports veteran psychologists as they navigate new demands and engage in novel service delivery. Supervision provides essential supports for implementing contemporary evidence-based assessment and intervention protocols. Thus effective supervision provides critical benefits for practitioners at all levels of experience and promotes quality state-of-the art services for the welfare of the public we serve.

Supervision as a Distinct Professional Competency

APA (2011, 2015a) has identified supervision skills as core professional competencies; and NASP (2010d, 2011a) promotes the need for supervision not only for preservice training but throughout psychologists' professional careers. This means that all psychologists should receive training in supervisory skills. It is essential that clinical supervisors possess strong clinical skills; however, by itself, this is insufficient to be an effective supervisor. Specific competencies in supervisory skills, methods, and processes are required for effective supervision. Similar to other professional competencies, training in supervision skills requires knowledge of best practice and contemporary research, application of skills under (meta)supervision, collegial supports, and continuous professional development. This text will focus on these issues. We will present a framework for supervision in line with current best practice; delineate behaviorally specific methods and processes, describe structures and activities for supervision training and ongoing professional development for graduate students, early career professionals, and veteran psychologists; and define a research agenda to advance our empirical understanding of best practice in supervision.

Focus on Supervision in School Psychology

Most of what has been written about clinical supervision comes from counseling and clinical psychology. There is a critical need for a school psychology-specific formulation for best practices in supervision. The unique diverse roles and wide breadth of professional practice domains specific to school psychology require nuanced and specialty-specific supervisory practices. Core elements of supervisory practices are shared across psychology disciplines and are applicable to social work, professional counseling, and other related service personnel as well. However, the unique demands of the school setting and the broad diversity of roles, functions, and service requirements for school psychologists necessitate the development of a school psychology-specific model for supervision. As we articulate the dimensions of this model, we will in turn be influencing best practice in related disciplines; particularly when, regardless of the practice setting, these professionals work with children and families and collaborate closely with educators.

Practical Applications

Supervision models must be theoretically sound, informed by available research, and consistent with best practice in both service delivery and professional training. Most importantly, they must facilitate practical applications of prescribed methods and processes to the daily challenges of clinical supervision. To this end the Developmental, Ecological, Problem-solving (DEP) model described in this text includes behavioral markers and specific activities that demonstrate effective supervisory practice. During internship supervision a critical task is to integrate theory, research, and practice. We strive to achieve this integration for supervision practices relevant to every career stage. We use multiple case examples and provide supervisor reflection exercises throughout the text. We share many forms and practice tools to support the practice of supervision. The DEP model provides readers with a comprehensive supervision model rooted in contemporary best practice that is operationalized through specific practical supervisory strategies. The application of this approach results in a purposeful and reflective approach to supervision particularly applicable to practice in school settings.

Who Will Benefit From This Book?

In line with the NASP (2010d, 2011a) principle that clinical supervision should be available for all psychologists throughout their professional careers, this book addresses a broad audience. Field supervisors of practicum, intern, and postdoctoral programs are the first professionals who will benefit from this text. The DEP model was developed in the context of our extensive work with intern and practicum supervisors. These field-based practitioners helped to refine and validate its central elements. The DEP model provides a blueprint for supervision of graduate and postdoctoral students. This text also serves as a companion to workshops on best practices in supervision for clinical supervisors of both graduate students and credentialed psychologists. It provides a framework for training and is a desk reference for self-monitoring the implementation of best practices in providing clinical supervision. We are particularly concerned that both early career and veteran psychologists have access to the supports of clinical supervision. Supervisors and mentors of early career professionals seeking the National School Psychologist Certification (NCSP) credential can be guided by the DEP framework.

We also address supervision of psychology service programs. We believe it would be beneficial for school psychologists to receive their administrative supervision from an expert psychologist and describe how to blend the combination of administrative and clinical supervision when they are provided by the same professional. Since most current supervisors have not received formal training in clinical supervision, we outline a variety of training formats and initiatives that directors of university training programs and leaders in state professional associations can employ to address the need for quality supervision and the professional development of current supervisors.

This text is also designed for use in graduate courses in supervision. Preparation for becoming an effective supervisor should begin in preservice training. Supervision skills are defined as a core professional competency for all psychologists. Graduate training in the DEP model will prepare supervisees to take best advantage of their field-based training experiences and in turn begin the preparation for their eventual role as supervisors.

Finally, while we present a school psychology-specific model of supervision, its core principles and practices apply to supervision within related clinical and counseling psychology and social work disciplines as well. This is particularly true for mental health practitioners who work with children and adolescents and collaborate closely with schools.

Organization of This Book

This book will outline the Developmental, Ecological, Problem-solving (DEP) model for supervision in school psychology. Part I explores the foundations for effective supervisory relationships by examining supervisor and supervisee roles and responsibilities, characteristics of effective supervisory relationships, routine collaborative processing of the supervisory relationship, and ethical practice. Part II delineates the DEP model with a comprehensive description of each component and how they are integrated for effective supervision. Particular focus centers on specific practical supervisory structures, skills, and activities that implement the model and guide daily practice. The DEP model will initially be delineated in relation to practicum and internship supervision. Case examples will illustrate the practical application of this supervisory framework. Part III will extend the application of DEP to professional development for credentialed psychologists and psychological service delivery systems. Supports and strategies for professional development of supervisors will be addressed including metasupervision and other collegial support networks. Part IV will conclude with a look toward the future of supervision in school psychology. This section will examine needs for training and research to refine school psychology supervision and more effectively prepare the next generation of clinical supervisors.

Why Do We Write This Text?

Clinical supervision has been a key focus of each of our professional careers for many years. We are both licensed school and clinical psychologists. One of us (Mark) has been a university educator including a program director of a doctoral- and specialist-level preparation program, practicum and university internship supervisor for specialist and doctoral interns, coordinator of professional development programs, and been involved in both national and state initiatives focused on quality supervision and graduate training. The other (Dennis) has been a field practitioner in both elementary and secondary school settings; supervisor of practicum, specialist, doctoral, and postdoctoral students; and director of a public therapeutic day school where he provided both administrative and clinical supervision to school psychologists and other educators.

Both of us have taught graduate courses in clinical supervision. The combination of our field and university experiences enriched our collaboration for professional development workshops on supervision and stimulated the development of the DEP model.

For the Children and Families

In the end, effective clinical supervision is meant to benefit the clients we serve. Quality supervision benefits children, adolescents, families, and educators who benefit from all forms of psychological service delivery. Effective supervisors expand the number of lives touched by their psychological careers exponentially. Every client who benefits from a supervisee's future practice and eventual role as a supervisor has benefitted from the professional contribution and expertise of her or his supervisor. In the end, psychology's heightened focus on competent supervision is a commitment to the children and families we serve.

ACKNOWLEDGMENTS

Our own training and professional development was supported by outstanding mentors and supervisors. These professionals had a lifelong influence on our careers and our development as supervisors: Frank Cimarrusti, John Shack, and Wes Lamb (Dennis) and Tom Fagan, Harvey Clarizio, Bill Rice, and Jim Mooney (Mark).

We are indebted to our colleagues who collaborated with us in many workshops on supervision and in our original conceptualization of the DEP model: Tracy Cruise, Brenda Huber, and Daniel Newman. University educators like Lynne Golomb and Ruth Kelly and the leadership of the Illinois School Psychologists Association have vigorously supported supervision training initiatives in our home state of Illinois.

Under the leadership of Brenda Huber, the Illinois School Psychology Internship Consortium (ISPIC) has become an exemplary doctoral internship program because of its focus on effective supervision practices. Many of the principles and strategies described in this text were field tested in ISPIC. The program's supervisors and interns have contributed greatly to the practical application of the DEP framework.

We have been privileged to engage in clinical supervision with scores of practicum students, interns, early career, and veteran professionals who have in turn nurtured, challenged, and informed our understanding of best practices in supervision.

We are particularly grateful for the support and contribution to this text by Daniel Newman, Routledge Series Editor, collaborating author, and substantial contributor to the field of supervision. His delineation of the joys, challenges, and supervision needs experienced by early career psychologists is a significant contribution to the field. His support of our work and expert editorial consultation is greatly appreciated.

Kathy Kapp-Simon's extensive review and editorial suggestions greatly improved this text and ensured its applicability to fields related to school psychology.

We appreciate the support and expertise of the Routledge editorial team, Daniel Schwartz, Matthew Friberg, Rebecca Novack, and their colleagues, throughout every step of this project.

Most importantly we thank our spouses, Kathy (Dennis) and Peggy (Mark), whom we have relied upon for support in this project, for their love, and as our partners in all of life's endeavors. They have been excellent supervisors in their own fields (Kathy, psychology, and Peggy, special education).

Introduction

.

1

THE STATUS OF SCHOOL PSYCHOLOGY SUPERVISION

Current Perspectives and Core Principles

The increasing interest in defining effective supervisory practices in psychology is long overdue. For many years, it was assumed that competent practitioners were automatically effective field supervisors. The field of clinical supervision has begun to examine the specific factors that contribute to successful supervision (Bernard & Goodyear, 2014; Corey, Haynes, Moulton, & Muratori, 2010). The discipline of school psychology requires a unique diverse set of roles, responsibilities, and competencies. This means that supervision in school psychology presents distinct challenges specific to its practice demands and diverse core competencies (Harvey & Struzziero, 2008; Newman, 2013; Simon, Cruise, Huber, Newman, & Swerdlik, 2014). This chapter begins our examination of supervision in the specialty of school psychology. We will explore current perspectives on supervision; summarize standards and guidelines articulated by the National Association of School Psychologists (NASP), the American Psychological Association (APA), the Association of State and Provincial Psychology Boards (ASPPB), and other key professional organizations; define needs for training in a school psychology supervision model; and propose core principles to guide the practice of supervision.

Current Status of Supervision in School Psychology

Limited Early Models

Until fairly recently, treatment of supervision in school psychology was limited. Early models of psychology supervision originated in clinical psychology and were associated with specific theories of psychotherapy (Bernard & Goodyear, 2014). Supervision focused on the practice of counseling and psychotherapy and was conceptualized within psychodynamic, behavioral, client-centered, cognitive-behavioral, systemic or other frameworks depending on the orientation of the supervisor or practice setting. While these models could support case conceptualization within a specific therapeutic orientation, they had limited applicability to other domains of psychological practice. As the contemporary focus on evidence-based practice emerged, singular orientations did not always incorporate the full range of empirically supported therapeutic interventions. These models also risked creating confusion regarding the nature of the supervisory relationship as a form of training or therapy. Singular therapeutic approaches are insufficient for providing a comprehensive framework for the diverse professional tasks that are the focus of training, particularly within school psychology.

Although Knoff (1986) provided an early call for supervision models focused on school psychology practice, the discipline continued to rely on supervision models developed within clinical and counseling psychology and clinical social work. Drawing attention to this dilemma, McIntosh and Phelps (2000) highlighted the complexity of the supervisory process, noted the challenges in defining supervision focus and tasks, and called for research to define effective supervisory practice. Unlike other disciplines, school psychology prepares and supports practitioners at both specialist and doctoral levels. This creates additional complexity for designing supervision models particularly for internship training. The daily practice of school psychology requires diverse roles and distinct competencies. Supervision models in the field must address requirements for competent practice across the full range of professional practice domains both for preservice training and to support professional practice.

Identification of Supervision as a Priority

Effective practice of supervision has now been identified as a priority for school psychology. The NASP (2010a) *Model for Comprehensive and Integrated School Psychological Services* specified 10 domains of practice: data-based decision-making and accountability; consultation and collaboration; interventions and instructional support to develop academic skills; interventions and mental health services to develop social and life skills; school-wide practices to promote learning; preventive and responsive services; family-school collaboration services; diversity in development and learning; research and program evaluation; and legal, ethical, and professional practice. In recognition of the breadth and complexity of these professional activities, the model called for supervision and mentoring not only for trainees but for all school psychologists to ensure the provision of effective and accountable services. The goals of supervision were not only the professional development of supervisees at every level of practice but improved service delivery to enhance outcomes for students and the school community. This NASP Practice Model was designed to define contemporary school psychology. Its practice domains delineate the core curriculum for graduate training and expected areas of professional competency required for credentialing of school psychologists. The introduction to this policy document directly linked this service model to NASP documents on graduate preparation and credentialing: *Standards for Graduate Preparation of School Psychologists* (NASP, 2010b) and *Standards for Credentialing of School Psychologists* (NASP, 2010c).

The NASP (2011a) position statement on *Supervision in School Psychology* extends the conceptualization for supervision by promoting "professional supervision of school psychologists by school psychologists at all levels of practice (e.g., student, intern, early career, and expert) as a means of ensuring effective practices to support the educational attainment of all children" (p. 1). This approach recognizes that supervision should not only be part of preservice education and early career development but contribute to lifelong professional development. Importantly, supervision's function is directly linked to student and client outcomes. The NASP Practice Model requires a focus on measurable outcomes to ensure effective service delivery. From this perspective, supervision is designed to support effective practice, promote accountability, certify sufficient competency for entry into the profession, and promote continuous professional development for the benefit of the profession and those it serves. Effective clinical supervision not only promotes competency and professional development for the supervisee, but it also protects the welfare of the public.

Supervision supports development of entry-level professional competencies for graduate students; but it also focuses on the professional development of credentialed professionals. NASP has focused particular attention on the supervision needs of early career psychologists during their first 5 years of practice (Silva, Newman, & Guiney, 2014). To qualify for the Nationally Certified School Psychologist credential (NCSP), NASP requires at least 1 year of supervision or mentoring by a senior professional. Routine clinical supervision in subsequent years supports development of broad professional competencies and eventually prepares the next generation of professionals for supervisory practice.

Too often the practice of school psychology is conducted in isolation from psychologist colleagues. Some practitioners serve multiple schools, and others may be the only psychologist in their school district. Isolated practice limits opportunities for collegial consultation and exposure to new methods of practice; and the absence of direct support can increase risks for professional burnout. A common dilemma faced by many school psychologists is that professional performance reviews are often not completed by psychologists but rather by an administrator from a different educational discipline (Curtis, Castillo, & Gelley, 2012). Unfortunately less than 30% report receiving supervision or mentoring through formal school district programs (Curtis et al., 2012). Lacking a systematic approach or organizational support, school psychologists must seek out peer consultation and mentoring relationships on their own. Rather than a systematic approach to professional development, they may seek consultation only in relation to their most challenging cases.

Competency-based Training and Evaluation

Over the last 15 years, new directions in professional preparation emphasized identification and evaluation of entry-level competencies required for effective psychological practice and thus for professional credentialing (Kaslow, 2004). While graduate course credit and completion of specified training activities remain essential, the competency initiative strives to evaluate readiness for independent practice based on demonstration of professional core competencies. Significant effort has concentrated on identifying and assessing a universal set of competencies as the target for training, credentialing, and accountability across the field of psychology (Kaslow, 2004; Kaslow et al., 2004). APA workgroups convened to define specific foundational and functional skills deemed essential to all professional psychological practice (APA, APA Task Force, 2006). These core skills were identified as the core curriculum for all levels of training. To graduate to professional status, interns are required to demonstrate measurable outcomes matching defined behavioral criteria in these competency domains. Competency benchmarks were developed to create behavioral markers (Fouad et al., 2009). "Competency assessment toolkits" were assembled to delineate evaluation methods for competencies (Kaslow et al., 2009).

NASP produced similar initiatives in *School Psychology: A Blueprint for Training and Practice III* (Ysseldyke et al., 2006) and the *Standards for Graduate Preparation of School Psychologists* (NASP, 2010b). *Blueprint III* proposed functional and foundational domains of competency. Functions related to professional activities for enhancement of cognitive, academic, social, behavioral, and emotional competencies through data-based decision-making and systems-based service delivery. Core foundational competencies identified included ethical and social responsibilities, diversity awareness, interpersonal and collaborative skills, and technological applications. This delineation foreshadowed the NASP Practice Model (2010a) and the *Standards for Graduate Preparation* (2010b). While these initiatives defined the areas of practice that would become the target for training and supervision, they did not operationalize skills nor provide assessment tools. Harvey and Struzziero (2008) stressed that professional skill development needed to be understood within a developmental context. They noted that expected competency levels vary greatly from novice to experienced practitioners and suggested that 5–10 years of practice are likely necessary to achieve broad competencies across the multiple delivery systems prescribed within the NASP Practice Model. This is consistent with the premise that clinical supervision should be available not only for trainees but for credentialed practitioners. However, it underscores the challenges for supervisors in defining, teaching, and evaluating expected professional competencies.

As the competency initiative for training continues to evolve, many challenges remain. APA is attempting to define training and supervision competencies that are appropriate across clinical, counseling, and school psychology (APA, 2015a). However it is not clear that these core competencies account for all of the specialist competencies required by the broad professional activities required within the practice of school psychology (Daly, Doll, Schulte, & Fenning, 2011). A Work Group of the Council of Directors of School Psychology (2012) made efforts to adapt these broader professional psychology competencies to the specialization of school psychology. Their doctoral-level internship guidelines require a breadth of training that includes the full range of practice activities promoted by NASP (2010a, 2010b, 2010c) practice, training, and credentialing documents. The complexity and diversity of the skill set required by school psychologists complicates reliable and valid operationalization and assessment of functional and foundational professional practice skills. Significant empirical investigation will be required to ensure effective training and evaluation of competencies.

Phelps and Swerdlik (2011) urged school psychology to incorporate the competency initiative into internship training while recognizing the need for specialty adaptations. They highlighted the need to identify and prioritize school-specific competencies that are relevant to daily tasks within school settings and then use this delineation to inform graduate training. Newman (2013) emphasized the importance of balancing breadth and depth of experience during internship training to ensure sufficient acquisition of core entry-level competencies. We believe it is important for school psychology to embrace the broad interdisciplinary professional competencies defined by APA, but also define additional school psychology specialty competencies that relate more directly to practice in schools. The supervision model outlined in this text will be compatible with the competency initiative but will focus on school psychology-specific training and supervisory practices.

Evidence-based Practice and Outcome Monitoring

Both APA (2008) and NASP (2010a) have called for implementation of evidence-based practice (EBP) which integrates research on effective intervention strategies with clinical expertise. This focus on empirically supported practice defines a significant dimension of the competencies taught and monitored within training and supervision. It not only defines some of the content of supervision but underlines expertise required by supervisors. To be a competent supervisor requires up-to-date knowledge and skills in EBP and the ability to support supervisee application of evidence-based strategies within the complexity of the field setting. This means that in addition to a focus on practitioner interpersonal skills like empathy, technical skills like data-based decision-making, and the application of evidence-based interventions (EBI), client outcomes must be monitored to ensure effective results. NASP training standards focus on the achievement of outcomes for clients (NASP, 2010b). Thus supervisors must incorporate the supervisee's ability to improve outcomes for the children and adolescents they serve into training and professional development progress monitoring and evaluations. The supervision model described in this text integrates intern competency development into best-practice service delivery models within the framework of evidence-based practice.

Identification of Supervision as a Core Professional Competency

The focus on defining professional competencies required for credentialing and effective practice has necessitated an examination of supervision competencies required to support training and professional development (Falender & Shafranske, 2004). NASP (2011a), APA (2015a), and ASPPB (2015) have all called for identification, research, and training in supervisory competencies. While in the past, competency for supervision was primarily assessed in terms of expertise in areas of practice, there is a growing recognition that effective supervision requires specific supervisory skills (Bernard & Goodyear, 2014; Falender & Shafranske, 2004; Harvey & Struzziero, 2008). APA's (2011) revised competency benchmarks identified supervision as a core professional competency. As a core competency, supervision skills should be incorporated into professional training both at the preservice level and as part of ongoing professional development. Similar to other targeted competencies, development of proficiency proceeds on a developmental trajectory.

The challenge for the profession is to define supervision competencies so they can be taught, applied with fidelity, and evaluated. Falender and Shafranske (2004) called for the development of science-informed theory and practice to guide competency-based supervision. Relative to other areas of professional practice, research on effective supervision practices remains fairly limited.

APA (2015a) developed *Guidelines for Clinical Supervision in Health Service Psychology* to delineate essential practices in supervision within a competency-based framework. These guidelines were intended to address supervision in clinical, counseling, and school psychology organized across seven domains: supervision competence; diversity; supervisory relationship; professionalism; assessment/evaluation/feedback; professional competence problems; and ethical, legal, and regulatory considerations. Supervisor competence was delineated in terms of knowledge, skills, attitudes, and values. ASPPB (2015) drafted *Supervision Guidelines for Education and Training Leading to Licensure as a Health Service Provider* using a similar framework. These documents described supervision knowledge and skills in broad terms including the following: professional competency in the areas being supervised; understanding of models and methods of supervision; knowledge of evidence-based practice in service delivery and in supervision; understanding and application of ethical and legal requirements for clinical practice and supervision; diversity competence; the ability to form a supervisory alliance; skills for providing feedback and evaluation to support supervisee development and self-monitoring; and the ability to integrate theory and research into practice. Attitudes and values included: modeling professionalism; ensuring an appropriate standard of care for clients; establishing a collaborative supervisory relationship that is developmentally sensitive, strength-based, and growth-oriented; understanding professional limitations and seeking consultation when necessary; balancing the needs of clients, supervisees, and the service agency; and commitment to lifelong professional development in both clinical and supervisory skills. To develop a competent supervisor, both the APA and ASPPB guidelines call for specific coursework and ongoing professional training in supervisory skills providing metasupervision of supervision which includes direct or recorded observations of supervisory practice.

Writing in NASP's latest volume of *Best Practices*, Harvey, Struzziero, and Desai (2014) describe similar knowledge, skills, and values requirements for effective supervision within school psychology. They emphasize three overarching variables as critical elements: building a strong working alliance; using a goal-directed, problem-solving model; and using progress monitoring and effective evaluation procedures.

Across professional psychology a consensus has emerged that supervision is a core professional competency requiring a defined set of knowledge, skills, attitudes, and values. The breadth and depth of competencies required is expansive. Designing curriculum and methods to train, support, and evaluate supervisors in these areas will require clearly delineated operationalization of supervisory skills. Further work is necessary to validate reliable tools and procedures for assessing outcomes of supervisee progress toward competence, for integrating client outcomes into evaluation of supervisee competence, and studying the impact of various supervisory practices on both supervisee development and client progress. The school psychology supervision model described in this text will present behavioral markers and specific supervisory activities that indicate fidelity of implementation of the Developmental, Ecological, Problem-solving (DEP) approach to supervisory practice.

Procedural Regulations and Requirements From Credentialing Organizations and State Licensing Boards

Requirements for preservice training (practicums and internships) and postdoctoral supervision clinical experiences and supervision are offered by various professional organizations involved in accreditation of university programs and field-based training, i.e., APA (2015b); ASPPB (2015); Association of Psychology Postdoctoral and Internship Centers (2011); CDSPP (2012); NASP (2010b, 2010c). In general, requirements for internship supervision call for a minimum of 2 hours per week of face-to-face individual supervision by an appropriately credentialed psychology professional. Doctoral internships generally require an additional 2 hours of supervision that may include group supervision or supervision by additional supervisors (APA, 2015b; CDSPP, 2012). NASP (2010b, 2010c) requires a minimum of 1200 hours for specialist-level interns and 1500 hours for doctoral candidates. APA (2015b) requires 1 year of full-time training during internship that must be completed in no fewer than 12 months or 10 months for school psychology. Table 1.1 summarizes requirements of these professional organizations and credentialing bodies.

Individual state licensing boards and departments of education may require somewhat different standards for internship and credentialing. APA's *Model Act for State* Licensure (2010b) and NASP's NCSP credential are intended to guide licensing practices nationally, but individual differences remain from state to state. It is important for supervisors and supervisees to familiarize themselves with individual state regulations. Both APA and NASP present updated state by state information on their websites.

Pressing Needs for Supervision in School Psychology

School Psychology-Specific Model of Supervision

The reflective and purposeful practice of supervision requires a sound conceptual framework or model that informs the practice of supervision (Bernard & Goodyear, 2014; Corey et al., 2010). A sound supervision model integrates theories of learning and development and research on best instructional practices with goals for training and professional development and the empirical best practice literature. Clinical and counseling psychology models of supervision have largely focused on counseling and therapeutic activities. School psychology has evolved to require a diverse and complex set of professional roles and skills that is broad and in many domains unique to this specialty (Harvey & Struzziero, 2008; Simon et al., 2014). The practice of school psychology requires direct and indirect service delivery, individual and systemic interventions, proactive instruction in social/emotional learning, the integration of academic and behavioral supports, early intervention, crisis intervention, universal screening for mental health, intense therapeutic interventions, and networking with community resources (Reschly, 2008; Sheridan & Gutkin, 2000).

The breadth of the professional responsibilities and activities delineated within the NASP Practice Model challenges university preparation, field work and internship supervision, and supervision and mentoring supports for career-long professional development. To address these challenges and support the development and enhancement of professional competencies at all levels of training and experience, there is a need for the development of a supervision model specific to school psychology. It would be influenced by models of supervision prominent in the clinical and counseling literature but would be specifically designed for the multidimensional practice of school psychology. To address this need, this text will describe the Developmental, Ecological, Problem-solving (DEP) model of supervision for school psychology. The components of the model will address the full scope of practice in schools. Case examples will illustrate applications to supervision. Descriptions of supervisory skills and activities will include behavioral markers that indicate implementation fidelity. This model has been applied

TABLE 1.1 Internship Requirements of Professional Organizations

Organization	Required Internship Hours	Required Hours of Supervision	Primary Supervisor Qualifications	Permission for Telesupervision	Intern to Supervisor Ratios
APA	1 yr. full time	4 hours; at least 2 are individual face-to-face with primary supervisor	Doctoral licensed at independent practice level for jurisdiction of internship	No more than 50%	Not specified
APPIC	1500 hours	1 hour for every 20 internship hours	Doctoral licensed for jurisdiction of internship	NA	Minimum of 2 interns per site & 2 doctoral licensed supervisors per site
ASPPB	1500 hours	10% of total time worked each week	Doctoral licensed at independent practice level for jurisdiction of internship	No more than 50% & only after 1st hour is in person face-to-face	No more than 3 interns per supervisor
CDSPP	1500 hours, no less than 10 months full time	4 hours; at least 2 are individual face-to-face with primary supervisor	Doctoral license at independent practice level for jurisdiction of internship & state school psychology license for school-based hours	No more than 50% & only after 1st hour is in person face-to-face	Not specified
NASP	1200 for Specialists & 1500 for Doctoral (at least 600 in school setting)	2 hours of individual field-based supervision per week	State school psychology credential & 3 yrs. of full time experience	Some acceptable	Not specified

at both the specialist and doctoral levels of training and refined by feedback from field supervisors. It is the framework for supervision within the Illinois School Psychology Internship Consortium where it has been applied by supervisors who are licensed in both school and clinical specialties. While it focuses on school psychology-specific supervision needs, many of the tenets of the DEP model are applicable to clinical, counseling, and social work practice particularly when they involve interventions with children and adolescents that affect school functioning. The principles and practices of the DEP model apply to professional development at all career stages. The model's particular relevance to supervision for early career school psychologists will be discussed.

Training in Supervision Skills

To prepare the next generation of supervisors, coursework in effective supervision practice should be incorporated into preservice training. Transparent delineation of a supervision model by supervisors at the onset of practicum and internship training experiences coupled with routine processing of the supervisory relationship provides opportunities for supervisees to reflect on supervisory practices and their effectiveness. Developmentally appropriate opportunities for supervision of intervention activities by school staff and/or casework by less experienced graduate students under close metasupervision can foster initial competencies in supervision. Additional training in supervision skills is necessary when young professionals acquire sufficient experience to supervise students in field placements.

It is also necessary to provide professional development and ongoing support to current field supervisors. Most practicing supervisors have had limited exposure to supervision models and the literature on best practices (Harvey & Struzziero, 2008). There are advantages to conducting portions of supervisor training with supervisors and supervisees examining best practices together. We will share sample training activities within the DEP framework. We will also describe large-scale statewide training initiatives for supervisors in Illinois that have attempted to advance training of internship supervisors at all levels of supervisory experience (Cruise, Kelly, Swerdlik, Newman, & Simon, 2012; Kelly, Wise, Cruise, & Swerdlik, 2002).

Once trained in core supervisory practices, supervisors require ongoing collegial support and professional development. Similar to case consultation in other areas of professional practice, supervisors can benefit from structured supports for refining skills, sharing resources, responding to challenging supervision dilemmas, and remaining up to date with best practice. Collaboration with university trainers and participation in metasupervision support groups will be highlighted in this text.

Creating Clinical Supervision for Credentialed Psychologists

NASP (2011a) called for the availability of clinical supervision for psychologists at all levels of practice. Supervision and mentoring by school psychologists for school psychologists would provide essential collegial support, enhance skills and practice outcomes, and support professional competencies in the ever evolving concepts of best practice. Unfortunately, only a minority of practitioners currently receive ongoing clinical supervision (Curtis et al., 2012). This is of particular concern for early career psychologists where only 38% report access to clinical supervision (Silva, Newman, Guiney, Valley-Gray, & Barrett, 2016). The DEP model can provide a framework for supervision or mentoring for credentialed psychologists. In addition, we will examine applications to supervision of school psychological services delivery.

Empirical Study of the Effectiveness of Supervisory Practices

As noted above, there is a growing consensus on the skills, knowledge, attitudes, and values required for effective supervision. However, research is needed to further confirm these elements and to determine the impact of specific supervisory skills and practices. We are only beginning to differentiate the additional characteristics specific to supervision in the specialty of school psychology (Milne, Sheikh, Pattison, & Wilkinson, 2011; Ward 2001). The concluding chapters of this text will suggest training and research agendas to refine school psychology supervision practices.

Core Principles of Supervisory Practice

The core principles that serve as a foundation for supervisory practice and the DEP Model are consistent with NASP standards and best practice documents (Harvey, Struzziero & Desai, 2014; NASP, 2010a, 2010b, 2010c; Sullivan & Conoley, 2008) and APA (2015a) supervision guidelines. Their integration into the DEP supervision model presented in this text was shaped by our personal experiences as field supervisors, university educators, and program directors and influenced by the supervisors and supervisees that we have been privileged to work with and learn from during workshops and consultations. Particularly important to the development of these principles has been our collaboration with the supervisors, interns, and university trainers associated with the Illinois School Psychology Internship Consortium (ISPIC), an APA-accredited doctoral training program that has field tested and adopted the DEP model, and the specialist-level field supervisors we have trained in collaboration with the Illinois School Psychologists Association and the Directors of University School Psychology Programs.

Core principles that serve as the foundation for effective supervisory practice include the following:

- Supervision is rooted in the supervisory relationship that is characterized by empathy, commitment, a healthy interpersonal alliance, mutual respect, and a focus on the professional growth of the supervisee.

- Supervision must be characterized by a primary responsibility for ensuring the welfare of the client and in its gatekeeping role the protection of the public.
- Supervision is a structured relationship with clear delineation of expectations, roles, and responsibilities of both the supervisor and supervisee.
- Formative feedback and summative evaluation are core supervisory activities that support competent practice, foster supervisee professional growth, and promote development of supervisee self-reflection and monitoring.
- Supervision is a developmental process that requires different structures, supports, and methods at various levels of supervisee development and is oriented toward increasingly competent independent functioning by the supervisee.
- Supervision teaches problem-solving methods that employ data-based decision-making to assess needs, inform intervention planning, and monitor progress.
- Supervision teaches systematic approaches to case conceptualization and problem-solving that the supervisee will be able to apply to independent practice.
- The school psychology internship requires training in the full range of psychological skills that includes prevention, assessment, progress monitoring, intervention, multidisciplinary problem-solving, program development, and system change.
- Supervision integrates theory and research to promote evidence-based practices with an emphasis on application in field settings with vigilant monitoring of student outcomes.
- Supervision fosters the development of ethically, culturally, and diversity competent practitioners.
- Clinical supervision for school psychologists should be provided by appropriately credentialed school psychologists to foster lifelong professional development informed by research on best practice to ensure competent service delivery.
- Clinical supervision is a core professional competency requiring specific training and supports and can be guided by a supervision model that integrates the *developmental* process of training, the *ecological* contexts that impact practice, and evidence-based *problem-solving* strategies.

Summary

Supervision is a core professional competency requiring specific training for the benefit of supervisees, clients, and the profession. It is no longer assumed that competent practitioners are automatically effective field supervisors. It is necessary to examine specific factors that contribute to successful supervision. The discipline of school psychology requires a unique diverse set of roles, responsibilities, and competencies. This means that supervision in school psychology presents distinct challenges specific to its practice demands and diverse core competencies. In this introduction, we delineated core principles of supervisory practice which will be covered in depth in the chapters that follow. A school psychology-specific model of supervision must integrate the *developmental* process of training, the *ecological* contexts that impact practice, and evidence-based *problem-solving* strategies.

PART I

Foundations of Effective Supervisory Relationships

2

CLINICAL SUPERVISION

Roles and Responsibilities

School psychologists who provide clinical supervision assume a myriad of roles and responsibilities to their supervisees, to the supervisees' clients, to their schools or organizations, and to the profession. Effective supervision is characterized as well by the supervisee assuming a number of roles and responsibilities. This chapter will discuss various definitions of supervision including its varied purposes and then address the diverse roles and responsibilities associated with clinical supervision for both the supervisor and the supervisee.

Definition and Purposes of Supervision

Definitions of Supervision

A variety of definitions of supervision exist, which are influenced in part by the particular specialty for which the supervision is provided. From a clinical or counseling psychology perspective, Bernard and Goodyear (2014) defined supervision as a distinct intervention provided by a senior member to a junior member of the same profession. Their definition included that the relationship is evaluative, extends over time, and has a variety of purposes. These purposes include increasing the knowledge and professional skills of the junior members, monitoring the effectiveness of the psychological services provided by the junior members to their clients, and serving as a gatekeeper for entry into the profession.

As noted in Chapter 1, school psychologists, who have earned entry-level credentials, are encouraged as part of their ethical responsibility to seek continuing supervision (NASP, 2010d). McIntosh and Phelps (2000), two school psychologists, advanced a definition of supervision that can be relevant for school psychologists at any level of experience. Their definition does not reference the experience level of the supervisor or the supervisee but rather focuses on the nature and purpose of the relationship:

> Supervision is an interpersonal interaction between two or more individuals for the purposes of sharing knowledge, assessing professional competencies, and providing objective feedback with terminal goals of developing new competencies, facilitating effective delivery of psychological services, and maintaining professional competencies.
>
> (McIntosh & Phelps, 2000, pp. 33–34)

This definition of supervision suggests that supervision is not always provided by a senior practitioner to a junior member of the profession but rather should reflect areas of expertise.

Purposes of Supervision

There are a variety of purposes for supervision. All have the common goals of developing the professional skills of the supervisee and insuring the welfare of their clients.

Supervisee Growth

Supervisee growth in both professional knowledge and skills represents a major purpose of supervision. This growth is focused on a number of different areas of professional functioning which represent the professional competencies articulated by the school psychology-specific or broader health service psychology professional organizations and licensing boards as referenced in Chapter 1 (APA, 2015a; ASPPB, 2015; NASP, 2010a, 2010b, 2010c; CDSPP, 2012).

Client Welfare

Consistent with our profession's ethical codes (APA, 2010a; NASP, 2010d), assuring client welfare represents a major purpose of supervision. As part of the supervision process supervisees must fully disclose their work with their clients; and supervisors must assure that these clients are receiving appropriate services. This purpose becomes paramount when a client of the supervisee is expressing thoughts or engaging in activities that reflect a risk of harm to self or others.

Gatekeeping

Particularly for preservice supervisees, the assessment of their "fit" to enter the profession represents a major purpose of supervision. This can be particularly challenging when the supervisee may be competent in most areas of professional functioning but not ready for independent functioning in others. For example, a school psychology intern who at the end of her internship is competent for independent practice in the competencies related to data-based decision-making/ assessment role but not in those related to counseling/therapy. Going beyond consideration of the welfare of the supervisee's current clients, the gatekeeping responsibilities of the supervisor are meant to protect the public and ensure the quality of the service by the profession going forward.

Restorative/remedial

Supervision also includes assessing and addressing competencies that are in need of remediation. For example, experienced school psychologist who has not remained current with recent advances in the evidence-based practice literature related to interventions with children with anxiety disorders would be in need of supervision to address this professional competency.

Empowering Self-reflection/Monitoring

Giving supervision away is the goal of every effective supervisor. Supervisors want their supervisees to develop self-reflection skills in order to monitor their own practice to decide when they need to seek additional supervision. For example, a school psychologist who has never provided counseling services to an adolescent dealing with transgender issues should seek supervision when called upon to treat this student.

Defining Needs for Future Professional Development

NASP (2010d) and APA (2010a) ethical codes and professional standards stress the need for lifelong learning. The half-life of knowledge or the amount of time that acquired information can be considered current and relevant in school psychology is now 9 years and with recent advances in evidence-based practices is soon to be 8 years (Kaufman, 2015). This requires an individual entering the profession of school psychology to make a commitment to lifelong learning. Thus the identification of needs and priorities for future professional development represents another important purpose of supervision. Within a strong supervisory relationship, supervisees can begin to articulate their needs for future professional development based in part on their professional interests and self-assessment of their knowledge and skill sets.

Preparing for Future Role as Supervisor

Another purpose of supervision is to begin to prepare supervisees for assuming their future role as supervisors. This can be accomplished by supervisors and their supervisees analyzing the process of supervision during their sessions. These discussions would include reflections on the supervisory model and methods employed and an exploration of the supervisory characteristics and strategies the supervisees have found most effective and would like to provide for their future supervisees. At this time within school psychology, preservice training in supervision is only required for doctoral-level graduate students; however, since most supervision is provided by specialist-level practitioners, it is essential that all school psychologists achieve competencies required for effective supervision.

Opportunities for supervised practice of supervision during the graduate training program and the internship experience, coursework and professional development programs in effective supervision, and routine processing of supervisory experiences represent necessary components of this preparation.

SUPERVISOR REFLECTION ACTIVITY: THE ROLES AND PURPOSES OF SUPERVISION

Reflect on your own experience as a supervisee. How would you define the purposes and roles played by your supervisor?

If you have been a supervisor, how have you explained your role to your supervisee? What expectations did you communicate as necessary for an effective supervisory relationship?

Diverse Roles and Responsibilities

Supervisor Roles

The school psychology supervisor assumes roles that have some commonalities but also major differences with that of a teacher, therapist, consultant, and mentor. We will now explore each of these roles in more depth.

Teacher

Similar to teaching, supervisors instruct their supervisees exposing them to new knowledge and then evaluate their knowledge and performance. However, unlike university classes, where the content of a class is driven by a predetermined curriculum, the content taught in supervision is determined by supervisee and client needs. In both situations, teaching may include didactic methods. Supervisors' role as teachers also requires that they evaluate their supervisees. Finally, supervisors must also serve a "gatekeeper" role which requires recognition of when supervisees are not prepared to move forward in their training or enter the profession.

Therapist

The supervisor/supervisee relationship also has some similarities to the therapist/client relationship. The therapist and the supervisor both address problematic thoughts, feelings, and behaviors of the client or supervisee. However, in supervision the therapeutic work has the goal of increasing the supervisees' competency in therapeutic interventions with clients; while in therapy the goal is personal growth for the client. Supervision also involves a strong evaluative component while in therapy the therapist is nonevaluative. Finally, clients generally choose their therapists while supervisees are assigned supervisors.

Consultant

Supervision and consultation share the goals of increasing the supervisees' and consultees' professional effectiveness. In fact, consultation and supervision may look the same for more advanced trainees who are engaging in more peer-like supervision and are functioning at or near an independent practice level. Differences between consultation and supervision include the following. Consultation is non-hierarchal while supervision presents a power differential due to the evaluative role of the supervisor. Consultation may be a one time or brief occurrence while supervision is ongoing. Consultation is typically voluntary, while supervision is generally mandated by accrediting bodies and licensing boards. Typically, in consultation the consultee is free to accept or reject the suggestions of the consultant, while supervisees are not due to the legal liability the supervisor has for all of the activities of the supervisee.

Mentor

Similar to supervision, mentoring requires school psychology discipline-specific knowledge. Both have the goal of supporting the supervisee/mentee in professional practice; and both can serve a restorative function that fosters professional development and prevents burnout. However, unlike supervisors, mentors do not typically have an evaluative role nor are they directly responsible for their mentee's decision-making. The mentor has no direct liability for the mentee's work (Silva et al., 2016).

This wide variety of roles that a supervisor can assume may change based on the supervisory agenda, developmental level of the supervisee, and intended or required client and supervisee outcomes (Corey et al., 2010). Functional and systemic factors of the agency or school settings in which the supervisee and supervisor work also affect the particular roles a supervisor can play at any particular time in the supervisory relationship. For example, a supervisor may plan a more teaching role when the supervisee has little knowledge about working with a particular type of client; however, the supervisor may apply a more consultant approach when the supervisee is providing psychological services to a client who is dealing with a problem that the supervisee has sufficient knowledge and skill to address.

Supervisor Responsibilities

Supervisor responsibilities vary widely and include responsibilities associated with professional skill development of the supervisee, the welfare of clients, and development of supervisees' professional identity and self-care.

Supervisee Professional Growth

The supervisory relationship is focused on supporting supervisee growth to prepare the supervisee for competent independent practice. This growth should be evident across multiple domains of professional functioning. The supervisor ensures that supervisees learn case conceptualization, assessment practices, strategies for direct and indirect intervention, appropriate professional role and demeanor, emotional awareness, and self-evaluation (Holloway, 1995, 2016). To maximize supervisee growth, supervision must occur within the context of a strong supervisory relationship. The topic of developing effective supervisory relationships that support maximum supervisee growth will be addressed further in Chapter 3.

Feedback and Evaluation

Feedback and evaluation represent critical responsibilities of the supervisor and are ethical (APA, 2010a; NASP 2010d) and legal obligations reflected in a number of psychology licensing laws (e.g., Texas). This responsibility represents a central component of supervision for fostering professional growth for the supervisee and ensuring healthy and effective practices within the profession of school psychology. Effective feedback and evaluation practices must occur during the supervisory relationship for the supervisee to develop into an independent practitioner. Evaluation must be both formative and summative. Formative evaluation refers to feedback that is ongoing during the course of supervisees engaging in professional activities and that suggests actions to guide next steps in immediate professional activities. Summative evaluation summarizes overall effectiveness across multiple domains of practice at key developmental time periods of the training experience (e.g., quarterly) and generally includes written feedback across multiple domains of practice. This summary evaluation is also shared with the university for intern and practicum students. The topic of evaluation and feedback will be addressed in greater detail in Chapter 7.

Due Process Information for Supervisees

Related in part to providing formal evaluations to supervisees, supervisors have the responsibility to provide due process policies and procedures to their supervisees. Supervisors must provide information about the process and procedures for disputing an evaluation provided by the supervisor; seeking solutions if the supervisor is not providing the level or intensity of supervision required by accrediting bodies and licensing boards (e.g., less than 2 hours a week of face-to-face supervision); and/or if personality conflicts are interfering with developing productive supervisory relationships.

Model Effective Communication, Problem-solving, and Self-care Strategies

Modeling, teaching by example, represents a powerful learning tool for supervisees. Supervisors can teach their supervisees much about effective practice by *thinking or problem-solving aloud* to demonstrate clinical evaluation and decision-making approaches. Modeling effective communication strategies in interactions with supervisees, children, parents, teachers, and administrators provides a practical example for supervisees to emulate. Is the supervisor dismissive when communicating with parents or teachers or does he or she demonstrate respect? Does the supervisor engage in impulsive or more reflective problem-solving, carefully considering options before taking action? The answers to these questions can have a significant impact on their supervisees' learning. In addition to communication and problem-solving strategies, supervisors also model self-care strategies. What do supervisees observe in terms of their supervisors' efforts to balance their personal and professional lives? How does the supervisor handle the multiple stresses associated with the role of the school psychologist?

Promote Diversity and Cultural Competence

Just as acquiring ethical knowledge and demonstrating ethical behavior represents a core professional competency so does developing diversity and cultural competency (APA, 2011; NASP, 2010a). Supervisors have the responsibility to provide their supervisees with opportunities to work with children and families as well as consultees who represent diverse backgrounds or minority characteristics. These cases give their supervisees an opportunity to demonstrate their developing knowledge and skills in this important area. Consistent with promoting ethical knowledge and behaviors, it is important for the supervisor to model sensitivity to and knowledge of effective strategies to use with diverse clients and consultees during the problem-solving process.

Integrate Systemic Contexts into Intervention Planning

Many school psychologists subscribe to an ecological model (Bronfenbrenner, 1977) in conceptualizing student problems. This model includes the various social relationships and "systems" that impact child development and behavior. For school psychologists, these systems include those closest to the child and ones with whom children have the most contact. The microsystem has the greatest impact on the child and includes home and school and interactions with family, peers, and other caregivers such as teachers. The mesosystem includes interactions between the different people in the child's microsystem. An example would be the relationship between the child's parents and the child's teacher. The next level, the exosystem, does not directly involve children as active participants but can impact them. For example, exosystem would include the impact on a child when a parent loses a job. The next level is the macrosystem, which includes the cultural environment in which the child lives and all other larger systems that impact the child. These systems include the economy, cultural values, and political systems. One example of how the macrosystem can impact a child occurs when a child from a military family has one of his parents deployed.

Through the problem-solving process, supervisors assist their supervisees in appreciating these larger contexts or systems and incorporating them into intervention planning. For example, a child who is bullying other children may be impacted by the reactions of peers in the classroom or neighborhood, parents and siblings in the home, the norms or rules operating in the classroom, and the school culture as a whole. An analysis of these various systemic factors is an important part of understanding the context of the bullying behavior and then choosing appropriate multifaceted evidence-based interventions to address it. Best practices in contemporary school psychology target both individual and systemic interventions (Simon, 2016). The DEP model incorporates ecological considerations into supervision and problem-solving.

Promote Accountability/Risk Management

Supervisors have the responsibility to promote effective accountability practices that manage the legal risk for both themselves and their supervisees. Risk management refers to those practices that focus on the identification, evaluation, and treatment of problems that might injure clients, lead to the filing of an ethics complaint, or a malpractice action (Corey et al., 2010). These practices include for example documentation of when supervision occurred, summaries of those sessions, documentation of what activities the supervisee is engaging in, and development of a comprehensive written supervision contract that specifies supervisor and supervisee responsibilities. A more detailed discussion of developing a supervision contract and other risk management strategies is provided in Chapter 7.

Ensure Welfare of the Client

Supervisors maintain the primary responsibility for their supervisees' clients. This responsibility influences activity assignments for supervisees, intensity of case monitoring, and degree of direct involvement by the supervisor in service delivery.

Vicarious Liability

Based in large part on the position of authority and control the supervisor has over the professional work of their supervisees, supervisors assume full responsibility for all of the professional work of their supervisees in terms of client welfare. Supervisors need to be fully aware of this responsibility since they can be held liable even when they do not have specific knowledge about the supervisees' client. The concept of vicarious liability is discussed further in Chapter 5.

Know and Monitor All Supervisee Cases

Since supervisors are ultimately legally and ethically responsible for the welfare of their supervisees' clients, supervisors have the responsibility for monitoring all of their supervisees' cases in order to be fully knowledgeable about them. This monitoring is important not only to assure client welfare but also to be informed to provide feedback to supervisees regarding their strengths and areas that need to be targeted for growth.

Promote Ethical Knowledge and Behavior

A core competency at both the specialist and doctoral levels of school psychology preparation relates to acquiring knowledge of professional ethical codes and promoting ethical professional behavior (APA, 2011; NASP, 2010d). Although on-campus university coursework facilitates the acquisition of ethical knowledge, it is the field-based training particularly during practica and internship that provides an opportunity for supervisees to integrate and apply that knowledge and demonstrate how it is incorporated into their professional behaviors. It is the responsibility of the supervisor to provide frequent opportunities to discuss ethical dilemmas employing a systematic decision-making model as they occur in the field setting and to monitor the demonstration of ethical behavior (Jacob, Decker, & Hartshorne, 2011). It is also important for supervisors to recognize that they serve as influential models of ethical decision-making and behavior as they provide case supervision to their supervisees. Ethical and legal issues will be addressed in more detail in Chapter 5.

Supervise within Scope of Competence and Monitor Supervisees' Competence

Supervision competence is two-pronged and includes knowledge of effective supervisory practices and clinical expertise. When supervising particular cases or other professional activities of their supervisees, it is important that supervisors both monitor their own competency to supervise this particular type of case (i.e., do they have the training and/or experience with similar cases) as well as the supervisees' competency level to work with the assigned clients. It is important to monitor the supervisees' work with their cases adequately, including the progress or lack of it, to both ensure client welfare and that supervisees are only assigned tasks that they are competent to perform with supervision. If the supervisor does not possess the expertise to supervise a particular case or work activity, the supervisor has the ethical responsibility to seek supervision or transfer supervisory responsibility to someone who does.

Promote Professional Identity and Self-care

Special challenges occur when supervising interns and practicum students who are experiencing the multiple professional demands inherent in their professional roles for the first time. These challenges include added stress, performance anxiety, lack of familiarity with the various professional roles and functions required in an applied setting, and assumption of a professional adult identity for the first time.

Supervisors must monitor supervisee personal development as it affects professional practice and personal self-care. During the supervisory relationship, the supervisee is not just expanding professional knowledge and skills but personal development is also simultaneously occurring. Areas of growth related to personal development can include the supervisee's increasing maturity, sense of self-efficacy, and ability to manage stress. The latter is critical, as the role of the school psychologist can be stressful (Huebner, 1992). Unmanaged stress can lead to burnout and problems in professional competence. Personal development also requires that supervisees learn about personal self-care, particularly the importance of maintaining a sense of balance in one's life, which in turn enhances professional functioning. Maintaining this balance is particularly important given the stressors inherent in working as a school psychologist with its multiple tasks and clients/consultees (i.e., students, parents, faculty, and administrators). This healthy work-life balance enables school psychologists to be more effective with all those with whom they work and provides more rewards in all parts of their lives.

Supervisee Diverse Roles and Responsibilities

A major responsibility of the supervisee is to be an active learner with shared responsibility for creating a beneficial supervisory relationship. Proactive supervisees assume responsibility to maximize their learning and contribute to effective supervisory relationships (Newman, 2013). This role can be accomplished in a number of ways, which are discussed below.

Proactively Seek Out Information and Opportunities

A significant behavioral marker for active learners is that they ask many questions and seek out additional opportunities for involvement. During a video or audio recording review of the supervisee's work, a supervisee assuming the role of an active learner would be observed verbalizing as much or more than the supervisor. The verbalizations would include requesting specific feedback, asking for additional resources on topics discussed, and volunteering to engage in a variety of activities to gain more experience.

Engage in Self-advocacy and Self-care

Related to proactively seeking out information and activities, active learners in supervisory relationships engage in self-advocacy and self-care. They advocate for themselves in terms of what they need from their supervisors such as more or less structure, more or less independence, or greater involvement in different types of activities. These supervisees also engage in self-care. Similar to the supervisor responsibility to monitor and teach through modeling effective self-care strategies, active learners implement these self-care strategies and use supervision as a place where they can discuss ways to promote their physical and mental health as it relates to fulfilling their professional responsibilities (Corey et al., 2010).

Hold Supervision Time Sacred, Be Punctual and Prepared

As is also true of supervisors, supervisees must communicate that their dedicated supervision time is valued. This can be communicated to the supervisor by not scheduling other activities that conflict with supervision, only canceling sessions in emergencies due to sickness or unavoidable circumstances (e.g., car breaking down), and being punctual in arriving to supervision. Being prepared for supervision is essential. Preparation is best accomplished by completing a supervision session planner in advance of a supervision session. This form includes the supervisees' goals for the supervision session, topics for discussion, and cases for focused review. Case and activity summary notes that specify the supervisees' current activities and projected next steps with their clients prepare the supervisee and supervisor for the upcoming session. Both of these planners will be discussed in more detail in Chapter 7.

Identify Professional Strengths and Weaknesses and Develop Goals for Supervision

As noted earlier in this chapter, one of the responsibilities of the supervisor is to empower the supervisee to develop self-reflection/monitoring skills. Self-reflection and monitoring includes the ability to identify professional strengths and weaknesses. Supervisees should engage in continuing self-assessment of their strengths and weaknesses and share this information with their supervisors. The discussion of these professional skill strengths and weaknesses, including professional behaviors, should lead to the modification of existing supervisee goals and/or the development of new goals for supervision around the outcomes of this assessment. Active learners engage in continual self-assessment and do not wait for formal feedback or evaluation from their supervisors. When the supervisor provides an assessment of strengths and weaknesses, the supervisee integrates this information into future self-monitoring. Supervision sessions discuss how the supervisee's self- perceptions are consistent or inconsistent with what has been observed by the supervisor. This process contributes to the development of effective self-monitoring skills.

Work Toward Developmentally Appropriate Self-monitoring and Independence

Related to the above, active learners work towards exhibiting both developmentally appropriate self-monitoring and independence in their professional work. Supervisees articulate clearly to their supervisors how they are self-monitoring their clinical work and their needs for more or less independence.

Monitor the Internship Plan with the Supervisor

A written internship or practicum plan consists of the objectives of the training experience and activities the supervisee will engage in to reach those objectives. Often these training plans collect dust in desk drawers and are only reviewed when required, such as when the university program representative visits an internship or practicum site. Active engagement in the supervisory experience includes the supervisee understanding the importance of this written plan, keeping it up to date in terms of activities completed, discussing it frequently with the supervisor, and modifying it when appropriate.

Share All Casework with the Supervisor

As noted earlier supervisors are responsible both legally and ethically for all of their supervisees' clinical work. Supervisees therefore also have the legal and ethical responsibility of full disclosure to their supervisors. It is very important to communicate to supervisees that even though the particular clinical activity they might have engaged in (e.g., a counseling or assessment session) may not reflect positively on the supervisor's assessment of their level of competency, they must share all relevant information with their supervisors.

Review Assessment/Intervention Plans with Their Supervisor Prior to Implementation

Specifically related to the responsibility of sharing all casework with supervisors, supervisees are required to review their assessment/intervention plans with their supervisors prior to their implementation. The level of detail they must go into will be dependent on their developmental status with more advanced supervisees likely having to share fewer details than a less experienced supervisee. However, it is the supervisor's decision not the supervisee's to determine the level of detail necessary based on the developmental level of the supervisee and to clearly communicate expectations to the supervisee.

Obtain Supervisor's Signature When Required

Legally and ethically all relevant case documents such as psychoeducational reports, case summaries, progress notes, and other similar documents related to their clients must have both the supervisee's and the supervisor's signature. These signatures must be obtained prior to the distribution of the document to confirm that the supervisor has reviewed it, as it is the supervisor who has the legal and ethical responsibility for all of the supervisee's clinical work.

Engage in Evidence-based Practice

The assessment and intervention plans reviewed by the supervisor should be consistent with evidence-based practice and reflect an effort by the supervisee to integrate all prior theoretical and skills training. This will allow the supervisor to obtain a more reliable assessment of the supervisee's current knowledge and skill set and result in more accurate and useful feedback and evaluation. Evidence-based practice is both a clinical and ethical responsibility.

Accept and Act Upon Supervisor's Guidance and Directives

Supervisees have the legal and ethical responsibility to accept and act upon their supervisors' directives. The supervisee can certainly disagree with a proposed plan advanced by the supervisor to implement with one or more clients; and the supervisee has the responsibility to share these concerns and discuss them openly. However, the final decision regarding the course of action with a particular client or how to proceed in a professional work activity is up to the supervisor.

Monitor Defensiveness

Since supervisee defensiveness reduces acceptance and subsequent implementation of constructive feedback and evaluation provided by the supervisor, supervisees have a responsibility to monitor their own defensiveness. If defensiveness becomes an issue, it is the responsibility of both supervisor and supervisee to bring this into the open and discuss thoroughly, as defensiveness in the relationship can inhibit learning.

Share Difficulties and Ask for Help When Needed in a Timely Manner

It is the supervisees' responsibility to share with their supervisors any difficulties they are experiencing related to completing their work responsibilities. Rather than waiting for the problem to increase in severity, supervisees should ask their supervisors for assistance in a timely manner. Whether or not supervisees will fulfill this responsibility will be dependent in part on the strength of the supervisory relationship and the level of trust between supervisor and supervisee.

Immediately Inform the Supervisor of All Risk-of-Harm Situations

To ensure client welfare and to minimize risk of supervisor liability, supervisees have the responsibility to immediately inform their supervisor (or designated back-up supervisor) of any situation where clients are at risk of doing harm to themselves or others. Supervisors have the responsibility to inform their supervisees when they will be unavailable when their supervisees are engaging in assigned professional activities and whom the supervisee should contact when they suspect the risk of harm to self or others.

Provide Feedback to the Supervisor

Feedback is a reciprocal responsibility in a supervisory relationship. Although supervisors have the responsibility to provide ongoing feedback and conduct periodic evaluations of their supervisees, supervisees share a responsibility to provide feedback to their supervisor particularly around unmet supervisory needs or responsibilities not being fulfilled by their supervisors. Supervisees should share concerns with supervisors when they are uncomfortable about any aspects of their supervisory relationship or the process of supervision. The likelihood of the supervisee meeting this responsibility will depend in part on the level of trust developed in the supervisory relationship.

Complete Tasks within Required Timelines

Supervisees have the responsibility to complete all assigned tasks within designated timelines. Punctuality in completing work tasks represents an important professional behavior that needs to be developed during the training experience. If a supervisee cannot complete a task within the agreed upon timeline, he or she has the responsibility to inform the supervisor and negotiate a new due date.

Know and Follow All School District and University Policies

Supervisees must be aware of and follow all school district or other agency and university policies. If policies are unclear, the supervisee has the responsibility to raise questions and initiate a discussion with the supervisor. District, university, and/or other agency administrators typically expect trainees in their settings to follow all designated policies and procedures.

Uphold APA and NASP Ethical Standards

In addition to following all state and federal legal regulations relevant to the practice of school psychology in their particular setting, supervisees are expected to uphold the ethical standards of relevant professional organizations including APA and NASP. Supervisees have the responsibility to raise ethical dilemmas in supervision and collaboratively problem-solve them with their supervisors using a systematic legal-ethical decision-making model (Jacob et al., 2011). This will be discussed further in Chapter 5.

Summary

While various definitions of supervision emphasize different characteristics of the role, most share in common that it represents a professional interaction focused on increasing the professional skills of the supervisee and ensuring client welfare and that supervision is evaluative and extends over time. As school psychologists are encouraged by our professional codes to seek supervision no matter our level of experience, the seniority level of the supervisor or supervisee is not critical to the definition of supervision adopted by us for this text. Just as definitions are varied, so are the purposes of supervision. These purposes include supporting supervisee growth, ensuring client welfare, gatekeeping (depending on the experience level of the supervisee), remediating competency problems, empowering self-reflection/monitoring, defining professional development needs of the supervisee, and preparing for the future role as a supervisor. Supervisors and supervisees each have a number of diverse roles and responsibilities. For supervisors these roles and responsibilities include aspects of teaching, supporting, consulting, and mentoring. The responsibilities center around those related to the professional skill development of the supervisee and include: supporting supervisee professional growth, providing feedback and evaluation, modeling effective communication, problem-solving and self-care strategies, promoting cultural and diversity competence, appreciating the role that larger systemic contexts play in individual interventions, and demonstrating accountability/risk management. Ensuring the welfare of clients represents the second category of supervisor responsibilities and includes vicarious liability, knowing and monitoring of all cases, promoting ethical knowledge and behavior, supervising only within the scope of one's competence, and evaluating and monitoring the supervisee's competence. The last category of supervisor responsibilities includes monitoring the supervisee's personal development as it affects professional practice and promoting professional identity and self-care.

Supervisee roles and responsibilities include: being an active learner, sharing all casework with their supervisor, accepting and acting upon the supervisors' guidance and directives, monitoring their own defensiveness, sharing difficulties and asking for help when needed in a timely manner, informing their supervisor (or designated back-up) of all risk of harm situations, providing feedback to the supervisor, completing all tasks in a timely manner, knowing and following all relevant school district and university policies, and upholding APA and NASP ethical standards. The extent to which supervision can fulfill all of these stated purposes and supervisors and supervisees can effectively assume all of their diverse roles and meet all of their responsibilities is very much dependent on having a strong supervisory relationship. We now turn our attention in Chapter 3 to the characteristics of an effective supervisory relationship.

3

CHARACTERISTICS OF EFFECTIVE SUPERVISORY RELATIONSHIPS

Supervision represents a complex interpersonal relationship that is impacted by the personal attributes and professional skills of the supervisor, supervisee characteristics, the dynamics of the supervisor-supervisee relationship, and the types of supervisory processes employed by the supervisor. Who is the effective supervisor represents a critical question when considering what contributes to an effective supervisory relationship (Barnett, Erickson Cornish, Goodyear, & Lichtenberg, 2007). Ladany, Mori, and Mehr (2013) studied supervisee perceptions of effective therapy supervisors in the field of counseling psychology and identified four key characteristics of effective supervisors and supervisory relationships. These characteristics included the quality of the supervisory alliance, the ability to foster inquiry and autonomy in the supervisees, the clinical expertise of the supervisor, and their ability to provide their supervisees with positive and challenging feedback. This chapter will address these and other aspects that contribute to an effective supervisory relationship and fulfill the purposes of supervision discussed in Chapter 2.

Supervisor Characteristics

Personal Attributes

Effective Interpersonal and Communication Skills

One of the most critical elements of effective supervisory relationships is the ability of supervisors to establish a positive connection with their supervisees (Bernard & Goodyear, 2014; Carifio & Hess, 1987; Corey et al., 2010). The outcome of a positive connection can be attributed in large part to the interpersonal and communication skills of the supervisor.

Effective supervisors possess strong interpersonal and communication skills both verbal and nonverbal. They exhibit multicultural and diversity competence reflected in their ability to work with supervisees from diverse backgrounds and developmental levels. They demonstrate well-developed active listening skills for both verbal and nonverbal communication as well as the ability to communicate trust, support, acceptance, empathy, genuineness, and honesty with the capability to provide constructive feedback in a nonjudgmental manner. All of these attributes and skills contribute to creation of a safe environment for learning and a strong supervisory alliance. Effective supervisors take the time to get to know their supervisees and spend time in rapport building helping the supervisee to feel comfortable in the supervisory setting and thus more willing to disclose challenges and take the risks that are an essential requirement for professional development. Effective supervisors are also skilled in conflict resolution both when ruptures occur in the supervisory relationship or if conflicts develop with other staff members. Effective supervisors are respectful of their supervisees' input including feedback about the supervisory relationship; they listen carefully to their supervisees' concerns; create a supportive atmosphere in which their supervisees can ask questions and express their opinions; and encourage their supervisees' independence in their professional functioning (Corey et al., 2010; Harvey & Struzziero, 2008; Harvey, Stoiber, & Krejci, 2014).

A number of interpersonal and communication skills that are deleterious to the supervisory relationship have been identified (Corey et al., 2010; Ladany et al., 2013; and Lowry, 2001). These characteristics include rigidity, being judgmental and excessively critical, lacking compassion, and arrogance.

Self-care

Self-care is defined as attending to one's own physical and psychological wellness (APA, 2015a). Underlining the importance of self-care, it is included in Principal A of APA's Ethical Code (2010): "Psychologists strive to be aware of the possible effect of their own physical and mental health on their ability to help those with whom they work" (2010a, p. 3). Promoting wellness through self-care is increasingly recognized as preventing professional burnout among school psychologists, stress-related illnesses, unprofessional behaviors and/or ethical violations, and promoting more effective service delivery (APA Board, 2016; Huebner, 1992; Huebner, Gilligan, & Cobb, 2002).

There exist a number of occupational hazards encountered by psychologists working in any setting. Those most likely to impact school-based school psychologists include working with students and parents in distress; varied and quickly changing role demands; working in isolation as the only school psychologist in the building and/or district; frequently changing demands of the profession; multiple demands from the varied consumers of school psychological services with different "agendas" including students, parents, teachers, and administrators; and the interactions between personal stress and work demands.

What are some warning signs of occupational stress which supervisors should monitor? Some of these signs may include feelings of dissatisfaction with work, depression reflected in sleep or appetite disturbance or negative mood, substance abuse, anxiety, difficulty concentrating, workaholism, increased clinical errors, and chronic irritability and impatience.

Effective supervisors recognize the importance of self-care; and they model these self-care behaviors for their supervisees (Newman, 2013). Authentic modeling by the supervisor of proper work-life balance and personal stress management prepares the supervisee to manage the long-term pressures inherent in the profession of school psychology.

The APA Practice Directorate (2016), in collaboration with the APA Board of Professional Affairs Advisory Committee on Colleague Assistance, developed a series of brief online articles that focused on self-care. These articles included specific suggestions for how to address this important area. They can be classified into physical, cognitive, emotional, and financial (Baird, 2008). Suggestions include: making self-care a priority (cognitive); conducting a realistic assessment of psychological and physical health with a focus on prevention rather than waiting to remedy problems (e.g., poor nutrition) when they occur (physical); spending time engaging in restorative activities such as exercise, massage, and pleasurable reading (emotional); identifying and using sources of social support (emotional); establishing and utilizing professional connections to discuss the nature of job stressors (emotional); developing realistic and reasonable expectations for work performance and the ability to meet them such as reducing case load (cognitive); monitoring the balance in work, rest, and play and being prepared to say "no" to additional commitments (emotional); nurturing interests outside of work as a psychologist (cognitive and emotional); conducting a cost-benefit analysis of work and health (financial); and being proactive in enhancing career satisfaction by diversifying professional activities and increasing collaboration with colleagues (emotional).

Self-care should be a priority impacting professional lifestyle from the beginning of a career. Taking a more long-range perspective (cognitive) and beginning to engage in self-care as an early career professional was also recommended. Establishing self-care as a habit at the onset of a career proactively builds it into the foundation of a professional lifestyle. This last recommendation to begin engaging in self-care as an early career professional is why this represents an important topic for discussion during supervision. It also underlines how important it is for supervisors to be more cognizant of the self-care practices they are modeling for their supervisees. Page (2008) developed the *Healthy Lifestyle Assessment* survey which supervisors can use to self-monitor work-life balance and self-care. (See Appendix 3A.)

In addition to supervisors modeling effective self-care strategies for their supervisees, they also play a very important role in preventing and reducing their supervisees' stress (Newman, 2013). A number of supervisory strategies, based on the DEP model, can be employed to reach the goal of preventing and reducing stress.

A first step involves accurate identification of the developmental level of the supervisee, assessment of the professional skills required in the task, and then employment of appropriate supervisory methods to match the supervisee's skill levels. For example, if a risk assessment of a client is necessary and the supervisee has never conducted one, the supervisor can use role-playing and/or cotherapy to conduct the risk assessment jointly rather than relying on verbal self-report after the supervisee conducted the risk-assessment independently. Engaging in this activity without proper skills would likely be very stressful for the supervisee.

Second, it is important to assure a match between the demands of the training site and the skills of the prospective practicum student or intern. Supervisors should advocate for being included in the interview process to ensure selection of a potential supervisee who has the prerequisite knowledge and skills to match the demands of the training site.

A third focus is the development and maintenance of a strong supervisory relationship. Consistent with information presented in this chapter, developing a strong supervisory relationship will help prevent or reduce the supervisee's stress. The supervisory relationship should be characterized by open communication, explicit and transparent expectations, supervisee input into the goals of the supervisory experience, and encouragement for the supervisee to move outside of professional comfort zones while the supervisor still provides support or a professional safety net.

A final focus involves navigating institutional stresses. As will be discussed in more detail in Chapter 8 (ecological component of the DEP model), schools are complex organizations. As such they pose challenges for those with less experience to navigate. An important supervisory practice to prevent or reduce supervisee stress would be to openly discuss these challenges and provide strategies to address them. Letting your supervisee know it is appropriate at times to say "no" to taking on additional responsibilities and facilitating cooperation and collaboration with other professionals in the school can go far in preventing or reducing stress. This focus prepares the supervisee to have the ability to cope with institutional barriers and constraints that inevitably impact and add stress to professional practice.

Motivated and Committed to Training and the Development and Advancement of the Profession

Effective practicum and internship supervisors are strongly committed to training the next generation of psychologists (Carifio & Hess, 1987). They view supervision as a way to give back to their field and "touch the future" of their profession; and they communicate this value to their supervisees. Those who supervise or mentor early career school psychologists or others who are later in their careers are also committed to advancing best practices in the field. Supervision represents one of the primary mechanisms by which to advance our specialty of school psychology and the field of education (Harvey & Struzziero, 2008; Sergiovanni & Starratt, 2002). Supervisors demonstrate this commitment to supervision to individual supervisees by their commitment to and execution of best supervisory practices, routine solicitation of feedback regarding supervision effectiveness, and explicit incorporation of training in supervision competencies into the supervision experience.

Unrelenting Focus on the Good of Children and Their Families

Effective supervisors have a strong commitment to meeting the needs of their clients and families and are described as passionate by their supervisees. This is evident in how supervisors interact with their clients and how they approach their role as a supervisor. This attitude is communicated clearly to supervisees both by how supervisors communicate about their supervisees' clients and their close attention to monitoring supervised activities and interventions.

Professional Skills

Knowledgeable and Possessing Effective Clinical Skills

Effective supervisors possess a strong knowledge base and effective clinical skills in all of the domains of school psychology practice (NASP, 2010a); and this is considered an important factor that impacts the supervisory relationship (Bernard & Goodyear, 2014; Carifio & Hess, 1987; Corey et al., 2010; Holloway, 1995, 2016; Ladany et al., 2013; Spence, Wilson, Kavanagh, Strong, & Worrall, 2001). However as noted above, well-developed clinical skills and knowledge of evidence-based practices will not in itself create a productive supervisory experience for the supervisee. Much like an ineffective consultant who may be skilled in consultative processes but lacks a knowledge base related to an issue brought up by the consultee, a clinical supervisor cannot provide valid supervision in areas beyond personal expertise.

Sufficient Experience Base

In addition to a strong knowledge base and effective clinical skills, an effective supervisor must have sufficient experience to draw upon when engaging in supervision (Barnett et al., 2007; Carifio & Hess, 1987; Ladany et al., 2013). The nature of the setting in which the supervision is occurring presents an important contextual factor that impacts what occurs in supervision including the supervisory relationship (Holloway, 1995, 2016). Consider the situation in which supervision is provided to an intern in a building in which there is significant staff conflict over how to handle the management of children exhibiting challenging behaviors. This conflict will impact the school climate, which in turn affects staff, students, and families and the supervisee's ability to provide direct and indirect interventions to these clients and consultees. The supervisor's experience with dealing with these types of building climate issues and their impact upon a range of student problems would be an important factor in providing effective supervision.

The supervisor's experience in dealing with a wide range of student issues will also impact the nature of supervision and the supervisory relationship. The amount and types of experiences the supervisor can draw upon can have a significant impact on the effectiveness of supervision provided. As further evidence of the importance of experience to an effective supervisory relationship, professional organizations and professional licensing boards require a certain level of licensed experience to qualify as an internship supervisor (see Table 1.1 in Chapter 1 for specific requirements).

Effective Problem-solver

Effective supervisors are skilled in problem-solving. They appreciate the value of a systematic problem-solving model in their own school psychology practice; and it is the *modus operandi* of the way they conduct supervision. Systematic problem-solving refers to addressing the four stages of problem identification, problem analysis, plan implementation, and plan evaluation (Cates, Blum, & Swerdlik, 2011). Effective problem-solving can be applied to all problems encountered by the school psychologist. Since problem-solving is the core activity of professional practice, supervisors must be skilled in problem-solving, able to apply those skills to the supervisee's cases, and capable of teaching methods that the supervisee can apply to eventual independent practice. It is so critical to effective practice in school psychology that it represents a key component of the DEP model that is discussed in more depth in Chapter 9.

Strong Metacognitive Skills

Related to excellent problem-solving skills, effective supervisors exhibit strong metacognitive skills. These are higher order thinking skills that help them plan, organize, and monitor problem-solving activities. This means they are able to use prior knowledge for planning how to address particular tasks, such as developing an assessment plan for a child or designing an intervention, for engaging in the necessary steps to complete tasks, for evaluating results, and, if necessary, for modifying approaches. Effective supervisors not only are able to utilize these metacognitive skills in their own practice but can model them by verbalizing them for their supervisees.

What follows is an example of the supervisor using metacognitive skills for prospective planning with the supervisor thinking aloud about how to plan a particular assessment. A supervisee early in the internship is discussing a student who is being considered for special education eligibility and is preparing for the Domain Meeting at which decisions will be made as to what additional assessments need to be conducted. The supervisor begins "thinking aloud" to model necessary questions to raise at the meeting. These questions include: "What are the particular referral questions that need to be answered by this assessment?" "What areas (e.g., academic achievement, cognitive, social-emotional) are related to these questions?" "What data utilizing the RIOT matrix (R=Review, I=Interview, O=Observation, and T=Test, Hosp, 2008) are currently available?" "What specific assessment approaches might be utilized to fill in any gaps in the data necessary to answer the referral questions?"

This second example involves the supervisor utilizing metacognitive strategies for a retrospective analysis of what occurred in a parent interpretive conference the supervisor and supervisee conducted together. The purpose of this conference was to discuss the results of the recent comprehensive assessment the intern had conducted with their 5th grade student. The parents participating in this conference were divorced but still both actively involved in raising their child. The supervisor "thinks aloud" about what she was processing during the conference when the father (the noncustodial parent) became disengaged because the mother spent a great deal of time criticizing the father. The supervisor shares with the supervisee that she noted the father had become very quiet and his body language suggested disengagement and escalating annoyance (looking away and arms crossed by his chest). She then redirected the conversation by asking the father specific questions about his interactions with his son and how these interactions reflect the positive relationship they have established with each other. Only after this positive redirection does she ask him to identify specific concerning behaviors. The supervisor then asks the mother to do the same.

Perceives Complexity but Is Able to Suggest Concrete Paths of Action

Dealing with complex situations involving consulting with school staff and dealing with challenging student issues is the norm for school psychology supervisors. Typically much information is available for analysis; and effective supervisors are able to perceive the complexity of the data available yet still make practical recommendations. They are able to "see the forest for the trees." Effective supervisors can model for their supervisees the ability to analyze a significant amount of complex data gathered from multiple sources and methods as inputs into their case conceptualizations and then develop specific intervention plans or approaches to address student or staff issues being discussed in supervision (Carifio & Hess, 1987). As was true with modeling problem-solving and effective metacognitive strategies, effective supervisors verbally model this skill for their supervisees. Effective supervision teaches the supervisee to address both individual and systemic factors impacting problems and to take effective action even when there are substantial barriers to success.

Integrates Theory and Research into Practice

Effective supervisors integrate current theory and research of evidence-based practices into their supervision. Effective supervision includes efforts to integrate current theories of human behavior into case conceptualizations and in the eventual selection of intervention or prevention strategies. Supervisors, by modeling this approach to decision-making, also challenge their supervisees to do the same as they become more independent in their clinical practice. Effective supervisors also utilize evidence-based assessment, intervention, prevention, and consultation strategies in their own clinical work. A focus on linking assessment findings with evidence-based interventions and encouraging supervisees to verbalize these links as they apply to their clinical work is a characteristic of effective supervision.

Engages in Ongoing Professional Learning

To remain effective as a supervisor, it is necessary to routinely participate in professional development activities that ensure that professional skills continuously improve and reflect contemporary best practice. This commitment to continuing education applies to enhancement of skills for supervision as well. A supervisor's commitment to continuing professional development models the importance of this practice for supervisees. Professional development regarding supervision competencies communicates to supervisees the importance placed on supervisory responsibilities.

Process Skills

Engages in Effective Supervisory Process

Effective supervisors engage in effective teaching methods to facilitate the learning process for supervisee professional development rather than merely providing directives or telling the supervisee what to do (Barnett et al., 2007; Carifio & Hess, 1987; Ladany et al., 2013). These supervisors use supervisory strategies such as the Socratic strategy of inquiry and discussion in dialogue between the supervisor and supervisee. This method is based on asking and answering questions to stimulate critical thinking and to illuminate different approaches to clinical practice (Overholser, 1991). The Socratic method challenges and guides the supervisee to assess and evaluate data and options for problem-solving. It parallels the cognitive-behavioral therapy strategy that encourages self-discovery and critical analysis skills (Friedberg & McClure, 2015).

These supervisors also use scaffolding which refers to a variety of instructional techniques such as questioning, verbal or live modeling, or systematic rubrics or templates to organize data analysis and intervention planning. All of these supervisory strategies have as their goal to move the supervisees to progressively greater understanding and, ultimately, to greater independence. The goal of scaffolding is to provide sufficient structures and supports for the supervisee to learn new ways of interpreting data or implementing a particular intervention or consultation approach. Scaffolding matches supervisory supports to the supervisee's developmental learning curve and current competencies. Without scaffolding supports, the foundation for learning complex skill sets would not occur. Matching supervisory methods to emerging supervisee competencies will be addressed in detail in Chapter 7 on the Developmental component of the DEP model.

Another example of effective supervisory process involves encouraging dialogue between the supervisor and supervisee about the supervisory relationship by routinely requesting feedback from the supervisee. We have identified this previously as an important interpersonal or communication skill and value that is to be communicated by an effective supervisor to the supervisee. Routine processing of the supervisory relationship models a variety of clinical skills that are taught in supervision including progress monitoring, reciprocal feedback with clients, and attention to the interpersonal dynamics that influence collaborative problem-solving. It also fosters the development of self-monitoring skills in the supervisee. The next chapter will examine this approach in greater detail.

Other effective supervisory processes such as communicating clear expectations through contracting and various structures for accountability such as the completion of a supervision planning document by the supervisee and supervision notes by the supervisor will be discussed in more depth in Chapter 7. These processes add more structure at the early stages of the supervisory relationship.

Flexible and Available

Effective supervisors communicate the importance of the supervision hour holding supervision times "sacred" by not scheduling other meetings that conflict with these supervision sessions nor allowing interruptions such as responding to texts, emails, or answering phone calls during the supervision session. These interruptions can damage the working alliance in supervision (Angus & Kagan, 2007; Shulman, 2006). To communicate the sacredness of the supervision hour to others, including their supervisees, supervisors can hang a sign on their door such as "In Supervision—Please do not disturb except in an emergency."

Effective supervisors are also flexible if a supervision meeting needs to be rescheduled and are also available for additional supervision if requested by the supervisee. Reflecting these processes, supervisees are told that if an emergency situation occurs or the supervisor or supervisee is ill necessitating the canceling of a supervision session, all sessions will be rescheduled at a mutually convenient day and time unless both agree that it is not necessary to meet that week. It is important for supervisors to explicitly communicate both verbally and nonverbally to their supervisees these values related to the sacredness of the supervision hour and procedures for rescheduling and requesting additional supervision. This will be discussed in further detail in Chapter 7, which includes a discussion of the components of the written supervision contract.

Sets High Goals

Effective supervisors set high goals for themselves and their supervisees. However, they are also explicit in communicating these goals to their supervisees and hold themselves to the same high standards as their supervisees. For example, supervisors model effective professional behaviors for their supervisees such as completing tasks within the required timelines and engaging in respectful communication with children, parents, and school staff. Self-assessment and progress monitoring of goals represent important professional skills for school psychologists; and supervisors provide their supervisees with multiple opportunities throughout their supervision to set professional goals and then self-assess their progress towards those goals (Carifio & Hess, 1987; Corey et al., 2010; Harvey & Struzziero, 2008; Holloway, 1995, 2016). During these goal setting and progress monitoring activities, supervisors communicate their high expectations for their supervisee. They also provide their assessment of their supervisees' progress towards their goals with subsequent discussion focused on comparing the supervisees' self-assessments with their supervisors' perceptions of their progress.

Respect for Boundaries

Effective supervisors respect boundaries in supervision (Barnett et al., 2007; Spence et al., 2001). Supervisors need to possess the personal and professional maturity to manage multiple roles and responsibilities as these might negatively impact a supervisory relationship. Multiple relationships occur in supervision when a supervisor is engaged in a number of professional roles and at least one more role in addition to supervisor, either professional or nonprofessional, with the supervisee (Corey et al., 2010). These multiple roles might involve a university-based clinical supervisor who is also the supervisee's thesis or dissertation chair or his or her graduate assistantship supervisor. Another example is a supervisor who develops a friendship or social relationship with the supervisee. If a supervisor also became the supervisee's therapist, role confusion and a boundary issue would occur resulting in a compromising dual relationship. While it is impossible to avoid all multiple relationships in supervision, it is the supervisors' responsibility to respect these boundaries, determine the advantages and disadvantages of each of the multiple roles and how each might impact their objectivity and judgment related to their trainees. The supervisor-supervisee relationship is a hierarchical one with a power differential. Because supervisors have a responsibility to evaluate their supervisees and in the case of preservice school psychologists to serve as gatekeepers for the profession, multiple relationships can become problematic. It is virtually unavoidable to not engage in multiple relationships with licensed peers who are seeking supervision hours for licensure or certification (Corey et al., 2010). The ethical dilemmas that can arise in the context of multiple relationships will be covered in detail in Chapter 5.

Manages Organizational Demands and Advocates for Their Supervisees

There exist many demands on the time of both the supervisor and the supervisee in the typical school or other practice setting. There are assessments to complete, teacher and parent consultations to conduct, reports to write, and a variety of meetings to attend from IEP and 504 meetings to manifest determinations. Supervisors with effective organizational skills enable their supervisees, depending on their developmental level, to organize these tasks and be successful by protecting them from too many simultaneous demands limiting their effectiveness. Effective supervisors advocate for their supervisees by protecting them from inappropriate requests to ensure that they gain access to experiences critical for their training.

For example, early in the internship, the building administrator asks the supervisee to serve in the role of a one-on-one personal classroom aide for a student who is particularly disruptive in order to control the student's behavior. This would represent an inappropriate request; and the effective supervisor would discuss with the building principal that serving as the classroom personal aide would interfere with the intern's training experience, which needs to be broad.

In a building in which the supervisor does not provide any counseling services but his intern requires this training experience, the effective supervisor could negotiate with the building social worker for the intern to access referred students to provide these counseling services and arrange for appropriate supervision. This would be an example of the supervisor facilitating access to needed training experiences. As supervisees move towards greater independent professional functioning, they are encouraged to employ their own organizational skills to effectively manage the multiple demands of the setting.

Fosters Movement from Dependency to Competent and Mature Independent Functioning

Effective supervisors facilitate their supervisees transitioning from more dependent to independent functioning. Supervisors at the practicum and internship levels typically engage in the learning sequence of: "I (supervisor) do, we do (Supervisor and Supervisee), and you do (Supervisee)" (Newman, 2013, p. 87). The practicum and internship experience typically begins with observing the supervisor complete a variety of professional tasks then transitioning to completing tasks collaboratively and then moving into more independent functioning first with isolated professional tasks and then with all of the tasks associated with the role and function of the school psychologist (Alessi, Lascurettes-Alessi, & Leys, 1981; Newman, 2013). Historically, this represents the basis of the developmental models of supervision (Loganbill, Hardy, & Delworth, 1982; Stoltenberg, McNeill, & Delworth, 1998; Stoltenberg & McNeill, 2010), which are briefly described in Chapter 6. The developmental nature of effective supervision also represents one of the three pillars of the DEP school psychology supervision model, which is the focus of Chapter 7.

Delegates Responsibility and Trusts Their Supervisees

Effective supervisors are able to delegate responsibility trusting their supervisees to engage in problem-solving. However, they also closely monitor their supervisees' clinical work and engage them in systematic problem-solving as a component of effective supervisory process. Effective supervisors view training as a developmental progression toward the final goal of competency for independent practice. Thus, while a supervisor always closely monitors a supervisee's involvement in assessments of risk for harm-to-self or others, it is essential that by the end of supervision the supervisee has the opportunity to individually conduct this critical assessment. In this case, supervision presages the consultation that is routinely required in risk assessment.

Teaches Case Conceptualization and Problem-solving

Effective supervisors teach an explicit process of case conceptualization directly linked to problem-solving (e.g., Cates et al., 2011; Simon, 2016). Case conceptualization represents a major goal or supervision task and therefore needs to be explicitly taught and monitored with feedback provided to supervisees related to their progress in developing this skill (Holloway, 1995, 2016).

Encourages Emotional Awareness and Self-evaluation

Two of the major outcomes of effective supervision are the development in the supervisee of emotional awareness and the ability to engage in self-evaluation (Holloway, 1995, 2016). Emotional awareness refers to the supervisees' awareness of their own feelings, thoughts, and subsequent actions that occur during their work with students, parents, or teacher/administrative consultees. It is important to recognize one's own emotions and the personal history that can trigger those emotions when engaging in counseling. If one is not aware of these emotions, they can interfere with the supervisee's objectivity while engaging in these professional activities.

Supervisees must also be aware of their emotions as they relate to their work with clients, the supervisory relationship, and what occurs in supervision. For example, a supervisee's self-awareness that she is getting frustrated with an oppositional adolescent in counseling assists her in avoiding potentially counterproductive responses. Similarly, a supervisee who is aware of a tendency to hypersensitivity to critical feedback can inform the supervisor and ask her supervisor to help her prevent it from interfering with her ability to take in constructive recommendations. Finally, emotional awareness can help a supervisee who may have had some difficult relationships with authority figures openly discuss differences of opinion with her supervisor in the context of their hierarchical relationship.

The development of self-evaluation skills refers to the supervisees' ability to assess their own effectiveness in working with clients or supervisees in order to determine if their approach needs to be modified. Further, as a primary ethical responsibility, supervisees need to self-evaluate their own skill levels in an effort to recognize the limits of their competence to handle particular issues. Thus goals of supervision include both awareness of potential influences on professional activity from personal history and personality factors and the sound judgment to seek consultation when cases are beyond experience or competency.

In a study conducted by the NASP Graduate Education Workgroup on characteristics of effective school psychology intern supervisors (Harvey, Stoiber, & Krejci, 2014), it was reported that supervisors and supervisees agreed on the following supervisor characteristics which were rated as most important: respectful of the supervisee's input, feedback, and ideas; listens when a supervisee has a concern; provides a supportive setting in which the supervisee can ask questions and express his or her opinions; and encourages the supervisee to develop his or her own ideas. The characteristics that were rated as least important by the supervisor and the supervisee included prompt in reviewing reports and providing feedback; raises challenging questions to facilitate additional conversation and problem analysis; and helps the supervisee to define and achieve specific concrete goals during the training experience. The study also addressed the mismatches between the self-ratings of the supervisor and the supervisees' ratings. These mismatches included: the developmental needs of the intern not matched by the supervisor; supervisor and supervisee differences in terms of desired supervision structure, time allocation, theoretical orientation, or reliance on empirically based decisions; disclosures made during supervision sessions not kept private by the supervisor; and the supervisee with multiple supervisors receiving conflicting expectations. The DEP model discussed in depth in Chapters 6–9 addresses these mismatches by focusing on evidence-based practice, structural processes and requirements within supervision, and close attention to developmental considerations of the supervisee.

Supervisee Characteristics

Since reciprocity within the supervisory relationship is critical to its effectiveness, it is important to note what supervisors have identified as characteristics of an effective supervisee (Berger & Bucholtz, 1993; Corey et al., 2010; Harvey & Struzziero, 2008). The essential characteristics highlighted below are also based on our conversations with experienced supervisors with the Illinois School Psychology Internship Consortium (ISPIC) and with those supervisors enrolled in our supervision training workshops and minicourses. In fact these characteristics are such an important aspect of forming an effective supervisory relationship that at our universities a module in the introductory seminar in school psychology focuses on this topic of characteristics of effective supervisees. Most entering school psychology students have not had any experience with clinical supervision and are unaware of these characteristics and behaviors and how they will impact the development of a positive supervisory relationship. When supervisors share with supervisees their personal experiences of what supervisee behaviors have contributed to successful supervisory relationships, they are in effect teaching them how to be effective learners in this field experience.

These supervisee characteristics include allowing oneself to be a "learner" and a willingness to acknowledge fears, self-doubts, or anxieties by discussing them with their supervisor. Other characteristics include: supervisees recognizing their legal and ethical responsibility to share all information about a client with their supervisors; coming to supervision prepared; demonstrating timeliness in the completion of tasks and keeping their supervisors informed of their progress in task completion; providing feedback to supervisors about the supervisory process including sharing what is going well (what I like and find beneficial in supervision), what is not going well with specific suggestions on how to improve supervisory process; takes an idea and "runs with it"; takes the initiative by embracing opportunities to get involved in different activities and views every opportunity as a learning experience; asking "why" questions and understanding there are no "stupid questions"; realizing there is no perfect solution; being eager to receive feedback, curious, and energetic; recognizing that the supervisor is not the only one with the answer and being willing to share their impressions; being reflective and willing to identify their own strengths and weaknesses; engaging in a collaborative manner in identifying the needs of the community and working with their supervisors on meeting them; exhibiting a good sense of humor; expressing clearly what they need from supervision; and teaching their supervisors by sharing new and innovative ideas related to case conceptualization and intervention development.

Summary: The DEP Perspective

Based on our review of the effective supervision literature coupled with our own experiences as university-based and field-based school psychology supervisors, we have identified the following list of essential characteristics of an effective supervisory relationship. In many respects the supervisory relationship is parallel to the concept of a therapeutic alliance with strong attachment. In combination these characteristics contribute to effective and purposeful supervision practices. Each of these characteristics are integrated into the DEP model so that supervisors can consistently apply best supervision practices.

1. The supervisor possesses interpersonal and clinical skills for engagement, empathy, encouragement, and support.
2. A supervisor establishes a professional relationship that is rooted in trust, focused on learning, and serves as a platform or base for professional growth in areas of inexperience or relative weakness.
3. An effective supervisory relationship is characterized by structure with flexibility. There exists a clear delineation of roles and expectations within a written contract as well as specific structures, protocols, and tools for organization of supervisory practice and sacred scheduled supervision times with additional flexible capacity for "as needed" supervision. These structures include multimethod supervision, supervision session planners, essential documentation and recordkeeping, and protocols for crisis response and back-up supervision. These structures and essential supports will be discussed in more detail in Chapter 7.
4. The supervisor possesses strong clinical skills guided by up-to-date evidence-based practices for problem-solving.
5. The supervisor is able to link theory, research, and practice and communicate this integration to the supervisee.
6. The supervisor is an effective problem-solver who fosters the supervisee's growth in problem-solving and teaches effective case conceptualization.
7. The supervisor possesses a developmental perspective focused on supervisee growth to competent independence.
8. The supervisor possesses competency in understanding and responding to the complex interactions between individuals and systems and teaches the supervisee how to integrate individual and systemic issues into assessment, intervention planning, and consultation.
9. The supervisor exhibits diversity and multicultural competence.
10. The supervisor possesses system change agent skills addressing interactions among individual, familial, school, and community systems.
11. Supervision processes include: clear mutual goal setting; provision of effective and routine formative and summative feedback; encouragement of supervisee self-discovery and engagement in problem-solving (i.e., the supervisor is not just the "answer person"); a focus on supervisee growth toward independent competence, challenging the supervisee to grow and engage in new activities, trust in supervisee engagement in new professional practice while remaining supportive; maintenance of supervisory support; and incorporation of

an ecological perspective and sensitivity, and competency in understanding and responding to the complex interactions between individuals and systems.

12. As an effective supervisory relationship is based on the interaction between supervisor and supervisee, there are also supervisee characteristics that contribute to a positive relationship. These include personal attributes and behaviors of the supervisees such as emotional awareness and capacity for self-evaluation, enthusiasm and initiative, professional work behaviors such as timeliness of completing tasks and fulfilling responsibilities, and commitment to keeping their supervisors informed of their progress. It is important for supervisors (at the university and/or in the field) to educate their supervisees about these attributes and professional work behaviors.

13. Continuing professional development related to supervision, including didactic training and collegial consultation through metasupervision, are important for the development of supervisory competencies for school psychologists. This training and additional support through collegial consultation will advance the quality of the practice of supervision by enhancing purposeful supervision and fostering self-reflection and self-monitoring of supervisory practice. These continuing professional development activities will also serve to build a network of support for supervisors. The topic of building networks for collegial support is addressed in more detail in Chapter 10.

SUPERVISOR REFLECTION ACTIVITY

Consider the characteristics of your most effective supervisors. Compare and contrast these characteristics with those described in this chapter. How would you describe your most productive and least productive supervisory relationships and how do characteristics of each compare with what was discussed in the chapter? Ten years from now how will your supervisees describe you as a supervisor and the nature of their supervisory relationship with you?

SUPERVISORY PROCESS ACTIVITY

Engage in a discussion with your supervisee or if in a supervision class role-play with one of your classmates playing the supervisee. Discuss your supervisee's outlook on supervision. What does the supervisory relationship mean to your supervisee? What does your supervisee want or expect from you as the supervisor? What does your supervisee expect to contribute to supervision? What are your supervisee's expectations or goals related to the supervision he or she will be receiving? What are your supervisee's previous experiences with supervision? What was positive and what would your supervisee change?

4

PROCESSING SUPERVISORY RELATIONSHIPS

Previous chapters have emphasized the critical importance of the supervisory relationship as the foundation for an effective supervisory experience for both the supervisee and the supervisor. In an effort to ensure a satisfying and productive supervisory relationship, it is important for both the supervisor and supervisee to continually reflect on the nature of their relationship and the various supervisory processes that contribute to building a strong supervisory relationship. This chapter will review these various processes and provide practical strategies to allow the supervisor and supervisee to process or review their relationship leading to any corrective actions should that be necessary.

Transparent Structure and Routine Process

A positive supervisory relationship is facilitated by clear expectations for both the supervisor and the supervisee. These expectations would include: frequency of supervision sessions; time and location; rescheduling missed supervision sessions; roles and responsibilities of both parties including the supervisee's role in preparing for supervision and who will determine the agenda and be expected to lead the discussion; the issue of vicarious liability and its implications for what is discussed in supervision; and the methods, frequency, and timeline for evaluation. It is the evaluation role of the supervisor that generates the most anxiety for supervisees; therefore, both parties must be clear about how the evaluation will be completed. Developing a written contract and then implementing it with integrity is the most efficient and effective way to be transparent in terms of communicating the structure, routine procedures, and expectations to the supervisee. Discussion related to the contract also begins the all-important process of establishing trust between the supervisor and supervisee. The development and execution of written supervision contracts will be covered in detail in Chapter 7 and include sample contracts.

Routine Direct Review and Discussion of Supervisory Relationship

Due to the importance of the supervisory relationship for a productive supervision experience for both the supervisee and supervisor, it is important to frequently discuss the relationship. As trust develops in the relationship, the expectation should be established that processing the relationship will become a routine part of supervision sessions. This processing would include identifying what is going well in the relationship and what can be improved. The extent that the supervisee can be truthful in sharing perceptions of the effectiveness of the supervisory relationship provides an index of the degree of trust that has been established. The authors in their roles as supervisors recall having supervisees provide honest constructive feedback related to the supervisory relationship that lead to improvements and the strengthening of the relationship. For example, supervisees have commented on the need for more feedback, more opportunities to present their ideas prior to the supervisor providing comments, and more modeling demonstrations of particular skills by the supervisor. During these sessions the supervisees also had an opportunity to comment on what they thought was going well in supervision. The extent to which we as supervisors listened to this feedback and acted upon it was directly related to increases in trust and strengthening of the supervisory relationship.

Establishing a Foundation for Feedback and Evaluation

Routine processing of the dynamics of the supervisory relationship establishes a foundation for productive dialogue regarding feedback and evaluation from the supervisor, a central function of supervision. These discussions build trust and encourage a climate in supervision sessions that is focused on self-reflection and improvement. From the onset of the supervisory relationship, the supervisor provides frequent formative feedback regarding strengths and weaknesses, areas requiring additional focus, specific suggestions for improvement, and the quality of participation in the supervision process. Routine formative feedback and processing of the supervisory relationship ensure that supervisees will never be surprised by summative evaluation comments; and similarly, supervisors will not learn about supervisee concerns too late in the training cycle to make changes.

Addressing Blind Spots and Transference Issues

One of the roles of supervisors is the identification of professional "blind spots" of supervisees. Self-awareness regarding the potential impact of interpersonal style, personal issues, and biases is essential for psychologists to minimize any interference in judgment, attribution, or responses in work with clients. The monitoring and addressing of any transference, countertransference, or parallel process issues that may occur in the supervisory relationship is an important aspect of this role as well. These concepts have been extensively studied in relation to supervision of psychotherapy (Borders & Brown, 2005; Corey et al. 2010; Ekstein & Wallerstein, 1972; Loganbill et al., 1982; McNeill & Worthen, 1989; Searles, 1955; Stoltenberg & Delworth, 1987). Blind to the supervisee's awareness, all involve the supervisee responding in one setting as though the supervisee were relating to a different individual in a different setting. Unresolved issues supervisees experience in other relationships can inadvertently contaminate relationships with clients or supervisors and interfere with sound clinical judgment. These responses can occur in work with clients in therapy or consultation or within the supervisory relationship. Drawing these issues to the attention of the supervisee increases self-awareness and fosters self-monitoring.

Transference is a psychodynamic therapy term that refers to a client's unconscious transferring of feelings, attitudes, and behaviors from reactions to significant others in their lives to their therapists. Typically, these are more distorted, exaggerated, irrational, or unrealistic reactions (Harvey & Struzziero, 2008); for example, a client can transfer negative feelings they have towards their parent to the school psychologist.

Countertransference can occur when a psychologist unintentionally responds to a client based on his or her own unresolved interpersonal or emotional issues. For example, countertransference occurs when a school psychologist unknowingly transfers negative feelings towards an ex-husband or wife onto an administrator who reminds the school psychologist of his or her spouse. Countertransference can also occur in supervision when the supervisee transfers feelings, attitudes, and behavioral patterns from other significant relationships to the supervisor. In supervision, it is common for supervisees to begin to idealize their supervisors due to the assistance and emotional support they receive from them and their own lack of self-confidence in their professional skills. However, it is also possible for unresolved authority issues to emerge as part of the supervisory relationship due to the supervisor's authority role related to evaluation and gatekeeping.

Transference and countertransference can also occur on the part of the supervisor toward the supervisee. Unresolved personal issues and problem areas of supervisors can be triggered when interacting with their supervisees. Schools can be stressful environments. At times, the intense role demands of school psychologists can be overwhelming. Supervisors may inadvertently transfer their frustrations with others in their personal or professional lives to their supervisees. Sometimes supervisors can become unrealistically impatient with the progress of supervisees toward independent functioning when workloads peak or problem situations requiring more intense supervision emerge. Supervisors' self-monitoring and healthy emotional awareness assist them in avoiding inappropriate emotional reactions to their supervisees during stressful periods and when personal issues may interfere with effective supervision.

Some specific areas supervisors should monitor in terms of reactions to their supervisees include: maintenance of realistic expectations; avoidance of unwarranted rescuing responses that foster dependency (e.g., allowing supervisees to experience challenges and struggles in problem-solving activities); comparisons to prior supervisees; the need to have all the answers; favoritism within a supervisee cohort; and parental responses to supervisees who may be of similar age to the supervisor's own children.

When supervisors recognize that their own personal issues may be interfering with supervision, they carry an ethical responsibility to seek out their own supervision, consultation, or personal therapy to address these concerns (Corey et al., 2010; Norcross & Guy, 2007). Typically, it is supervisors who should seek consultation with a colleague rather than sharing the countertransference issues with their supervisees, which can be overwhelming to them as their energy is focused on developing competency as a school psychologist. However, depending on the nature and impact of the countertransference and after consulting with a colleague, it may be appropriate to share it with the supervisee and explore some aspects of the supervisor's reactions to help the supervisee understand the supervisor's interactions with them. The developmental level of the supervisee should be a factor in considering whether or not to share countertransference issues with a supervisee with it being contraindicated with less experienced supervisees (Borders & Brown, 2005).

The cognitions, affect, and behaviors associated with transference and countertransference in supervision typically manifest themselves early in supervision although it may take a longer time for the supervisor to recognize them. Productive processing of these issues can strengthen the supervisor-supervisee relationship and help the supervisee establish better relationships with clients and consultees.

The most frequent domain for examining limitations in emotional awareness and the interference of personal reactions or issues lies within the supervisees' work with clients. It is important not to cross a boundary that would turn supervision into therapy; however, it is equally critical for supervisees to learn self-monitoring skills to improve dispassionate clinical judgment and avoid letting personal beliefs, attitudes, behaviors, or issues interfere with professional work. For example, when working with an angry student who may be projecting their anger at a teacher or parent upon the supervisee during a crisis intervention, the supervisee must be careful to avoid reenacting the counterproductive responses of these other adults. In another example, it is a natural tendency of novice supervisees to assume too much responsibility for the success of their clients and to risk enabling or overprotective responses (i.e., protecting them from the natural disciplinary consequences earned by student actions). Feedback in supervision addresses these interpersonal dynamics and promotes supervisee self-awareness for the benefit of their clients.

Discussing observations related to transference, countertransference, and parallel process can help supervisees gain important insights into their work as school psychologists. Rather than perceive them as negatively impacting clinical work or supervision, supervisors might think of them as potentially useful tools that signal areas that need to be addressed. At times, they may indicate deficient clinical skills to be addressed with targeted training; while at other times these issues may need to be addressed in personal counseling outside the supervisory relationship. Attending to these issues must be done carefully and judiciously keeping in mind the welfare of clients and the growth of the supervisee. While noting the importance of monitoring these issues in supervision, Corey et al. (2010) cautioned against an overly intense focus on transference issues. However, examination of these interpersonal dynamics does provide a mirror to understand ways that these feelings impact supervisees' work with clients in counseling or how the supervisee's unresolved personal issues may negatively impact the supervisory relationship. Enhancing supervisees' self-awareness fosters development of their own sense of competence and their ability to solve problems.

How can discussions of these processes be initiated? Corey et al. (2010) provided some examples of questions or statements that can be used to explore transference, countertransference, and parallel process issues in the supervisory relationship. These questions include:

- What similarities do you see between our supervisory work and the relationship you share with your client?
- We have talked about your wanting my approval as a supervisor. It appears to me that you are hesitant to challenge your client lest she not approve of you.
- Think aloud for a bit about what purpose your client's resistance might be serving.
- You appear to be having a very strong emotional response to your client; where and with whom else in your life might you experience this emotion?

(p. 81)

Processing as Preparation for Supervisory Role

Examination of the process of supervision and the key elements of supervisory practice help prepare supervisees for their eventual role as supervisors. For supervisors who adopt the DEP supervision model articulated in this volume, the authors have created an instrument to assess the strength of the supervisory relationship and the integrity of implementation of the various behavioral markers that characterize each component of the DEP supervision model.

The *DEP Self-reflection and Supervisor Feedback Survey (DEP-SSFS)* is intended to be completed by both the supervisor and the supervisee at various stages of the supervisory relationship. This instrument provides a mechanism to structure feedback from the supervisee regarding the supervisory relationship and practices within the DEP framework and self-reflection on the part of the supervisor. This instrument will be discussed in detail in Chapter 10 after a full description of the DEP model. It can be found in Appendix 4A.

Summary: Processing the Supervisory Relationship

Processing of the supervisory relationship is of critical importance in ensuring an effective and satisfying supervision experience for both the supervisee and supervisor. Early in the supervisory relationship, it is important for the supervisor to develop a transparent and routine process for supervision. This transparency begins with a written contract. Supervisors are encouraged to routinely review and discuss the dynamics of the supervisory relationship. This can include reviewing the benefits of supervision in order to identify any areas of concern or possible ruptures in the relationship followed by discussing corrective measures. These discussions contribute to establishing a foundation for the central role of reciprocal feedback in the supervisor relationship. Any supervisee blind spots or transference issues can negatively impact supervisees' client relationships as well as the supervisory relationship itself. Directly addressing these issues fosters the development of supervisee self-awareness and ensures that personal issues do not interfere with clinical work. Supervisors and supervisees should also periodically review the process of supervision so that the supervisee learns skills related to competent supervision. The DEP-SSFS provides a mechanism for supervisors to self-reflect and monitor the quality of their relationships with their supervisees and the fidelity of their implementation of the DEP supervision model. The instrument is designed to be completed by both supervisors and their supervisees and then discussed.

SUPERVISORY PROCESS ACTIVITY

Consider ending each supervision session with a request for feedback from your supervisee. This feedback can be structured to include the following: (a) On a 1–5 scale rate how effective we were in meeting your needs/accomplishing what you had hoped to accomplish in this supervision session? (b) How can we work more effectively together to earn a rating of 5? and (c) How can we strengthen our supervisory relationship?

5

ETHICAL AND LEGAL ISSUES IN SUPERVISION

Although most trainees as part of their on-campus didactic training are exposed to legal mandates and the ethical principles related to the practice of school psychology, it is during their field-based training and subsequent professional practice that they have the opportunity to integrate and apply this knowledge. Teaching and modeling ethical and legal psychological practice represents a core task of supervision. Supervision itself also presents unique ethical challenges to both supervisees and supervisors (Goodyear & Rodolfa, 2012) and is highly susceptible to ethical infractions (Koocher & Keith-Spiegel, 2008). Ethical decision-making in supervision can often be more complex than clinical decision-making (Storm, Todd, Sprenkle, & Morgan, 2001). There exists a number of frequently encountered legal-ethical issues in the practice of clinical supervision. This chapter explores the relevant legal mandates and ethical principles impacting supervision, provides suggestions for addressing this core task with supervisees, and presents some of the common ethical dilemmas clinical supervisors may face in the process of working with their supervisees.

The Relationship between Ethics and Law

Ethics and law represent related but distinct concepts. Professional organizations strive to define ethical or moral principles for professional activity. These ethical principles represent standards of behavior and those behaviors that deserve punishment. Disregard of ethical standards can lead to sanctions or even removal from professional organizations.

Legal and statutory regulations provide guidelines for practice designed to ensure eligibility for services and the protection of consumers of services. Disregard of legal requirements can result in legal consequences such as fines or even prison terms.

In general, ethical and legal guidelines align. However, at times issues might arise when there is conflict among principles of ethics, law, and personal belief. This may be more likely to occur for supervisees who are just beginning to internalize professional practice standards. These challenging circumstances must be addressed in supervision. However, before these challenging cases can be addressed, it is necessary to provide full coverage of ethical and legal responsibilities within the profession, which are an essential focus of supervision. Near the end of this chapter, case examples will cover a number of these complex and challenging dilemmas.

School psychology is striving to define its practice within a social justice framework (Shriberg et al., 2008) which not only requires ethical practice but professional advocacy on behalf of those in need of services or disenfranchised from full social participation. At times this requires advocacy to change regulatory or district procedures. For example, if a school district is not providing appropriate services for English Learners and a large majority of these students are failing and dropping out of school, a social justice framework requiring professional advocacy would indicate that the school psychology supervisor and supervisee should advocate for these services with the administration of the school district.

Legal and Ethical Codes of School Psychology Related Organizations

Standards for legal and ethical practice emerge from professional organizations and from legal and regulatory entities. We will summarize the relevant ethical codes and discuss in more depth those standards that pertain specifically to supervision. For a more detailed discussion of legal-ethical principles that impact the practice of school psychology the reader is referred to Jacob, Decker, and Hartshorne's (2011) text on ethics and law for school psychologists.

Ethical codes are based on core moral principles that are accepted obligations unless they compete in a particular situation with an equal or stronger obligation (Bersoff & Koeppl, 1993). These moral principles include Beneficence and Nonmaleficence, Fidelity and Responsibility, Integrity, Justice, and Respect for Autonomy (APA, 2010a; Bersoff & Koeppl, 1993). A definition for each follows with an example. Beneficence refers to contributing to the welfare of others and maximizing benefits over risks. Examples would include the ethical requirement of competence. Nonmaleficence is the moral principle that above all one should do no harm. Again, the ethical requirement of competence addresses this moral principle. Loyalty and keeping our promises is reflected in the moral principal of fidelity. Fidelity and responsibility are reflected in the ethical requirements related to not abandoning our supervisees. For example, when a supervisor facilitates the development of a remediation plan when a supervisee's skill deficits or professional behavior problems are observed, both fidelity and responsibility are demonstrated. Integrity refers to honesty in the professional supervisory relationship and would be reflected in the ethical standard related to fully disclosing to the supervisee the responsibilities of the supervisor for evaluation of the supervisee including the gatekeeping function. Justice refers to fairness and the ideal distribution of risks and benefits and would be reflected in the ethical requirement related to specifying due process procedures for a supervisee. Respect for autonomy refers to respecting the right of individuals to make their own choices and would be reflected in ethical requirements related to informed consent of the supervisee to engage in supervision with the supervisor.

National Association of School Psychologists

The NASP *Principles for Professional Ethics* (2010d) includes four overarching principles. The first is Respect for the Dignity of Persons that includes subsections on self-determination and autonomy, privacy and confidentiality, and fairness. The second principle is Professional Competence and Responsibility and includes subsections on competence and responsibility. Honesty and Integrity in Professional Relationships and Responsibility to Schools, Families, Communities, the Profession, and Society represent the third and fourth overarching principles.

The NASP guidelines specifically related to supervision include Standard II.2.4, which states that when supervising graduate students' field experiences or internships, school psychologists are responsible for the work of their supervisees. In addition to being an ethical standard, this responsibility refers to the legal concept of *vicarious liability*. Supervisors may be held liable for the work of their supervisees under the doctrine of *Respondeat Superior*. This legal doctrine holds that a supervisor who is in a position of authority or control over a supervisee may be held legally liable for damages caused by the supervisee. It is important to recognize that this liability can be found whether or not the supervisor did anything inappropriate and also extends to an employer-employee relationship.

NASP Standard IV.4.2 states that school psychologists who supervise practicum students and interns are responsible for all the professional practices of their supervisees. This refers to the same legal principle of vicarious liability noted above. The standard goes on to state that supervisors ensure that practicum students and interns are adequately supervised as outlined in the NASP *Graduate Preparation Standards for School Psychologists*. Interns and graduate students are identified as such; and the supervising school psychologist cosigns their work. Acceptance of membership into NASP commits the supervising psychologist to adhere to these principles.

American Psychological Association

The *APA Ethical Principles of Psychologists and Code of Conduct* (2010a) delineated five guiding moral principles for ethical practice including Beneficence and

Nonmaleficence, Fidelity and Responsibility, Integrity, Justice, and Respect for People's Rights and Dignity.

In the *Ethical Principles of Psychologists*, the American Psychological Association (APA, 2010a) included several statements relevant to supervision. These include requirements for assessing supervisee performance and providing the supervisee with information about this process at the beginning of supervision, and the prohibition of engaging in sexual relationships with those with whom they have or likely have evaluative authority.

Acceptance of membership in the APA commits the supervising psychologist to adhere to these principles. In addition, these principles may take on the force of law when they are incorporated into licensing laws for psychologists, which occurs in many states.

Other sources of guidance related to ethical professional behavior include other organizations concerned with training and supervision such as the Association of State and Provincial Psychology Boards (ASPPB, 2015). Because of their aspirational nature, these guidelines lack the enforcement power of the ethical principles.

The APA *Guidelines for Clinical Supervision in Health Service Psychology* (2015a) addresses the Domain of Ethics, Legal, and Regulatory Considerations and more extensively comments on training for ethical practice. These guidelines include that supervisors are responsible for acculturating supervisees into the ethical practice of the profession. The primary obligation of the supervisor is the welfare of the client. The gatekeeping role of the supervisor for entry or continuance in the profession is an essential role for the protection of present and potential future clients, for the good of the profession, and for the welfare of the supervisee. The guidelines for supervision specify that parameters of supervision should be clearly outlined in a written supervision contract (see Chapter 7). Documentation of supervisee progress toward competency and professional development is also required.

Other Related Professional Organizations

The American Counseling Association (ACA) Code of Ethics (2014) addressed supervisory ethics in the section: Supervision, Training, and Teaching. These ethical standards include standards similar to APA and NASP but go farther to include requirements for training the supervisor in supervision methods and techniques and to complete required continuing education activities related to supervision. The standards also address the role of multiculturalism and diversity in the supervisory relationship.

There exist differences in levels of specificity among the attempts of the various professional organizations to address ethics in relationship to supervision. As there is increased focus on the practice of supervision, increased attention to the role of the supervisor in modeling and fostering ethical practice for supervisees is being delineated. Ethical practice is defined as a critical competency within the movement to define professional competencies for training and supervision.

Association of State and Provincial Psychology Boards (ASPPB)

Although not a professional organization per se but rather comprised of member state and provincial boards of psychology with the goal of promoting excellence in regulation and advancing public protection in psychology, the ASPPB (2015) has recently published *Supervision Guidelines for Education and Training Leading to Licensure as a Health Service Provider.* The first edition of these guidelines was published in 1998; and they are intended to assist state and provincial psychology boards in developing their own supervision requirements consistent with "best practice." The Guidelines are also meant to offer guidance regarding appropriate expectations and responsibilities within the supervisory relationship.

One of the five areas addressed in this document includes Ethics of Supervision. This ethics section draws upon the ASPPB (2013) *Code of Conduct,* the *Ethical Principles of Psychologists and Code of Conduct* of the American Psychological Association (APA, 2010a), *the Canadian Code of Ethics for Psychologists* of the Canadian Psychological Association (CPA, 2000), the American Psychological Association *Guidelines for Clinical Supervision in Health Service Psychology* (APA, 2015a), and the CPA (2009) *Ethical Guidelines for Supervision in Psychology: Teaching, Research, Practice, and Administration.*

The development of these regulations in supervision is particularly dependent on the ethical principles of respect, beneficence (welfare of the client as the highest priority), integrity, competence in both psychological practice and supervision, informed consent, confidentiality, multiple relationships, and ethical issues around the use of technology. Further, special attention to the ethical code sections relating to education and training (APA, Section 7, 2010a; CPA, 2000) and cultural diversity (APA, Principle E, 2010a) is important. As the supervisor's highest duty is protection of the public, ethical dilemmas may arise in which the supervisor is required to balance this duty with supervisee development, supervisory alliance, evaluative processes, and gatekeeping for the profession (Bernard & Goodyear, 2014; Falender & Shafranske, 2004, 2007). Although supervisors need to balance the goals of client welfare and supervisee learning, the welfare of the client remains primary. The utilization of interns or practicum students must be focused on learning and not misused to merely address staffing shortages.

As the ASPPB provides one of the more detailed treatments of ethical standards related to supervision drawing upon a variety of ethical codes, we now turn our attention to the Ethics of Supervision section of these guidelines. The specific areas addressed by the ASPPB (2015) are confidentiality including limits of confidentiality, informed consent, competence, evaluation, multiple relationships, and technology.

Confidentiality

Confidentiality represents a key domain to be addressed within supervisory practice. Confidentiality includes limits of confidentiality regarding abuse and risk of harm to self and others and the duty to warn and protect. The Tarasoff (*Tarasoff* v. *Regents of California*, 1974, 1976) decisions and follow-up state-level interpretations require that psychologists provide warnings to parties who might be threatened by one's client. In Tarasoff the supervisor was found to have vicarious liability for the lack of appropriate practice by the supervisee when the supervisee did not inform the individual who was the target of a threat of intended harm. The supervisee's client subsequently murdered this third party. State laws should be consulted as they do differ in terms of when confidentiality should be broken and when third parties who are threatened with harm need to be warned and protected.

Also related to confidentiality, the special circumstances and recommended protocols for explaining confidentiality to clients who are minors need to be addressed. A minor generally has no legal right to confidentiality independent of his or her parents. However, a transparent discussion with the child and parents of the limits of confidentiality needs to occur. In a counseling situation, children require an explanation at their level that what they discuss with the school psychologist will be confidential. Confidential in this situation means that the school psychologist will not tell the child's parents what the child shares during counseling unless the child indicates they intend to hurt themselves or someone else at which time the school psychologist will need to inform their parents or others to protect them. Further, the school psychologist should share with the child that there may be other issues unrelated to harm to self or others or abuse that may need to be shared with the parents. However, if the psychologist believes one or more of these issues (beyond harm to self or others or abuse) needs to be shared with the parents, the child will also be informed prior to the discussion with the parents. It should be noted that the limits of confidentiality will also be different when the main purpose of the school psychologist working with the child is to conduct a psychoeducational assessment in a school setting as compared to what occurs in a counseling situation. When conducting a psychoeducational assessment, the school psychologist may explain to the minor that the results of the assessment will be shared with both the child (with the extent of detail depending on the child's age) and the child's parents and teachers; but nothing specific the child shares with the school psychologist will be repeated, only general impressions, unless what the child shares indicates the child is a danger to him or herself or others. Examples can be provided to clarify these limits to confidentiality. For example if the child indicates that he or she does not like a particular teacher, the school psychologist would not share that specific information with the child's teacher but would share general impressions about the child's attitudes towards school. Attention must also be paid to both school and mental health codes related to confidentiality as they may differ in requirements. For example, in some states the mental health code allows any minor 12 years of age or older to request and receive counseling services on an outpatient basis for up to five sessions without the consent of the parents, while the Family Rights and Privacy Act of 1974

(FERPA; 20 U.S.C. 1232g; 34 C.F.R. Part 99) states that until a student reaches the age of 18, the parents have a right to give or deny consent.

Also as part of a written contract, supervisors have an ethical responsibility to discuss the limits of confidentiality related to personal disclosures and evaluation. Supervisees should be informed who will have access to these personal disclosures and their performance evaluations such as their faculty members in their graduate training program, other clinical supervisors and/or program faculty, administrative supervisors in the practice setting, and state licensing boards. Supervisees should also be informed about what types of records will be created regarding what occurs in the supervisory sessions and procedures for storing and destroying these records. Related to limits of confidentiality, the supervisees' clients must also be informed of their trainee status, the name of their supervisor, and that the supervisor is responsible for all of the clinical services the supervisee provides and has access to all client records.

ASPBB ethical guidelines for supervision also include obtaining informed consent from the supervisee. This has a narrower interpretation than obtaining informed consent from clients for clinical services. This interpretation is based on training and accreditation standards, school, agency or other practice setting requirements, and state laws governing the practice of psychology. In addition, through the written contract (see Chapter 7) the supervisee should be informed of supervisor expectations related to supervisee responsibilities, requirements for supervision, and the parameters of supervision of which the supervisee must be informed and provide consent.

Competence

Competence in providing *both* the clinical services provided by the supervisee *and* in the provision of supervision is required. Supervisors must also demonstrate competence in modeling the highest level of ethical practice, which should be incorporated into supervisory practice. This ethical practice includes multiple foci such as ethical practice for the benefit of the client. The welfare of the client is paramount as is the use of evidence-based practices on behalf of the client. Practicing within one's competency also includes the supervisor knowing when to seek consultation and incorporating collegial consultation into one's practice routine.

Essential ethical competence for supervisors also includes appropriately assigning clients based on supervisee competency and client needs. Consistent monitoring of their supervisees' progress and professional development is also required. Related to the latter, supervisors should have the professional competencies to effectively provide an assessment of supervisees' competencies and the skill to provide effective feedback based on a supervisory review of supervisees' clients' progress. This assessment of supervisee competence provides ongoing data to guide the supervisors' assignment of clients to the supervisees as well as gauging the intensity of supervision required.

Evaluation

As noted in previous chapters, evaluation is a necessary role of the supervisor; and providing feedback is a critical task of supervision. However, psychologists experience challenges in providing constructive feedback to supervisees (Hoffman, Hill, Holmes, & Freitas, 2005). For example, supervisors may wait too long to begin providing feedback, struggle with giving critical feedback, or not include sufficient behavioral descriptors. However, training in supervision improves the process of providing this critical feedback to supervisees (Milne, Sheikh, Pattison, & Wilkinson, 2011). Related to evaluation, due process must be available and clearly delineated for supervisees. Feedback and evaluation must be honest, appropriately administered, and timely. Systems must be in place to ensure that supervisees can address concerns about the supervisory relationship, training experience, and character or conclusions of evaluations with external resources. The written contract, discussed in Chapter 7, should reference due process procedures and the schedule and responsibilities of the supervisor for feedback and evaluation. The topic of providing effective feedback and evaluation to supervisees is addressed in more depth in Chapter 7.

Multiple Relationships

Some multiple relationships are unavoidable and should be evaluated on the degree to which they can impair the objectivity of the supervisor. Due to the power differential between supervisor and supervisee and the supervisor's responsibility for evaluation including gatekeeping, multiple relationships in supervision need to be carefully considered. Multiple roles in supervisory relationships (e.g., dissertation supervisor and practicum supervisor) must be focused on establishing mature professional relationships and be consistent with the developmental status of the supervisee.

Supervision teaches appropriate management of multiple relationships with clients and with educational colleagues who are consultees. Supervisors should directly discuss and then monitor multiple relationships between themselves and supervisees. Supervisory relationships are primarily defined as professional relationships, have a power differential, are evaluative, and are focused on professional growth of supervisees but are not therapy relationships. Although school staff periodically engage in social activities, supervisors should cautiously approach individual social relationships with supervisees. Sexual intimacies between supervisors and supervisees are *never* appropriate.

Due to the power differential, supervisees may not be able to refuse to participate in a multiple relationship or withdraw from the supervisory relationship. The ASPPB (2015) ethical code related to supervision specifies a number of problem-solving frameworks to conduct a risk/benefit analysis of the particular multiple relationships that might be entered into by the supervisor or supervisee (Burian & Slimp, 2000; Gottlieb, Robinson, & Younggren, 2007).

Technology

Unique ethical issues and challenges are raised related to providing supervision using telecommunication technologies. The ASPPB in collaboration with the APA, and the APA Insurance Trust (APAIT) formed a joint task force and developed specific ethical principles addressing the practice of telepsychology (APA, 2013). Drawing upon these guidelines, the ASPPB (2015) also developed ethical principles related to offering supervision using telecommunication methods. These ethical guidelines include requiring the supervisor to be knowledgeable of the limits and risks to confidentiality and that the supervisor needs to be informed about the security of the connection or any electronic breaches. Other ethical standards include: (a) confirming the identity of the supervisee and the identity and age of the client and securing parent or guardian permission if necessary; (b) being aware that nonverbal communication and emotional reactivity of the client may be impacted by communication mode; (c) establishing emergency provisions since the supervisor would not be readily accessible to intervene in risk of harm or similar situations; (d) communicating the limits of confidentiality in the use of electronic methods such as video recording including delineation of who has access to the recordings, where they are stored, and when they will be destroyed; and (e) explicitly discussing with the client and/or parent/guardians of a minor child the use of technology for supervision, the precautions taken for security of information, and the required consents.

The supervisor also needs to review with the supervisee the ethics of using social networks and online communication including "friending" of clients and the supervisor on Facebook or other social media. It is important to instruct supervisees that it is inappropriate to post anything on social media related to their clients whether or not their identities are masked. Specific safeguards must be delineated regarding all use of electronic communication with clients or their families such as email or voicemail. A confidentiality and electronic communication access policy was developed by the school psychology program at Ball State University. It addresses many of the electronic communication ethical issues discussed above. It can be accessed from: http://cms.bsu.edu/-/media/www/departmentalcontent/edpsych/pdfs/school%20psychology%20doctoral%20handbook.pdf.

Despite these ethical requirements discussed above, a study by Ladany, Lehrman-Waterman, Molinaro, and Wolgast (1999) found that over 50% of supervisees reported that their supervisors did not follow at least one ethical guideline with many lapses centering around standards of competency in providing supervision such as performance evaluation, monitoring of the supervisee's activities, defining limits of confidentiality in supervision issues, session boundaries, and respectful behavior. Other practices inconsistent with ethical guidelines of the provision of supervision include negatively impacting the supervisory relationship due to the power differential as well as client welfare, supervisee development, and supervisee wellbeing.

Federal and State Laws Impacting the Practice of School Psychology

A detailed discussion of federal laws such as the Individuals with Disabilities Improvement Act of 2004 (IDEA, Pub. L No. 108–446, 34 C.R.R. Part 300), the Family Educational Rights and Privacy Act of 1974 (FERPA, 20 U.S.C. 1232g; 34 C.F.R. Part 99), Section 504 of the Rehabilitation Act of 1973 (Pub. L No. 93–112, 29 U.S.C.794. 34 C.R.R. 100), and relevant state laws and regulatory codes for special education and mental health services and school records impacting the practice of school psychology is beyond the scope of this chapter. For a more thorough discussion of these laws, we refer the reader to Jacob et al.'s (2011) text on ethics and law for school psychologists. However, a discussion of their implications for supervision follows.

An essential supervisory responsibility is to assist supervisees in understanding and adhering to legal requirements related to the practice of school psychology. Supervisors must thoroughly understand legal requirements impacting their practice and adhere to them as they serve as powerful models.

Legal principles influencing professional practice directly bear on supervisory practice. A fundamental legal concept is *Standard of Care* that refers to what the typical school psychologist would do faced with a particular set of professional circumstances and decisions with similar resources. Standard of Care relates directly to definitions of best practice both in terms of service delivery to clients and the practice of supervision and training. There are several sources that would be consulted to determine standard of care in the practice of school psychology. These would include but are not limited to the NASP Practice Model (2010a), NASP *Best Practices Guidelines for School Psychology Intern Field Supervision and Mentoring* (2014c), NASP *Standards for Graduate Preparation of School Psychologists* (2010b), and APA *Guidelines for Clinical Supervision in Health Service Psychology* (2015a) discussed previously. Standard of Care requires the application of evidence-based practice and thus evolves over time; and the supervisor must continue to be current in empirically supported practices. Supervisors should model and teach the responsibility to stay professionally current including professional development in supervisory practice.

When this standard is observed, there should be a reduction of the tension that can emerge when a supervisee has been exposed to state-of-the-art practice in graduate training; but it is less evident in the practices of a training site. Supervision is responsible for implementation of appropriate Standard of Care activities. It falls within the supervisor's responsibility to integrate theory, research, and practice and ensure best practice by the supervisee (see Chapter 2). Engaging in advocacy and pursuing system change represents an ethical responsibility when a school district is not fully supporting contemporary best practice.

Moral principles underlying the establishment of Standard of Care have a direct relationship with ethical principles articulated in the APA Ethical Code (Barnett, 2008; Corey et al., 2010). These principles were referenced earlier and include: *Autonomy* or promoting self-determination and the freedom of clients to choose their own direction; *Beneficence* or promoting the good of others; *Justice* which involves fostering fairness or a means of providing equal treatment to all people; *Fidelity* which refers to making honest and realistic promises and honoring commitments to those served; *Veracity* involves truthfulness and honesty with clients; and *Self-care*. Barnett (2008) emphasized that taking care of ourselves is essential so that we are capable of executing appropriate standard of care for clients. Supervisors must model self-care and support its development in supervisees.

The legal concept of *liability* results primarily from not following appropriate professional Standards of Care. Examples would include how crisis intervention is handled for a student at risk for suicide or utilization of an appropriate evidence-based assessment protocol. Key legal principles affecting supervisory liability are *Direct* and *Vicarious Liability*. Direct liability for a supervisor can arise from improper actions or negligence in suggesting a particular approach for a supervisee to use with a client. A supervisor can be negligent by not properly executing supervisory responsibilities such as inadequate monitoring of the supervisee's activities, repetitive failure to convene supervisory sessions, or assignment of clients inappropriate for the training level of supervisee. Vicarious liability was discussed earlier in this chapter.

Risk Management

Risk management refers to the "practice of focusing on the identification, evaluation, and treatment of problems that may injure clients, lead to filing of an ethics complaint, or a malpractice action" (Corey et al., 2010, p. 182). Our previous discussion of direct and vicarious liability suggests that there are risks in taking on the role of a supervisor but that its benefits and satisfaction outweigh these risks. Building safeguards into the supervisory process minimizes risks and helps to prevent any ethics complaints or legal actions. These safeguards include several previously discussed: (a) developing a comprehensive supervision contract that is signed by both the supervisee and supervisor at initial stage of training relationship (see Chapter 7); (b) balancing intern training needs and responsibility for child welfare; (c) insisting on supervisee transparency in self-disclosures related to professional activities, particularly related to challenges, questions, and problems; (d) the supervisor and supervisee practicing within their level of competence and seeking supervision and consultation when necessary; (e) being consistently available for the supervisee with professional back-up specified when unavailable; (f) maintaining appropriate confidentiality standards, which can be particularly challenging in a school setting when working closely with classroom teachers and school administrators; (g) being accountable and engaging in appropriate and responsible recordkeeping, including documenting assessment activities, intervention plans, recommendations, and supervision sessions which are discussed further in Chapter 7; (h) providing close oversight of the supervisee's activities; (i) maintaining an outcome focus regarding client and supervisee growth and development; (j) employing multiple methods of supervision as self-report alone is no longer acceptable (these multiple methods of supervision are discussed in more depth in Chapter 7); (k) implementing a feedback and evaluation plan that is timely and transparent; (l) soliciting feedback from your supervisee regarding his or her experience of supervisory process and its benefits and shortcomings; (m) conducting scheduled reviews of progress on the internship plan and/or agreed upon goals for the supervisory experience; (n) appraising administrators (and, when required, legal authorities) of student risk for harm to self or others.

As a note of caution, legal advice for risk management must be monitored in terms of its implications for the welfare of the client. Educational lawyers will sometimes prescribe risk management strategies designed to protect school district liability that might not be in the best interests of children or may not match psychological best practice. Examples would be the common practice of excluding students from school who express suicidal ideation when in fact that exclusion may increase their risk for self-harm, or suspending students out of school for substance abuse infractions when this increases not only their risk for continued abuse but may increase risk for classmates. In another example, financial pressures on special education departments may cause some districts to compromise eligibility standards to reduce special education costs.

Teaching a Systematic Approach for Ethical and Legal Decision-making

There exist a number of legal-ethical decision-making models including those developed by Jacob et al. (2011), Koocher and Keith-Spiegel (2008), and Remley and Herlihy (2010). Building upon a model proposed by Corey et al. (2010) and our knowledge and experience supervising interns and practicum students in both university and field settings, we find the following 8-step decision-making helpful with our supervisees.

1. Define potential ethical or legal issues in the problem situation.
2. Research ethical and legal guidelines from professional organizations and federal and local regulations.
3. Consult with colleagues (if necessary with school district or university legal counsel).
4. Consider the rights, responsibilities, and welfare of all affected parties including the supervisee and supervisor.
5. Employ common sense, mindful of the overriding responsibility toward client welfare and avoidance of harm.
6. Propose multiple courses of action and evaluate their impact on the welfare of the client and their ethical and legal consequences.

7. Make a decision and implement an action plan using common sense.
8. Monitor and evaluate outcome and implications of decision and action plan and use these data to decide if further action is necessary and to guide future decision-making.

Murky Waters: Unique Challenges and Complications

Ethical principles, legal requirements, and personal beliefs are related but may at times be in conflict or at the very least difficult to reconcile. For example, personal beliefs of supervisees regarding issues such as homosexuality, abortion, and women's roles and rights may conflict with the profession's standards or legal safeguards. When this occurs, supervision must directly address these conflicts, teach the supervisee how to monitor potential interference of personal beliefs with intervention work, ensure that the profession's ethical guidelines are safeguarded and followed, decide when a supervisee should remove himself or herself from a specific case, and transparently evaluate whether the supervisee has developed sufficient diversity and multicultural competency required for entrance into the profession demonstrated by not permitting personal beliefs to interfere with service provision.

Cases Presenting Ethical Dilemmas

What follows are a series of ethical dilemmas related to supervision. For three cases we go through our proposed 8-step legal-ethical decision-making model. For the remaining dilemmas in Appendix 5A, we encourage you alone or as a joint activity with your supervisee to use the information from this chapter together with the cited ethical codes to apply the legal-ethical decision-making model to each scenario.

Issues Related to Confidentiality

A. Angela, a high school sophomore, receives psychological counseling services in school as designated in her IEP. Dan, a school psychologist intern, is assigned to provide this therapeutic service. Angela has a history of depression, which has been judged to significantly interfere with her academic progress. When depressed she shuts down academically, demonstrates minimal work production, becomes socially withdrawn, and even sometimes shows deteriorating self-care skills. In the course of a counseling session, she tells Dan that she has something critical to disclose but wants him to promise again and in advance that he will keep it confidential. Dan assures her that her disclosures are confidential. She proceeds to tell Dan that she has an eating disorder that she does not believe anyone is aware of because she has hidden her symptoms so well. Dan is alarmed at the severity of her symptoms. He presents this case to you in supervision the next day. How do you respond and how do you think Dan should respond?

Authors' Analysis

1. Define potential ethical or legal issues in the problem situation.

   The central issue in this case involves the limits of confidentiality, which is both a legal and ethical requirement. Dan did not discuss the limits of confidentiality as he told Angela everything she shares with him during their counseling sessions is confidential. Dan is concerned that Angela's eating disorder poses a danger to her health.

2. Research ethical and legal guidelines from professional organizations and federal and local regulations.

   Ethics codes of both NASP (Principle 1.2) and APA (Standard 4) address confidentiality and that there are limits to confidentiality. The legal principles/ restrictions related to confidentiality and its limits are reflected in FERPA (as this counseling is occurring in the school setting) as well as relevant state education or mental health codes (e.g., Illinois School Code and Illinois Mental Health Code). Although Angela has some rights to confidentiality they are limited when she indicates she is engaging in behaviors that pose a danger to herself or others (i.e., her eating disorder). As Angela is a high school sophomore and likely a minor, her parents also have a legal right to information about her treatment consistent with FERPA and relevant state and mental health codes.

3. Consult with colleagues (if necessary with school district or university legal counsel).

   In this case, Dan is consulting with his intern supervisor who maintains vicarious liability for all of Dan's clinical work including his counseling with Angela. The supervisor might also want to consult with the school nurse if there are questions specifically about the impact of the eating disorder on Angela's overall health.

4. Consider the rights, responsibilities, and welfare of all affected parties including the supervisee and supervisor.

   The supervisor assumes vicarious liability for the therapeutic work Dan is doing with Angela. Dan has the responsibility to explain to Angela the limits of confidentiality in their counseling relationship and to share information that suggests that Angela is engaging in behaviors (i.e., associated with the eating disorder) that can pose a risk to her health or safety.

5. Employ common sense, mindful of the overriding responsibility toward client welfare and avoidance of harm.

   With an overriding responsibility to assure client welfare, it is important to determine to what degree Angela's eating disorder represents a "risk of harm" and balance this with the potential negative impact of disclosing this information to the parents on the counseling relationship.

6. Propose multiple courses of action and evaluate their impact on the welfare of the client and their ethical and legal consequences.

    a. Dan can do nothing which could cause harm to Angela and also lead to Dan's supervisor being legally liable if it is determined that the standard of care is that Angela's eating disorder would be considered a danger to her health and her parents should have been told so they could seek treatment for their daughter. As telling her parents about her eating disorder represents a salient issue for Angela, Dan sharing this information with them may damage his relationship with Angela and/or cause her to decide to terminate counseling. It is clear that Angela's social-emotional health and academic functioning require counseling services and breaking confidentiality may serve as a barrier to her receiving the services she needs to address these needs.

    b. During the next counseling session, Dan can revisit the issue of confidentiality apologizing to her for his lack of clarity and this time include the limits of confidentiality. More specifically, Dan can describe to Angela which information disclosed during the session would be confidential and what types of information would be disclosed to parents or guardians and perhaps teachers. These limits to confidentiality would include when Angela shares anything that could pose a danger to herself or others. Information would also be shared with appropriate staff such as the state's child protection agency if Angela was being abused or neglected by any caregivers including parents or teachers consistent with the state's child abuse and neglect laws.

        Related to the above, depending on the severity of the eating disorder and subsequent consultation with the school nurse, the degree to which Angela's eating disorder represents "risk of harm" can be determined. However, this determination represents the judgment of Dan and his supervisor. It is important for the supervisor to direct Dan to initiate ways to guide Angela to understanding that the involvement of her parents in this issue is necessary. If not in immediate danger, it would be best if Dan can work with Angela to disclose her eating disorder to her parents as treatment will be dependent on the parents being involved (see c. below).

        After addressing risk of harm and abuse situations, Dan can also share with Angela that there may be other issues that arise that in his judgment might warrant some form of communication with her parents or teachers, but that these would be discussed with Angela prior to disclosure. If this should occur, it would be Dan's responsibility to help Angela understand the benefits of such disclosure and guide her to participate fully in the disclosure to facilitate treatment outcomes. Dan can also share with Angela that an additional option would be for him to update the parents and/or teachers every few weeks on Angela's general progress in counseling without providing specific details of what Angela discussed. He would share with Angela the general comments he is sharing with her parents and/or teachers.

c.   If her eating disorder is more severe and represents a "risk of harm" to Angela, she must be referred for a medical evaluation and/or outside agencies specializing in the treatment of eating disorders to be sure her needs are addressed by competent professionals. School-based treatment of the depression with Dan can continue with consistent collaboration with external service providers.

7.   Make a decision and implement an action plan using common sense.

a.   In consultation with his supervisor, Dan should share with Angela and her parents the limits to confidentiality explaining why this is important to ensure Angela's welfare. If Dan is not comfortable explaining this to Angela and meeting with the parents and Angela together, he can role-play communication in these meetings with his supervisor. If the supervisor remains concerned about Dan's ability to conduct these sessions independently, he or she would join as a cotherapist. It is also important for Angela and her parents to understand that all information shared with Dan, due to his status as an intern, is also shared with you as his intern supervisor due to vicarious liability and the supervisor's responsibility to ensure Angela's welfare.

b.   Dan should obtain more detailed information about Angela's eating disorder including a complete description of symptoms and associated behaviors. Consultation with the school nurse may be helpful in determining if her eating behaviors represent significant risk of self-harm. In addition, if the eating disorder is more severe, resources must also be provided to Angela and her parents to treat the eating disorder.

8.   Monitor and evaluate outcome and implications of decision and action plan and use these data to decide if further action is necessary and to guide future decision-making.

It would be important for Dan's supervisor to monitor this case very closely to determine the degree of risk of harm the eating disorder as well as her depressive symptoms pose to Angela and the need to inform the parents.

Supervisory Issues and Strategies

Initially you can resummarize the appropriate actions your supervisee took including praising Dan for sharing Angela's symptoms and recognizing that this may be a "risk of harm" situation that would require breaking confidentiality to assure client welfare. The fact that Angela shared this very personal and significant information with Dan also reflects the strength of their therapeutic relationship and his developing counseling skills. Dan should also be praised for recognizing what the implications of breaking confidentiality may be for his client as well as bringing all of these issues to your attention in supervision. You would also want to assess Dan's awareness of confidentiality and its limits in terms of both ethical and legal requirements. Depending on the results of your assessment, you would want to review appropriate procedures regarding confidentiality and the limits of confidentiality which should occur at the initiation of treatment. The next issue is to help Dan recover from his error of failing to discuss the limits of confidentiality with Angela at the start of counseling with a focus on what is for the good of the client. You can also role-play with Dan how he might address this issue with Angela and then bring her parents into the discussion. If in your judgment as supervisor, Dan is not ready to respond to this situation competently, you can sit in on the sessions with Angela and then with her parents as a cotherapist.

Issues Related to Consent, Confidentiality, and Provision of Therapeutic Services to Minors

B. *Lynn is seeing your intern, Bob, in a high school counseling support group for students whose parents have recently gone through a divorce. Lynn finds the group to be very helpful. She comes to Bob's office after school with a friend of hers, Sandy, who wants some help from Bob too. Sandy describes intense conflicts between her parents and a hostile relationship between herself and her parents as well. She goes on to describe horrible outbursts at home that have resulted in police responses due to concerns for domestic violence. Sandy asks to meet with Bob to receive support and figure out how to survive the family conflict, but she does not want her parents to know she is receiving counseling at school. Bob asks you if he can provide services for Sandy without telling her parents and if so under what terms and conditions. How do you respond to Bob? What courses of action do you advise him to take? What are Sandy's rights for counseling and what are the limits to her confidentiality regarding this requested therapeutic relationship?*

Authors' Analysis

1. Define potential ethical or legal issues in the problem situation.

   The issues presented in this case include consent to provide counseling without parent permission, limits to confidentiality, and provision of therapeutic services to minors.

2. Research ethical and legal guidelines from professional organizations and federal and local regulations.

   NASP Ethical Standard I.1.2 indicates that parental consent is a prerequisite for ongoing individual or group counseling. Standard 1.1.3 also indicates that in instances of self-referral without parental consent, the school psychologist is allowed to conduct "one or several meetings" with the student to assess the need for counseling services as well as to determine the student's degree of risk for harm.

Relevant specifically for Illinois but used here as an example, 405 ILCS 5/ et. seq section 3–501 of the *Illinois Mental Health and Developmental Disability Act* indicates that psychologists or social workers can legally conduct five counseling sessions with children ages 12–17 prior to obtaining parental consent. This principle has also been adopted by the Illinois State Board of Education (ISBE, 2007). It is important for supervisors to know the legal considerations required in their state.

Ethics codes of both NASP (Principle 1.2) and APA (Standard 4) address confidentiality and that there are limits of confidentiality which must be discussed with clients at the start of any professional relationship between the school psychologist and the client. The legal principles/restrictions related to confidentiality and its limits are reflected in FERPA (as this counseling is occurring in the school setting) as well as relevant state education or mental health codes (e.g., Illinois School Code and Illinois Mental Health Code). The state's child abuse and neglect act should also be consulted. In Illinois, domestic violence is included in the definition of abuse and neglect; and Bob is a mandated reporter. Bob is therefore required to break confidentiality when provided with information such as Sandy shares which includes repeated exposure to interpersonal violence in the home.

3. Consult with colleagues (if necessary with school district or university legal counsel).

    Bob is consulting with his intern supervisor.

4. Consider the rights, responsibilities, and welfare of *all* affected parties including the supervisee and supervisor.

    There may be risk of harm based on the level of interpersonal violence in Sandy's home so it will be important to follow up on this issue as Bob (and his supervisor) are mandated reporters. Failure to assess this may cause possible harm to Sandy and liability for Bob's supervisor. Placing this example in our state of Illinois, counseling may not be provided for more than five sessions without parent consent and the focus should be on understanding the needs of the student. If Bob provides more than five sessions he (and his supervisor due to vicarious liability) can be found in violation of several legal regulations and ethical principles.

5. Employ common sense, mindful of the overriding responsibility toward client welfare and avoidance of harm.

    The overriding responsibility would be to assess degree of risk of Sandy's home situation and to keep her safe. It is also critical to Sandy's welfare to assist her and other family members to reduce and manage more effectively the level of interpersonal hostility in the home.

6. Propose multiple courses of action and evaluate their impact on the welfare of the client and their ethical and legal consequences.

   a. Bob and his supervisor may decide that this case is more appropriate for an outside agency and refer Sandy to a community resource. However, Sandy has already disclosed information to Bob and sought him out through her friend Lynn. Sandy may not accept this referral and could continue to be at risk of harm in her current home environment. After more information is obtained, a decision can be made whether or not an outside referral would be more appropriate than working with Sandy in the school setting or whether a combination would be beneficial. Maintaining a counseling relationship with Sandy with consent to collaborate with a therapist outside of school makes it more likely that continued participation in treatment could be monitored.

   b. Bob could meet with Sandy for up to five sessions prior to obtaining parental consent. Through these meetings Bob could determine the risk of harm her current home situation presents. In addition, Bob would utilize active listening skills to build a supportive relationship as rapidly as possible to facilitate trust with the goal of getting parental involvement and beginning to assist Sandy and family members to problem-solve family issues more effectively.

7. Make a decision and implement an action plan using common sense.

   Meet with Sandy for up to five sessions to assess the degree of risk of harm in her current home situation and to facilitate her talking with her parents to gain parent permission for counseling (if it is determined school-based counseling is more appropriate than an outside resource) or to refer Sandy and her parents to an outside resource with consent to share information and permission to periodically check in with Sandy at school for ongoing support.

8. Monitor and evaluate outcome and implications of decision and action plan and use these data to decide if further action is necessary and to guide future decision-making.

   It will be critical to determine if a report needs to be made to child protective services. It will also be important to monitor the effectiveness of Bob's discussion with Sandy related to obtaining parent consent.

Supervisory Issues and Strategies

a. Discussion with your supervisee of issues related to his understanding of consent, confidentiality, and limits to confidentiality drawing upon relevant APA, NASP, and Illinois (since Bob is practicing in an Illinois school) laws and regulations including those related to child abuse and neglect and being a mandated reporter. Through discussion and role-playing, you can assess Bob's ability to explain confidentiality, limits to confidentiality, and his responsibilities as a mandated reporter to Sandy and her parents as well as his comfort with the steps required if a report to child protective services is necessary.

b.   As you are suggesting that Bob meet with Sandy for up to five sessions during this time, you would work with Bob on therapeutic strategies to facilitate Sandy becoming comfortable well before the five session limit with obtaining parental consent and involving her parents in the treatment process. This could be accomplished through role-playing, close case monitoring, and discussion in supervision.

c.   During Bob's meetings with Sandy, he will need to assess her level of safety and the services she may require. Bob will need to assess risk of harm of her current living situation; and he may need both instruction and modeling of approaches to conduct this assessment.

> *C. Raymond, your school psychology intern, is working with a student service organization as an associate sponsor because he supports its cause and you and he thought it would be a good way to observe a different element of the school population. Raymond discusses his role in this student group in supervision periodically. He keeps bringing up Rachel, a high school senior and one of the student group's members, in conversation, with a frequency that makes you begin to wonder if he might be at risk for some boundary issues or might even be sexually attracted to her. How, if at all, do you respond to this intuition? Would you respond differently if Raymond initiated a conversation about his discovering that he is sexually attracted to Rachel? In general, how do supervisors counsel trainees regarding admission of sexual attraction to clients? When does it cross a boundary that requires termination of the trainee's working relationship with that student?*

Authors' Analysis

1.   Define potential ethical or legal issues in the problem situation.

Raymond's possible boundary violations can lead to possible exploitation of the client or negatively impacting the client in terms of clinical decision-making.

2.   Research ethical and legal guidelines from professional organizations and federal and local regulations.

APA Code of Conduct 3.02 prohibits psychologists from engaging in any type of physical, verbal, or nonverbal conduct that is sexual in any way and that could be offensive, unwanted, or abusive. NASP Standard III.4.3 prohibits the exploitation of clients, supervisees, and graduate students and forbids any sexual harassment of children, parents, or other individuals for whom the school psychologist has authority over. NASP Principle IV.3 states that school psychologists are responsible for the monitoring of their own and others' conduct in the school.

3.   Consult with colleagues (if necessary with school district or university legal counsel).

The intern supervisor may consult with colleagues if necessary.

4. Consider the rights, responsibilities, and welfare of *all* affected parties including the supervisee and supervisor.

   If Raymond does have feelings about Rachel that risk boundary issues, the potential exists for behaviors to emerge that would risk the welfare of the client (i.e., sexual harassment). Any inappropriate behaviors that might occur can also lead to reportable ethical and legal transgressions committed by the supervisee for which both the supervisee and supervisor would be responsible. Inappropriate feelings can also negatively impact the school psychologist's judgment including clinical decision-making although the feelings in and of themselves are not a reportable offense.

5. Employ common sense, mindful of the overriding responsibility toward client welfare and avoidance of harm.

   Although you (as the supervisor) do not have any direct evidence that there has been any inappropriate contact between the intern, Raymond, and Rachel, the client, it is certainly appropriate to be concerned; and you are bound to investigate and explore this issue further.

6. Propose multiple courses of action and evaluate their impact on the welfare of the client and their ethical and legal consequences.

   a. You could ignore the situation and not bring anything up. This could jeopardize client welfare and lead to your vicarious liability.

   b. You could share your concerns with your intern, Raymond, and make efforts to prevent any transgressions caused by Raymond acting on his feelings. These feelings can also impact clinical decision-making. By addressing these issues with Raymond, you would protect client welfare that is your first responsibility. This would also represent important learning for your intern.

7. Make a decision and implement an action plan using common sense.

   As a supervisor you should discuss this issue with Raymond. During a regularly scheduled supervision session, the supervisor would ask about the group and how it is going. Then the supervisor would listen carefully to see if Raymond brings up Rachel and, if so, would share the concerns and also add that the supervisor has also observed this frequent mentioning of this one student during previous supervision sessions. The supervisor can begin by complementing Raymond on his commitment to the group. The supervisor would ask directly about Raymond's feelings about Rachel. If he denied any sexual feelings towards the student, the supervisor would still share his interpretation that the frequency of his mentioning her raises concerns about risk of impropriety or compromised clinical judgment. The supervisor stresses how important it is for Raymond to be mindful of his feelings and subsequent behaviors and how these feelings can also impact his clinical decision-making related to this student.

8. Monitor and evaluate outcome and implications of decision and action plan and use these data to decide if further action is necessary and to guide future decision-making.

It would be important to carefully monitor Raymond's behavior with Rachel and to continue to discuss how his feelings may be impacting his clinical decision-making.

Supervisory Issues and Strategies

It is the responsibility of the supervisor to point out professional "blind spots" of the supervisee. If Raymond is unaware that he is enamored with Rachel or has any sexual feelings toward her, then the first supervisory task is providing your data for raising a concern and helping him explore it. If in fact Raymond cannot manage these feelings, he needs to remove himself from contact with the student. In the absence of wrongful behavior, it might stop here with additional attention to be paid to monitoring future relationships with close supervision and any personal issues that might interfere with Raymond's ability to practice and manage boundaries appropriately. As part of this discussion, it is also important for the supervisor to discuss the difference between thoughts, feelings and behaviors. It is inappropriate behavior that can lead to reportable ethical transgressions. There is a difference between finding someone sexually attractive and taking inappropriate actions. If Raymond denies any feelings of attraction toward the student, the supervisor might still increase his self-awareness and prompt more self-monitoring by reiterating the basis for raising the concern and by reflecting on the potential impact of his verbalizations on decision-making. There is an opportunity here for Raymond to increase his sensitivity to his own reactions to clients and learn how to monitor their potential impact.

Summary

Teaching ethical and legal psychological practice represents a core task of supervision. Supervision itself presents unique ethical challenges as supervisors balance supervisee development, client welfare, and risk management. Ethical and legal considerations in complex school cases can present significant decision-making challenges but are excellent opportunities for learning ethical practice. Ethics codes of professional organizations and risk management strategies must be applied within a systematic decision-making model that considers the rights, responsibilities, and welfare of *all* affected parties including the supervisee and supervisor. This chapter applied an 8-step ethical decision-making model to diverse case examples delineating supervisory issues and strategies. While ethical principles, legal requirements, and personal beliefs are related, at times they may be in conflict or difficult to reconcile presenting unique challenges to supervision. Ethical practice places the welfare of clients at the core of psychological service delivery.

PART II

The Developmental, Ecological, Problem-solving (DEP) Model

6

INTRODUCTION TO THE DEVELOPMENTAL, ECOLOGICAL, PROBLEM-SOLVING (DEP) MODEL

Supervision Models as Essential Guideposts

Effective supervision is anchored in a theoretically sound and practical model of supervision. It is important to have a coherent framework to conceptualize, organize, and execute supervisory tasks linking theory, research, and practice. A supervision model provides an organizational framework to guide practice and ensures that supervision will be purposeful, reflective, comprehensively address all professional skill sets, and focused on training outcomes. In the absence of a model, the supervisor lacks a template for defining the goals, processes, and methods of supervision. Lacking a big picture road map, the supervision journey meanders along trails without a clear destination and no way of determining progress. In this case, supervision is reduced to clinical instinct and often centers solely on problem-solving related to individual cases.

NASP's (2011a) and APA's (2015a) call for training in supervisory skills does not delineate a specific model for supervision but emphasizes the necessity of a strategic organization for supervision that is purposeful, goal-oriented, systematic, and transparent. The competency initiative and the NASP Practice Model point toward outcomes for training. A supervision model delineates the process, curriculum, and methods for achieving those outcomes. A model outlines supervisor and supervisee roles and tasks, the content and process of their interactions in supervision, and the interface with the contexts within which supervision occurs. The context is multidimensional including the training setting, the university or employment requirements for supervision, and the evolving professional consensus on best practice. An effective supervision model is guided by current formulations of best practice and, to the extent possible, empirically informed. Within school psychology, the overarching emphasis on data-based decision-making, evidence-informed problem-solving, and outcome monitoring must be applied to the supervisory process. These central activities apply to work with clients, the development and evaluation of supervisee skills and development, and the application of supervision practices. A supervision model provides an integrative framework for the content and process of supervision.

Similar to other domains of professional practice, supervision requires a blend of art and science. There is no session by session manual for supervision; and individual client or consultee needs and supervisee characteristics require flexible application of proven methods. However, a core supervision model provides essential principles, values, and activities to guide practice. An effective model provides a sufficient framework for defining best practice implementation across multiple supervisors, supervisees, and settings.

Models of Supervision from Clinical and Counseling Psychology

Psychotherapy-based Models

As noted in the introduction to this text, early models for clinical supervision originated within clinical and counseling psychology specialties and focused on the application of specific approaches to psychotherapy, (e.g., person-centered/humanistic (Farber, 2010; Lambers, 2007), psychodynamic (Sarnat, 2010), behavioral/cognitive-behavioral (Reiser & Milne, 2012), solution-focused (Hsu, 2009), and so forth). Limitations to this approach are readily apparent (Bernard & Goodyear, 2014). A supervisee's training was orientation-specific with limited exposure to other approaches. As psychology's focus on evidence-based practice emerged with an attempt to define "what works for whom under what circumstances," singular orientations were not always capable of addressing the diversity of client needs in a comprehensive fashion. Focusing supervision with a psychotherapeutic model increased risks that the boundaries between supervision and therapy for supervisees could be blurred. As clinical psychology activities diversify particularly with increased collaboration with other professionals in integrated healthcare, therapy-specific models of supervision may lack sufficient scope to guide practice. While therapeutic interventions have an important role in school psychology practice, psychotherapeutic models could not address the multiple diverse roles within this specialty nor within evolving clinical and counseling practice.

Developmental Models

Developmental models of supervision emerged as an alternative approach (Loganbill, Hardy, & Delworth, 1982; Stoltenberg & McNeill, 2010). Drawing from theories of learning, cognitive, and social development, this approach centered on the development of professional identity and skills of the supervisee.

Stoltenberg and associates' Integrated Developmental Model (IDM) has had a significant impact on the conceptualization of supervision (McNeill & Stoltenberg, 2016; Stoltenberg, McNeill, & Delworth, 1998; Stoltenberg & McNeill, 2010). Similar to stage theory in cognitive development, IDM outlines stages of supervisee development from novice to advanced beginner to competent to proficient to expert. As supervisees grow in skills and professionalism, they grow in awareness, motivation, and autonomy. Over time, performance improves; self-efficacy grows; the ability to respond to complex challenges is enhanced; capacity develops to not only apply technical skills with precision but to take into account multiple contextual and systemic factors; and eventually competent independent practice is demonstrated.

IDM matches supervisor strategies and supports to the supervisee's developmental level. At novice stages, supervisors provide more structure, modeling, and direction. As competency grows, supervisees function more independently; and supervisors assume more of a consultant role. It is noteworthy that this developmental model describes professional development and supervision from early training through advanced professional practice. Rønnestad and Skovholt (2003) take this a step further and propose a lifespan developmental model focusing on the career-long development of therapists. The developmental perspective on supervision has much to offer to conceptualization of supervision and is consistent with school psychology's call for the availability of clinical supervision for all levels of training and credentialed practice (NASP, 2011a). Focused on supervisee development, a potential limitation of developmental models lies in their relatively limited focus on the content of professional tasks and minimal attention to cultural and other forms of diversity and systemic factors.

The Discrimination Model

The discrimination model (DM) of supervision, originally proposed by Bernard (1979) is an eclectic model that conceptualizes the supervisor's task as discriminating what the focus of supervisee skill development is at a given moment of supervision and then matching the supervisory role or approach to this assessment. DM focuses on three categories of supervisee skills: intervention, conceptualization, and personalization (Bernard & Goodyear, 2014). Centered on the development of counseling competency, supervisory attention may address observable intervention skills, conceptualization of the underlying processes or patterns occurring within a counseling session, and the contribution and integration of personal style into practice. Within DM, the supervisor intentionally adopts different roles or postures to match the supervisee's needs. Supervisors differentiate their approach to the supervisee as a teacher, counselor, or consultant depending upon the ability of the supervisee in the essential skill categories. Bernard and Goodyear (2014) describe DM as a process-oriented model of supervision that is flexible and capable of addressing the shifting dynamics within supervisory sessions. DM's attention to matching skill focus and supervisory roles is congruent with a developmental perspective. While not focused on a specific therapeutic orientation, it remains focused on professional competency in counseling.

Systems Approach to Supervision

Holloway's (1995, 2016) systems approach to supervision (SAS) incorporated the importance of context in understanding the supervisory process. She emphasized the complexity of the supervisory process and the dynamic interaction among functions, tasks, and system requirements. Holloway details seven dimensions within SAS with the character and process of the supervisory relationship at its core. The second dimension centers on the tasks of supervision: counseling skills, case conceptualization, professional role, emotional awareness, and self-evaluation. The third dimension delineates the function(s) of supervision: monitoring/evaluating, instructing/advising, modeling, consulting, and supporting/sharing. Holloway describes tasks as the *What* of supervision. These are skills and attitudes supervision strives to advance. Functions represent the *How* of supervision. The supervisor attempts to match supervisory functions to the tasks being addressed. For example the supportive function may be applied to discussions of the supervisee's emotional reactions to the client and the client's self-disclosures. In this case the supervisor empathetically assists the supervisee in enhancing and monitoring self-awareness so that personal reactions and feelings do not interfere with the therapeutic relationship. On the other hand, the instructing function would be appropriate to address specific interviewing strategies for evaluation of a client's risk for harm to self or others.

However, as the supervisor strives to match functions to tasks in the context of the supervisory relationship, Holloway highlights the necessity of understanding the influence of contextual factors which form the other four dimensions of SAS. In addition to the supervisor, the trainee, and the client, the institutional context influences the process of supervision. Context can include personal histories, cultural backgrounds, the professional experience and theoretical orientation of the supervisor and supervisee, organizational structures, institutional goals, and characteristics of the work setting. Figure 6.1 provides Holloway's representation of the dynamic influences that reciprocally influence the supervisory process with the interpersonal supervisory relationship at its core. This image captures the complexity of the supervisory process while still attempting to match supervisor actions to supervisee needs. The major contribution of SAS is the incorporation of contextual and systemic factors in understanding the process of supervision. These systemic variables interact with each other and impact the character of the supervisory relationship as a whole. Systemic factors influence interactions and the selection of tasks and functions within an individual supervision session.

Although Holloway was focused on the development of counseling skills, her approach can readily be adapted to other professional skills. Her conceptualization

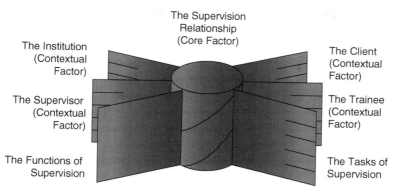

FIGURE 6.1   A Systems Approach to Supervision: Seven Dimensions
Source: From Holloway, E.L. (1995). *Clinical supervision: A systems approach.* Thousand Oaks, CA: Sage. Copyright 1995 by Sage Publications. Reprinted with permission.

proves to be a good fit with contemporary school psychology's focus on simultaneously addressing individual and systemic factors. The critical importance of the character of the supervisory relationship was described in Chapter 3. Chapter 8's description of the ecological component of the DEP model extends SAS's recognition of the importance of contextual factors within the practice of school psychology and within the supervisory relationship.

Supervision for Diverse Psychologist Roles

The broad scope of professional responsibilities and activities within school psychology and the unique setting of the school context require a multidimensional and integrative supervision model. The diversity and complexity of contemporary practice challenges university preparation and clinical supervision at practicum-, specialist-, and doctoral-level training. Licensed school psychologists are often required to extend their work to new target populations, (e.g., shifting assignment from a standard education population and work with students with higher incidence disabilities, such as specific learning disabilities, to specific specialized programming for children with autism). Veteran professionals may assume responsibility for domains of practice that were not addressed in their own graduate training, (e.g., implementation of school-wide social-emotional learning curriculum).

Fortunately there are some common skill sets and professional requirements across the diverse practice domains that can help to define an appropriate school psychology supervision model. The diverse roles and activities all require strong interpersonal skills, assessment and intervention practices that are linked and data-driven, psychoeducational skills for instruction in social and coping skills, therapeutic skills for mental health interventions, implementation of evidence-based practice in all domains, a commitment to integrated individual and systemic interventions, and the utilization of structured problem-solving methods. The problem-solving process that links data-based assessment with evidence-based intervention resides at the core of contemporary school psychology practice and permeates all of these activities (NASP, 2010a; Tilly, 2008). Empirically supported problem-solving and wellness/prevention activities are not limited by a specific intervention orientation or approach to counseling and psychotherapy. Rather than defining a one-size-fits-all approach to intervention, a collaborative problem-solving process is defined that utilizes a wide range of empirically supported strategies differentiated to address diverse problems and the uniqueness of individuals and systems. Problem-solving requires an analysis of specific presenting concerns that can be linked to empirically supported intervention strategies. However, recognizing that problems may vary in severity, present with unique and complex configurations, and be resistant to standard solutions, problem-solving may require the introduction of innovative or novel strategies; but these modifications originate from whatever empirical base is available and are systematically monitored and adjusted by ongoing data collection (Forman et al., 2013; Kratochwill & Shernoff, 2004).

This scope and complexity of practice necessitates quality supervision while illustrating the challenges inherent in the supervisory role. Supervisors need to demonstrate broad professional competencies, be capable of helping supervisees resolve case-specific problems, and teach individual- and systems-level approaches to collaborative problem-solving that can be applied systematically and independently to circumstances the supervisee will face in the future.

A Supervision Model for School Psychology: The Developmental, Ecological, Problem-solving Model (DEP)

We believe it is necessary to develop a model of supervision that is specific to the specialty of school psychology. We propose a model that is consistent with the diverse professional requirements of school psychology practice, applicable to the school context, and appropriate for specialist and doctoral training as well as career life span clinical supervision and professional development. It takes elements from clinical and counseling supervision models and integrates them with supervision strategies specific to school psychology. While it is certainly necessary to expand well beyond psychotherapeutic models of supervision, their focus on intervention competence and fidelity, and monitoring the influence of the supervisee's self-awareness and personal reactions within the intervention process remain appropriate. Supervision must assist the supervisee in understanding and managing personal blind spots, potential countertransference, and parallel processes. However, counseling is only one role among many for school psychologists; and intervention fidelity is monitored in terms of evidence-based strategies rather than fidelity to a singular intervention orientation. Although developed for school psychology, the multifaceted DEP framework is applicable to other specialties that practice within the school setting.

Developmental models contribute significantly to our perspective on school psychology supervision. The developmental perspective mirrors the field's understanding of effective teaching and learning for school children and for professional development of educators as well as parents. Developmental schemas match supervisory strategies to the experience and competence level of supervisees. This approach's differentiation of stages of initial training and lifelong professional development is applicable to the progression from practicum to internship and from specialist to doctoral levels of field-based training. This is consistent with NASP's (2011a) call for supervision at all levels of practice and all career stages and APA's (2010a) ethical requirements for lifelong learning in the context of an evolving body of professional knowledge.

Holloway's (1995, 2016) SAS approach incorporates contextual and systemic variables into supervisory practice. This systemic perspective complements school psychology's focus on system's change and ecologically sensitive interventions. The SAS model strongly influences our DEP conceptualization; however, the number of systems relevant to problem-solving within a school environment is even more expansive than accounted for in the SAS conceptualization.

The DEP model incorporates developmental and systemic perspectives into supervisory practice and integrates them into the primary problem-solving role that is central to school psychology practice. A comprehensive yet flexible framework is required to integrate individual and contextual factors impacting the clients of supervisees and the professional training and career development of supervisees themselves.

The three principal components of the DEP model make distinct contributions but must be effectively integrated to implement quality supervisory practice. The *Developmental* component assesses supervisee competencies, needs, and goals and provides essential structure to supervision. This domain attends to the required supports appropriate for the developmental level of the supervisee that are necessary to ensure client welfare and promote supervisee growth. Supervisory methods are matched to the problem-solving requirements of individual activities and the relative competencies of the supervisee in the skill sets required for intervention in each circumstance. Formative feedback and summative evaluation are central supervisory activities for guiding supervisee development in professional skills and identity. Evaluation data monitors developmental progress toward independent practice and in the case of preservice training is essential to the gatekeeping process for licensing and credentialing. Critical tasks related to accountability, recordkeeping, and risk management are addressed early in the developmental process. Ethical and legal considerations are infused throughout supervision but the nuances inherent in complex cases are more readily addressed at later stages of development. Similarly, across all practice activities, the developmental perspective guides the supervisee to integrate isolated skills into comprehensive yet flexible intervention strategies that can account for the complex variables inherent in challenging problem-solving scenarios. As the supervisee progresses in competence the role of the supervisor adapts to foster increased independence and self-monitoring.

The *Ecological* component incorporates examination of the multiple systems that impact any problem-solving challenge or program development. It is impossible to truly understand and intervene with an individual student without taking into account the environmental influences of the family, the classroom, peers, culture, and other systemic variables (Brofenbrenner, 1979; Sheridan & Gutkin, 2000). Training in diversity and multicultural competence is focused within the ecological domain and addressed within the supervisory relationship and all intervention planning. Particularly germane to school psychology but also critical to other psychological specialties, the ecological perspective requires integrated intervention plans that simultaneously address both individual and contextual factors (Forman et al., 2013; Kratochwill & Shernoff, 2004). School psychologists involve parents, teachers, and administrators in problem-solving and strive to alter behavior management and emotional supports within each critical life context of the child. Evidence-based intervention protocols for serious mental health issues for children and adolescents routinely require multisystemic interventions (Simon, 2016). It is this ecological framework that has contributed to the emerging emphasis on system change and wellness-oriented social-emotional learning curriculums within school psychology (NASP, 2010a; Tilly, 2008). The challenge within supervisory practice is to draw the supervisee's attention to both individual and systemic concerns and view all problem scenarios within their environmental contexts.

The *Problem-solving* component within DEP focuses on the core activity of school psychology. Supervision teaches systematic case conceptualization (Simon, 2016) and effective processes for collaborative problem-solving (Pluymert, 2014). Data-based decision-making that links assessment to intervention to progress monitoring is utilized to address individual, classroom, school, and family issues. Sensitivity to ecological factors requires problem-solving efforts to address both individual and systemic issues. The application of multitiered systems of support teaches the supervisee system-wide approaches to prevention and remediation and is a significant focus in school psychology supervision. Commitment to scientific practice models requires the application of evidence-based intervention (EBI) protocols. Given the unique challenges present in diverse school environments, a major task of clinical supervision is to assist the supervisee in flexibly adapting EBI to individual circumstances while maintaining core implementation integrity. With this focus, the problem-solving domain focuses on the critical task of integrating theory and research into real world practice. Particularly within practicum and internship training this is a core supervisory activity.

These three components of the DEP model each require specific attention in supervision. However, they must be integrated into a comprehensive approach to preserve training and professional development. Effective problem-solving must incorporate developmental and ecological considerations into intervention planning. Supervisors are responsible for routinely integrating developmental, ecological, and problem-solving into the fabric of all supervisory activities.

Summary and Preview

Supervision models are essential guideposts for conceptualizing and implementing effective supervisory practices. Clinical and counseling psychology models of supervision have contributed to the foundation of supervisory practice but are insufficient for the diverse professional requirements and unique school setting of school psychology practice. A school psychology-specific model of supervision is required. We have created the DEP model to address the unique requirements of supervisory practice within school psychology (Simon et al., 2014). The next three chapters will present each component in significant detail. We will delineate the theory and assumptions that are the foundation of each component. However, the focus will remain on practical application of the model to daily supervisory practice. Specific supervisory activities will be highlighted. Behavioral markers that indicate fidelity of application of the DEP model will be delineated. The integration of each component into a theoretically comprehensive model that guides practical application will be supported by numerous case examples.

The DEP model will be delineated primarily in relation to specialist-level and predoctoral internship supervision, the capstone professional training experiences in school psychology. However, DEP applies to practicum, early career, and postdoctoral supervision as well. Chapter 11 will apply DEP to supervision of licensed professional psychologists.

7

THE DEVELOPMENTAL COMPONENT

Structuring and Supporting the Development of Professional Competencies

The Developmental Perspective

As noted in the introduction to the DEP model in the prior chapter, a developmental perspective helps us understand a supervisee's evolving needs, status, and progression during training and the coinciding roles and methods of the supervisor required to support development in professional skills, attitudes, and identity. Building upon the work of Stoltenberg and his associates (Stoltenberg & McNeill, 2010), we extend the developmental perspective to preservice training and professional development within school psychology. In the process we identify specific supervisory practices that provide the essential conditions for the supervisee's development and the selection of approaches and methods that match current competencies and foster growth toward independent practice. We will use internship supervision as an example to lay out the principles and methods of the DEP model, but the framework applies to professional development at all levels of professional practice.

Variable Development

Supervisee development does not need to be viewed in discrete stages nor routinely evaluated across the totality of skill development. Interns come to their final preservice field experience with a variety of skills and different emphases in their graduate preparation. They may have significant experience and solid foundational skills in some areas of practice but limited exposure or competencies in others. Development and professional growth may occur unevenly as well. The developmental process of supervision is designed to initiate training at the functioning levels in each competency domain assessed at the start of the internship.

Consistent with the practice of establishing competency benchmarks (Fouad et al., 2009), supervisory approaches systematically prepare supervisees for overall readiness to enter professional practice at the conclusion of their internship year.

Supervision Structure and Supports to Match Intern Development

At the onset of the internship, the supervisor must provide significant structure to organize all aspects of the training experience. Expectations, goals, roles, methods, and supports are delineated in a written supervision contract and thoroughly discussed in supervision sessions. The supervisor provides a structured approach for entry into the school setting, assumption of a professional-in-training role, and the supervisory relationship. At the beginning of a training experience, there can be considerable dependence on the supervisor for direction and support; but as the internship progresses, there is a gradual phased progression toward eventual independent functioning. The goal is achievement of competencies for effective entry into professional practice.

Structure promotes learning and accountability. The process begins with a discussion of roles, responsibilities, procedures, and supports required during the field experience and within the supervisory relationship. The supervisor engages the supervisee in an assessment of entry-level skills across all NASP practice domains (NASP, 2010a). An internship plan is outlined that recognizes that professional skill sets will be unevenly developed. Together, the supervisor and supervisee define training needs, set goals, and delineate field activities and supervisory supports that will eventually guide the intern toward professional entry skill levels in all essential school psychology practice domains.

Since different stages of development require different levels of support and guidance, supervision must utilize multiple methods tailored to the competency of the intern for specific professional activities. In areas with limited experience, the supervisor may need to teach and model skills; while in areas in which the intern demonstrates emerging competencies, the supervisor may serve as more of a coach or consultant and overseer. Throughout training, supervision does not merely rely on intern self-report but involves co-intervention and observation.

Feedback and Evaluation as Tools for Development

The professional development of the intern is guided by frequent and direct performance feedback from the supervisor. Routine formative feedback shapes the intervention and consultation activities of the supervisee and ensures that best practices are applied for the welfare of all clients. Scheduled summative evaluation enables the supervisor and supervisee to assess the big picture and overall progress of the supervisee across professional practice domains. These comprehensive evaluations monitor progress including assessing whether the intern is functioning at an appropriate developmental level of competency given the stage of the training year. In preservice training, evaluation is critical to the gatekeeping function of supervision. Extensive treatment of effective feedback and evaluation will occur later in this chapter.

Developmental Continuums

It is possible to visualize the multidimensional continuums that describe the developmental progression of supervisees across a training cycle. These continuums describe development across a broad range of behaviors, performance dimensions, training and supervisory tasks, and professional roles. The developmental perspective recognizes that professional skills can be assessed on a continuum; and that while a competency benchmark may be achieved, skills are constantly evolving and being refined.

During progression from early to late stages of internship, supervisory actions progress from highly directive to less directive. As the year unfolds, the intern gradually takes more initiative and executes interventions and consultations with less step by step direction and increased freedom and trust to design and adapt strategies. While still requiring supervisor approval, in the latter part of the training year, the intern may begin to independently recognize and define needs of clients, classrooms, or the school system and propose interventions and new program development. Increasingly recognized by school staff as a competent practitioner, the intern may also be sought out for consultation, problem-solving, or participation in new program initiatives. As this developmental evolution occurs, the intern continues to engage in assigned and circumscribed duties but begins to increase initiative and function less as a trainee and closer to an independent professional.

The corollary development in the supervisory relationship is from significant dependence to increasingly independent functioning. With the encouragement of the supervisor the intern seeks out a broader support network. The intern has been taught to recognize limitations and seek consultation from other experts and identify a wide range of support resources. This development can be fostered by the supervisor's establishment of collaborative supervision relationships that are often task-, case-, or setting-specific but enable the supervisee to learn from other professionals.

The character and content of supervision sessions changes over time as well. Early supervision sessions may be task-specific, focused on an isolated skill, intervention, or assessment instrument. Over time the content of sessions gradually shifts focus to the selection and integration of skills and multifaceted intervention strategies. The supervisor becomes less didactic or prescriptive and more consultative, guiding the supervisee in a Socratic fashion toward case conceptualization and subsequent intervention. Similarly there is a progression from a singular focus on individual clients to a more comprehensive understanding of environmental influences and the role of systemic factors. As supervisees' assessment skills mature, they begin to understand the big picture that includes the dynamic interaction among individual, familial, peer, school, and community variables. At this stage of development the supervisor guides the intern toward intervention plans that simultaneously address individual and systemic factors. It is not until advanced stages of development when foundational skills are more naturally and automatically applied that the supervisee can effectively assess the need for and execute plans for system change. In essence, it is necessary to be able to clearly see the forest *and* the trees to successfully contribute to the nuances required for the development of multitiered models of service delivery that address individual and systemic concerns and challenges.

Over time as the professional competency of the supervisee matures, the agenda for supervision sessions becomes less supervisor-driven and increasingly the responsibility of the intern. Supervision methods evolve toward less reliance on direct observation or cotherapy/consultation and more trust in intern self-report and independent clinical practice. Explicit feedback from the supervisor continues, but increased emphasis is placed on self- reflection and self-monitoring. Expert supervision avoids prematurely shifting the supervisee-supervisor relationship to the status of a colleague; but the central role of the supervisor gradually shifts from teacher to mentor to consultant as the intern's competency grows.

The developmental progression during internship training culminates in a supervisory relationship that approaches the status of a junior colleague supported by a senior consultant. A successful supervisory relationship deepens the intern's respect for the supervisor. However, the intern achieves a healthy recognition of the limitations as well as the strengths of the supervisor's personal and professional skills. This less idealized view gives confidence to the supervisee that professional competency is attainable and requires neither special charisma nor perfection. At the same time the maturing supervisee recognizes the continued need for supervision beyond the internship, collegial consultation, and lifelong professional development. While the character of clinical supervision for licensed psychologists may modify this dynamic, supervision is always geared toward development and recognition of independent competence continuously supported by professional colleagues.

Since supervision is a defined professional competency (APA, 2015a; ASPPB, 2015; Falender et al., 2004; NASP, 2011a), the beginning development of supervisory skills is a goal targeted in the latter stages of the internship and may be an explicit focus in professional development of licensed psychologists. This is a specific expectation for doctoral-level interns. In early phases of supervision this goal is addressed not only through modeling by the supervisor but by clearly defining transparent expectations, processes, and methods of supervision. Routine processing of the supervisory relationship including reciprocal feedback about the effectiveness of the supervisory relationship introduces the supervisee to examination of effective supervisory processes. It is at later stages of development that the intern may be provided opportunities to supervise under close metasupervision.

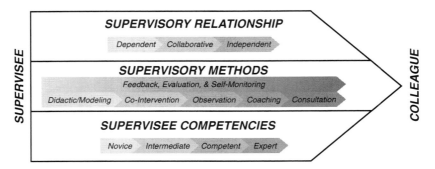

FIGURE 7.1 The Developmental Progression within Supervision

Interns may supervise a practicum student, a teacher's implementation of a social-emotional learning curriculum, paraprofessionals, or staff implementing other activities that are solidly within the intern's competency range.

In summary, the developmental process within supervision assesses the supervisees' skill levels and training needs, sets goals, plans activities, matches supervisory methods to developmental status, provides feedback and evaluates progress, and proceeds to systematically prepare interns across required competency domains to establish and certify readiness to enter independent professional practice by the end of the training cycle. Figure 7.1 summarizes the key developmental progressions that occur during a successful supervision experience.

Key Supervisory Elements within the Developmental Domain

The remaining sections of this chapter will delineate the key elements of supervision that are required in the Developmental component of DEP. We will begin with an examination of the supervision contract which sets the ground rules and establishes the structure of the supervisory relationship. The specific organizational strategies to support training will be outlined including preparation tools for supervision sessions, requirements and methods for monitoring and documenting supervisees' activities and the content of supervision, and processes for risk management. Then coordination with collaborating supervisors will be addressed to ensure consistency and purposeful integration of supervisory activities. The assessment and goal setting process will be delineated. Feedback and evaluation within supervision will be discussed in detail. The application of multiple methods of supervision will be examined. Finally, closure for the supervisory relationship and transition planning for the next steps in professional development will be covered.

Supervision Contract

As previously noted the developmental component of the DEP supervision model includes the assumption that the supervisee will require more structure and support earlier in the supervisory relationship. One vehicle to provide this needed structure is for supervisors to provide supervisees with a written contract. This section will describe the advantages and the necessary components of a written supervision contract (Osborn & Davis, 1996).

A supervision contract represents a written agreement between school psychology supervisors and their supervisees that specifies the parameters of the relationship. A contract is critical to the development of an effective supervisory relationship (Goodyear & Rodolfa, 2012; Harvey & Struzziero, 2008). A written contract is also necessary according to supervision guidelines promulgated by the Association of State and Provincial Psychology Boards (ASPPB, 2015), the American Psychological Association *Guidelines for Clinical Supervision in Health Service Psychology* (APA, 2015a), and by state boards of psychology such as Texas (Texas Board of Examiners of Psychologists, 2015).

Advantages of the Written Contract

The contract provides a blueprint of what is to occur in supervision. It increases transparency and decreases the mystery of the process by specifying ground rules and guidelines for both the supervisor and the supervisee as well as defining supervision and its goals.

It was noted earlier that feelings of anxiety on the part of the supervisor and supervisee are common at the initiation of a supervisory relationship. In particular, anxiety is generated around the evaluative and gatekeeping functions of supervision. As noted in earlier chapters, evaluation of the supervisee is a critical role of the supervisor and a core function of the supervisory process. Structure tends to mitigate anxiety; and the contract provides this degree of structure for both parties. More specifically, the contract provides predictability in terms of when and how evaluation and feedback will be provided and communicates that evaluation and feedback is the norm and an expected part of any supervisory relationship. The contract also allows for negotiation of roles and expectations providing the supervisee some control, which also lessens anxiety. For example, supervisors can ask their supervisees if there are any parts of the contract with which they are uncomfortable and how these sections might be modified. The structure provided by the written contract allows for a more purposeful channeling of the energy of both parties minimizing anxiety.

We have also noted earlier that the supervisory relationship is critical to effective supervision. A contract produces an open discussion of what makes for an effective supervisory relationship. It specifies responsibilities regarding communication and support that are building blocks for an effective relationship. For example, the contract requires that the supervisees will inform their supervisors of any difficulties they are having in the areas of delivering clinical services to clients; and in turn the supervisor commits to both a defined supervision schedule and flexible availability as needed. These and other terms of the contract help to establish the trust that is essential to an effective supervisory relationship.

Having a written contract increases the probability that supervisees will act in accordance with expectations. For example a contract will outline the supervisees' ethical responsibility to share all information about their clients with their supervisors. Often failure of the supervisee to meet these types of expectations occurs because of a lack of understanding rather than willful ignoring of the responsibility. Contracts clarify these expectations in writing.

A written contract also promotes trust by communicating clear expectations and reducing ambiguity. Supervisees come to trust the supervisor because he or she is sharing what is expected of the supervisee. Sharing these expectations also communicates that the supervisor wants supervisees to be successful; and sharing the information contributes to this success.

A supervision contract promotes shared responsibility. The contract should include not only expectations for the supervisee but for the supervisor. This communicates to supervisees that they share with the supervisor responsibility for developing a productive supervisory relationship.

A written contract represents an important risk management tool for the supervisor. Not only does the contract minimize the chances of the supervisee experiencing difficulties by not meeting their supervisor's expectations; but it can also provide direction when difficulties arise. Supervisors can refer back to expectations put in writing in the contract; and supervisees cannot say they were uninformed about particular clinical responsibilities.

Essential Components of a Written Contract

There exist a number of essential components of an effective written supervision contract. These will now be discussed and sample contracts prepared for a school psychology practicum and for a school psychology internship will be shared.

Goals of Supervision Including Credentialing, Licensure, or Professional Organization Requirements

The overarching goals of supervision should be clearly specified in the contract such as to monitor and ensure the welfare of clients and to provide for the professional and personal growth of the supervisee. This section should also include any particular requirements articulated by a licensing board or professional organization such as the number of required hours of the practicum or internship and/or for individual face-to-face supervision.

Definition of the Roles and Expectations of both the Supervisor and Supervisee

The contract should include a clear delineation of the roles and responsibilities for both the supervisor and supervisee. For the supervisors these would include providing formative and summative evaluations of the supervisees' development of professional skills and assisting supervisees to explore and clarify thoughts and feelings which impact their practice. For the supervisees the expectations would include being prepared for both client sessions and supervision and that the supervisee will inform their supervisor of any difficulties they are having in the areas of delivering services to clients, completing paperwork, or coordinating with other agencies or providers such as schools or independent practitioners.

Sacredness of the Dedicated Supervision Hour

The contract should include the specific day/time schedule for supervision and rescheduling procedures if there is a need to cancel a session. The contract is a vehicle to communicate the supervisors' value of the importance of the supervision hour. This can be accomplished by clearly specifying that the supervisor assures a minimum of 2 hours of face-to-face supervision per week and listing the day and time of their regularly scheduled supervision sessions. It might also be noted that supervision will only be canceled in rare circumstances such as sickness and will always be made up unless it is agreeable to both the supervisor and the supervisee to cancel their supervision session that week. The supervisor can also include in the contract that these supervision hours will be uninterrupted and neither will be taking phone calls or texting unless an emergency arises.

Process for Requesting Additional Supervision Time

It is often very confusing to supervisees what to do if they feel they need additional supervision time. They are hesitant to ask for additional time as they may worry this may suggest inadequacy in their professional knowledge or skills. By including a section in the contract that addresses this situation, these feelings can be alleviated; and the norm will be created that this need for additional supervision will likely occur. The contract can communicate that there will be times when the supervisor will feel their discussion during the supervision hour about a particular case or situation is unfinished and the supervisor needs to request additional time with the supervisee. Alternatively, the supervisee when reviewing what was discussed in supervision realizes he or she is confused and additional supervision time is needed. It is in these types of situations that it is the responsibility of either the supervisor or the supervisee to request additional supervision time; and this is perfectly normal and does not communicate any inadequacy on the part of the supervisee.

Multiple Methods to be used in Supervision

Later in this chapter a number of methods of supervision will be identified and discussed in detail. The written contract should include a listing of these methods to normalize their use. For example, the supervisor can indicate that live or audio/video recording or role-playing will be used as a method of supervision. It can be communicated that this does not indicate any inadequacy on the part of the supervisee; but rather it is the norm and provides vehicles for the supervisor to provide feedback to the supervisee.

Clarification of the Supervisory Process

The written contract can also include a description of the supervisory process such as a brief description of the supervision model employed by the supervisor. For example it can be noted that the clinical supervisor is an experienced person with advanced training who oversees the clinical work of the supervisee and who is responsible, with the supervisee, for the quality of the supervisee's clinical work. Clinical supervision focuses on the services the supervisee provides to clients and includes such areas as client welfare, the therapeutic relationship, assessment, diagnosis, mental health/educational interventions, prognosis, appropriate referral techniques, and advocating for the client with other agencies in the community. This is all accomplished through a set of supervisory activities that include demonstration, direct instruction and training, consultation, and feedback and evaluation.

Legal, Ethical, and Liability Issues

It is important that legal, ethical, and liability issues be clearly stated in the written contact including the responsibilities of both the supervisor and the supervisee that result from them. For example, it is important that supervisees understand the legal concept of vicarious liability, that their supervisor is both legally and ethically responsible for all of the clinical work of their supervisees. This leads to the supervisee having the responsibility to keep the supervisor informed of everything that is occurring with their clients. In addition, protocols for risk of harm situations should be clearly described in the contract. This should include that the supervisees will contact the supervisor immediately if they suspect risk of harm to self or others. Further, it should be clearly communicated that the supervisor will always identify back-up supervisors if the supervisor cannot be contacted in these situations. Legal-ethical responsibilities related to supervisees and the requirement to only practice within the scope of professional competency are the responsibility of both the supervisor and supervisee.

Evaluation Procedures

Evaluation is the most anxiety provoking aspect of supervision. The written contract provides an opportunity to provide more structure to the evaluation process reducing anxiety. The contract can include a preview of the process of evaluation including its purpose, when it will occur, and due process procedures for addressing problems, disagreements, and deficiencies. Including these items in the contract can normalize the process. This section can also make it clear that it is the responsibility of the supervisor to provide this feedback and conduct formative and summative evaluations; but it is also the responsibility of supervisees to request additional feedback if they feel they are not receiving enough. This also is an example of the shared responsibility that occurs in a supervisory relationship. An effective contract is characterized by reciprocity. The supervisor and supervisee bear responsibilities to each other regarding the supervisee's performance review. Additionally the supervisor requests feedback from the supervisee regarding the supervisory process.

Sample Contracts

The components of an effective supervision contract discussed above together with other suggested components can be found in the sample contracts provided in Appendices 7A and 7B at the end of this book. As the goals and developmental levels of the supervisees are different for practicum and internship, sample contracts are provided for both a practicum and internship.

Documentation and Recordkeeping for Effective Practice and Risk Management

Organizational Strategies and Recordkeeping Forms

Structure and organization help the supervisor to maximize the benefits of the training experience. There exists a reciprocal relationship among recordkeeping, preparedness for supervision, and liability and risk management. Utilizing various systematic forms allows supervisors to focus their efforts, ensure accountability, and build in progress monitoring to support supervisee growth and effective clinical practice. The use of these forms also facilitates supervisee preparedness for supervision, sets an agenda for the supervisory process and intervention implementation, and teaches the supervisee appropriate documentation and effective risk management. These tools contribute to a systematic review of all of the supervisee's casework. These forms document cases and activities, supervisee progress, essential next steps for clients and the supervisee, and provide for the full range of observation and quality control supervisory strategies beyond case consultation. A supervision file, which should include these documents, should be kept for a minimum of 7 years (APA, 2007).

These forms can be divided into those for which the supervisee is responsible and those which the supervisor takes responsibility for completing. Forms the supervisee completes include: the Supervision Session Planner, Supervisee Client/Activity Session Planner, and Supervisee's Client Summary/Progress Notes. The supervisor would be responsible for completing the Supervisor's

TABLE 7.1 Supervisory Session Recording*

Supervisee Responsibilities	Supervisor Responsibilities
Supervision Session Planner	**Supervision Progress Notes**
• Preparation for meeting with supervisor	• Documentation of supervision session
	• Key session points
	• Recommendations
	• Follow-up agenda
Client/Activity Session Planner	
• Planning for intervention, consultation, problem-solving activities	• Case review comments
	• Supervisee skill development next steps
Client Summary/Progress Notes	
• Documentation of activities and progress reports	• Review of overall progress (the "big picture" — not completed after every session)

* A confidential summary file of this documentation can be kept electronically through an exchange or ledger through file sharing. Alternatively when using paper forms, the supervisor can complete Supervision Session Notes on the reverse side of Supervision Session Planners.

Supervision Notes. These forms will be described further below and are summarized in Table 7.1.

Supervision Session Planner

The supervisee completes the Supervision Session Planner in preparation for each meeting with the supervisor. It includes sections such as what topics need to be followed up from the last supervision session, a description of the activities the supervisee has been involved in since the last supervision meeting, specific cases or activities the supervisee would like to review, and questions/concerns or feedback requested of the supervisor. The supervisee would not be restricted to only these questions; but these topics systematically address key content areas for supervision sessions. Although not completed each session, the supervisee should also include a self-assessment of his or her progress, which would include strengths and areas of need. This form should be shared with the supervisor prior to their supervision session, which would assist the supervisor in preparing for the meeting. Appendix 7C includes a sample of this Supervision Session Planner.

Client/Activity Session Planner

Whereas the Supervision Session Planner focused on planning for the supervision session, the Client/Activity Session Planner provides an opportunity for supervisees to prepare for and share their plans with the supervisor for their next client session or other activity. This is applicable to an assessment, intervention/therapy session, group activity, or consultation. The planner includes all of the referral questions/concerns for the particular case, the specific objectives of the session with the client, the specific plan of activities to accomplish with the client such as if a particular psychological test will be administered or a particular treatment strategy employed, what the supervisee needs to do to prepare for this session such as reviewing a particular psychological test or treatment manual or reading a chapter in a textbook, and any questions/concerns they want to raise with their supervisor. As was true for the Supervision Session Planner, the supervisee would not be limited to these questions; but the form provides a process for supervisees to begin to think of questions they have for their supervisor. Similar to the Supervision Session Planner, the supervisor should also have a copy of this form in advance and can use the form to record notes on during the supervision session. The supervisor's notes can include recommendations made to the supervisee to review certain reference materials such as books or articles. A sample of the Client/Activity Session Planner can be found in Appendix 7D.

Supervisee's Client Summary/Progress Notes

After each client session the supervisee should complete a summary/progress note. This document includes the supervisee's description of the session content such as topics and themes that were expressed during the session; a description of process such as therapeutic techniques and skills training that occurred; an assessment of client progress; plans for the next session; and information the supervisee wants to bring up in supervision related to this client. A sample of this form is provided in Appendix 7E.

Supervisor's Supervision Notes

This last form provides a mechanism by which supervisors can monitor short- and long-term professional skills development of their supervisees. It includes a section completed by the supervisor related to a summary of content presented during the supervision session which can include follow-up items from the last session, critical case/activity reviews, supervisor initiated agenda, feedback, concerns, and other notes related to professional development. Other sections of this form include a process summary of the supervision session including supervisee self-presentation, session dynamics, supervisory strategies employed, a summary of feedback/recommendations related to skills and intervention/activities for the intern to follow up on, and next steps/future action which might include suggestions for interventions such as homework/research, skill practice, case follow-up, or activity prescription. The final section of the Supervisor Supervision Notes includes a developmental status summary recording the supervisor's assessment of the supervisee's overall progress, key goals for improvement and professional development, and formative feedback.

These notations will prove to be a particularly helpful resource when writing summative evaluations or letters of recommendation. While this final progress assessment section is typically not completed after each supervision session, it focuses the supervisor's attention on the larger picture of the supervisee's developmental progress. A sample Supervisor Supervision Notes form is provided in Appendix 7F.

Streamlining and Managing Planning and Recordkeeping

The utilization of all of these approaches to planning and documentation are intended to ensure planful approaches to the supervisee's work and to the supervision process. These practical quality control tools can be implemented without the undue burden that is often associated with paperwork. Based on our experiences working with school psychology supervisors who have adopted use of these forms a number of strategies appear helpful. Some supervisors prefer hard paper copies of the Supervision Session Planner and Supervisor's Supervision Notes which can be printed back-to-back on a single page for ease of recordkeeping and thus be readily completed and filed immediately after supervision session. Some interns and supervisors are using Google Docs (or a similar document or file sharing system) to exchange and file the intern's Supervision Session Planners and Client/Activity Session Planners; and then follow-up notes can be added by both the supervisor and supervisee. When the supervisor adds his supervision notes to these documents at the end of a session, a file is created that summarizes the supervision for required documentation and risk management responsibilities.

CASE EXAMPLE: A COMPLETED SUPERVISION SESSION PLANNER

SUPERVISION SESSION PLANNER

Date: 12/2/15   Supervisor: Dennis Simon / Supervisee: Mark Swerdlik

Last supervisory session follow-up (i.e., what was agreed upon during the last supervision session):

- use of relaxation exercise (deep breathing) with 5th grader with social anxiety;
- use of Good Behavior Game in consultation with kindergarten teacher having classroom management problems;
- use of "one downmanship" strategy when consulting with kindergarten teacher.

Activity summary since last supervision (i.e., how time spent):

* continued routine teacher consultations and counseling activities;
* initiated systems-level consultation around implementation of PBIS in Solomon Elementary School;
* researched evidence-based practice for child with school phobia;
* met with parents who are concerned about their child being bullied.

Cases/activities to review:

* system-level consultation related to staff concerns about implementing PBIS school-wide;
* parent consultation about their child being bullied.

Questions/concerns/feedback requested of Supervisor:

* strategies to work with parents and teachers of child who is being bullied;
* planning for upcoming progress review meeting with my university supervisor;

Self-assessment of progress:

(Not completed every time. Include strengths and areas of need)

Strengths

* Academic assessments of students experiencing academic difficulties
* Ability to build rapport with students and staff
* Initiative
* Reliability and timeliness in completing tasks

Areas of Need

* Counseling children with externalizing problems
* Dealing with teachers feeling too overwhelmed to introduce new class-room management strategies

---

SUPERVISORY PROCESS ACTIVITY

Review the practicum or internship contract presented in Appendices 7A and 7B. Review Section III of the sample contract related to duties and responsibilities of the supervisor and supervisee. Review and discuss this section of the contract with your supervisee or, if enrolled in a graduate class, role-play with another student playing the role of the intern or practicum student (e.g., was it helpful by providing more structure, did it increase or lessen anxiety, answer my questions, etc.).

Assessment and Goal Setting

Assessment of the supervisee's skills and professional development needs is an early task in establishing the agenda for the supervisory relationship. Consistent with other areas of school psychology practice, the supervision experience begins with an assessment of current functioning. Data are collected from all relevant sources including the supervisee, the university program, and letters of reference. Then the assessment data are linked to a supervision plan. Throughout the supervision experience progress is monitored in comparison to the initial baseline data and the training goals established for the internship. As initial goals are met, new ones may be initiated.

Linking Assessment to Goal Setting: The Internship Plan

For the internship this assessment process includes a review of graduate training, practicum, and other relevant field-based training. The capstone internship experience is designed to prepare the student for entry-level competency across all NASP practice domains (NASP, 2010a) and for doctoral internships across all APA (2011) competency benchmarks as well. Thus the assessment should address each of these domains. These areas are commonly covered within the university or state internship plan which can serve as a partial guide for goal setting and a reference for the content of progress monitoring. Appendix 7G contains a sample internship plan from the Illinois School Psychology Internship Consortium, an APA-accredited doctoral internship program. The NASP practice domains (NASP, 2010a) summarize the principal training areas that are targets for professional preparation and summarized in the internship plan.

Data collection for the entry-level assessment for supervision starts with intern self-report. This discussion begins broadly with the intern sharing his or her perspective on strengths and weaknesses, training needs, and personal goals for the internship. Then the formal internship plan is reviewed to systematically address all critical practice domains. The intern should record self-assessment across each practice area which then becomes a reference point for progress monitoring and ongoing formative evaluation.

The assessment process then moves on to a review of the professional knowledge base and skill areas which were the focus of university education and the nature of all prior field-based training. The supervisor works with the supervisee to identify any gaps in exposure to core practice areas either in terms of theoretical preparation or experience within practicum settings. Even the best graduate programs will have different points of emphasis in curriculum; and practicum experiences can be expected to provide exposure to either limited student populations or circumscribed areas of practice. For example, a supervisee may have extensive experience in the application of curriculum-based measurement to consultation regarding academic instruction but no or limited exposure to universal screening and brief progress monitoring strategies for social-emotional functioning. Practicum experiences may have exposed the intern to work with the general population of students but not included significant experience with students on the autism spectrum. Typically there are limited opportunities prior to the internship for experience with crisis intervention activities. It is also important to identify any special professional interests the intern has to see if they can be explored and enhanced in training, for example, work with students with mood disorders or program development for universal screening of social-emotional concerns.

Collaboration with University Liaisons

A second valuable source of assessment data as a foundation for supervision is the university internship liaison. Unfortunately, letters of recommendation while likely to delineate strengths, seldom shine sufficient light on training needs. The new Standard Reference Form from APPIC addresses this issue for doctoral internship candidates by specifically asking for recommendations regarding training needs and areas of improvement (APPIC, 2015). At this time, no such standard form exists for specialist-level candidates. In our experience, an informal conversation with the university internship liaison near the start of the internship can provide a more complete picture of the intern's strengths and weaknesses and can include helpful recommendations for crafting the internship plan. Establishment of an early connection with university faculty is beneficial in many ways, but is particularly important for the limited number of cases where an intern displays significant problems.

Strengths-based Assessment

The supervisor's assessment of the intern's strengths, weaknesses, and needs should be comprehensive but with particular attention to current strengths. Every opportunity for articulating how a personal strength or competency can be a foundation for further professional development in new areas of practice can motivate the intern and reduce performance anxiety that is typically heightened in entry to a new field-based experience.

Systems-focused Conceptualization and Skills

The assessment process examines professional skills and competencies for case-specific intervention and consultation activities. It also explores the supervisee's understanding of systemic issues and the tensions inherent in all school systems and other practice settings as they evolve to incorporate new conceptualizations of best practice. This focus contributes to goal setting regarding the essential competencies of program development and change agent skills. It also provides an important opportunity for discussion of the challenges of implementation of best practice approaches that may be the center of on-campus university training but might still be a work-in-progress in the context of field-based experiences.

Interpersonal Style

Observations during the intern's initial activities provide indicators that may modify self-assessment data. The interpersonal style of the intern plays a significant role in all professional practice and is readily observed early in the internship experience. It is important for supervisors to recognize that a variety of interpersonal styles besides their own can be effective for the role of school psychologist. Further, some supervisee's interpersonal strengths may not be fully evident until they have attained a sufficient comfort level within the new school setting. However, interpersonal skills and characteristics are central elements within this human service field and should be assessed and examined within the context of their impact on professional practice. Most often over the course of an internship, the supervisor will be challenging the intern to display underutilized strengths with increased confidence; but sometimes modifications in interpersonal style or self-presentation may boost professional competency (e.g., an impatient and overly intense focus on change may contribute to resistance from clients) (Holloway, 1995). It remains important to maintain the distinction that supervision is not therapy for the supervisee. If there are significant interpersonal issues that require therapeutic support, these should be addressed in a separate therapeutic relationship with a different professional. This role distinction was discussed in greater detail in Chapters 2 and 3.

Performance Anxiety

It is expected that entering a new field experience would at least temporarily elevate performance anxiety. This can be explored as part of this initial assessment process. The supervisor can ask the supervisee to share how she or he typically enters a new culture or work site. What level of performance anxiety is experienced? What strategies are applied to reduce anxiety and to gain comfort within the setting and with new colleagues? What has been helpful in past field experiences? What anxiety is there regarding evaluation by the supervisor or informally by other faculty or practitioners? Normalizing the occurrence of initial anxiety and discussing it openly can be helpful. Additionally it prepares the intern for another level of self-reflection and emotional awareness that will be expected throughout the supervisory relationship. Finally identification of adaptive approaches to management of anxiety and assimilation into new settings will prepare interns for their first independent professional experiences. As a standard part of the initial assessment process at the onset of supervision, the examination of performance anxiety may also alert the supervisor to additional supports required for a successful launch of the internship and its supervision experience.

Learning Styles

We all have unique learning styles that apply specifically to supervised field-based experiences. It is helpful to prompt interns to self-reflect and then share how they learn best in field-based training experiences. This includes a discussion of past supervisory relationships and an exploration of what proved most helpful or unsatisfactory in the past. In turn, supervisors share what they perceive to be the key supervisee attitudes and actions that result in a successful internship experience. (See coverage of effective supervisee characteristics in Chapter 3.) Supervisors offer a description of their supervisory style, share their model of supervision, and what they believe has contributed to successful training experiences and supervisory relationships with past interns. (See *Supervisory Process Activity* in Chapter 3.)

Assessment Sets Tone for Supervision and for Self-monitoring

In summary, the assessment process is multifaceted. It covers current skill levels and competencies, defines needs, and sets goals. It incorporates interpersonal dimensions related to practice and the potential influence of performance anxiety. It models the overall foundational practice standard of school psychology that links assessment to intervention to outcome monitoring. The focus on self-reflection and assessment and emotional awareness sets a foundation for the process of feedback and evaluation within this supervisory relationship and for the essential skills of self-monitoring that will guide all future professional development.

CASE EXAMPLE: ASSESSMENT AND GOAL SETTING

Beth engages her supervisee, Ann, in a discussion about her emerging professional skills and personal goals for supervision. Ann's self-reflection indicates that she is comfortable with Response to Intervention (RtI) approaches to academic consultation but has less experience with consultation regarding individual or classroom-wide behavior management. She did have positive experiences with supervised individual counseling cases at her practicum site, but this work did not include direct consultation or intervention work with parents or guardians. The counseling work centered on student concerns with anxiety or depression, but she did not have any cases that addressed anger management or disruptive behaviors.

Ann notes that her practicum supervisor was attempting to introduce multitiered systems of support into district practice, but that efforts were met with significant resistance. Ann is interested in collaborating with her internship supervisor on new program development; and she is excited that a pilot for universal screening for social-emotional concerns is being considered for the current school year. She would like coaching on managing barriers to new program implementation.

Beth leads Ann through a review of her university's or the state-wide internship plan to systematically assess prior training and field experience and self-assessment of competencies across all core domains of school psychology practice. Together Beth and Ann discuss opportunities within this internship site that can provide supervised experience in areas that have been identified as training needs and those that are of particular specialty interest for Ann.

Beth explores with Ann her levels of confidence and anxiety as she begins this capstone field experience. The discussion also highlights Ann's perception of her interpersonal or self-presentation and field-based learning styles. Ann describes herself as naturally quiet and appearing introverted in new situations but gradually able to assert herself and become an active contributor even leader in work teams. This is consistent with the feedback that Beth received from her university supervisor who noted that Ann's social style is naturally introverted and can lead coworkers to initially underestimate Ann's skills. However, team members fairly quickly see her strengths and appreciate the depth of insight she brings to problem-solving tasks. Beth asks Ann to share what kind of supervisory supports helped her feel comfortable in new situations more rapidly and with less anxiety. Ann highlighted the benefits she has received from supervisor modeling including advance role-playing for new situations.

Beth and Ann summarize their mutual understanding of needs and goals and related training activities for the internship. Beth notes that this assessment process is not a one-and-done activity. Using the internship plan and their notes from this initial assessment and goal setting, they will together routinely monitor progress and adjust goals, Ann's internship activities, and Beth's supervision approaches.

SUPERVISORY PROCESS ACTIVITY: ASSESSMENT AND GOAL SETTING

Supervisory Process Activities suggested in this text can be directly implemented as part of the development of the supervisor-supervisee relationship. In the context of supervision training, activities can be enacted through role-plays with supervisors taking turns as supervisor or supervisee or in a graduate class with students taking turns in both roles.

Goal Setting

The intern shares one area of self-assessed professional strength, then one area in need of further development, and finally one personal professional growth goal for the internship year.

Learning Style and Field-based Supervision

Interns share: "How do I learn best in a field-based training experience?" and "What do I look for in a supervisory relationship?" Supervisors share: "What are the key intern attitudes and actions that result in a successful internship experience?" and "What do I value most from an intern in a supervisory relationship?"

Feedback and Evaluation

Feedback and evaluation are central components of supervision for fostering professional growth and ensuring healthy and effective practices within the profession of school psychology. These activities are critical for several aspects of supervision. Feedback is a primary teaching and coaching tool for fostering supervisee skill development. Evaluation contributes to this process but also involves the gatekeeping role that supervisors must perform for the benefit of the public and the profession. Addressing supervisory relationships, the APA (2010a) ethics code states: "psychologists establish a timely and specific process for providing feedback to students and supervisees. Information regarding the process is provided to the student at the beginning of supervision" (7.06a). Supervisors have ethical obligations to provide timely and substantive feedback to supervisees. The process, frequency, and disclosure regarding which other professionals will have access to this information (i.e., collaborating supervisors and university supervisors for internships) should be delineated in the written contract and discussed in the orientation to the supervision relationship. NASP's (2010d) ethics code also addresses evaluation requiring school psychologists who supervise or train professionals to provide appropriate working conditions, fair and timely evaluation, constructive supervision, and continuing professional development opportunities (Standard IV.4.3). Some state licensing laws also identify evaluation as a required component of supervision (e.g., Texas).

Addresses All Dimensions of Training and Competency

The contract for supervision must make it clear that *all* dimensions of training and areas of professional competency will be addressed by feedback and evaluation. This includes not only professional skills but professional dispositions which involve commitment, values, and ethics evident in work activities and relationships with clients and collaborating professionals. Timeliness of reports, attendance at meetings, appropriate completion of responsibilities, taking initiative, and executing a fair share of the workload on professional teams are all areas subject to feedback and evaluation. Interpersonal style and the quality of relationships with clients and colleagues is also an essential domain. While supervisors often find this last area very challenging to address, the ability to build rapport, establish collegial relationships, and engage effectively in teams is essential for competent psychological practice. For example, a supervisee may demonstrate excellent technical skills regarding assessment; but if she or he is consistently unable to establish rapport with students, then assessment results may prove unreliable or invalid. In this case feedback and coaching would target the interpersonal dimensions involved in assessment.

Corey et al. (2010) provided a summary of important targets for evaluation that go beyond technical skills and knowledge. These include the following: the character of relationships with staff and with clients, which in schools would include children, parents, teachers, other specialists within the school and community; diversity competence; professional judgment and maturity; ethical and legal practice; recognition of limitations and when to seek consultation; and responsiveness to supervision and openness to personal development. The last characteristics are evident by the character of the supervisee's participation in the supervisory relationship. They include an acknowledgment that professional development is a continual journey. A supervisee who appropriately accepts feedback then adjusts professional practice and who seeks out collegial supports when necessary indicates a commitment to ethical practice within personal competencies; and these attitudes and behaviors can be viewed as predictive of dedication to continued career long professional development for the benefit of clients.

Gatekeeping, Supervisee Rights, Due Process

Since evaluation in clinical supervision may serve a gatekeeping function that can impact either entry to or continuance in the profession, the supervision contract should detail the timetable for evaluation and the supervisee's recourse for contesting an evaluation's content. The rights and due process procedures for responding to or even appealing a negative evaluation finding should be transparently delineated at the onset of supervision. For internship training, the roles of the collaborating university supervisor and other cooperating supervisors who may supervise the intern in an alternative setting or for a short rotation should be clearly described.

Internship Plan and Assessed Goals

The internship plan provides a summary framework for defining the target skill areas and competencies for professional preparation and thus summarizes the primary content for feedback and evaluation. This plan should reflect all practice domains delineated in the NASP Practice Model (2010a) and the APA competency areas (2011). Upon entry to supervision, the supervisor engages the supervisee in a collaborative assessment of skills across these professional domains and establishes goals for supervision that will become a focus of feedback activity and be subject to formal evaluation. During internship training, the entry-level assessment of the supervisee's knowledge and skills will typically reveal uneven preparation and/or experience across the required domains of practice. Since broad competencies are required of school psychologists, feedback and evaluation should particularly focus on areas requiring improvement and additional supervised experience to ensure eventual readiness for independent practice upon completion of the internship. For supervisees who have extensive field experience and demonstrate strong competencies early in the internship year, it remains important to not only affirm their strong abilities but to continue to challenge them to grow to additional levels of competency and to improve skills in leadership.

Formative Feedback and Summative Evaluation

Evaluation and feedback are continuous processes throughout training and supervision. These processes involve the provision of *formative feedback* to shape and improve performance and *summative evaluation* which rates performance against expected standards. Formative feedback provides prescriptive and evaluative comments during the course of activities or in proximate performance reviews. For example, a supervisor may provide feedback to a supervisee regarding the character of her or his contributions during a problem-solving team meeting, specific suggestions on how to improve behavior management in a counseling group, or technical corrections about administration of a standardized test. This feedback evaluates the supervisee's performance with the intent to shape improvements in performance until she or he gradually meets expected competencies.

Summative evaluation summarizes overall effectiveness at key developmental time periods. During internship training, this should be at least quarterly and would include structured written feedback to the university across multiple domains of performance. Summative evaluation provides a picture for the supervisor, supervisee, and university liaison of the intern's level of performance at each developmental stage of training relative to expectations for eventual progression to entry-level professional competencies across all required practice domains. When an evaluation reveals a serious concern about a specific area(s) of competency that has been subject to significant formative feedback, supervisory focus will intensify in this area; summative evaluation in this domain might be scheduled more frequently; and if necessary a structured remediation plan would be developed.

Self-monitoring

A primary goal of feedback and evaluation is development of self-assessment and self-monitoring skills by supervisees (APA, 2015a). These skills are important for all professionals, but particularly in the field of school psychology where so many practitioners are one-of-a-kind professionals in their schools. Routine self-monitoring creates a reflective posture for all service delivery and predisposes practitioners to be aware of when they need to seek additional case consultation. The interplay between self-assessment and supervisor feedback and evaluation helps supervisees judge the accuracy of their self-evaluations. Wise et al. (2010) note that research suggests a cautionary approach to assuming the accuracy of self-assessments while at the same time emphasizing its importance as a skill to be developed as one dimension of defining the need for lifelong learning.

One way to create dialogue regarding self-assessment and formative feedback is to routinely ask supervisees to assess their performance in various tasks and then provide supervisory formative feedback for comparison. In a similar fashion, in preparation for summative evaluation reports, it can be beneficial to ask supervisees to rate themselves across the same competency domains that are subject to evaluation. For example, a review of the internship plan with a comparison of supervisee self-assessment ratings and supervisor evaluation input can provide feedback on the accuracy of self-assessment skills while simultaneously providing a summary of the supervisee's self-confidence levels in key practice domains. While there is concern regarding the potential for supervisees to overrate their competencies, in our experience competent supervisees are frequently too hard on themselves and their growth is enhanced by attention to their strengths. In either case, the dialogue in supervision hones self-monitoring skills and helps to define an agenda for supervisory focus.

Characteristics of Effective Feedback and Evaluation

Both in psychology and in education much has been written about the characteristics of effective feedback (see Bernard & Goodyear, 2014; Corey et al., 2010; Falender & Shafranske, 2004; Harvey & Struzziero, 2008). We draw from this literature, our own experiences as supervisors, and extensive dialogue with both specialist- and doctoral-level clinical supervisors to define characteristics for the effective practice of feedback and evaluation.

Feedback is best accepted when it is embedded in a trusting supervisory relationship (Karpenko & Gidycz, 2012). Chapter 3 delineated the characteristics of an effective supervisory relationship. The factors covered there describe the necessary foundation for a supervisory relationship that enables the supervisee to accept and utilize feedback. The provision of feedback is effective when it is direct and specific. Clear descriptions of observable behaviors coupled with specific suggestions for improvement are required. When necessary, examples modeled by the supervisor may add to the clarity of communication and expectations.

Effective feedback is delivered in a timely manner in close proximity to the supervisee's performance. Novice supervisors are often hesitant to provide feedback particularly when it involves a challenging critique. Formative feedback should be frequently given starting from the very beginning of the supervisory relationship. The more feedback becomes a routine anticipated part of supervisory sessions, the more likely it is to be become a natural dialogue that can improve performance; it increases the likelihood that feedback will be balanced in terms of positives and negatives. As frequent feedback becomes the norm, it is less likely to produce performance anxiety in the supervisee who may come to appreciate its benefits for professional development.

Feedback should be communicated in a calm, respectful manner but with a directness that provides clarity. It should be honest but balanced in terms of strengths and weaknesses. Supervisors need to be sensitive and empathic as they provide feedback. One common strategy, the *sandwich method*, recommends placing corrective feedback between two positive comments (Daniels, 2009). Cantillon and Sargeant (2008) propose a four-step approach that begins with supervisee self-assessment: (a) the supervisee states what was positive about his or her performance; (b) the supervisor states areas of agreement and elaborates on positive performance; (c) the supervisee states what was not as well done or could have been improved; and (d) the supervisor states what he or she thinks could have been improved and makes recommendations. It is important to be conscious of the fact that in preprofessional training some supervisees who have excelled in the classroom may only be used to outstanding reviews of performance; but they may now be experiencing a dose of prescriptive feedback that is more significant and in their eyes more critical than they have encountered before. The protection that limits the possibilities of overwhelming a supervisee is built from accurate assessment of current skill levels and appropriate matching of training activities to skill levels. A strong trusting supervisory relationship supports receptivity to feedback.

SUPERVISORY PROCESS ACTIVITY: FEEDBACK AND EVALUATION

This exercise is designed to be the stimulus for a dialogue between the supervisor and supervisee regarding their personal experiences of receiving feedback. It can set the stage for direct discussion about the feedback and evaluation that will occur within this supervisory relationship. As an individual reflection exercise for supervisors, these stimulus questions can foster increased self-awareness of how their personal experiences being evaluated may influence their supervisory style in this area.

1. Think about a time when you received *positive feedback*. What was it about the communication or the relationship that helped you accept or reject that feedback?
2. Think about a time when you received *negative feedback*. What was it about the communication or relationship that helped you accept or reject that feedback?
3. Share with each other what might be helpful for you in this supervisory relationship to clearly understand and accept feedback.
4. What concerns if any do you have in either the supervisee or supervisor role regarding formal evaluations of performance?

Effective feedback critiques behavior and technical execution of skills not the person. It includes an expression of confidence that the supervisee can indeed master professional competencies. Particularly early in training, practicum and intern supervisees are prone to feeling overwhelmed by the complexity of professional skill sets required for competency. They may require the experienced perspective of the supervisor and reassurance that over the course of the training cycle they will begin to master essential skills.

Whenever possible feedback should be followed by time for reflection and questions. Thus feedback needs not only be timely but be given time to be processed and discussed. If the supervisee struggles with critical feedback or disagrees with the supervisor's perspective, ample time for discussion should be provided; and opportunities for follow-up activities should be made available to permit the supervisee an additional opportunity to demonstrate positive performance in areas in question. These additional opportunities may be limited by the necessity of putting a client's welfare first if in the supervisor's judgment the supervisee's resistance to feedback is unrealistically distorted; and he or she requires more training to engage in the activity in question immediately. Constructive feedback is the foundation upon which alternatives for improvement are derived. Frequent feedback provided in a supportive supervisory relationship is the cornerstone of an effective supervisory relationship.

Direct Observation and Multirater Feedback

In the next section of this chapter, we will highlight the critical importance of employing multiple methods in supervision and not merely relying on supervisee self-report. In terms of feedback and evaluation, direct observation or collaborative review of recordings of performance provide the best data for feedback from the supervisor. The APA (2015a) *Guidelines for Clinical Supervision in Health Service Psychology* straightforwardly asserted that: "Live observation or review of recorded sessions is the preferred procedure [for providing feedback]" (p. 19). This document goes on to note that direct access to supervisees' professional performance increases both the accuracy and the helpfulness of feedback; and, importantly, direct observations are associated with enhanced outcomes for supervisees and their clients. Direct observation reduces legal risk if a supervisor's execution of the supervisory gatekeeping role is questioned or challenged; and it satisfies the requirements for monitoring appropriate standard of care for clients and for the supervisory process. To ensure inclusion of feedback for the full range of expected competencies, selections of activities for observation and materials for review should be collaboratively decided upon by the supervisor and supervisee.

Particularly during preprofessional training, it is best practice for the primary supervisor to gather feedback from other professionals. Engagement of the expertise of other psychologists and related professionals to participate in case supervision or other aspects of the training experience can improve the entire training and supervision experience. Obtaining feedback from collaborative supervisors increases the breadth of supervision, serves as a check against potential biases or blind spots by the primary supervisor, and extends feedback to cover areas in which the primary supervisor has limited expertise.

Supervisors are not immune to potential bias in evaluation. Karpenko and Gidycz (2012) note that the character of the supervisory relationship can influence the character of supervisor feedback. Within a strong positive relationship a leniency bias can emerge; while in difficult supervisory relationship with reduced supervisor-supervisee alliance, a tendency to overly critical feedback may develop. Receiving confirmation or extensions of feedback regarding supervisees from collaborating supervisors can help limit the influence of blind spots. School psychologists spend their entire careers focused on assisting clients in overcoming obstacles and achieving beyond their own and others' expectations. This "helpful bias" can occasionally compromise effective feedback and evaluation in supervision. Supervision is a hierarchical relationship and while a friendship relationship may evolve after supervision concludes, supervisors must be mindful of maintaining sufficient boundaries in supervisory relationships to promote increased objectivity. When supervisors and supervisees have diverse backgrounds including but not limited to racial or cultural differences, it is incumbent on the supervisor to ensure that inadvertent biases do not interfere with objectivity of feedback and evaluation throughout the supervisory process (Christiansen et al., 2011).

Assuming the responsibility to provide both positive and challenging feedback from the beginning of supervision and seeking the feedback of collaborating supervisors can negate bias. The responsibility the supervisor bears for protecting the public requires objectivity and dispassionate judgment in evaluating readiness for independent practice. In some cases it may be in the best interests of both the supervisee and the publics served by the profession to withhold certification of readiness for independent practice.

Summative Evaluation and Assessment of Competencies

Inevitably the process of evaluation includes both subjective and objective elements. The concern within the field has been to devise and employ more objective measures of performance that are behaviorally specific and increasingly criterion-referenced (Bernard & Goodyear, 2014; Corey et al., 2010). Psychology has moved toward evaluation of professional competencies that are commonly defined and anchored in observable behaviors (Falender & Shafranske, 2004; Fouad et al., 2009; Kaslow et al., 2009). APA (2011, 2012a) has developed a system of competency benchmarks, guidelines for their application, and toolkits of measurement instruments. These benchmarks focus on defining competencies required for readiness for practicum, internship, and entry to professional practice respectively. While APA's intent was to define competencies across all psychology specialties, the system does not adequately capture all required elements of school psychology preparation. Additional benchmarks and behavioral markers would be required not in place of what exists, but in addition to what has been delineated to clearly capture the full range of school psychology competencies required in daily practice. A Council of Directors of School Psychology Programs (CDSPP) task force has outlined practicum competencies for school psychology (Caterino et al., 2010). Nevertheless the APA competencies, evaluation tools, and benchmarks contribute toward a more unified, comprehensive, behaviorally specific, and thus objective approach to evaluation.

In addition to the APA measures, various authors have proposed rubrics, scales, and checklists for evaluation of supervisees (Bernard & Goodyear, 2014;

Harvey & Struzziero, 2008). These tools attempt to define professional skills and attitudes in a systematic manner with explicitly defined characteristics or examples. University programs, internship consortiums, and state-wide internship plans may provide formal instruments for summative evaluation of supervisees that may incorporate elements of this approach. Consistent with the APA benchmarks, competencies can be rated on a continuum. It is anticipated that supervisees will continue to present with relative strengths and weaknesses even at the endpoint of the supervision cycle; but it is required that by the end of internship they demonstrate broad entry-level competencies across the NASP practice domains and for doctoral candidates the APA competencies as well.

The field supervisor of practicum and internship supervisees is likely to be presented with a formal final evaluation form by the student's university or the participating internship consortium. It is likely to include elements of rubric and benchmark tools similar to what was just described. Clinical supervisors of credentialed psychologists are likely to receive generic school district personnel review forms that broadly address professional performance for a diverse group of educators. The supervisor should receive this form in advance of the training cycle and review it with the supervisee at the onset of training.

All that has been written about feedback in general applies to summative evaluation. If formative feedback has been frequent, concerns directly addressed and noted, specific supervisory attention and monitoring paid to any areas requiring improvement, then the summative evaluation should merely be a recap of what has been discussed in supervision throughout the training cycle. There should never be any surprises or new data entered into final summative evaluations. Any concerns should have been transparently communicated and addressed prior to completion of this summary review. The unique objective of summative evaluation is to summarize professional competency in relation to standards and criteria required to successfully advance to either the next level of training or entry into the profession. Reviews of credentialed professionals typically address standards related to tenure, retention, and needs for professional development. Summative evaluations are shared with university supervisors and/or district administrators.

Summative evaluations generally contain affirmations of the progress and attainments of supervisees. As preparation for summative evaluation, the supervisor can review supervision session notes as a reminder of achievements, issues, and progress throughout the year. Whenever a narrative description is required, it should use behaviorally descriptive language with appropriate examples. It is a sign of an effective supervisory relationship when the supervisor and supervisee share a similar perspective on the assessment of competencies as described by the supervisor in the evaluation form. Every summative evaluation should point toward next steps in professional development and describe the resources or methods necessary for further growth.

Problems of Professional Competence

Unfortunately, some supervisees exhibit significant problems in professional competence. When formative feedback is frequent and the first quarter summative evaluation is comprehensive, these challenging supervisory situations may be apparent early in a supervision cycle; and these concerns should be addressed directly and as soon as they emerge. It is important to distinguish between problematic behavior that is developmentally anticipated, such as performance anxiety at a new training or work site, or transitory and remediable, thus able to be addressed through additional support and/or training. Transitory issues may emerge if a supervisee is experiencing significant temporary personal stress due to a life event (e.g., the onset of a terminal illness of a parent) or when a supervisee is overwhelmed by a new challenge (e.g., first time working in a low SES environment, first experience with a violent student episode, and so forth).

Historically the literature used the term *impairment* to describe severe problematic behaviors; however, concerns were raised that this term could be confused with the formal definition of impairment described in the Americans with Disabilities Act (1990) (Collins, Falender, & Shafranske, 2011; Elman & Forrest, 2007; Schwartz-Mette, 2011). In light of the competency initiative, the term *problems in professional competence* has replaced this term; and when we address issues that may require remediation plans or exercise of supervisory gatekeeping responsibilities, we are referring to significant problematic behaviors that go beyond developmentally anticipated and transitory concerns.

Significant problematic behaviors can be identified when any of the following conditions are evident. The supervisee does not acknowledge, understand, or address the problem when it is identified. The problem is not merely a reflection of a skill deficit that could be addressed by additional academic or didactic training. The quality of services delivered by the supervisee is sufficiently negatively affected and results in concerns about the welfare of clients. The problem is not restricted to one area of professional functioning but broadly impacts professional competencies. The problematic behavior does not change as a function of feedback, and/or remediation efforts. Of particular concern are behaviors in supervisory sessions that communicate active and persistent denial or opposition to recommendations for change. Often, the supervisor will begin to receive critical concerns from not only collaborating supervisors but other school staff regarding performance. Finally, a disproportionate amount of attention and time is required by the supervisor and other training personnel with minimal signs of improvement.

Problems of professional competence may emerge in any of the skill or practice areas defined in the NASP Practice Model (2010a) and the APA (2011) competency benchmarks, and outlined in the internship plan. Various schema have been proposed to organize and define professional competence (Kaslow et al., 2007). Lamb and Swerdlik (2003) described three primary categories: (a) acquisition and

integration of relevant professional standards (e.g., ethical behaviors and incorporation of APA and NASP standards of care); (b) development of appropriate professional skills; and (c) monitoring of personal functioning (e.g., professional dispositions, stress management, and psychological health as it impacts performance).
While each of these categories should be addressed in feedback and evaluation,
they are not discrete nor unrelated areas of performance. Assessment of significant
problematic behavior requires an integration of these factors into a total picture
of performance (Cruise & Swerdlik, 2010).

In our experience working with supervisors, the following areas may present
challenging supervisory situations that are capable of escalating to serious levels
of concern. Skill deficits or gaps in training become significant concerns when
they severely compromise performance and impede client welfare and if they are
unresponsive to even intensified supervisory intervention (e.g., persistent difficulties in appropriate administration, interpretation, and reporting of standardized
assessments). Continued unresponsiveness to supervision is an alarming behavioral
marker not only because it interferes with current professional development, but
because it is indicative of a poor prognosis for the development of future competencies and a commitment to lifelong professional development essential for an
effective career. Problems in professional behaviors may be evident in irrespon-
sible work habits (e.g., chronically missing deadlines and appointments or not
following through on responsibilities to collaborative teams). Interpersonal and
communication style can become problematic if they repeatedly interfere with
collaborative problem-solving or the establishment of essential consultation and
therapeutic alliances (e.g., consistently abrasive or critical demeanor or limited
display of empathic skills necessary for effective engagement with clients). Finally,
significant problems in professional competence can emerge when supervisees'
psychological health or stress management style and capacity consistently interfere
with professional judgment, execution of professional responsibilities, and recep-
tiveness to supervision (e.g., a supervisee's clinical level of depression creates blind
spots in providing therapeutic support for students, interferes with work production, and blocks supervisory support and recommendations).

As noted above, every training program must define expected professional
competencies, evaluation procedures and timelines, and due process procedures for supervisee objections to evaluation process and/or content. Any rating tools and evaluation instruments should be as objectively defined as possible
and reviewed at the beginning of the supervisory relationship. These rating scales
should be included in a training handbook and/or included in the appendices of
the supervision contract. University graduate programs or internship consortia
are required to carefully outline and review these standards and procedures with
supervisors and supervisees (APA, 2015b; NASP, 2010b).

It is important to provide formative feedback and summative evaluation
according to the guidelines described earlier in this section. As soon as sufficient
data indicate the need for a remediation plan, concerns should be summarized

both verbally and in writing. Cruise and Swerdlik (2010) recommend beginning with an action letter that describes problematic behavior in language that is observable and measurable and compares performance to explicit criteria and standards. The content and support for the stated concern should be able to be backed up by routine supervision notes that summarized formative feedback, performance concerns, responsiveness to supervision, and any prior summative evaluations. Providing the supervisee with a detailed action letter prior to verbal discussion in a supervision session provides an opportunity for the supervisee to digest the content, prepare questions and responses, and effectively participate in a discussion of the concerns and the eventual remediation plan. The tone of action letters should communicate both concern and a commitment to support improvement.

Remediation plans should be individualized to address the specific professional competency concerns raised in the evaluation. The plan's language should be unambiguous, specify time frames for further evaluation, delineate expectations for performance improvement and utilization of supervisory supports, define the extra supervisory and training supports that will be provided, and specify any rubrics, rating scales, or other measurement instruments that will be utilized to evaluate improvement (Cruise & Swerdlik, 2010). While it is important to indicate the gravity of the concerns and the potential consequences for falling short of expectations, a remediation plan should provide a positive and constructive framework for improvement that encourages hopeful expectations and dedicated commitment by the supervisee. The APA Task Force on Assessment of Competence in Professional Psychology provided guiding principles and recommendations for the assessment of competence (Kaslow et al., 2007). APA's website provides both a list of resources related to trainees with problems of professional competence and a sample outline of a remediation plan: www.apa.org/ed/graduate/competency-resources.aspx.

Initiating a remediation plan is a very stressful activity for supervisors (Bernard & Goodyear, 2014). The following factors can assist in stress management: (a) close positive collaboration with the university supervisor or district administrator; (b) involvement of collaborating supervisors in confirming the need for remediation and in executing the support plan; (c) solicitation of support from fellow supervisors through individual contacts or metasupervision groups; (d) direct support of school district administrators; (e) review of the ethical responsibilities for supervisee development and public welfare; and (f) extra attention to personal self-care needs.

Remediation plans require timely review and direct input from the supervisee regarding the nature of required supports. Plans may need modification to ensure they are providing sufficient supports for the supervisee and ensuring appropriate service delivery. In the unusual event that upon final evaluation, a supervisee cannot meet acceptable professional standards, the gatekeeping function of either terminating training or requiring an additional internship or other remedial training experience should be exercised in conjunction with the university supervisor or, in the case of credentialed personnel under remediation, with the appropriate school district administrator. Care should be taken to provide the supervisee with resources for support and future planning. Appendix 7H provides an example of a remediation plan.

Reciprocal Feedback

While we have focused on the provision of feedback to supervisees, it is equally important to provide opportunities for the supervisee to give feedback to the supervisor regarding the supervisory relationship. The supervisee should be routinely prompted to provide suggestions for how supervision could be more helpful. Building reciprocal feedback into the process of supervision not only helps the supervisor; but this process establishes the norm that professionals should remain continuously open to feedback from clients and collaborators regarding improvements in professional practices. A healthy reciprocity models openness and acceptance of feedback and sets a tone that can increase the supervisee's receptivity to a broad range of feedback. The DEP Self-reflection and Supervisor Feedback Survey (DEP-SSFS) can be completed by the supervisee and the supervisor and then discussed in a supervision session to review supervisory practices and implementation integration of the DEP model (see Appendix 4A). During a year-long training cycle, we recommend use of this survey and subsequent dialogue occur at the halfway point of supervision and at the time of final summative evaluation of the supervisee.

Feedback to University Graduate Programs

Field supervisors are in a unique position to offer feedback to the university programs who send them intern and practicum students. Particularly if a supervisor has worked with multiple interns over a period of time from the same university, he or she is in a beneficial position to give feedback to university supervisors about general preparation for field placements. Even the best of graduate programs tend to have strengths and weaknesses in areas of preparation and can benefit from both positive feedback and constructive suggestions. This process serves to complete the reciprocal loop of feedback among the supervisee, supervisor, and the university.

Case Examples

We will now present three case examples that present challenges related to providing feedback. For each case, there are suggestions provided regarding supervisory approaches. Appendix 7I presents multiple additional cases without author commentary. These additional case provide opportunities for further reflection and practice regarding feedback and evaluation.

CASE EXAMPLE A: FEELING DEFENSIVE

After your intern presents her report at a Child Review Meeting, the parents express strong disagreement with the test results, suggest that her findings are wrong, and (not so subtly) raise doubts whether she is experienced enough to assess their child.

The intern quickly becomes defensive and responds to the parents by stating that she has received extensive training in these assessment tools and that results have been rechecked several times and reviewed with you, her supervisor. She emphatically asserts that their child indeed does have a disability and qualifies for special education services. Trying to shift the focus of the parental "attack," you and other staff team members intervene on her behalf; but the parents are still not convinced and persist in expressing their dissatisfaction.

What Type of Feedback Would you Want to Provide to your Intern?

SUPERVISORY APPROACHES: The supervisor begins by providing empathy to the intern regarding her sense of being challenged and devalued and in response to the stress she experienced while being confronted in a meeting in front of other faculty. It can be helpful to ask the intern to share and process her reactions during the meeting. What thoughts did she have when the parents challenged her and her findings? What feelings was she experiencing during that part of the meeting? With some distance from the moment, does she have any other reactions? Is there anything she wishes she might have done different? Then it would be appropriate to ask her to reflect on the feelings and thoughts the parents might be experiencing when they hear for the first time that their child might have a disability and then how could she have responded empathically to their stress. If necessary, the supervisor can model an active listening response to the parents that responds to their concern and anxiety about the evaluation results. Noting that the parents may still remain overwhelmed and continue to suggest that her testing results are invalid, the supervisor can suggest ways she can continue to respond empathically to their feelings, matter-of-factly summarize the conclusions of the findings, note to the parents that the information is difficult to hear, and offer to meet with them again with the supervisor after they have had time to digest the results. Care would be taken to continually phrase concerns in terms of the good of the child.

Next, the supervisor provides direct feedback about how she appeared defensive in the meeting. The feedback should be as behaviorally specific as possible commenting on both verbal and nonverbal communication. If necessary, the supervisor could ask the intern to replay the situation in a role-play to practice an empathic and less defensive response style. Afterwards the supervisor might provide additional coaching regarding appropriate responses in this difficult situation. During the review process, the tone should emphasize that this is a learning experience; and there will be more opportunities to gain comfort in what would be a stressful experience for even a seasoned professional. Finally, it may be useful to explore the intern's experience and comfort level in working as a professional with parents who are likely considerably older than she is.

How might this situation be processed differently if you had been pulled out of the meeting for a crisis and were not there to hear the parents' comments and your intern's reaction and thus could not provide support in the moment?

CASE EXAMPLE B: UNPROFESSIONAL APPAREL

It is the beginning of the school year; and you notice that your intern has been coming to work in attire that you would not deem professional. For example, he seems to be dressing in a casual style that would be more appropriate for a social setting. You are concerned that some might even judge him as unprofessional or trying to appear as one of the students. You worry about the impact on work with adolescent students and how his personal presentation is viewed by parents and staff. (Please note that there could be a similar example with a female intern.)

How do you address this concern with your intern? What concerns might you have about addressing this issue? What might you say?

SUPERVISORY APPROACHES: Keeping in mind the principles that feedback should be timely, direct, behaviorally specific, and delivered in a tone that connotes respect and expectation of growth, the supervisor directly raises her concerns about her intern's nonprofessional dress style. She notes specifically what style elements are of concern. The supervisor is careful to frame the concern in terms of its impact on professional effectiveness both in terms of working with adults and students. Like most school districts there is a general dress code for staff when students or parents are present. The nature and purpose of the dress code are noted by the supervisor. To be sure there is no ambiguity regarding expectations, the supervisor describes examples of attire that would be professionally appropriate for this school setting. The supervisor then invites the supervisee to explore not only reactions to this feedback but what it is like to assume this adult professional role for the first time. An opportunity may develop to discuss boundary issues in general that impact psychological practice. (It is worth noting: if the supervisor is of a

(Continued)

(*Continued*)
different gender than the supervisee, the supervisor may feel more comfortable providing feedback regarding dress style in the presence of a supportive colleague, such as another staff psychologist, who is both known to the supervisee and the same gender as the supervisee.)

CASE EXAMPLE C: PERSONALITY ISSUES

Your intern has demonstrated an effective grasp of technical professional skills for his training status. However, his *interpersonal style* is rubbing staff the wrong way and significantly harming effectiveness. Staff complain to you that he can be overly blunt in his opinions and/or dismissive of theirs (not really listening); not sensitive to their challenges, needs, or time constraints; and not viewed as a warm and collaborative member of their classroom teams.

How do you directly, supportively, and effectively provide feedback to him regarding his personality style, its impact on his work, and what staff members are raising as concerns?

SUPERVISORY APPROACHES: At the beginning of the training year when reviewing feedback and evaluation targets specified in the internship contract, the supervisor had noted that interpersonal style, communication effectiveness, and the ability to positively establish working alliances in professional relationships were competencies subject to evaluation. The supervisor begins her feedback by commenting on the demonstrated proficiency in technical skills that has been observed, providing specific examples. Then the supervisor reminds the intern that the interpersonal professional characteristics noted in the beginning of training are equally important. In a supportive, yet direct manner with specific behavioral illustrations, the supervisor shares personally observed examples that note these concerns. Then if necessary, she shares some feedback received from colleagues. Because this is particularly difficult feedback to receive, the supervisor is particularly sensitive to the reactions of her intern. She responds with empathy as appropriate, notes that this is difficult feedback to receive, but expresses her belief that the intern can address these issues and improve his effectiveness as a result. The supervisor asks if he has received similar feedback before and, if so, how he digested it and responded to it. The supervisor acknowledges that this topic will require further discussion. She communicates what she would like her intern to work on; and she notes that she will focus a portion of her feedback on these characteristics until they are no longer of concern. Since the supervisor has heard direct examples from faculty regarding interpersonal style at team meetings, she recommends that they plan to engage in some role-play situations that permit practice in these areas.

Seven additional case examples are available in Appendix 7I. These practice cases are written to be addressed by the reader without our commentary.

Multimethod Supervision

Beyond Intern Self-report

A central tenet of the Developmental component of the DEP model is the requirement for utilization of multiple methods of supervision that match the developmental competencies of supervisees, enhance learning, ensure client welfare, and contribute to risk management. Studies of supervisory practices within school psychology (Ward, 1999) and clinical and counseling psychology (Amerikaner & Rose, 2012) report that intern self-report is overwhelmingly the most frequent method used in supervision. In Amerikaner and Rose's (2012) survey of supervision methods, 73% of supervisees reported that verbal case presentations of their own selection were the exclusive or primary supervision activity. Only 11% reported that supervisors observed recordings of their work and less than 10% had the opportunity to observe supervisors' clinical work. Ward (1999) reported similarly that intern self-report was the dominant method within school psychology supervision. While 14% of supervision time involved direct observation of interns, only 0.5% of supervision activity involved review of recordings of school psychology supervisee activity.

Supervisee self-report and case selection ensures that the intern's concerns and questions are addressed. This method proactively encourages intern responsibility for the primary agenda of the supervision session. However, overreliance on supervisee self-report has significant limitations (Bernard & Goodyear, 2014; Harvey & Struzziero, 2008). Self-report is dependent upon the accuracy of the intern's recollection and perception. Unintended distortions or omissions limit the reliability of case data. Additionally, inexperienced supervisees risk inappropriate selection of material to highlight in supervisory review; and they may inadvertently omit critical information. Since a supervisory relationship is evaluative in nature, unintentional positive biases may seep into self-reports. Supervisors who rely primarily on intern self-report create risk management vulnerability since they may not be fully informed regarding clinical work for which they carry vicarious liability.

Supervisee self-report is an essential method in supervision practice but should be only one of many methods employed. Multimethod supervision provides an increased variety of learning strategies and ensures enhanced reliability in case monitoring. Self-report may become a primary method of supervision for practice domains for which the intern has consistently demonstrated observed competencies. This may occur naturally in latter stages of training when supervision focuses on areas of relative weakness or inexperience while consultation becomes the supervisory approach for areas nearing independent practice levels of competence.

Unfortunately in our experience, there are occasionally times when supervisees have had limited exposure to either direct observations or review of recordings of their work. This can create significant initial anxiety. It is important to include in the supervision contract, discussed earlier in this chapter, and to establish in the beginning of the supervisory relationship that multiple methods of supervision will be utilized to enhance learning; and that these methods will include direct or recorded observations, review of work samples, co-intervention/consultation work, and solicitation of feedback from appropriate professional colleagues.

Multimethod supervision begins at the onset of the supervisory relationship. If there is a significant delay and initial sole reliance on self-report, the delayed introduction of additional methods may heighten anxiety and lead the supervisee to mistakenly fear that more direct supervision methods are being introduced in response to concerns about inadequate performance. Creating the expectation for and executing multimethod supervision as a standard operating procedure for advanced learning fosters trust and openness to supervisor feedback.

Within the developmental component of the DEP model, the selection of supervision methods is designed to match the developmental progression of skills acquisition by the supervisee. Methods are varied to bring depth to learning but generally are selected in relation to supervisees' needs, complexities of clinical tasks, and demonstrated competencies. Supervision naturally progresses from frequent modeling and didactic presentations with an emphasis on direct instruction to co-intervention to direct observation to consultation and coaching formats.

Modeling and Direct Instruction

Modeling and demonstration are supervision methods which are used throughout the internship but most frequently at the beginning of training or when a new skill is introduced. At the onset of the field experience, modeling may simply involve shadowing the supervisor both to learn the logistics of the psychologist's role in the setting and to observe the supervisor's presentation and skills in typical practice encounters. As a teaching tool, modeling requires explicit delineation of skills and expected behaviors. This is followed by the supervisee's practice of those skills while being monitored by the supervisor. Skills can be demonstrated and then practiced in role-plays within supervision. The supervisor and supervisee take turns in the roles of psychologist and client and process the application of targeted skills.

Sometimes it is necessary to review and provide direct instruction in core helping and counseling skills that are applicable to all psychologist activities (i.e., active listening, direct communication, cognitive restructuring, and collaborative problem-solving). The supervisor must differentiate between personal style and defined skill strategies, but demonstrate to the intern not only what it takes to empathically connect with clients or consultees but how to effectively engage them in problem-solving to produce adaptive changes. Foundational clinical and interpersonal skills can be operationalized, shaped, and selectively applied to various intervention and consultation challenges (Simon, 2016).

Cotherapy and Coconsultation

The supervisor and intern can work together in interventions and consultations to combine *in vivo* modeling and training by the supervisor with direct observations of the intern. For example, when they collaborate as cotherapists in a counseling group, the intern can view the intervention strategies of the supervisor in real time. Observing the supervisor's strategy selection and implementation in response to directly observed individual and group dynamics can be a powerful learning tool. When the intern provides interventions as a cotherapist, the supervisor is present and can observe verbal and nonverbal communications and the immediate impact of the intervention. Following the cotherapy experience, the supervisor and intern can process the group dynamics, critically review their implementation of any manualized group curriculum, and assess the impact of their interventions. The supervisor can articulate the decision-making process behind intervention selection and provide feedback to the intern concerning therapeutic work.

Co-intervention work is particularly appropriate when cases are complex as in the case of parent conferences that intend to create coordinated home-school behavior management plans. They also should be considered when strong resistance to problem-solving activities or new approaches is anticipated such as a classroom consultation with a teacher with a rigid instructional and behavioral management style.

Co-intervention work provides the flexibility for the supervisor to either increase leadership in the intervention or defer to the intern to take more responsibility and initiative. The activity level of the supervisor is influenced by concerns for the welfare of the client, the developmental skill level of the intern in this area, and the stage of the internship. Consistent with the DEP model's developmental framework, the anticipated progression would be for the supervisor to assume more leadership in early stages and gradually cede control of intervention activities to the intern. Increased supervisor activity would be utilized to model interventions and demeanor and to respond to the particular severity of risk factors for an individual child. Over time, the supervisor and intern demonstrate more balanced interventionist roles and shared responsibility. Eventually the supervisor assumes a supportive but less active posture that is primarily observational but could still serve as a back-up interventionist when necessary. In our example of a counseling group, the supervisor might initiate the group and serve a very active role in the beginning, gradually cede responsibility to the supervisee, and might eventually withdraw as regular cotherapist. Newman (2013) refers to this transition as a progression from "I do" to "we do" to "you do."

An additional benefit for co-intervention supervision methods is the demystification of the intervention process. Many interns expect that an expert would demonstrate unachievable skills that rely on intuition and charisma that is beyond their achievement. What is discovered is that effective interventions can indeed be dynamic but are not magical and are part of a skill set that can be learned and effectively implemented. The benefits of the supervisor and intern directly observing each other's work in a commonly shared context are significant.

Live Observation or Recording

Both live observation and audio or video recording provide opportunities for the supervisor to directly observe the supervisee's work. Recordings have many advantages over other methods but are challenging to implement due to logistical and confidentiality issues. Once the intern and the client are comfortable with the presence of the equipment, recording is less obtrusive than live observation. The supervisor can review the recording and replay parts of it in supervision. As the supervisor and intern review a section of the recording, they can examine the intern's internal process, self-talk and decision-making considerations, as well as the observable intervention dynamic. The impact on the client of a singular intervention and the totality of an intervention session are readily observable and available for discussion. During this review, the supervisor also focuses attention on the development of the intern's skills in self-assessment.

Informed and signed consent is necessary to gain permission for recording. The consent should include an indication that recordings would be reviewed only by the supervisor and permanently deleted at the conclusion of the training period with a specific date noted. Video recordings have distinct advantages over audio recordings; but the logistics and technical requirements are seldom easily managed in the school setting. Unlike university-based clinic settings that are clearly defined as training centers and have built-in infrastructure for recording assessment and intervention activities, schools are seldom properly equipped for this training mode. While attitudes may vary from one community to the next, the culture of the public schools typically is less supportive of recording of any kind even for supervision purposes. The advantage schools present for mental health work is the normalization of therapeutic problem-solving and the demystification of mental health services. The process of arranging for consents for recordings might reduce this advantage and be viewed by families as particularly intrusive and even prohibitive.

While direct observation can appear more intrusive than recordings, it is more likely to be acceptable to clients and school administration. For observation to be effective, several conditions are required. At the beginning of any intervention or consultation relationship, interns must identify themselves as professionals in-training and specify the name of their clinical supervisor. It is important to note to clients not only that work will be reviewed by the supervisor; but that the supervisor might from time to time be directly involved in service delivery. For parents and students, it is advantageous to introduce the supervisor in person early in the relationship when possible. The more the potential occurrence of an observation is anticipated and experienced as routine for quality control and training purposes, the less intrusive the supervisor's presence will be perceived during an observation.

During observations the supervisor sits at a distance that enables a view of the supervisee and client but avoids the likelihood of persistent direct eye contact. A structured observation format that records the character of supervisee interventions is a useful tool for systematically organizing an approach to the observation and for an effective and efficient review within a subsequent supervision session. When using a written recording system while viewing a counseling session, it can be helpful to note at the beginning of the session that the observer will be taking notes focused on the work of the intern not the disclosures of the client. The intervention plan prepared for either an individual, group, or parent session would have been discussed in advance by the supervisor and intern. Since all assessment and intervention plans require flexibility in application, the timing and appropriateness of deviations from the plan are worthy discussion material for the follow-up supervision session.

During a structured observation of a counseling session, the observing supervisor can record the therapeutic skill or strategy applied in each interchange. The supervisor can use an abbreviated method of summarizing the client communication and then labels the response of the intern in a brief code. For example, if the intern uses active listening, it would be recorded as "AL," open-ended questioning as "OQ?," role-playing as "RP," and so forth. Appendix 7J provides a schema for recording counseling strategies for this purpose (Simon, 2015a). The supervisor can note suggested alternative responses in the same code as well and review their potential differential impact during supervision. This structured coding method can also provide data regarding what specific skills require more focus or additional training in supervision. Egan (2016) and Friedberg and McClure (2015) provide further background on counseling skills identification and training.

Most of this counseling coding system is applicable to consultation activities as well. Active listening (AL), information gathering (IG), challenging perceptions (CP), evaluation of pros and cons to various course of action in problem-solving (PS-PC), collaborative problem-solving (CPS), expert advice (E), and summarizing (S) are examples of helping skills frequently applied in consultation work. Consultation coding systems might require site-specific coding schemas that fit an individual school's structured multidisciplinary problem-solving conference format. Cates and Swerdlik (2005) developed a *Problem-solving Team Observation Checklist* that provides a form for direct observation of problem-solving teams (see Appendix 7K). Reviewing this observation form in supervision helps the intern understand and monitor the key elements required for successful problem-solving teams. When the intern has an opportunity to facilitate a problem-solving team, it can serve as a structure for providing feedback on team leadership skills.

Supervisory observations focus on the application of specific skills contributes to the operationalization of competencies required for progress monitoring during the internship. Additionally, it reinforces the essential perspective that counseling and consultation practice require reflective and purposeful interventions that are change oriented and monitored to ensure positive outcomes.

Live supervision is a variant of passive observation or review of recordings for supervision (Bernard & Goodyear, 2014). In live supervision, the observing supervisor will periodically intervene to redirect the supervisee or reinforce or amplify positive supervisee interventions. This approach was applied extensively in family therapy training (Liddle, Breunlin, Schwartz, & Constantine, 1984) and has been utilized in university training with the availability of one-way mirrors and bug-in-the-ear technology providing supervisors who are not seen by clients to comment on test administration or counseling interventions. While these technologies are not generally available in school settings, live supervision can be an alternative to passive observations. However, its appropriateness should be determined by the developmental status of the supervisee and the risk factors present at the moment of the intern's intervention. Even in a passive observation focused on coding and recording an intervention, the supervisor may need to intervene if an unanticipated risk for harm situation emerges and is not effectively managed. On the other hand live supervision risks compromising the intern's spontaneity and responsibility if he or she becomes hesitant and repeatedly defers to the supervisor for direction. For this reason, we would suggest that co-intervention or structured passive observation are generally preferable supervision strategies within a school setting. The developmental progress of the intern in a particular practice area will dictate the choice of supervision strategy with the *caveat* that the welfare of the client remains the paramount responsibility throughout supervision.

Effective Self-report

In our opening comments about supervision methods we noted that supervisee self-report and case consultation were the most frequent supervision methods employed within school, clinical, and counseling psychology. We discussed the advantages and disadvantages of this supervisory approach and emphasized that overreliance on this method can limit the effectiveness and benefits of supervision and potentially compromise the welfare of the client. Nonetheless when properly used, self-report is an important method for supervision and most clearly ensures that the intern's questions and concerns will be addressed within a supervision session.

Earlier in this chapter we recommended the use of an advance Supervision Session Planner to prepare both the supervisee and the supervisor for a supervision session. This approach organizes priorities for self-report and prepares the supervisor to address issues and concerns that might require preparatory use of reference and consultation resources. In general the more structured and account-able supervisees are for assessment and intervention planning and recording, the more effective self-report can be as a supervision method. It is important that supervisees are directed to report what went well in assessment and intervention activities in addition to raising questions or concerns. This balanced approach counters the tendency of too many interns to be too hard on themselves and thus limit their opportunities to learn from successful strategies that might be relevant for other work. When supervisors begin an intervention or case review by asking supervisees to reflect upon and evaluate their performance, they are fostering the development of self-monitoring and self-evaluation skills that are an essential goal of the entire supervision process. Reflection and review of the intern's selection of self-report materials can assist the supervisor and supervisee in identifying pat-terns of strengths and weaknesses. This review also reveals further training goals for the internship and prepares supervisees to define their professional develop-ment needs for lifelong career development.

Particularly when the agenda for supervision is driven by the supervisee, it is important to conclude sessions by asking the supervisee to comment on the helpfulness of the supervision session. For example, the supervisor can simply ask the supervisee to rate the supervision session on a 1 to 3 scale (i.e., very help-ful, helpful, not very helpful) and then propose what might make sessions more effective in the future. Examination and reciprocal feedback on the process of supervision can influence supervisor responses and intern self-report strategies for future sessions.

Effective self-report methods are rooted in a trusting supervisory relationship, require the intern to take responsibility for their learning, benefit from structured advance preparation, can be shaped by supervisor feedback, and prepare the intern to identify future professional development needs. As already noted, self-report will be a more effective method when it is balanced by sufficient direct observa-tion strategies.

Consultation and Coaching

The developmental progression toward independent practice outlines a movement from close monitoring and supervision to eventual near-independent practice with the supervisor serving more as a consultant, coach, or sounding board for the supervisee. Throughout the internship the principle of vicarious liability applies so knowledge and monitoring of all intern activities remains essential. However, in areas evaluated as competent at all stages of development and in a more compre-hensive manner in the last stages of training, the supervisee should begin to assume a role more similar to junior colleague; and the methods of supervision should center on consultation approaches that mirror what the intern will need to proactively seek out for future professional support and development when fully licensed.

Throughout training, the intern may be directed to seek consultation from other staff members who may have particular expertise in a specific client concern or system issue. This prepares the intern to recognize the lifelong need for collegial consultation. Within the Developmental component of the DEP model, it is an essential part of the termination process for the intern to exercise increasing autonomy and independence in clinical practice. Supervision largely shifts to a consultation role which still fills gaps in expertise and suggests alternative approaches but places primary responsibility on the intern to decide how to incorporate this information into intervention planning. One cautionary note is necessary. Due to expanded supervised practica experiences and advancements in graduate education, many if not most interns demonstrate high levels of proficiency early in the second half of their internship year. It is important that they are not prematurely viewed as independent colleagues and thus only receive reduced supervision. Supervisors maintain a responsibility to challenge even the most competent interns to reach their personal fullest potential. This can be ensured by maintaining significant structure in supervision activities, continuing to employ multimethod supervision, and by challenging the intern to achieve competencies in additional areas of practice or to acquire further depth of skills in specialty areas.

Group Supervision Formats

Supervision is commonly considered in terms of a one-on-one session with a supervisor and single supervisee. For internship supervision, there is a requirement of 2 hours per week of face-to-face individual supervision. Substantial benefits can accrue from providing additional group supervision during preservice training; and group formats may be the best available or most appropriate format for some supervision of licensed school psychologists.

Group supervision presents many advantages and some limitations. Advantages for a group format include that it is time, cost, and resource efficient; provides opportunities for vicarious learning; normalizes challenges faced by supervisees; increases the breadth of cases that supervisees consider; expands the diversity and quality of feedback and suggestions beyond the individual supervisor; provides additional perspectives on supervisees particularly in terms of relationships with peer colleagues; exposes supervisees to collegial supports; and promotes learning of supervisory skills (Bernard & Goodyear, 2014; Harvey & Struzziero, 2008).

Limitations of group supervision include reduced individual case consultation time; the potential for interference by negative group dynamics if undue competition, member conflicts, or insensitive peer feedback occur; and additional challenges for maintaining case and supervisee confidentiality (Bernard & Goodyear, 2014). Group supervision may make it more difficult to directly process the dynamics of the supervisory relationship. While group collaboration may normalize the vulnerability that supervisees often feel particularly in preservice training, the group context might also make some supervisees more guarded for fear of appearing less competent to their peers. In the case of the participation of a supervisee who may be on a remediation plan due to consistent concerns regarding competencies or professional demeanor, the group format may prove beneficial due to positive peer modeling or harmful if this participant's issues contribute to defensiveness that impairs the overall group climate.

We believe that for preservice training, group supervision can add benefits to individual supervision. For the doctoral-level internship APA (2015b) requires 2 hours of individual supervision but 4 total hours of supervision. Group supervision can provide some of this additional required supervision and can benefit specialist-level interns as well. In addition to the advantages just described, the group format can foster a climate of support among a cohort of supervisees within the same setting. In some situations, multidisciplinary groups that include social work or counseling trainees can provide additional perspectives and bolster preparation for future collaboration across disciplines. Group supervision can also prepare preservice trainees for participation in future collegial consultation case discussion formats.

For licensed professionals, group supervision formats may frequently be the most economical option for creating time and for engaging an expert supervisor. As a path to increasing accessibility to supervision for licensed professionals, group supervision might provide one vehicle for addressing the discrepancy between the need for clinical supervision and its limited availability (Curtis et al., 2012; Silva et al., 2016).

Group supervision can be structured in a variety of ways. It can focus on individual supervisees' activities with members receiving supervision in rotation. The supervisor facilitates the discussion and provides primary supervision while simultaneously encouraging peers to provide collegial consultation. At the conclusion of a case consultation, the group can reflect upon and discuss the implications drawn from this case to their own activities. During preservice training within a developmental perspective, the supervisor may be more active, make more recommendations, and provide more direction earlier in the training year and gradually cede more responsibility to the group for consultation as time progresses and competencies emerge. In latter stages of an internship, this shift to greater collegial consultation becomes part of the preparation for future roles as consultants and supervisors.

Multimethod supervision can be applied within a group format as well. In addition to supervisees' self-report for case consultation, recordings can be reviewed, role-plays enacted, or techniques modeled. Varying methods enhances learning, engages attention, and counters the limitations of sole reliance on self-report.

Newman and colleagues have outlined a protocol for structured peer group supervision (SPGS; Newman, 2013; Newman, Nebbergall, & Salmon, 2013). They have applied this format to consultation and supervision training, but it has potential for professional peer group supervision for licensed practitioners as well. SGPS is highly structured in a way that supports positive group dynamics (Newman, 2013). It is organized into a five-step process: (1) *Request for Help* by member; (2) *Asking Questions or Seeking Clarification* by colleagues; (3) *Feedback* from colleagues while supervisee is silent but takes notes; (4) a *Pause/Break* for reflection on feedback by supervisee; (5) *Response Statement* by supervisee to feedback and disclosure of implications for next actions, and *Discussion* of issues surfaced in the process as time permits. This degree of structure may be particularly helpful for graduate students. While more flexibility and some adaptation would be required by practicing school psychologists, it is important to remember that structure can maintain focus and reduce anxiety in collegial consultation at all practice levels.

Holloway (1995) provided an extended illustration of the application of her SAS model within a group consultation format for training supervisors. She utilized the terms and conceptualization of SAS as a common language and filter to explore supervision. Consistent with the SAS focus on contextual factors, three relational contexts are a focus: the counseling relationship between the supervisee and client, the supervisory relationship between the supervisor and the supervisee, and the consultative group of supervisors with the training supervisor. Focus of analysis may shift from one context to another, but each influences the others. The training supervisor assists supervisors in reflecting how an intervention directed to one context will influence the others.

We will address group supports for supervisors in Chapter 10 when we share our experiences with building networks for collegial supports for supervisors including metasupervision groups. Similar to Holloway's (1995, 2016) example, we have realized the benefits that an overarching model provides with a common framework and consistent language for discussing supervisory practice.

Summary of Multimethod Supervision

In summary, multimethod supervision is an essential requirement for effective supervision. In addition to supervisees' self-report, various co-intervention/consultation and direct observation strategies ensure client welfare and appropriate guidance toward professional competency. From the developmental perspective, supervisory methods are selected to match the training needs and developmental skill progression of the supervisee. Supervision begins with highly structured close supervision and ends with primary reliance on consultation approaches.

CASE EXAMPLE: JANE'S APPLICATION OF MULTIMETHOD SUPERVISION

Nearly half of the internship year has passed. Jane's intern Steve is involved in a variety of clinical activities. His experience and competency levels vary across these activities. From the beginning of Steve's internship Jane has employed a variety of supervision methods. She reflects on two key activities that Steve is involved in this month and what supervision methods she will apply. Other activities in established competency areas will be reviewed this week from Steve's self-report.

She and Steve are cotherapists for an anger management group that uses Larson and Lochman's (2011) *Anger Coping* curriculum. While she exercised primary leadership at early stages of the group, she has now reduced her activity level and has concentrated instead on preparing Steve to execute this manualized curriculum. Steve is responsible for outlining the intervention approach for the next session and reviews it with Jane prior to the group. During the group Steve assumes the primary instructional role; and Jane concentrates on assisting with behavioral management. She supports him in implementing the role-play activities that are the core of this session, but leaves the introduction, demonstration, and primary monitoring responsibilities to Steve. Afterwards, she jots down notes to prepare her for providing Steve feedback during their next supervision session.

Jane also has a parent conference scheduled with the mother of one of the group's participants. The principal reports that this parent is frequently defensive and protective of her son and often blames school staff for his difficulties. This parent conference was requested by the student's homeroom teacher to attempt to design a coordinated home-school intervention plan. Responsibility for leading the parent conference is Jane's but since Steve works with the student in the group program she has invited him to the session. Before his internship, Steve had limited field experience with problem-solving-oriented parent-teacher conferences (Sheridan & Kratochwill, 2010). Under Jane's supervision he has increased his involvement in family interventions but has not dealt with complex or conflictual cases. Jane will lead the problem-solving in the conference and facilitate communication among the parent, teacher, and student. Her supervisory goal is to model the clinical skills required to manage a challenging parent conference and guide it toward an effective home-school problem-solving plan. She delineates the general principles of her approach prior to the session and will review and debrief with Steve during their next supervision session.

SUPERVISOR REFLECTION ACTIVITY

Informally review the frequency with which you use different supervision methods. Is there a difference in selection of methods as the training year progresses? Which intern activities would be most important to directly observe for your current supervisee? What are barriers to introduction of more direct observational methods to your supervision practice? Devise a plan for how you could apply a direct observation method to a key intern activity.

Preparation for Supervisees for Eventual Role as Supervisors

Supervision skills are now considered an essential professional competency (APA, 2015a; NASP, 2011a). One of the final stages in the developmental learning progression during internship supervision involves initial preparation for supervisees for their eventual role as supervisors. The NASP (2011a) Position Statement on Supervision in School Psychology specifies at least of 3 years of full-time experience to qualify to be a supervisor; and many states require a minimum number of years of licensed experience to supervise internship training (i.e., Illinois requires 3 years). However, it is not uncommon for interns to have their first experience as a primary supervisor very early in their careers.

The most significant influence on supervisees' eventual practice as supervisors is often the character, quality, and methods of their capstone internship supervision. The DEP model promotes a transparent structure and process for clinical supervision and encourages frequent processing of the supervisory process and relationship. Participation in a written contract, recordkeeping and risk management activities, collaborative assessment and goal setting, routine feedback and evaluation, and multimethod supervision prepare the intern to apply these same strategies in their supervision practice. Interns who experience ecologically sensitive problem-solving training and evidence-based case conceptualization and intervention training are likely to incorporate these approaches into their practice as supervisors. The DEP supervision model identifies specific training approaches and activities that can be replicated in supervision across the field of school psychology.

To address supervision training as a core professional competency in the final stages of the internship year, the supervisee should have opportunities to provide supervision under close metasupervision by the supervisor. The availability of supervision experiences will vary from site to site but may include any of the following: supervision of an activity of a practicum student, a teacher-implemented social-emotional learning curriculum, paraprofessionals supporting students with special needs, graduate students in service learning programs, or student peer support activities. The review of supervision strategies and experiences would occur within supervision.

Even with a graduate course in supervision and specific focus on competency in supervisory skills, further training and metasupervision are required to ensure competent practice as a supervisor. Part IV of this text will propose a variety of approaches for future training of supervisors and address these issues in more detail beyond internship training.

Closure and Termination for Supervisory Relationships

The final developmental task within a supervisory relationship addresses the impending termination of supervision. In many ways, achieving healthy closure in this final stage of a supervisory relationship parallels the process of ending other teaching or therapy relationships; however, differences do exist. Supervisory relationships often involve more intensity and interpersonal closeness than in other instructor-student relationships. Termination in therapy relationships generally ends contact between therapist and client. On the other hand collegial, social, or even continuing mentor relationships may eventually develop between supervisors and supervisees. They will be members of the same professional organizations and in some cases may even work together; but all of these future relationships will have a different character and diverse role definitions. It is important as the period of supervision ends to establish healthy closure specific to the supervision relationship.

Addressing termination in a supervisory relationship is an opportunity to model for the supervisee direct healthy communication regarding the close of all client relationships and transitions. Just as it was necessary to be explicit regarding roles, expectations, and responsibilities at the beginning of the supervisory relationship, it is important to directly recap the professional growth of the supervisee and the development of the supervisory relationship. Any discussion of the supervisor's final summative evaluation of the supervisee should contain "no surprises" because the supervisor should have provided frequent feedback and formative assessments throughout the year. Closure discussions must also provide an opportunity for sharing feelings that both the supervisor and supervisee are experiencing as the supervisory relationship comes to an end.

An essential part of closure involves a discussion of the supervisee's immediate and long-term professional development needs. Recognition by the supervisee of ongoing training needs is one sign of a successful supervision experience. The supervisor can provide recommendations for pursuing continuing education and supervision. Sometimes supervisees may wish to continue a mentor or consultant relationship with the supervisor. The supervisor must honestly communicate his or her interest, ability, and availability. Besides addressing opportunities, boundaries, and limits, this discussion should note the differences in the character of future collaboration. Elements specific to supervision like vicarious liability and formal evaluation will not be part of a relationship that may be best described as consultation or mentoring. Indeed, the supervisor may wish to seek consultation in the future regarding a specialty competency area in which the supervisee possesses exceptional expertise.

There are occasions when a supervisee is hired to work as a school psychologist in the same district where supervision occurred. When this is the case, it is important to discuss how roles will be different and for interns to recognize that there will be a transition period for recognition of the new full professional designation by other staff. There will also be a transition within the relationship with the supervisor as roles change to full professional colleagues. The supervisor commends the intern for earning this transition, promises reasonable ongoing collegial support, and highlights the anticipated different evolution of their relationship.

Closure also includes direct feedback to the supervisor about the character, quality, and fidelity of supervision. The DEP Self-reflection and Supervisor Feedback Survey (DEP-SSFS) initially discussed in Chapter 4 is a systematic tool for reviewing the supervisory relationship and assessing fidelity to the DEP model. Completing and reviewing this survey organizes closing feedback to the supervisor and provides data to inform future supervisory practice.

Implementation Integrity of Developmental Component: Behavioral Markers

The DEP supervision model not only provides a theoretical framework for supervision but defines specific approaches and activities for the day to day practice of supervision. As with any core training or intervention strategy, there are behavioral markers that can be monitored to ensure implementation integrity. We will now summarize these supervision activities or markers for the Developmental component of the DEP model. A similar summary will occur after the Ecological and Problem-solving component chapters. These behavior markers are incorporated into the DEP-SSFS described in Chapter 4 and located in Appendix 4A.

Structure

The supervisor provides significant structuring at the onset of supervision that clearly defines roles and expectations. This is implemented by utilization and review of a detailed written supervision contract. Supervisory activities include a protected meeting schedule. The supervisee has the responsibility of completing a Supervision Session Planner to prepare for supervision; and the supervisor records supervision notes. Appropriate case, activity, and consultation planning and recordkeeping documentation is required to ensure purposeful evidence-based practice and support risk management.

Developmental Assessment

A formal assessment of entry-level skills and training needs is conducted as a basis for goal setting and selection of supervisee training activities. This assessment covers all NASP practice domains and APA competency areas for doctoral training and reviews the state or university internship plan. Schedule and methods for progress monitoring are delineated.

Feedback and Evaluation

The provision of routine formative feedback that builds upon the supervisee's strengths, shapes skill acquisition, and ensures client welfare is the central activity of supervision. Scheduled summative evaluation measures developmental progress and informs supervisory methods and training activities. Progress monitoring is a dimension of feedback and evaluation that assesses behavior markers of professional competencies and outcomes of all prevention, intervention, consultation, and program development activities. This includes routine review of progress on the internship plan relative to the stage of the training cycle. In the extraordinary case of serious competency issues evident in preservice training, formative and summative evaluation may require the development of a more intensive remediation, support, and evaluation plan. When required, summative evaluation may necessitate the supervisor executing a gatekeeping role for the welfare of the public, the profession, and the supervisee.

Multimethod Supervision

Multiple methods of supervision are employed that are appropriate to various stages of the supervisee's development and different skill levels for specific professional tasks. Supervision methods vary in relation to case novelty, complexity, and risk factors. Multimethod supervision is also tailored to the learning style of the supervisee and the setting in which supervision occurs.

Metasupervision of Supervisee's Supervisory Practice

Creation and close metasupervision of an opportunity for the supervisee to engage in supervisory practice is a behavior marker for a later stage of supervisee development.

Closure

Implementation integrity is evident when the impending termination of the supervisory relationship includes a discussion of the following: a review of developmental progress; direct discussion of the emotions surrounding the end of the training year and the personal supervisory relationship; delineation of future supervision and professional development needs; and the nature of the postsupervision relationship between the supervisee and the supervisor. The DEP-SSFS should be completed by both the supervisor and supervisee and discussed as a closure activity to inform future supervisory practice.

Summary

The Developmental component defines the structure and supports required for the development of professional competencies of supervisees. A developmental perspective matches supervisory roles and methods to the supervisee's training goals, current skills, evolving needs, and progression toward competent independent practice. Supervision is a structured learning experience with goals, methods, roles, and expectations clearly defined in a written supervision contract. The supervisor provides sufficient structure and supports to simultaneously promote supervisee learning and ensure client welfare. Multiple methods are used in supervision consistent with supervisee learning needs (i.e., modeling, co-intervention, observation, coaching, and consultation). Feedback and evaluation shape skill development and foster development of self-monitoring skills. Supervision's developmental goal is achievement of independent professional competencies. The DEP supervision model defines specific approaches and activities for the day to day practice of supervision. These behavioral markers are indicators for the implementation integrity of DEP.

8

THE ECOLOGICAL COMPONENT
Incorporating Contextual Factors

The Ecological Perspective

Human Ecology and Child Development

It is impossible to fully understand individual students, families, classrooms, and school communities without understanding their interaction with larger environments and systems. In his groundbreaking work on human ecology, the developmental psychologist Urie Bronfenbrenner (1979) emphasized the interconnectedness of individual and environmental influences in human development. Moving beyond the debate of the relative impact of nature versus nurture, his bioecological systems theory posited that child development occurs within the context of progressively more complex reciprocal interactions with the environment. From this perspective environment is the context for development. Its influence must be considered and understood. However it is not the sole determinant of development.

Bronfenbrenner (1979) described multiple levels of systems that impact development. These systems range from the immediate family system and local systems within schools and neighborhoods to macrosystems like culture, the economy, customs, and world events. While events in the immediate environment like a serious illness of a caregiver may have more impact than more distant influences like national events, the larger systems still provide the context for response to this stressor. For example, the cultural perspective on adjusting familial roles for the care and disruption of illness and the availability of extra-familial supports may all modify the impact of the effect of the caretaker's illness on the child's short and long term development. The behaviors and coping capacity of the child and the larger impact of this event on development can only be understood by accounting for the various larger systemic contexts.

Family Systems and Clinical Intervention

At the same time that Bronfenbrenner was exploring ecological systems from a developmental perspective, clinical family therapists were focusing on the impact of family dynamics and structures on social, emotional, and behavior problems (Watzlawak & Weakland, 1977). Minuchin (1974), Haley (1976), and other pivotal figures in the family therapy movement were applying systemic principles to therapeutic work with children and families. Their clinical intervention work focused on changing the structures and patterns of family interactions to remediate child and adolescent disorders. Rather than merely providing individual therapy to children and adolescents, they included families, sometimes even multiple generations, in sessions. Their belief was that it was necessary to change contextual influences and the system dynamics to modify individual behavior.

The foundation principles of Minuchin's (1974) structural family therapy paradigm have stood the test of time and have a significant influence on contemporary empirically supported family and systemic therapy approaches such as multisystemic therapy (Henggeler, Schoenwald, Borduin, Rowland, & Cunningham, 2009) and functional family therapy (Alexander, Waldron, Robbins, & Neeb, 2013). Each of these approaches expands interventions to include direct contact with schools and relevant community agencies. Intervention sessions may occur in a clinical office, the family home, the school, the probation center, or other important contexts. Interventions target changes both within individuals and within the contexts that influence and support behaviors both negatively and positively. The interactions between the individual and various social contexts become targets for change.

Social Learning Theory and Parent Training

Applying social learning theory to the study of youth aggression, Patterson and his associates examined coercive processes within families and other social variables that contributed to the development of aggression (Patterson, 1982; Patterson, Reid, Jones, & Conger, 1975). In response to their decades-long research findings, they developed parent training programs to teach behavior management strategies to change the aggressive behaviors of their children (Forgatch & Patterson, 2010). They discovered that changes in parenting practices can often have a more significant impact on child and adolescent functioning than individual counseling work alone. Parent intervention programs have expanded to address a wide range of both internalizing and externalizing disorders affecting children and adolescents and have been developed to promote healthy development for those deemed at-risk (e.g., Barkley, 2013; Webster-Stratton, Rinaldi, & Reid, 2011). Similar to family therapy approaches, the assumption is that it is necessary to directly intervene within the ecological context of children to improve functioning.

School Psychology's Focus: Collaborative Problem-solving and System Change

Consistent with the ecological perspectives described above, a central focus of contemporary school psychology involves collaborative problem-solving with parents and teachers (NASP, 2010a). Kratochwill and Bergan (1990) outlined a problem-solving model that has been incorporated into intervention team protocols to address behavioral and academic issues. Within contemporary multitiered systems of support, interdisciplinary problem-solving teams routinely examine both individual and systemic factors to plan interventions for children experiencing a variety of difficulties. Sheridan and Kratochwill's (2010) conjoint behavioral consultation protocol systematically engages parents and teachers in the development of coordinated home-school intervention plans. The most effective interventions for many social, emotional, and behavioral concerns require an integration of strategies that address individual, family, peer, and classroom variables (Simon, 2016).

Mental health services in schools are being reconceptualized to parallel public health intervention models that promote wellness and early intervention (Doll & Cummings, 2008). Consistent with this shift has been the development of programs to change school systems and peer contexts to promote healthy behavior and address problems. For example, Multitiered Systems of Support (MTSS) directly target changes in the school culture (Stoiber, 2014); and anti-bullying programs have been initiated on the premise that it is necessary to directly change peer cultures and faculty supervisory practices in addition to intervention with individual bullies and victims (Olweus, Limber, & Mihalic, 1999).

Ecological Perspective Informs Supervision Practice

It is clear to see that there is a convergence within developmental psychology, social learning theory, family therapy, and contemporary school practices to incorporate ecological considerations into all assessment and intervention planning. The implication for supervision is that the practice of the supervisee and the process of supervision must be ecologically sensitive and consider the influences of all environmental and contextual factors.

Training and professional development occur within multiple systemic contexts. The content and process of supervision is influenced by the profession of school psychology particularly its current perspectives and initiatives regarding best practices. To the extent that preservice training is similar to a professional apprenticeship, supervision is charged with preparing supervisees for competent practice in the daily psychological work required by school systems. At the same time, supervision strives to equip supervisees with the skills to change the systems they serve by promoting new practices to better serve children. In turn, these changes may alter some of the role definitions and daily practices of school psychologists. New national and state educational initiatives influence this process as well.

Local district, school, and classroom structures and cultures present the immediate ecology within which supervision happens. Participation in interdisciplinary faculty teams is another critical systemic context for practice and training. The school system is not an island but rather a center for community activity which is influenced by the larger community's culture, socioeconomics, and politics. All of these systems influence each other in a reciprocal fashion. Local school boards strive to imbue community values into local education. In turn educational practices influenced by universities and the regional and national educational community may impact local values and practices. For example, the rapid proliferation of anti-bullying initiatives in schools has contributed to local schools' re-examination of their supervision practices, discipline policies, and social-emotional learning curricula. These external initiatives are impacted by and in turn influence local student peer networks. Supervision is influenced by all of these systems and strives to assist supervisees in understanding, navigating, and influencing these systemic contexts.

This ecological perspective necessitates incorporation of contextual factors into supervision. Holloway's (1995, 2016) Systems Approach to Supervision (SAS) described in Chapter 6 provided one of the first comprehensive schemas for addressing contextual issues in counseling supervision. Contemporary school psychology practice increasingly focuses on systemic and contextual variables impacting students. Three critical areas of school psychology practice require substantial focus within supervision: diversity and multicultural competence, training in program development and systems change, and proficient application of multisystemic interventions.

Diversity and Multicultural Competence

Diversity and multicultural competence are core requirements for all professional activities and thus a central focus of supervisory practice (APA, 2003, 2008, 2015a; NASP, 2010a, 2010b). The APA (2015a) *Guidelines for Clinical Supervision in Health Service Psychology* describe diversity competence as "an inseparable and essential component of supervision" (p. 15). Supervising psychologists have a responsibility to strive to understand, respect, and support every aspect of diversity and its implications for individual clients, families, systems, and supervisees.

Complex Journey

Diversity competency involves understanding ethnicity and race but is much more complex and expansive than these two important variables. Additionally, it includes age, gender, gender identity, sexual orientation, disability, education, religion, spirituality, language, socioeconomic status, immigration experience including status of acculturation, and regional and local neighborhood variables. The breadth of these factors challenges supervisory competencies. Developing diversity and multicultural competency is a continuous journey and not a destination. In this sense achieving diversity competence can be viewed as a process. Supervisors must demonstrate sufficient competencies to purposely incorporate diversity variables into their own clinical work, the work of their supervisees, and the supervisory relationship itself. Understanding diversity and its influence on individual perspectives and development and its implications for psychological assessment and intervention is a continuous thread woven throughout the supervisory process.

Ethical and Social Justice Perspectives

Diversity competency can also be viewed through a social justice lens. The ethics principles espoused by APA (2002, 2010a) and NASP (2010d) require that welfare of clients be the critical concern in all psychological practice activities. Harvey and Struzziero (2008) note that in the absence of multicultural competencies, practitioners risk violating this standard even if they do so unintentionally. The ethical mandate to practice within one's area of competency requires school psychologists to develop multicultural competencies. Issues that arise in schools regarding disproportionality in discipline responses toward minority students and questions regarding potential over- or under-identification of educational disabilities require competent diversity-sensitive assessment and intervention practices. In addition these concerns may necessitate advocacy work by school psychologists that integrates diversity competency skills with change agency and other clinical skills as part of a commitment to social justice for students.

Understanding the implications of diversity within a social justice perspective is a critical task within clinical supervision. For example, it is important for supervisees to learn to pay attention to the additional risk factors and potential consequences for mental health that affect families with low socioeconomic status. Poverty and oppression can create coping and adaptation patterns that might not be readily understood by supervisees from middle class backgrounds. Educators may request additional homework support or behavioral supervision at home; but if the primary caretaker is a single parent required to work two jobs to pay rent and keep food on the table, this survival reality must be understood and accounted for. A creative support plan may involve other school-based interventions to support homework; and it may require work with the parent to identify other caretaking and supervision supports in the community or extended family given the reality of parental breadwinning requirements. Parent conferences to design supports and collaborative interventions may need to occur in the home or on the parent's schedule that may be different from standard school personnel work hours. Supervision guides the supervisee in understanding these unique challenges and in adapting intervention strategies to work within these constraints.

The histories and consequences of oppression and power differences may impact relationships with clients and the character of family relationships with school personnel. Building trust and fostering open and collaborative communication can be impacted by both personal and generational experiences of working with authority figures. Supervision strives to assist supervisees in understanding the implications of these factors and to communicate the empathy required to build collaborative and supportive problem-solving relationships. Recognition of power differentials in various relationships is an important step in this process. For example, consider the implications for school discipline conferences when deans of discipline are White and the student is African American or when an immigrant parent who does not have legal residency is hesitant to attend a school problem-solving conference. As clinicians, school psychologists must recognize that in their roles they may exercise a power differential in relation to clients. This applies directly to the supervisory relationship as well which is defined as an evaluative relationship; and the supervisor may exercise the power to prevent access to the profession.

Falicov (2014a) cautions that a sociopolitical lens is not limited to considerations of poverty or racism. She utilizes the example of an anorexic client. It is necessary to understand gender roles and expectations within a culture and the social pressures to be thin in young women to fully capture the dynamics that contribute to the eating disorder.

Falicov (2014a) goes on to describe effective therapeutic work as requiring *interactional justice*. This approach begins with communicating respect to all clients, striving to understand their experiences through their eyes, and not automatically assuming that cultural or other differences in thoughts and actions are dysfunctional because they might differ from the therapist's or the dominant culture. For minority clients she recommends direct exploration of personal experiences of unfair treatment and their responses to these events. This not only provides clinical cues for understanding coping strategies but provides an opportunity to empathize with the client's experience in a significant way. Helping clients adaptively respond to injustice empowers them and in itself can make therapeutic interventions acts of social justice. Supervision directs attention to these factors and promotes strategies that foster interactional justice.

Understanding Cultural Diversity

Ethnic and racial identities have a significant influence on personal history; social style, status, and acceptance; communication patterns; social perspectives; attributions; and worldviews. The development of multicultural competency requires psychologists to understand the culturally typical patterns of communication, problem-solving, familial structure, gender roles, child rearing, and other core behaviors and beliefs (Lynch & Hanson, 2011; McGoldrick, Giordano, & Garcia-Petro, 2005). For many interns, their field experiences may be their first opportunity for significant exposure to different cultures. Supervision guides the supervisee in understanding the perspectives, strengths, and nuances that are common within specific ethnic groups and might be somewhat different than his or her own. It is important to understand potential cultural differences regarding authority roles, gender roles, views of education, and perspectives on psychological disorders. Attitudes toward emotional expression and behavioral and emotional regulation may be apparent within different cultural perspectives. These differences may influence parenting styles and strategies and expectations for typical roles of fathers and mothers. These nuances are important to understand for successfully supporting students and engaging in effective problem-solving.

Recognizing Individual Uniqueness

While it is important to become familiar with and understand common broad cultural characteristics, it is essential to be mindful of individual differences and to avoid stereotyping based on cultural identification. Within all cultures there is significant variability in attitudes, perspectives, and behaviors. Supervisors support supervisees in balancing taking into account potential cultural influences and striving to understand the uniqueness of the individual client. It is important to investigate status of acculturation within immigrant families. It is not uncommon for different generations within the family to be at different stages of adopting or adapting to a new culture's patterns and procedures. There are unique pressures experienced by the adolescent who may be involved in integrating into a peer group whose membership largely mirrors the dominant culture in the country yet who simultaneously strives to remain connected within his own family.

Complications can also arise when language barriers create role reversals such as can be the case when a 5th grade student serves as a translator for his parents in discussions with school staff when bilingual supports are not available. The supervisor must guide the supervisee in the complex process of taking all of these variables into account. Sensitivity to the various perspectives and emotional experiences of each family member is required. Patience to take extra time in all meetings where communication involves translation is essential. Respect for the appropriate executive role of parents in family communication and problem-solving must be communicated and authentically incorporated into intervention planning.

The Challenges of Immigration

The United States is a country of immigrants that continually struggles to welcome and support each new wave of immigration (Noguera, 2009). In addition to the myriad challenges associated with movement to a new country and adaptation to a new culture, new immigrants too frequently cope with discrimination and a lack of acceptance. Public schools are one place where immigrant children encounter the larger social system of American culture. The stresses involved in migration can be overwhelming. They may be impacted by the reasons for the migration which can vary greatly from displacement by war, escape from oppression, economic survival, and personal family circumstances to many other reasons, some voluntary and some involuntary. Some families may be migrating with the support of family members who immigrated earlier; and others may arrive with no prearranged supports.

School psychologists are often required to provide supports for the stresses associated with the challenging transitions involved with immigration. The development of multicultural competency requires a basic understanding of potential stressors and trauma associated with this transition and its potential impact on psychological and educational functioning. In her text *Latino Families in Therapy*, Falicov (2014b) outlines the variations and diversity in the experience of migration. This again underlines the importance of not only understanding the commonalities associated with the experience of immigration but the unique factors impacting individual students and their families. Falicov outlines a variety of clinical roles and approaches that are important for psychologists including being a cultural observer and a social intermediary.

Schools are a potential resource for including families in the larger community or putting them in contact with potentially helpful community resources and institutional supports. School psychologists can provide therapeutic supports when family stressors are overwhelming and impacting students or when normal life cycle transitions such as emerging adolescence are intensified and complicated by competing needs for family cohesion and adolescent independence. All of these issues are important to address in supervision and are incorporated in the journey toward multicultural competency. While centered on Latino families, Falicov's (2014b) text provides an excellent overview of the variables associated with migration. Her delineation of practical clinical strategies can be extended to multicultural work in general.

Self-reflection and Cultural Humility

Even this brief discussion of key factors related to multicultural competency highlights the challenges for supervisors and supervisees in targeting and achieving growth in this area. The posture the supervisor models for the supervisee and routinely and purposefully promotes is one of self-reflection contributing to enhanced self-awareness. It is important to understand our own cultural foundations and its implications for assumptions, attitudes, beliefs, and patterns that may influence problem-solving. Supervisors accept but challenge limitations of their own cultural perspectives; this stance opens them up to less biased exploration of cultural meanings for clients (Falender, Shafranske, & Falicov, 2014).

Medical training has used the term *cultural humility* to define an approach to understanding the cultural perspectives of patients (Juarez et al., 2006). Applying it to supervision in psychology, Falender et al. (2014) integrate self-awareness of the clinician's own cultural predispositions with an openness to listening to the client share their experiences within their own cultural perspectives. Cultural humility suggests a posture that is respectful, supportive, and inquisitive. As clinicians strive to understand what it might be like to be in another's shoes, there is an acknowledgment that they can never completely succeed. This approach is empathic, builds trust and a working alliance, and fosters the client's own self-exploration of cultural issues with their strengths and limitations.

Expanding Perspectives Through Cross-cultural Dialogue

We are all at times enriched and at times constrained by our cultural experiences and perspectives. Cross-cultural dialogue can expand our horizons and broaden our perspectives in positive ways that are healthy and support both personal growth and social justice. Therapeutic interventions are often helpful by expanding the reflexive thinking and problem-solving patterns of clients to consider alternative perspectives and actions. Cognitive behavioral therapy strategies like Socratic dialogues, collaborative empiricism, and guided discovery are designed to assist clients in questioning unnecessarily limiting assumptions and restrictive behavioral responses to foster growth and expand effective problem-solving repertoires (Simon, 2016).

The therapeutic process is sensitive to cultural experiences but may assist clients in exploring perspectives and behaviors beyond their current cultural experiences. Psychologists strive to understand cultural standards but avoid supporting harmful limitations. Gender roles can serve as an example. Many cultures place limits on female roles and opportunities. While it is important to understand cultural perspectives on gender roles, psychologists strive to support their female students' strivings for equal opportunities. For example, in a high school parent conference focused on post high school planning, school staff might encourage parents to look beyond traditional expectations and roles and support their daughter's aspirations for collegiate and professional training. This intervention approach can be challenging to execute. The therapeutic stance is empathic and accepting, reframes perceived limits as opportunities, and challenges the family to expand their cultural perspective. The supervisor assists the supervisee in maintaining an accepting posture while challenging the family to explore new options for their daughter.

Exploring Potential Biases and Blind Spots

In supervision, supervisors assist supervisees in examining their own biases, encouraging their own self-awareness of personal attitudes and values that might unknowingly influence clinical practice. Supervisors provide feedback regarding potential blind spots and personal biases that may interfere with their work.

Frameworks for Multicultural Exploration

Even if an intern has had extensive classroom work focused on multicultural competency, it is in field experience that competencies can be engaged and enhanced. Bernard and Goodyear (2014) propose four dimensions that supervisors should address to foster multicultural competency. Two of the dimensions address distinct aspects of interpersonal awareness, one dealing with cultural identity and practices and the other dealing with expectations, biases, and prejudice. A third, the intrapersonal dimension, focuses on personal identity and self-definition examining the role of race, gender, and sexual orientation and their impact on relationships with others. The fourth dimension addresses social and political factors taking into account the level of privilege or oppression a person experiences based on any of several realities such as race, poverty, or sexual orientation. Bernard and Goodyear assert that each of these dimensions is important for understanding the supervisor, supervisee, and client independently and in interaction with each other. They suggest that it is the supervisor's responsibility to ensure that these dimensions are attended to routinely and appropriately in supervision. Through this process, the supervisee and supervisor can each grow in self-awareness and in multicultural competency.

Practical consideration of the dimensions formulated by Bernard and Goodyear touches many variables appropriate for supervision. For example, a field placement may provide the first opportunity for a novice trainee from an economically advantaged background to directly observe the impact of poverty, racial discrimination, and political oppression upon the educational and social-emotional development of children. Supervision would address these factors in terms of their impact on child welfare and their implications for psychological supports. Supervision would also examine the requirements for building an effective therapeutic relationship when the counselor's race, socioeconomic, and personal developmental experiences are completely different than the client's. If at the same time, the supervisor is of a different race and socioeconomic background from the supervisee, additional dynamics and perspectives may impact casework. Bernard and Goodyear suggest that the impact of diversity should be examined within the client and trainee and within the trainee and supervisor relationships.

Falicov (2014a, 2014b) proposed a multidimensional ecosystemic comparative approach (MECA) for understanding the place of culture in clinical practice and training. She originally outlined this schema in relation to family therapy supervision, but it is relevant to clinical and supervisory work in schools as well. Using a variety of approaches, MECA examines four domains: (a) family organization—nuclear/extended family, connectedness, hierarchies, and communication styles; (b) the family life cycle—ideals meanings, timings, and transitions; (c) the ecological context—community, work, school, and religion; and (d) migration/acculturation—separations and reunions, trauma, disorienting anxieties, and cultural identities. Cultural diversity is explored by examining family organization and family life cycle. Social justice is examined through the ecological context and migration/acculturation domains which focus on life conditions that are affected by socioeconomic status, contextual stressors, and discrimination. This conceptual approach can be applied to client, supervisee, and supervisor.

Similar to Bernard and Goodyear's (2014) dimensions for supervisory competency described above, Falicov defined these domains as essential targets for exploration, understanding, and sensitivity within both clinical work and supervision. Supervisors and supervisees can map out their own standing in each of these domains and compare similarities and differences discussing how each may affect the supervisory relationship in positive or limiting ways. This exercise builds sensitivity within the supervisee for understanding the influence of these factors in clients' lives and the potential overlapping and different influences that can affect clinical relationships. Enhanced cultural self-awareness enables the supervisee to view the client's challenges through a clearer lens with less personal distortion. This approach fosters the development of multicultural competency.

CASE EXAMPLE: EXPLORING CULTURAL AND DEVELOPMENTAL FACTORS IN CASE CONCEPTUALIZATION

Emily, a school psychology intern, is assigned a consultation case by the school's problem-solving team. The student's teachers are concerned that Maria, a 9th grader, has declining grades, is not completing all of her homework assignments, appears depressed, and seems increasingly withdrawn and disconnected from classmates. Maria tells Emily that she is indeed feeling depressed, lonely, and overwhelmed. Emily learns that Maria immigrated to this country from Central America when she was 7 years old with her mother, father, and two younger siblings. Sadly, her father had died in an accident 3 years ago. Since then her mother has been working evenings to support the family. In earlier grades, Maria had developed some friendships and would really like to participate in extracurricular activities through school. However, she is required to come home right after school to supervise her sisters and make dinner. That only leaves weekends for social activities; but rather than getting together with classmates, her weekends are centered on visits with extended family or church activities with other recent immigrant families where most of the children are much younger than she is.

Emily shares this information and her concerns for Maria in supervision. Before they discuss potential intervention plans, her supervisor, Sonja, prompts Emily to examine the influence of immigration and cultural factors on case conceptualization. She encourages her to examine these areas through a series of questions followed by discussion within the supervision session. Here are some of the questions she raises:

Try and place yourself in Maria's shoes and then in her mother's.
What pressures does each feel?
How are they similar and how different?

CASE EXAMPLE: RACIAL DIFFERENCES

In this case, the supervisee, Samantha, is Black; and her supervisor, Sarah, is White. The school district is in a rural community under economic duress with a largely White population. Samantha has prior experience in a field placement providing parent training to parents in a low income urban community where the population was very diverse, but primarily from minority racial backgrounds. Sarah and Samantha were aware that a couple of prospective parent participants had expressed hesitancies about working with a Black psychologist, particularly one who was new to the community. Sarah decided it was best to directly discuss with Samantha how the issue of being Black might impact her work with clients for whom that might be an issue. Realizing that racial discrimination was something that Samantha had undoubtedly encountered many times throughout her personal and professional lives, she asked Samantha how she was affected when issues like this arose and what she had learned from past experiences that helped her to cope and effectively respond to this kind of uncomfortable situation. She also asked her how being Black influenced her attitudes toward and work with those from the majority culture including herself as a supervisor who was White. Throughout the dialogue Sarah responded empathically and repeatedly reassured Samantha that she would support her when faced with racial discrimination including asserting that she would indeed remain the psychologist for this parent training program. She asked Samantha how she could be most supportive to her in processing and addressing these challenges acknowledging that these were not easy issues to discuss and would need to periodically be revisited. Samantha acknowledged how frustrating and challenging these situations were; but she indicated that it was very important to discuss this otherwise it would be the unaddressed "elephant in the room" both in terms of her field experience and her relationship with Sarah her supervisor. Samantha told her supervisor that she was not sure if anyone who was not of a minority racial background could fully understand the challenges Black professionals faced. It was clear to Sarah that this topic would require further discussion over time.

Supervision Regarding Sexual Minority Issues

An area of diversity that has been drawn into sharper focus lately and requires particular attention in supervision centers on sexual minority issues. Lesbian, gay, bisexual, transgender, and questioning (LGBTQ) students, faculty, supervisees, and supervisors face many challenges including discrimination resulting from their sexual orientation identification. In terms of clients, these issues are of particular importance to high school students who may be in the process of questioning or coming to terms with their sexual orientation. When they occur, differences in orientation between supervisor and supervisee may need to be discussed in supervision as part of building a trusting and affirming relationship similar to addressing gender or racial differences.

Affirmation

Both APA (2000, 2009, 2010a, 2012b) and NASP (2010d, 2011b, 2014a, 2014b) have developed policies and guidelines for supporting LGBT clients including a joint resolution on gender and sexual orientation diversity in children and adolescents in schools (APA & NASP, 2015). The profession recognizes diversity in gender identity and that all sexual orientations are valid and require affirmation. Sexual orientation status is not indicative of pathology nor should it be subject to conversion therapy. At the same time, professional organizations recognize that LGBT individuals may face additional stressors because of their minority status. These stressors may be exacerbated not only by direct discrimination but by the polarizing political and religious discourse prevalent in contemporary American culture. Unfortunately, too often insufficient training occurs to prepare supervisees with knowledge of sexual identity development and for work with LGBT clients (Bieschke, Blasko, & Woodhouse, 2014; McCabe & Rubinson, 2008).

Diversity Competent Supervision

Bieschke et al. (2014) outline several elements of supervisory practice that support diversity competency in this area. The most important starting point is the establishment of an affirmative environment within the supervisory relationship. Supervisors must have resolved their own value conflicts in this area, be comfortable discussing issues related to sexual orientation, and be prepared to affirm the sexual orientation of their supervisees. These authors emphasize the importance of supervisors being knowledgeable, skilled, and comfortable in working with LGBT clients prior to engaging in supervision. An understanding of the systemic issues challenging these populations not only in society in general but within the school setting in particular is essential; and these insights should be fostered in supervisees. LGBT students are at additional risk for being targeted by bullying. A national survey on school climate found 84% reporting verbal harassment and 40% physical harassment (Kosciw, Greytak, Diaz, & Barkiewicz, 2010). The need to address systemic issues as part of the process of supporting individual students is important. This is consistent with the ecological perspective outlined in this chapter that emphasizes the importance of addressing both individual and systemic issues that affect students.

Managing Conflicts Between Personal Beliefs and Professional Standards

One of the more challenging supervisory tasks emerges when a supervisee's personal and/or religious beliefs do not affirm diversity in sexual orientation. A first instinct might be to excuse the supervisee from participation in cases where clients are of sexual minority status. However, there are several difficulties with this approach. LGBT clients are a significant part of the population, and supervisees may have clients who are LGBT but have not revealed that in therapy either because it is not a central issue to the presenting problem or because they are cautiously waiting to do so until they feel assured that they would be affirmed by the therapist. Working in schools, supervisees are likely to work with students who are questioning their sexual orientation; and this is unlikely to be identified in a referral question. Bieschke and Mintz (2012) asserted that the responsibility of trainers is to ensure that trainees acquire both *demographic competency* (the ability to competently serve demographically diverse groups) and *dynamic inclusivity* (the ability to work with clients who may have different beliefs and worldviews). They recommend that psychologists should be prepared to competently work with diverse clients who may present with a full array of beliefs and worldviews that might differ from the psychologist's.

Diversity and multicultural competency requires professionals to be able to empathically and effectively work with clients who may have views contrary to their own belief systems. To frame this challenge in other content areas, this may include clients who make overtly racist comments or others who have committed heinous crimes. Since diversity competency is a core competency for entry to the profession, specific attention must be addressed to development and evaluation of this skill set. As in all skill training areas, the welfare of the client is the first priority. In some cases, supervisors may need to be cotherapists or coconsultants to model skills and ensure competent service. The eventual goal remains skilled independent functioning. Recognizing that for some supervisees this may be a process that takes some time, it is important to directly discuss preparedness for addressing diversity issues for sexual minority clients early in the supervision process and then develop an individualized supervision plan as necessary.

SUPERVISORY REFLECTION ACTIVITY: SEXUAL ORIENTATION DIFFERENCES

Reflect upon the case of Samantha coping with racial discrimination above and explore how it would be effectively approached by the supervisor, if in place of Samantha, the supervisee was James who was known to be gay by many in the school community. In this case the hesitant parents are expressing their discomfort with a psychologist leading their parent skills training sessions who is gay and that he did not and probably never would have kids of his own. Sarah, his supervisor, is heterosexual and has three children. Given the principles discussed in this chapter and explicated in the case of the supervisee who was African American in a largely White community, how would you express and explore these issues in supervision?

Never Defined Solely by a Singular Characteristic

While we have spent considerable time discussing particular elements of diversity, it is important to emphasize that no singular characteristic should define any individual. It is important to understand the influence of diverse characteristics, but they are only part of each client's story. For example, a child with a disability may present with strengths or challenges unrelated to the presence of a disability and would not want to be solely defined as disabled. An LGBT client may be struggling with a trauma experience unrelated to sexual orientation. Diverse characteristics may at times be in the foreground and at other times primarily in the background of collaborative problem-solving activities. This approach ensures that supervisees account for the implications of diversity but avoids pigeonholing or stereotyping clients. Indeed healthy social inclusion and nondiscriminatory practices recognize that we are all bound by the same human nature and share an essential commonality. In this regard, summary research on the applications of evidence-based interventions for ethnic minority youth are cautiously optimistic (Huey & Polo, 2010). Studies focused on African American and Latino youth show promise that empirically supported strategies can be effective for these populations. Culturally responsive adaptations may increase engagement and support implementation of interventions (Simon, 2016).

Intentionality in Supervision

In summarizing their view of training for competency in diversity and multicultural sensitive practice, Falender et al. (2014) highlight the intentionality of incorporating consideration of these issues into supervision and daily clinical practice. Since achieving competency in these areas is an extended dynamic process for both supervisors and supervisees, it is important to intentionally draw focus to these characteristics and to foster increased self-awareness and self-reflection related to the full range of diversity issues. Routine dialogue between the supervisor and supervisee can ensure that diversity factors are considered in work with clients, monitor potential personal biases that may inadvertently influence practice, and safeguard against harmful stereotyping based on singular client characteristics.

Rich Diversity in Public Schools

Public schools present an opportunity to experience the benefits and challenges inherent in working with diverse and multicultural populations in ways unmatched by most other institutions. Public schools are required to enroll and serve all students regardless of background or disability. This is part of what makes them exciting places to practice professional psychology. Internships in schools provide a unique opportunity to develop diversity competency.

Practical Supervisory Activities

Development of diversity and multicultural awareness and competency is an essential training goal established at the onset of the internship year. Supervisors pursue this goal by reviewing socioeconomic and cultural differences specific to the community of the school site. NASP *Standards for the Graduate Preparation of School Psychologists* (2010b) calls for training in strategies "for addressing diversity factors in design, implementation, and evaluation of all services" (p. 15). This requires supervision sessions to routinely review potential diversity and cultural factors that may impact assessment procedures, case conceptualization, and intervention planning. When appropriate, cultural factors that are potentially relevant to family functioning and engagement with the school should be considered prior to and in review of parent conferences. When possible, it is beneficial to create opportunities for interns to interact with school professionals with different cultural backgrounds. Supervisees can receive training and experience in cross-cultural problem-solving for mediation of peer conflicts. Psychological services for students from minority backgrounds may require advocacy and attention to school-wide systemic barriers. Supervisors can involve supervisees in change agency initiatives that foster social justice for all students.

SUPERVISORY PROCESS ACTIVITY: CULTURAL BACKGROUNDS

This activity involves reflection and dialogue initiated by the supervisor regarding personal cultural backgrounds and their potential impact on professional practice. The supervisor begins by sharing his or her personal cultural background. Strengths fostered by cultural and personal history factors should be highlighted. Additionally it is important to note characteristics that might limit perceptions or leave potential for blind spots, (e.g., raised in a White middle class family with minimal exposure to diversity). The supervisor invites the supervisee to share similar information. This activity should become a dialogue with the supervisor and supervisee taking turns and commenting on each other's disclosures. Domains to be addressed are not limited to but include the following: family of origin (characteristics, values, and structures); ethnicity; exposure and experience with diversity; current family and personal life cycle issues; and other relevant ecological contexts that impact worldview (i.e., work history, religious/spiritual background, training experiences).

This dialogue is followed by a discussion of the local community and the training site. The discussion compares and contrasts personal cultural background with cultural characteristics in the work community. The discussion concludes with an exploration of the potential implications of the information from this dialogue on diversity and cultural competent practice in this setting.

Training in Program Development and Systems Change

The NASP (2010a) Practice Model and the APA (2011) competency benchmarks incorporate attention to both student-level services and systems-level services. Domain 5 specifies engagement in school-wide practices to promote learning and mental health. This means that training and supervision do not merely focus on interventions for individual students but also must include strategies for developing programs that foster a positive inclusive school culture, enhance supports for learning for all students, and promote psychological wellness.

Sometimes *changing the system* is the central component of intervention planning. For example, when working with an individual student who is struggling with identity issues related to sexual orientation, it can become readily apparent that changes are necessary in the school culture to support many similar students. There may be a need for support programs for students who are questioning their sexual orientation or have identified themselves as lesbian, gay, bisexual, or transgendered. At the same time, it will likely be necessary to promote system-wide initiatives to address discriminatory aspects of the school culture and to promote educational practices that teach and value inclusion related to all manifestations of diversity. Supervision must routinely include examination of the larger contexts that influence the experiences of individual students and consider implications for potential systemic interventions.

Training in program development and organizational change skills is an important competency. While graduate training can provide the essential theoretical background and define the skill sets required to become an effective change agent, the ability to apply these principles and skills generally first occurs during the internship in collaboration with the supervisor. Since many programmatic initiatives require a lengthy process that generally covers more than a single school year, the first substantive opportunity to apply change agency skills is likely to occur during early career practice. This underscores the necessity of making clinical supervision available to this professional cohort.

Training in program development and organizational skills applies strategies similar to those involved in other problem-solving activities. The process begins with an identification of a need and an assessment of its prevalence and severity. A clear operationalized problem definition permits collection of baseline data that can later be a reference point for progress monitoring. Potential programmatic interventions are examined in reference to the current consensus for best practice within the field. An analysis of the system which is the target for change involves a broad examination of its culture including values, organizational structure, overt and covert decision-making practices, subgroup tensions, and politics. Supervisors guide supervisees through a systematic assessment of resources for and barriers to change and healthy development.

Change plans or program development initiatives must be directly linked to the problem conceptualization. The supervisor assists the supervisee in designing a comprehensive change plan that delineates any capacity building required for staff implementers, teaming methods, the implementation process and timetable, supportive resources, strategies for countering barriers, and mechanisms for modifying the plan based on the experience of initial implementation and progress monitoring data. Many change initiatives begin as pilot projects. No matter what the scale of initial implementation, it is critical to project what actions are necessary to sustain the initiative. This may involve anticipating what funding, personnel, or other resources might be required for successful long term implementation. This analysis may need to include what other roles or tasks staff may need to deemphasize, reassign, or eliminate.

This brief review of the process for new program development and systems change consultation reveals its complexity. While it still involves the same sequence of *assessment to intervention to outcome linkage* that characterizes all core psychological activities, systemic work must account for many more variables at each stage; and its success is largely dependent on the ability to marshal support from key stakeholders, form strong collaborative teams, and build and sustain the capacity of all implementers. Supervised field experience is the best training ground for developing these competencies; and supervisors must ensure opportunities for program development initiatives and provide supervision that fosters the required competencies for successful change agency. As in other areas of training and supervision, a well-delineated systematic approach improves learning and organizes supervisory guidance, feedback, and support. Table 8.1, *A Systematic Approach to Program Development and Systems Change,* provides a sample framework for organizing and processing program development and systems change initiatives (Simon, 2015b). Within the ecological perspective, faithful but flexible adaptations of empirically supported programs and best practice standards must incorporate attention to cultural and diversity variables impacting individuals and existing in school and community systems. For an extensive treatment of these topics, we recommend Forman's (2015) recent text on the application of implementation science to the development of mental health programs in schools.

CASE EXAMPLE: PERFORMANCE ANXIETY IN A HIGH ACHIEVEMENT HIGH SCHOOL

Cindy is completing her internship under Jody's supervision at Washington High School (WHS). WHS is a selective enrollment school in a large metropolitan area. It has an earned reputation for outstanding performance on state and national tests and a strong record of graduates securing admissions to top-level colleges. Jody received a referral from a science teacher regarding a student whom she had conferenced with after a surprisingly poor grade on a test. The teacher reported that the student, Maria, was very bright and hardworking, did well in classwork and homework, but performed poorly on tests. During the student-teacher conference, Maria appeared very stressed and anxious, was occasionally tearful, and frustrated that she was not being as successful as she had in the past. Jody thought this would be an appropriate counseling case to assign to Cindy under her supervision.

When Cindy shared her initial assessment of Maria's stressors in supervision, she was concerned that this student was experiencing excessive performance anxiety and that her struggles on tests were contributing to self-blame and escalating depression. Maria shared that she had always been the best student in her family and had planned to be the first one to attend college. Her struggles were impacting her sleep; and she was experiencing high and pervasive levels of stress throughout the day. During supervision, Jody directed Cindy to examine the impact of the school and family cultures on Maria's anxiety level. While she guided Cindy through individual intervention planning for Maria, she raised questions about the need for a program to address performance and test anxiety for many students who might be overwhelmed by the academic pressures and highly competitive atmosphere of WHS. Jody prepared Cindy to raise this question at the next student services department meeting.

At the meeting, several school psychologists and other counseling personnel reported an increase in referrals for anxiety. Jody suggested that Cindy, under her supervision, could systematically collect data on referrals for anxiety that had academic performance anxiety as a contributing feature, and then they could pilot an assessment of a segment of students who had not been referred for counseling to estimate the incidence in the student body as a whole. If sufficient need was demonstrated, development of a test anxiety program might be warranted.

Having guided her intern in an examination of the ecological factors impacting her client, Jody used this opportunity to provide Cindy with supervised experience in program development. She worked with Cindy to choose and develop assessment targets and instruments. They discussed the specific WHS systemic factors that may inadvertently exacerbate performance anxiety. They persuaded the science department to participate in the assessment process and subsequent pilot intervention programming. Cindy explored evidence-based curricula for addressing test anxiety. They enlisted an interested and well-respected teacher in the department to cofacilitate a pilot support group and provided her with the necessary training to ensure successful participation.

At each stage of program development, Jody helped Cindy examine the steps and skills necessary to initiate and eventually sustain new programming initiatives. Piloting this program proved to be an achievable training experience for the intern year. At the conclusion of the pilot, Cindy reported outcome data and shared potential next steps with members of the science

(Continued)

(Continued)

department. This initiative sensitized this academic department to brainstorm how they could better support all of their students in not only test preparation but in managing the pressures of this high achieving school culture. In Cindy's report back to the student services team, she was able to suggest that they more systematically collect data on referrals to see if other group intervention activities might be appropriate.

Innovation and change agency takes time to fully develop. This supervised experience in the early stages of program development equipped this intern with skills to apply in her future practice.

Multisystemic Interventions

The ecological perspective assumes that individual functioning cannot be fully understood without understanding the contextual variables that influence behaviors, thoughts, and emotions. Not only immediate environmental factors but the persistent influences embedded in critical social systems that the student participates in must be considered in assessment and intervention planning. These include the family, peers, classroom, school, neighborhood, and larger community. The implication of this perspective for psychological intervention activities is that problem-solving strategies should not only focus on the individual student but address change in the contexts and systems that contribute to behavioral concerns and academic issues. The implication for supervision is that supervisees must be trained to assess and intervene individually and systemically in an integrated plan. Supervisors assist supervisees in understanding the larger picture and designing strategies to alter systemic variables that can support student health and academic success.

Supervised intervention activities include classroom consultations, extensive collaboration with parents and caregivers, programming to address school and peer cultures, and collaboration with community resources. Multisystemic therapies (Henggeler, Cunningham, Rowland, & Schoenwald, 2012; Henggeler et al., 2009; Swenson, Henggeler, Taylor, & Addison, 2009) and functional family therapy (Alexander et al., 2013) provide evidence-based paradigms for coordinated intervention strategies that involve parents, school staff, and community resources. Wraparound social service initiatives provide an additional vehicle for helping schools marshal and coordinate a broad range of community support resources to assist students and their families (Eber, Breen, Rose, Unizycki, & London, 2008). Drawing from the best available empirically supported protocols, contemporary best practice in school psychology integrates intervention strategies for the student, classroom, family, school, and community (Simon, 2016). One key role of supervision is to assist supervisees in perceiving the linkage among these domains and then guide them in practical individual and systemic intervention planning and execution.

TABLE 8.1 A Systematic Approach to Program Development and Systems Change

I. Need identification
   A. Observational data
      1. Identification of persistent problems in a specific area
      2. Concerns over service gaps
      3. Absence of best practice
   B. Assessment
      1. Operationally define problem or need
      2. Find or develop assessment tools that both clarify need and anticipate progress monitoring and outcome data requirements
         a. Assessment tools must be user friendly, practical, and economical and include clear qualitative and quantitative descriptors
         b. Tap existing data collections and resources that might contribute to baseline data or measurement of change
         c. Include assessment of staff's capacity to respond to need and potential staff development needs
      3. Investigate relevant best practice standards
II. Analysis of system
   A. Culture
   B. Organizational structure
   C. Problem-solving style
   D. Procedures for implementing and supporting new initiatives
   E. Assessment of resources for and barriers to change
   F. Identification of respected and influential faculty who may be encouraged to provide vocal support and/or be enlisted to participate in pilot programming
III. Design new program or change plan
   A. Link plan directly to conceptualization of problem
   B. Investigate empirically supported programs to address need and then adapt to school context as necessary
   C. Delineate all aspects of change plan specifying required advance capacity building for staff, teaming methods, resource requirements, implementation process and timetable, mechanisms for modifying plan in response to experience during implementation and data from periodic progress monitoring
   D. Plan ongoing supports for implementers
   E. Plan for management of anticipated systemic barriers to change
IV. Project actions required to ensure sustainability of project or innovation beyond pilot stage
   A. Anticipate funding, personnel, and other resources necessary to sustain new program or change initiative
   B. Outline ongoing natural, professional recognition, and other incentives that support motivation and long term commitment of program implementers and change agents
   C. Keep all stakeholders informed of progress monitoring outcome data

This is the juncture where the ecological perspective and the problem-solving component of the DEP model intersect. The next chapter will extend this discussion to examine supervision of problem-solving activities, the core function within school psychology.

Implementation Integrity of Ecological Component: Behavioral Markers

The DEP supervision model not only provides a theoretical framework for supervision but defines specific approaches and activities for the day to day practice of supervision. As with any core training or intervention strategy, there are behavioral markers that can be monitored to ensure implementation integrity. We will now summarize these supervision activities or markers for the Ecological component of the DEP model. A similar summary occurs after the Developmental and Problem-solving component chapters. These behavior markers are incorporated into the DEP-SSFS described in Chapter 4 and located in Appendix 4A.

The following supervisory and supervised activities are consistent with the implementation of the Ecological component of DEP:

- Establish and define diversity and multicultural competency as a supervisory goal from the beginning of the supervisory relationship.
- Orient the supervisee to the school and community cultures.
- Orient the supervisee to the representative ethnic cultures present in the school community.
- Discuss supervisor and supervisee cultural backgrounds and their potential implications for psychological practice (strengths and limitations) and for the supervisory relationship.
- Discuss the influence of local socioeconomic factors and family histories of oppression and privilege within a social justice framework.
- Assess supervisee training and attitudes relative to psychological services for sexual minority students and implement supervisory and training activities as necessary to ensure diversity competency in this area.
- Incorporate attention to relevant diversity and multicultural issues into all practice activities.
- Provide feedback as appropriate for the interference of any blind spots, personal biases, or limiting cultural perspectives on clinical work.
- Provide supervised training opportunities in universal interventions designed to promote wellness and prevent psychological and academic problems (e.g., universal screening, PBIS, social-emotional learning curriculum).
- Provide sufficient opportunities for problem-solving parent conferencing and parent skills training activities.
- Provide sufficient opportunities for classroom behavioral management consultation.
- Provide supervised opportunities for program development and systemic change agency activities.

- Direct supervisee to research services and collaborate with community resources.
- Teach and employ a case conceptualization and problem-solving model that addresses both individual and contextual variables.

Summary

The ecological perspective assumes that individual functioning cannot be fully understood without understanding the contextual variables that influence learning, behaviors, thoughts, and emotions. Not only immediate environmental factors but the persistent influences embedded in critical social systems that the student participates in must be considered in assessment, consultation, and intervention planning. These include the family, peers, classroom, school, neighborhood, and larger community. The Ecological component of DEP focuses on the development of diversity and multicultural competency, ecologically sensitive assessment and consultation practices, integrated intervention planning that addresses individual and systemic factors, and training in program development and systems change. Specific behavioral markers indicate implementation integrity of the Ecological component of DEP.

9

THE PROBLEM-SOLVING COMPONENT

Core Activity of Psychological Practice

The third component of the DEP model is problem-solving. Empirically supported problem-solving is the central professional activity of school psychologists and thus a core focus within supervision. Problem-solving is involved in all aspects of psychological practice. It is intrinsic to assessment, intervention, consultation, program development, and systems change activities. Problem-solving activities incorporate consideration of all of the ecological factors reviewed in the last chapter. Diversity, multicultural, and environmental influences and other contextual or systemic factors must be addressed in the process of problem-solving. Supervisory practice focused on teaching problem-solving requires integration of all three DEP components. This integration is necessary both to ensure the provision of effective service for clients and to effectively connect theory, research, and practice for supervisees amid the complexities of the field setting.

Data-based Decision-making

The NASP (2010a) Practice Model describes data-based decision-making and accountability as practices that permeate all aspects of psychological service delivery. Data-based decision-making applies scientific principles to the problem-solving process. Systematic analysis of both individual and contextual factors occurs during assessment and intervention planning. Comprehensive multimethod and multisource data collection utilizing valid and reliable methods and instruments is the foundation for problem definition, problem analysis, solution generation, and intervention plan evaluation (Simon, 2016). This approach enables school psychologists to directly link assessment results to intervention. Accountability comes through the collection of routine progress monitoring and intervention outcome data. In turn this information may influence modifications of intervention strategies until desired results are achieved.

Evidence-based Interventions

Effective problem-solving requires the application of intervention strategies that are supported by research and tailored to the unique characteristics of clients and their presenting problems. Supervisors are responsible for guiding supervisees in the selection and application of evidence-based interventions (EBIs) that are consistent with assessment data and are appropriate for an individual student.

Individualized Applications of EBIs

EBIs must adapt to individual student differences and the contexts and systems within which they are implemented. Unfortunately, presenting problems are often complex and characterized by comorbid conditions (Mash & Barkley, 2006). EBIs proven efficacious in well-controlled research studies may require adaptation to be effective in applied school settings (Simon, 2016). A strong advocate for empirically supported interventions, Kendall (2012c) notes that they are not uniformly successful and often do not sufficiently take into account common comorbidities. Still they remain essential guideposts for interventions in all circumstances and are the foundation for problem-solving practices.

Evidence-based protocols are frequently manualized prescribing specific intervention strategies in a structured sequence. Recognizing that setting demands differ and that a one-size-fits-all approach can be a disservice to some clients, Kendall (2012c) recommends application of EBIs with *flexibility within fidelity*. He underlines the necessity of utilizing essential core intervention techniques consistent with the demonstrated change mechanisms of the EBI while creatively adapting therapeutic approaches to account for the unique characteristics of the client and setting.

Chorpita (2007) proposed a modular approach to implementation of manualized EBI protocols. He advocated for assessing the individual skill sets of the child and then selecting the modules in the intervention protocol that fit the individualized profile of his or her strengths and needs. For example, some students experiencing anxiety may require interpersonal skills training and anxiety management strategies to counter social anxiety and enhance social participation, while others may have sufficient social skills but still require extensive application of cognitive restructuring and exposure strategies. The supervisor guides the supervisee in defining assessment to intervention links that result in individually appropriate and parsimonious applications of EBIs.

Implementation Science

The emerging focus on implementation science is particularly relevant to clinical supervision (Forman, 2015). APA's Division 16 (School Psychology) study group outlined the need to focus research efforts on examining the essential components required for effective implementation of EBIs in school settings (Forman et al., 2013). The challenge is to adapt research supported intervention protocols, whose efficacy has been proven in controlled studies, to the complexity of problem-solving in daily school psychology practice where implementation of EBIs has been low (Kratochwill & Shernoff, 2004; McKevitt, 2012). While researchers may protest insufficient utilization of empirically supported strategies, practitioners question whether they can be effectively applied in the messier realities of schools and clinics (Kratochwill & Shernoff, 2004). Implementation science strives to bridge that gap by determining which implementation strategies will result in increased utilization and effectiveness in applications of EBIs. Relevant to our focus on clinical supervision, Forman (2015) emphasized the importance of technical assistance and coaching as methods to support implementation of EBIs. She noted that what is required is not only knowledge of the core features of an EBI but familiarity with the typical intervention approaches currently used by the implementing psychologist and the culture, context, and characteristics of clients in the setting. Clinical supervisors serve an important function by assisting supervisees in identifying relevant EBIs for specific cases and then coaching them to adapt and apply these research-based strategies to specific circumstances and settings. Supervisors combine their extensive clinical experience with their competencies in evidence-based practice to help supervisees integrate theory, research, and practice for individual clients, families, classrooms, and schools.

This same broker role must often be applied during practicum and internship training when supervisees encounter the differences between best practices defined in their graduate training and the actual degree and limitations of implementation in their field training site. Here the supervisor promotes supervisee development of the skills required to adapt classroom learning to best practice in the field. In each case, the supervisor insists on empirically supported best practices while guiding the supervisee to manage setting constraints.

Multidisciplinary Problem-solving Teams

School psychologists routinely function in collaborative multidisciplinary problem-solving teams. These teams bring diverse specialist expertise to a joint enterprise of assessing needs and planning integrated intervention strategies for students. Psychologists make a unique contribution to problem-solving teams but must be sensitive to and incorporate the perspectives of other professionals. As experts in data-based decision-making, systematic problem-solving, and collaborative group processes, school psychologists often have leadership or coordination roles in problem-solving teams. They ensure that decisions are based on the best available data and that intervention plans are routinely monitored for progress with data collection consistent with problem definitions and intervention goals.

Skills for rapport building, teaming, and collaborative problem-solving are essential targets for supervisee development in preparation for effective participation and leadership in problem-solving teams (Cates et al., 2011). Supervisors observe and provide feedback on these collaborative skills as essential competencies for effective school psychology practice.

A major benefit of problem-solving teams is their capacity to integrate interventions across contexts and disciplines. Supervisors are responsible for developing supervisees' facilitation skills that result in integrated intervention activities across home, classroom, and other peer settings and that address individual needs in academic, psychosocial, language, health, and other relevant domains (Simon, 2016).

Multitiered Systems of Support

Contemporary school psychology strives to practice within a framework of Multitiered Systems of Support (MTSS; NASP, 2010a; Stoiber, 2014). Consistent with public health intervention models, MTSS emphasizes the promotion of wellness in all realms of adaptive functioning, problem prevention, and early identification of at-risk behaviors to enable early intervention. Typically organized within three tiers of supports, academic and social-emotional-behavioral intervention services are matched to the level of needs exhibited by individual students.

Universal Supports and Progress Monitoring

The first tier provides universal supports and progress monitoring to the entire school population. A strong core academic curriculum, psychological education, and universal social-emotional learning supports are taught to all students. This maintains a focus on essential basic academic skills and includes integrating systematic social, coping, and problem-solving training into the general curriculum as core activities. School psychologists are involved in designing and implementing these services in close collaboration with teachers. School-wide support programs like Positive Behavior Interventions and Supports (PBIS) include school-wide and classroom activities, individual student monitoring and reinforcement strategies, and alternative approaches to discipline that focus on instruction in prosocial skills (Sugai, Horner, & McIntosh, 2008). Social-emotional learning (SEL) programs have been demonstrated to not only promote psychological health but to support academic achievement (Durlak, Domitrovich, Wessberg, & Gullotta, 2015). Learning implementation of evidence-supported SEL curricula is an essential supervisee goal similar to acquiring knowledge and skills of EBI therapeutic protocols. Supervisors also facilitate the development of supervisees' consultation skills in academic areas including analysis of academic concerns and applications of evidence-based academic interventions.

Universal screening for academic, behavioral, social, and emotional problems are essential first tier activities. Similar to early identification of reading or language problems, universal social-emotional-behavioral screening facilitates the provision of early intervention services for students at-risk for both internalizing and externalizing psychological problems. When school districts have not yet fully established universal screening programs, supervisors can work with their supervisees in program development activities to establish such screening programs.

Targeted Interventions

The second tier within MTSS targets early intervention for identified at-risk students. Students served at this level of support may be experiencing academic, social, emotional, or behavioral concerns that have been identified by routine screening data collection or through teacher or parent referrals to multidisciplinary problem-solving teams. Particular attention is paid to students with known risk factors such as exposure to trauma, recent loss, substance abuse history, chronic medical illness, low achievement, or repeated absences from school. While second tier interventions should be linked to targeted skill deficits and can take many forms, in the social, emotional, and behavioral arena, structured therapeutic support groups are a common intervention strategy (Simon, 2016). An exciting development in the field has been the expansion of empirically supported group programs that were specifically designed and validated for implementation in the school setting (e.g., Jaycox, 2004; Larson, 2005; Larson & Lochman, 2011; Stark et al., 2006). A comprehensive meta-analysis of CBT school-based group programs for anxiety and depression management strongly supported the effectiveness of these programs (Mychailyszyn, Brodman, Read, & Kendall, 2012). Rather than generic support groups, these EBI group programs employ structured intervention protocols that target specific symptom profiles such as depression, anxiety, anger management, or trauma (Simon, 2013). These programs are designed to integrate with classroom activities and include progress monitoring with teachers and parents. Even though these programs are designed for school-friendly implementation, they still require supervisory guidance for adaptation and utilization.

Similarly, there is a growing body of empirically supported interventions targeting academic skills including strategies for those who experience both behavioral and academic issues (Nelson, Benner, & Mooney, 2008). Summaries of evidence-based protocols for academic and social-emotional-behavioral problems can be located at websites such as Evidence-Based Intervention Network (http://ebi.missouri.edu), What Works Clearinghouse (http://ies.ed.gov/ncee/wwc/), and Intervention Central (www.interventioncentral.org).

Training and supervision should focus on these EBI programs that systematically address academic problems and specific social, coping, and problem-solving skills (Cates et al., 2011; Simon, 2013, 2016). Consistent with best practice, they are capable of linking assessment to intervention to outcome. Progress monitoring can include data on performance in the classroom, home, and other relevant settings. Second tier group programs provide an excellent opportunity for cotherapy or co-academic intervention work with supervisees. In our experience, the most challenging aspect of group leadership for supervisees is not the implementation of the prescribed curriculum but the simultaneous behavior management requirements that ensure effective child participation. Many EBI programs that teach social and coping skills specifically recommend cotherapy for group work (Larson & Lochman, 2011; White, 2011). Supervisors can model both intervention protocol implementation and behavior management. Consistent with the developmental component of DEP, supervisors can gradually cede primary leadership responsibility to supervisees and eventually be replaced by other support personnel. This coleadership experience enables direct observation of supervisees' therapeutic work with a variety of youth and thus provides content for review in supervision sessions.

Identification of at-risk students often occurs during crisis intervention activities, particularly when assessments are required for risk for harm to self or others, after a major behavioral episode, or a personal or school-wide traumatic event. Crisis intervention activities often generate service needs particularly at the second tier level of intensity (Brock, Reeves, & Nickerson, 2014). In terms of the Problem-solving component of DEP, supervision in crisis intervention is a core supervisory activity particularly for intern, postdoctoral, and early career supervisees. Crisis intervention often includes significant safety concerns and requires responsible risk management. Because of vicarious liability, supervisors may be tempted to limit supervisee participation in crisis intervention; however, this is a critical training activity that requires extensive practice with supervision. Supervisees should participate in crisis intervention appropriate to their developmental competencies for this skill set. Supervisees in preparation for independent practice should be provided with sufficient crisis intervention experience to ensure independent competency and a thorough understanding of when and how to seek consultation or supervisory support. When supervising crisis intervention activities, it is important to also address the emotional reactions of supervisees to engaging in these intense activities (Corey et al., 2010). The extended case example at the end of this chapter provides an example of supervision and training during internship in crisis intervention skills.

Intensive Services

The third tier of MTSS responds to students with intense needs that cannot be fully addressed with less comprehensive or specialized services. Some of these students are served in special education programs that provide multidimensional integrated academic interventions and social-emotional-behavioral supports at a high level of intensity. For students with significant mental health needs, it is necessary to intervene simultaneously in instructional and therapeutic domains for maximum benefit (Simon, 2016). At this tier, supervisees require development of skills for advanced collaborative problem-solving for the second stage of analysis of academic and/or behavioral-social-emotional concerns and for application of evidence-based therapeutic interventions for serious and complex psychological disorders and/or significant academic skill deficits. Many of these students present with comorbid conditions that require sophisticated multifaceted intervention protocols.

Casework at this intense level of service requires vigilant supervision. Key issues requiring focus in supervision include: comprehensive assessment to guide intervention; selection of appropriate evidence-based intervention approaches; management of potential resistance to treatments, including dividing and manipulating supervising adults; and coordination with relevant community resources. These students with complex mental health needs and poor academic performance often require multisystemic interventions with close coordination of teachers, parents, and community-based professionals (Alexander et al., 2013; Henggeler et al., 2012; Simon, 2016; Swenson et al., 2009).

These intense cases can easily overwhelm preprofessional supervisees and are the typical cases for which credentialed supervisees request consultation or supervisory guidance. The extensive clinical experience of supervisors enables them to see through the complexity of these cases and plan practical sequential intervention strategies. Talking through decision-making strategies first in cases managed by the supervisor and then in those assigned to the supervisee is an important supervisory method. Cotherapy and recorded or live observations are particularly relevant in these more challenging cases. The supervisory goal is not only to help the supervisee with case-specific problem-solving but to teach case conceptualization and problem-solving approaches that can eventually be independently applied to future cases.

These challenging cases often present with a great deal of complexity and may require innovative adaptations of EBI protocols (Forman, 2015). It is particularly in these situations that supervisees encounter the blend of art and science in intervention planning. Supervisors must ensure that supervisees maintain the core elements of empirically supported approaches; and when required to innovate or respond to problems minimally addressed in the research literature, supervisors make sure that supervisees monitor the outcomes of their revised strategies. The challenge is to know when to patiently stay the course and when to modify intervention plans. Supervisors' advanced clinical experience enables them to support supervisees in clinical decision-making.

Program Development and Systems Change

The degree to which individual school sites have successfully implemented MTSS varies greatly. Some school districts may have fully developed a comprehensive service continua while for others this framework remains largely aspirational. As noted in the chapter on the ecological component, program development and involvement in system change initiatives are important roles for school psychologists. As such, supervisees need to be provided opportunities to participate in these activities under supervision. Concepts defining best practice are continually evolving; and individual districts may have unique challenges to address. Supervision sets the tone for balancing individual and small group service delivery and systemic work while fostering a professional attitude that both embraces a commitment to implementing current best practice and an openness to continuous improvement in psychological service delivery.

Training Across All NASP Practice Domains

Particularly during practicum, internship, and postdoctoral supervision, it is important for supervisees to receive training across the complete realm of school psychology practice domains as articulated in the NASP Practice Model (NASP, 2010a) and delineated in the APA (2011) competency areas. This means that preprofessional supervisees should receive supervised experiences at all levels of MTSS and be involved in the full range of psychological practice activities. This includes assessment, consultation, intervention, collaborative problem-solving, and program development and work with students, faculty, parents, and community resources. While professional roles may specialize even during early career practice, entry-level psychologists should attain a broad foundation of competencies; but it may take from 5 to 10 years to develop particular expertise in any one area of practice (Ysseldyke et al., 2006). Often later supervision is required when a school psychologist moves into either a specialized area of practice or one targeting a population for which he or she has minimal experience.

Sharing Problem-solving Expertise

Supervision guides supervisees in the development of expertise in problem-solving both for individual casework and consultation and in the context of multidisciplinary problem-solving teams. Embedded in the MTSS framework is the assumption that all students and adult consultees should be trained to be competent problem-solvers. Universal services such as SEL programming teach these skills to students to promote healthy psychological development and coping capacity and to prevent problems. At targeted and intense levels of service, intervention goals continue to focus not only on remediation of the referral problem but on equipping students to independently respond to future challenges. This perspective of *giving problem-solving skills away* has been rooted in psychology for decades (G.A. Miller, 1969) and is a perspective to be embraced by supervisees. The development and validation of systematic skills training models for teaching effective coping and problem-solving skills has armed school psychologists with advanced tools toward achieving this goal (Simon, 2016). In addition to learning problem-solving skills in supervision and teaching psychosocial skills to students, supervisees can be provided opportunities to train teachers and parents in problem-solving skills both in the natural course of consultation work and in structured psychoeducational programs (e.g., Barkley, 2013; Fristad, Goldberg-Arnold, & Gavazzi, 2002).

Case Conceptualization

Since problem-solving is the core professional activity of school psychologists, teaching case conceptualization skills is likewise a core supervisory activity. Supervisors not only help supervisees in problem-solving focused on single cases but teach supervisees a framework for organizing case conceptualization to apply across the variety of case presentations. Consistent with the developmental component of supervision, the supervisory goal is to teach processes for eventual supervisee independent problem-solving regarding both individual and systemic issues.

Linking Assessment to Intervention

Problem-solving is rooted in data-based decision-making. Supervisors assist supervisees in collecting data from multiple sources utilizing multiple methods. In the behavioral realm, this could include: direct behavioral observations in a variety of settings over time; classroom and school-wide data from PBIS and other available sources; interviews of student, parents, and teachers; functional behavioral assessments (FBAs); and behavior rating scales and other psychological assessment instruments as appropriate. In the academic realm, assessment data could include classroom work samples, teacher reports, curriculum-based measurement data, referral-specific psychoeducational testing, and classroom observations. Assessment activity should be parsimonious but sufficiently comprehensive. The purpose of assessment is to collect data to address all referral questions, to form unbiased problem definitions, and to inform intervention selections. Assessment data also establish objective baseline performance information that provides a benchmark for progress monitoring regarding the effectiveness of intervention activities. There is a direct link from assessment to intervention to outcome evaluation.

Case Conceptualization within an Evidence-based Framework

It is important for case conceptualization to be delineated within an evidence-based framework. For social-emotional-and behavioral concerns, contemporary evidence-based practice relies heavily on cognitive-behavioral-systemic paradigms (Kendall, 2012c; Mash & Barkley, 2006; Weisz & Kazdin, 2010). These approaches are exceptionally compatible with practice in schools. CBT utilizes psychoeducational frameworks which are consistent with other forms of instruction in schools. CBT's emphasis on skill building through systematic instruction in social, coping, and problem-solving skills training integrates easily into school curricula; and thus when applied in therapeutic interventions, CBT strategies can lessen the stigmatization that is too often associated with psychological interventions. When schools develop adaptive skill building SEL programs, specialized applications of CBT for at-risk and severely needy students become more intense but build upon a coping and problem-solving framework that students have already experienced.

The systemic focus of contemporary EBI protocols is consistent with the paradigm shift in school psychology to address contextual and systemic issues that may contribute to or sustain social-emotional-behavioral problems (NASP, 2010a). Examples of this focus shift are seen in the organization of MTSS, in the development of school-wide programming like PBIS and trauma support programs like Cognitive Behavior Intervention for Trauma in Schools (CBITS, Jaycox, 2004), in attention to school supervision and support patterns for bullying prevention, in classroom management consultations, and in models for family-school problem-solving collaboration (Sheridan & Kratochwill, 2010; Simon, 2016).

Many student referrals are involuntary, initiated by teachers, parents, or other adults. Supervisors counsel supervisees regarding building therapeutic alliances and managing possible youth resistance to interventions. A particular risk for novice interventionists is to personalize oppositional behaviors from students. Supervisors can guide supervisees in applying motivational interviewing and similar strategies to engage challenging students who may fear change or loss of autonomy (W.R. Miller & Rollnick, 2012; Naar-King & Suarez, 2011; Reinke, Hermann, & Sprick, 2011).

School-centered Case Conceptualization: The Self-Understanding Model (SUM)

Case conceptualization in schools must be in line with contemporary best practice, capable of integrating EBIs into the school setting, practical, solution-focused, and problem-solving centered. Effective school-centered models must be capable of incorporating contextual and environmental variables into intervention planning. Clear linkage from assessment to intervention to outcomes must be maintained.

The important requirement within supervision is to teach a model that supervisees can eventually learn to independently use in their professional practice. There are a variety of case conceptualization models in clinical and school psychology literature. The Self-Understanding Model (SUM) meets the requirements just delineated and has been employed extensively in school settings (Kapp-Simon & Simon, 1991; Simon, 2012, 2016). We will use it as an example of a case conceptualization model appropriate for clinical supervision targeting social, emotional, and behavioral concerns.

Contemporary evidence-based therapeutic intervention is rooted in an integration of cognitive, behavioral, and systemic interventions (Kendall, 2012c; Simon, 2016; Weisz & Kazdin, 2010). Treatment assumptions include the following: Uncontrolled physiological reactions to stress interfere with effective coping and problem-solving. How information is processed through thoughts and cognitions directly impacts emotions. Understanding emotional experience and providing empathy are essential parts of effective therapy. Modifying the systems or the contexts that influence problem manifestation is often required to effect change and sustain improvements.

Building on these assumptions, the SUM case conceptualization model asserts the need to analyze symptom manifestation and maintenance by understanding the connections among a student's experiences, physical reactions to stressors, thoughts, feelings, and behaviors *and* the influence of context. Assessment must take into account each of these domains and then plan interventions as appropriate to address them in an integrated fashion. Guiding a student to gain awareness of the linkage among these factors will increase self-control and self-efficacy. For example, a student with social anxiety faced with a challenging social situation may experience intense *physical reactions* such as a racing heartbeat or tense stomach. His *thoughts* may quickly respond to these bodily reactions with a stream of negative self-talk and visual images of social failure. This will in turn exacerbate the intensity of his *feelings* of anxiety and may even escalate to panic. As his physical, cognitive, and emotional reactions accelerate, the *behavior* he displays is a rapid withdrawal from the social encounter as he isolates himself. Uninterrupted this pattern can become a self-reinforcing cycle escalating his anxiety and compromising any attempts at social interaction.

After this assessment in the SUM domains, an intervention plan in a CBT framework addresses each one of these domains. The student is taught physical self-calming strategies to control arousal. Cognitive intervention strategies are employed to help counter his overblown perception of threat. His instinctual flood of self-defeating thoughts is replaced with a self-instruction protocol that begins with an early recognition that his physical tension signals an emerging anxiety reaction. He learns a subvocal script to initiate his physical calming strategy followed by an individualized set of self-instructions to direct him to engage in planned coping responses. He uses behavioral rehearsal and role-plays to practice adaptive social participation skills; but they are paired with the coping responses in the other SUM domains.

SUM requires an assessment of systemic and contextual variables and an accompanying intervention plan as appropriate in these domains. For this socially anxious student, this process may involve a range of interpersonal skills training and social guidance activities such as the following: teacher-selected safe academic peer group; structured supports for any corollary performance anxiety; increased faculty supervision if his social awkwardness targets him for bullying; facilitated participation in noncompetitive social extracurricular activities (e.g., scouting, social service activities, etc.); and parent training to counter any unhealthy overprotection practices and to equip parents with skills to support social competency and prompt adaptive coping strategies. Contingent reinforcement plans can support healthy coping and social participation to counter the unfortunate temporary reinforcement gained through social withdrawal.

This brief assessment to intervention description demonstrates a comprehensive approach to case conceptualization that addresses individual and systemic factors

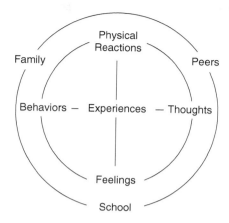

FIGURE 9.1   Case Conceptualization: The Self-Understanding Model
Source: Adapted from Simon, D.J. (2016). *School-centered interventions: Evidenced-based strategies for social, emotional, and academic success.* Washington, DC: American Psychological Association Press. Copyright 2016 by American Psychological Association Press. Adapted with permission.

in an integrated manner. School psychologists have the advantage of being able to design interventions that are integrated across individual, classroom, peer, and family domains. This multidimensional approach can significantly improve outcomes. EBI protocols for specific psychological disorders can be integrated into this approach (e.g., Kendall & Hedtke's [2006] Coping Cat program for anxiety).

This brief case example highlights a systematic and comprehensive case conceptualization protocol that can be taught to and then applied by supervisees. Early in training, the supervisor may take a more directive role in assessment and intervention planning. Consistent with the developmental component of DEP, supervisees should take increasing responsibility for intervention planning and monitoring the effects of problem-solving activities. The SUM schema provides an organizational format that can be used in supervision session planners. Facility with this process prepares supervisees for eventual independent case conceptualization and problem-solving. Figure 9.1 provides a graphic summary of the SUM components. Appendix 9A provides a sequential flow chart for applying the SUM approach. The *School-Centered Interventions* (Simon, 2016) text provides comprehensive treatment of this model with specific applications to the most common child and adolescent symptom profiles and a framework for intervention planning within a school setting.

Case Conceptualization for Academic Concerns

SUM provides a comprehensive protocol for case conceptualization for social, emotional, and behavioral concerns. A systematic approach to problem-solving is required for academic issues as well. For example, when a parent or teacher raises a concern regarding difficulties with reading skills, assessment must include collection of multimethod and multisource data regarding the various components of reading skills (i.e., phonemic awareness, alphabetic principle, accuracy and fluency in text, vocabulary, and comprehension; National Reading Panel, 2000). This process starts with teacher and parental reports followed by examination of student work samples, classroom assessment instruments, and curriculum-based measurement (CBM) data. Direct observation during routine reading instruction provides information on the student's participation, motivation, and skills in comparison to classmates; classroom climate and behavioral management variables that may influence learning; and the student's response to the teacher's class-wide instructions and individual interventions targeting his or her difficulties.

This initial analysis determines whether further assessment is required and points to what reading skills should be examined in greater detail. For example, if the initial data identify problems in reading fluency, then formal assessment may examine the subskills required for fluency. Then if test data reveal that weaknesses in phonics skills are central to fluency deficits, more intense and explicit instruction targeting phonics skills would be recommended. Instructional strategies would be prescribed from evidence-based approaches for both classroom and individualized instruction. Progress monitoring to assess the response to these additional interventions would involve frequent reviews of class assessment and CBM data and periodic formal assessment of phonics and reading fluency skills.

Since academic problems often co-occur with behavioral and emotional issues, it is important to routinely consider whether a student with academic challenges is also experiencing anxiety, depression, or other psychological concerns. When this is the case the SUM case conceptualization protocol can supplement information from the academic assessment and contribute to a comprehensive support plan for the student.

The similarity between the SUM and academic case conceptualization approaches is readily apparent. Each is multidimensional, collects data from various sources, addresses the subcomponents of the student's experience, and assesses contextual and systemic factors. Integrated assessment of academic and social-emotional concerns contributes to a comprehensive case conceptualization that guides selection of empirically supported interventions on behalf of the student. This permits a systematic link from assessment to intervention to outcome analysis.

Supervision of Consultation

As noted above, collaborative problem-solving has become a central focus within school psychology practice. Consultation skills are core competencies for school psychology and require specific focus within supervision (Harvey & Struzziero, 2008; Ysseldyke et al., 2006). An important advantage of effective consultation practice is that it benefits not only the client (generally the student) who may be the initial target of concern, but the consultee (i.e., teacher, parent, or adminis-trator) who works with and supports that client. When the skills of a teacher are enhanced during consultation, this increased expertise can be applied to other students and classroom instruction and management. Within consultation prac-tice, the consultee is primarily responsible for executing the intervention plan. This approach builds the professional capacity for the teacher and enables the school psychologist to influence a wider range of students.

Consultation relationships are defined differently from direct intervention rela-tionships. These relationships are voluntary and nonhierarchical. Both the con-sultant and the consultee bring expertise to the collaboration. Intervention plan-ning emerges from collaborative problem analysis, brainstorming of alternatives, and intervention selection. The consultee maintains the right to reject suggestions from the consultant. Even when a consultant is engaged with a request for shar-ing specific expertise (e.g., social supports for a child on the autism spectrum), the consultee has the responsibility for filtering the appropriateness and feasibility of recommended strategies and contributes classroom, school, or organization-specific knowledge regarding effective implementation. These defining param-eters of consultation practice are important to review in supervision. They influ-ence the character of the entry of the supervisee into a consultation relationship, foster a collaborative relationship, and define the dual purpose of consultation as assistance to student and teacher skill development. Understanding the shared responsibility in problem-solving collaboration can limit the tendency of novice consultants to feel like they must be the "answer person" with the wisdom to solve all aspects of psychological and instructional problems.

Supervision of skills for program development and consultation for systems change were addressed in Chapter 8's treatment of the Ecological component of DEP. Diversity and multicultural competence and multisystemic intervention strategies described there are applicable to consultation practice. The case con-ceptualization model provided above is relevant as well. Two common roles for consultation work will be addressed here: consultation with individual teachers and leadership/participation in multidisciplinary problem-solving teams.

Integration of Content and Process Skills

Consultation is an indirect form of service delivery that requires an integra-tion of content and process skills (Newman, 2012). All of the skills in assess-ment, instruction, intervention, and progress monitoring for both individual and systemic issues are required for effective consultation; but in addition, skills for engagement, collaboration, and motivation to support change and implementa-tion are essential. Similar to the importance of establishing an effective alliance with clients for direct service delivery, establishment and maintenance of effective collaborative relationships with consultees is of paramount importance and thus also a focus of supervision. Teachers are likely to request consultation when they feel stymied or even frustrated by a challenge in helping a student. It is important that supervisees form affirming consultation relationships founded on communicating empathy for the consultee, countering any unhelpful focus on self-blame or student-blame, and contributing positive energy that shared expertise will generate effective solutions.

Consultation requires both art and science. Supervisees benefit from learning a systematic framework for problem-solving. While the precise names of stages may differ slightly per consultation model, both behavioral and instructional problem-solving approaches generally include the following recursive steps: (a) problem definition, (b) data collection, (c) problem analysis, (d) intervention selection, (e) intervention implementation, (f) progress monitoring and intervention evaluation, (g) intervention modification as necessary (e.g., Kratochwill & Bergan, 1990; Rosenfield, 2014). The science of data-based decision-making and selection of evidence-based interventions is essential to this process; however, a mechanistic approach to collaboration that does not address professional support and relationship variables will prove insufficient (Rosenfield, Levinsohn-Klyap, & Cramer, 2010). Problem-solving is effective when it emerges from a creative and dynamic collaboration between contributing professionals with distinct expertise. Supervisors guide supervisees in the application of systematic problem-solving approaches with simultaneous focus on the interpersonal skills of empathy, productive inquiry, affirmation and trust building, integration of diverse points of view, and appropriate reinforcement for consultee effort and expertise.

Supervision Methods

Supervision methods applied to learning consultation skills are similar to those beneficial for other competencies. Rosenfield et al. (2010) described a process that matches methods to skill level of supervisee that is consistent with the DEP's Developmental component. Her progression moves from didactic presentations of concepts to modeling to simulation to direct practice under close supervision. Within supervision, she requires audio or video recording of consultation sessions and directs supervisees to complete process notes that highlight communication patterns, identify positive and problematic interactions, propose questions for supervision, and suggest next consultation steps. This approach is consistent with the DEP emphasis on self-reflection and monitoring. Segments of recordings are reviewed in supervision sessions with an attention to both process and content considerations.

Review of logs and recordings includes a focus on a variety of communication and problem-solving variables such as the following: empathy, encouragement, clarification, summarizing, checking for understanding, supportive nonverbals, collaborative language, information sharing, descriptive questioning, positive reinforcement, behavioral-specific problem formulation, and intervention recommendations. This approach is similar to observations of assessment and intervention work. Many elements of the *Counseling Skills Identification* recording system described in Chapter 7 and Appendix 7A are applicable. In his examination of supervision training for preservice consultants learning Rosenfield's model, Newman (2012) developed a coding system to analyze supervisee interactions with consultees and supervisor strategies. He found the dual focus on process and content to be beneficial and to contribute to appropriate developmental changes in supervisee skills and supervision focus. While review of both content and process is essential for supervision of consultation, it remains important to evaluate the outcome of consultation activities in terms of student progress, continued productive engagement with consultee, and, when available, reports of applications of strategies to additional students.

Managing Resistance to Change

Just as struggle with change can be evident in direct interventions, anxiety related to change or hesitancy to attempt new approaches can occur in consultation relationships. Supervisors can help supervisees ensure that their data collection and communication are clear and persuasive, that patience and persistence are necessary to achieve change, and that supportive intervention approaches such as motivational interviewing (W.R. Miller & Rollnick, 2012) are beneficial for challenging consultation relationships.

Tempering Consultant Anxiety

While novice consultants might fear resistance from consultees, our experience in supervision suggests that consultant anxiety can contribute to an unrealistic urgency in problem-solving. The need to quickly demonstrate competency and rapidly resolve student problems can have a negative effect if insufficient time and effort is placed in relationship building and careful problem definition. When this occurs, the consultant risks prematurely recommending interventions that might not address central concerns that would be revealed in a comprehensive problem analysis. Many problems that are initially presented as primarily behavioral concerns have learning or instructional match issues that contribute to problem manifestation; and certainly the reverse is true as well. Hasty intervention may miss the environmental or systemic aspects of problems and mistakenly focus strictly on within-student factors. Collaborative problem-solving should be focused and efficient but must involve accurate and complete assessment and data collection. Supervisory oversight monitors the efficiency, pace, and thoroughness of consultation activities.

Problem-solving Teams

The principles of consultation with an individual teacher are applicable to participation and/or leadership in school-wide problem-solving teams. Due to their expertise in data-based decision-making and problem-solving methods, school psychologists often serve as facilitators of multidisciplinary problem-solving teams. In addition to the skills already described, group leadership skills are required. Primary concern is to ensure that all members are able to contribute (i.e., managing monopolizers and drawing out reticent participants) and guiding the group process to remain faithful to systematic and empirically supported problem-solving methods. The *Problem-solving Team Observation Checklist* (Cates & Swerdlik, 2005) referenced in Chapter 7 and Appendix 7K is a tool for monitoring and supporting effective team functioning.

An additional benefit of team leadership is the ready identification of systemic needs and staff development requirements that emerges through repeated individual and single classroom problem-solving cases. For example, cumulative data developed in problem-solving teams might point to the need to examine particular areas of academic struggle. If written expression is a frequently raised academic concern regarding individual students, it may suggest the need to explore school-wide improvements in this area of curriculum or to research additional training and support resources for teachers. Similarly, if problem-solving teams discover that behavior incidents frequently occur in certain less structured or minimally supervised school locations, the consultant may bring this to the attention of administration; and faculty supervision responsibilities can be adjusted as a preventive measure. If in a high school with an intensely competitive and high achieving educational culture, problem-solving teams discover a high incidence of underachievement related to difficulties with stress management and performance anxiety, then, support programs might be developed school-wide to teach students coping and text taking skills. Within supervision, training in consultation skills progresses from a focus on core content and process skills for individual consultation and participation and eventual leadership in problem-solving teams to system-wide consultation and systemic intervention planning.

Problem-solving Supervision Incorporates Developmental and Ecological Components

Even though we have delineated each of the DEP components at length individually, in the process of problem-solving supervision, it is essential to integrate them within the supervisory process. When supervising problem-solving activities, the developmental status and case-specific skill levels of the supervisee will influence selection of supervision methods. Case conceptualization activities require and facilitate case planning, implementation, and outcome documentation which were initially designated as structured requirements in the developmental component. The formative feedback focus of the developmental component provides frequent direction for supervisees during problem-solving interventions. As supervisees gain competency in case conceptualization, they gradually function more independently. For the internship year, the developmental component's goals target independent functioning as a competent problem-solver across NASP practice domains and APA competency areas (for doctoral interns) by the conclusion of the training year.

The ecological component's incorporation of diversity and multicultural perspectives into problem-solving is essential throughout supervision in the problem-solving domain. The ecological perspective's emphasis on consideration of environmental, contextual, and systemic factors influences intervention selection. Engaging in problem-solving activities within an ecological framework requires employing interventions that address individual and systemic issues simultaneously. Analysis of ecological considerations also prompts program development and system change activities that go beyond a focus on individual intervention by implementing prevention and problem-solving initiatives that impact whole classrooms or the school-wide community.

Implementation Integrity of Problem-solving Component: Behavioral Markers

The following supervisory and supervised activities are consistent with the implementation of the Problem-solving component of DEP:

- data-based decision-making formats applied across intervention domains linking assessment to intervention to progress monitoring;
- application of a systematic case conceptualization model (must incorporate ecological considerations);
- intervention strategies targeting both individual and contextual or systemic variables in an integrated manner;
- consistent utilization of evidence-based strategies, monitoring fidelity of implementation, adapting to unique client and school setting needs as appropriate while maintaining core empirically supported intervention elements, collecting routine progress monitoring data to gauge effectiveness and guide decisions to modify protocols;
- supervisee involvement in intervention activity across multiple tiers of service delivery;
- application of problem-solving protocols to indirect service delivery through supervision of instructional and behavioral consultation.

Integrative DEP Case Example

We will now present a case example drawn directly from cases in our own clinical supervision experience that delineates the supervisory process and illustrates the integration of the Developmental, Ecological, and Problem-solving components of the DEP model. The within case commentary highlights supervisory responses that illustrate each component in action (D = Developmental; E = Ecological; and P = Problem-solving). All three are required for effective supervision.

CASE EXAMPLE WITHIN THE DEP SUPERVISION MODEL

The following case example illustrates the practical applicability of the DEP model for guiding the supervisory process. Sally, a school psychology intern in a high school placement, is approached by Pauline, a student she has begun to work with in a counseling support group. Pauline shares serious concerns about a friend, Mary, who has been depressed and begun talking about whether she would be better off dead. Pauline remembered that the school's universal suicide prevention program had addressed the important responsibilities that peers had for assisting each other when friends discussed harming themselves. This prevention program encouraged students to approach a trusted staff member or one of the presenting psychologists to share concerns about a friend in crisis. *[E: Intern participates in a systemic program that attempts to impact the culture of the school.]*

Pauline informs Sally that she is afraid for her friend but worried she will be angry at her for talking about it with a school staff member. Her friend has not specifically threatened suicide, but she is concerned over how depressed and withdrawn she has become. She asks Sally what she should do. Sally reassures Pauline that her concerns are valid and important and that she has taken appropriate action to seek help regarding her friend. As they discuss Pauline's concerns further, it becomes clear to Sally that despite the absence of a direct suicidal threat, this is a potentially serious situation requiring further assessment and intervention.

[P: Actively engaged in problem-solving activity.] She convinces Pauline to attempt to bring Mary in to see her together, making suggestions about how to encourage Mary, emphasizing how impressed she is with her concern for her friend, and noting that joining her in the meeting will make Mary feel more comfortable. While expressing confidence that Pauline's support will be successful in bringing Mary in for a session, Sally reassures her that she is committed to reaching out to Mary even if she is hesitant. Sally notes that she is in training as a psychologist, supervised by Ms. Grace Jones. *[D: As per supervision contract, intern identifies self as trainee and identifies supervisor and her role.]* She tells Pauline that she wants to make sure she is doing everything possible to be helpful to her and Mary and will be consulting with Ms. Grace Jones who may join them for the meeting to provide additional expert support.

Sally is in the second month of her internship. During the assessment stage in the development of her internship plan, Sally and her supervisor determined that one of her training goals would be to become more proficient in counseling skills. She has studied suicide assessment at the university but has never actually conducted a risk assessment. Her internship contract specifies that all concerns related to student safety must immediately be brought to her supervisor's attention. Right after meeting with Pauline, she contacts her supervisor to share the contents of this interview and consult about how best to proceed. Grace, her supervisor, takes time to review the situation with Sally and confirms that she has taken the correct action steps. Grace reviews the process of engaging in a suicide risk assessment and outlines the best way to proceed including planning ahead for following up with Mary's parents. Given the nature of the case, Sally's experience level, and the early stage of the internship, Grace decides she will join Sally in the session with the students. She encourages Sally to take the lead noting that she will lend support and ensure that the risk assessment is thorough and accurate. *[D: Entry-level assessment of intern skills levels defines focus of training. Supervision contract specifies actions to be taken in risk for harm situations. Supervisor provides direct instruction in suicide risk assessment (multimethod supervision). Supervisor provides formative feedback. Given critical nature of assessment and intern's early stage of training, supervisor will sit in next session.]*

Sally and her supervisor meet together with the girls. *[E: Involving peer in support of intervention is consistent with the ecological perspective.]* After Pauline expresses her concerns for her friend, Sally asks Mary if she would like Pauline to remain in the meeting for further support or whether she would like to explore these concerns privately. Still anxious about discussing these issues with unfamiliar school staff, Mary asks Pauline to stay for support; and the assessment process ensues. While Mary does not appear to be at immediate risk for self-harm, it is clear that she is clinically depressed and requires therapeutic intervention to address multiple concerns. She reports a recent break-up with a boyfriend, intense conflicts with her mother, significant academic difficulties, and some growing alcohol use "to try and take a break from my problems." When Mary initially resists Sally's recommendation that they meet together with her mother, Grace becomes more active. *[D: Since welfare of the client is the highest value, supervisor becomes more active to ensure positive outcome.]* She skillfully models an approach that not only achieves cautious agreement from Mary, but prepares her to appropriately share her concerns directly with her mother with their support. *[D: Supervisor modeling is part of multimethod supervision.] [E & P: Involving parents recognizes the need for a systemic intervention. This whole sequence is an example of problem-solving activity that will address both the individual and the context.]*

In a follow-up supervision session, Grace and Sally review the content and the process of the interview. They examine the content of Mary's disclosures and compare it to empirically supported suicide assessment protocols.

(Continued)

(*Continued*)

[P: Focus on evidence-based strategies is consistent with problem-solving component requirement.] The impact of the empathic interview and her friend's support and the dynamics of Sally's emerging relationship with Mary are processed. Grace guides Sally through a summary review of the interview exploring the connection between the data gathered and the decisions required for follow-up interventions. While Grace provides Sally with specific feedback and suggestions, she fosters her intern's self-reflection. *[D: Supervisor's feedback facilitates intern's self-monitoring.]* She repeatedly encourages Sally to share both her internal process during the session and her reflections on the intervention skills she demonstrated. They then plan the structure and approach for their upcoming meeting with Mary and her mother. *[P: Supervisor engages intern in specific practice in problem-solving.]* Finally, they summarize what other information and data would be required to begin to plan an intervention for Mary's depression and engage her in a multidimensional problem-solving process. They conclude the supervisory session with a review of their own process of working together. Grace and Sally comment on the dynamics of their cotherapy and the effectiveness of their postvention review. *[D & P: Processing the dynamics of their supervisory relationship is an important aspect of intern development. This dialogue models sound supervisory practice and collaborative problem-solving.]* Grace asks her intern if she has any further questions or needs at this time or any additional feedback regarding the supervisory process in this instance.

Documentation of student contacts is particularly important in circumstances like a suicide risk assessment. *[D: Practice is consistent with accountable recordkeeping and risk management.]* Grace directs Sally to draft a summary documentation of this intervention and share it with her. She in turn will document the supervisory process for her own records.

This case review illustrates the dynamic range of supervisory practice in school psychology. Within this single sequence, the supervisor engaged in multimethod supervision including direct instruction, modeling, cotherapy, live observation, and summary case review. *[D: Multimethod supervision is appropriate to case requirements and developmental level of intern.]* Complex developmental, ecological, and problem-solving dimensions of this case were addressed as they applied to the student's welfare, the context of her relationship to parents and peers, and the professional skill development of the intern towards competence in suicide risk assessment (e.g., Cramer, Johnson, McLaughlin, Rausch, & Conroy, 2013).

Developmental Considerations

In this example, the developmental perspective provided the supervisor with a framework for balancing her intern's training needs with the client's welfare. The supervisor prepared her supervisee for a critical intervention, provided her a developmentally appropriate level of responsibility, engaged in direct observation, modeled intervention strategies as a secondary cotherapist, facilitated processing the interaction, provided constructive feedback, and guided initial planning for problem-solving.

Ecological Considerations

Ecological considerations were evident on many levels. From the very beginning interventions were planned to address the individual and accompanying contextual factors. This student requires individual support for coping with her depression; but her debilitating affect cannot be remediated without attention and intervention in relation to familial, peer, and academic contexts. This systemic focus begins immediately with the joint session with her supportive friend and directly engages her mother's involvement at the outset of the intervention sequence. It will later need to address her academic stressors. Further assessment might indicate a need to address her involvement with peers that encourage underage drinking. This ecological perspective places Mary's issues with depression in context, provides a realistic picture of the complexity of the problems, and points to the multiple intervention targets required for effective problem-solving.

Problem-solving Considerations

The formal assessment of the student's suicidal risk and the identification of overwhelming stressors began the assessment and problem definition phase of the problem-solving domain. It can be anticipated that the session with the student and her mother will provide important insight into the nature and intensity of the student's depression, potential intervention requirements, and resources and barriers to change. Separate strands of intervention strategies need to be explored to address depression management, development of adaptive coping skills, resolution of family conflicts, healthy peer engagement, and academic support. Within each strand, the supervisor will guide the intern in collecting baseline data, choosing and implementing targeted EBI strategies, and monitoring the outcomes of their efforts.

Within each DEP domain, the supervisor demonstrated fidelity to the behavioral markers of this school psychology-specific supervision model.

Figure 9.2 provides a graphic summary of the DEP model. The arrows indicate the dynamic interaction among the developmental, ecological, and problem-solving components.

DEP Model of Supervision

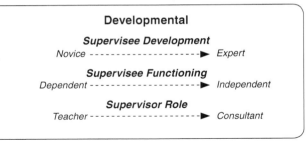

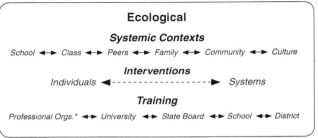

Orgs.* = Organizations

FIGURE 9.2   DEP Model of Supervision
Source: From Simon, D.J., Cruise, T.K., Huber, B.J., Newman, D.S., & Swerdlik, M.E. (2014). Supervision in school psychology: The Developmental/Ecological/Problem-solving model. *Psychology in the Schools, 51,* 636–645. Copyright 2014 by John Wiley and Sons. Reprinted with permission.

Summary

Empirically supported problem-solving is the central professional activity of school psychologists and thus a core focus within supervision. It is intrinsic to assessment, intervention, consultation, program development, and systems change activities. Problem-solving integrates all three DEP components to ensure the provision of effective service for clients and to effectively connect theory, research, and practice for supervisees amid the complexities of the field setting. Supervision teaches systematic case conceptualization that links assessment to intervention to outcome and prepares supervisees for independent problem-solving. DEP examines the integrity of delivery of evidence-based practices while addressing necessary adaptations to each unique school setting. The extended case example demonstrates the integration of the DEP supervision components and illustrates the behavior markers that monitor implementation integration of the Problem-solving component of DEP.

PART III

Professional Development for Supervisors and Credentialed School Psychologists

10

PROFESSIONAL DEVELOPMENT AND COLLEGIAL SUPPORT NETWORKS

School psychologists are well aware of legal-ethical mandates for continuing professional development (CPD) in order to maintain professional credentials such as the National School Psychologist Certification (NCSP) and state school psychology licenses required for school-based and independent practice. The supervisory skills explicated in this text require the same level of attention for ongoing professional development and collegial consultation as all other clinical skills. This chapter will discuss the rationale for continuing professional development related to supervision competencies and describe the various resources available to meet this need.

The Need for Continuing Professional Development

Consultation regarding supervisory practice is an essential professional responsibility. Targets of this consultation can include challenging cases or cases beyond the supervisor's area of expertise. Consultation regarding supervisory practice itself and challenges within the supervision relationship ensure best practice, increase the quality of support for the supervisee, and enhance supervisory skills for future practice. Engaging in this consultation also models for supervisees compliance with the ethical standard of not practicing beyond one's level of competency and responsible practice for the benefit of the supervisee.

When supervisors have a supervisee who is struggling with professional competencies, they face the challenge of balancing client needs, supervisee growth, and protecting the integrity of the profession. For example, supervising an intern who is resistant to feedback, has strained interpersonal relationships with staff, struggles to establish boundaries with adolescent clients, or has an unrealistic sense of self-confidence presents many challenges. Consulting with others who have worked with supervisees with similar characteristics can be very helpful in considering alternative approaches to addressing a particular concern, getting validation for current supervisory strategies, and addressing client and system needs. A supervisor may also be struggling with the high stakes gatekeeping function of supervision and would benefit from consultation when making the difficult decision of whether or not to approve for licensure a supervisee who is struggling to meet entry-level competency requirements.

Collegial support is essential even when supervisees are competent. Challenging supervisees to reach their fullest potential, supporting them in increasingly independent applications of psychological skills, and preparing them for competent work with complex individual and systemic issues requires supervisory expertise.

A supervisor's commitment to seeking professional development and consultation related to supervision models best practice for supervisees and underlines the importance of supervisory practice. When a supervisor seeks consultation regarding a challenging case or one beyond his or her personal competency, it can be beneficial to include the supervisee. When consultation relates to problems in supervisee professional competence, the supervisee would generally not be included but would still benefit from the supervisor's efforts to gain additional perspectives and strategies.

Self-assessment of Supervisory Skills

As noted above, school psychologists have a professional responsibility to self-monitor areas in which they need improvement and then seek out appropriate resources to address those needs. NASP offers an online self-assessment survey to assist school psychologists in identifying their professional development needs consistent with the 10 domains of the NASP Practice Model (2010a). (This survey can be accessed at http://apps.nasponline.org/standards-and-certification/survey/survey_launch.aspx.) However, this self-assessment does not address supervision competencies in any detail.

The DEP Self-reflection and Supervisor Feedback Survey (DEP-SSFS) (see Appendix 4A) was developed to specifically address supervisory practice within the DEP framework. It was primarily designed as a tool to facilitate self-reflection and communication between supervisors and their supervisees. This feedback form includes the behavioral markers corresponding to the various components of the DEP supervision model as described in previous chapters allowing the instrument to function as an integrity measure for implementation of the DEP supervision model. Sections include: (a) The Supervisory Relationship: Interpersonal Process; (b) Developmental Domain; (c) Ecological Domain; and the (d) Problem-solving Domain.

The DEP-SSFS is intended to be completed by both the supervisor and the supervisee. Supervisees can complete the survey and discuss results with supervisors to process the effectiveness of their supervisory relationship. This dialogue can improve the future character of supervisory sessions. It also models for the supervisee the importance of receiving feedback from clients. Supervisors can complete the survey to self-monitor their integrity of implementation of the DEP supervision model and to identify areas of supervision practice requiring more focus or continuing professional development.

Resources and Processes for Supervisor Professional Development

There are a variety of resources available for professional development in the area of supervision. Because the focus on supervisory competencies specific to school psychology is relatively new, it is necessary that supervisors actively seek out opportunities for enhancing their supervisory skills. We will now describe several resources and processes for supervisor consultation and professional development.

Self-assessment to Focus CPD Needs

Self-assessment is the first step in developing a plan for all professional skills areas (Armistead, 2014). Engaging in ongoing self-assessment and seeking targeted professional development related specifically to the competency area of supervision should represent as high a priority as the other areas of professional skills development. Supervisors should ask themselves the following questions related to their strengths, needs, and goals to identify their CPD needs:

- What are my strengths as a supervisor?
- What supervisor skills come easily to me?
- How can I build on these strengths?
- What areas of my supervision practice need improvement?
- What supervisor skills take significant energy and effort?
- How will I improve in areas that I find challenging or in which my skills are weaker?
- Identify one or more goals related to supervision between now and the end of the year.
- Identify one or more longer-term goals (i.e., beyond this year) for professional development as a supervisor.

Individual Collegial Consultation and District-level CPD Around Supervision Issues

Colleagues within a district represent a potential pool of possible consultants to draw upon for consultation around supervision issues. Supervisors seek out school psychologist colleagues with known experience and expertise in supervision who are willing to offer individual consultation or peer metasupervision. Concurrently, supervisors can also plan, develop, and participate in professional development about supervision in their school psychological services unit. If a supervisor is the only school psychologist serving a district, he or she can reach out to school psychologists working in neighboring districts or within the regional special education cooperative. For those in rural districts where the distance between districts is prohibitive to hold face-to-face meetings, phone or video conferencing (i.e., Skype, Google Hangout, etc.) or online discussion groups can be used.

As part of the individual- or district-level training and consultation, the supervisor can consider journaling, recording, and reviewing their supervision sessions with a colleague. Reviews of these types of work products related to supervision often lead to more productive consultation/peer supervision sessions.

Workshops and Online Discussion Groups or Electronic Mailing Groups

NASP, APA, and many state associations often sponsor supervision workshops. These professional development sessions not only provide supervisors with opportunities to learn new and sharpen existing supervision skills but also provide opportunities to connect with other supervisors who can serve as consultants and provide collegial support around supervision in the future.

NASP offers two options for peer consultation around supervision issues including the NASP Supervision Community and the NASP general electronic mailing list. The purpose of the NASP Supervision Community is to provide a forum and support for professionals with responsibility for supervising other psychologists. One can access this community at http://communities.nasponline.org/communities/community-home?CommunityKey=999cee2a-71f8-4cda-bc21-816f0c319dc5. NASP also has a general electronic mailing list that allows members to post questions. This forum has provided a medium for the discussion of a wide range of daily practice issues. It is likely that this group has many participants with supervision experience; however, we have rarely seen questions posted related to supervision. Perhaps *you* can begin the discussion!

Metasupervision Groups

Metasupervision groups are collegial support groups for sharing experiences related to supervision including both successes and challenges, discussing common issues, and engaging in supportive and collaborative problem-solving. Metasupervision groups can be facilitated by school psychologists with identified skill in supporting and training supervisors. These groups specifically focus on supervisory processes and skills; and their goals include: (a) promoting reflective practice as supervisors; (b) collegial support for professional growth as a supervisor; (c) consultation with colleagues about training and supervision issues; and (d) exchange of resources for training.

The multifaceted focus to these metasupervision groups includes both developing a range of supervisory skills and problem-solving specific challenging situations. Related to problem-solving, metasupervision provides support in addressing the multiple issues and challenges that emerge during supervision. Group members can seek ideas regarding specific client, system, or supervisory issues that are germane to supervision. Members share effective strategies, positive supervisory encounters, dilemmas, and resources. Importantly, metasupervision can provide significant support and consultation concerning specific challenges of cases that may require remediation and potential action consistent with the gatekeeper role of the supervisor. During collegial consultation that focuses on supervisory issues, attention is paid to the developmental stages of the supervisees based on their level of training, skill levels, and tasks occurring during a supervisory cycle. Metasupervision groups can also periodically address special topics such as interviewing interns or candidates for credentialed positions, writing letters of recommendation, dealing with specific problematic behaviors of supervisees, and providing feedback regarding interpersonal style and professional disposition issues.

Participating in a metasupervision group creates a culture that supports the professional growth of supervisors. However, in order to create this culture trust must be established between the participants. It is necessary to keep all discussions confidential and not shared outside of the metasupervision group. Assurance of this confidentiality will encourage participants to share not only their supervisee's challenges but also their own.

When supervisors share their participation in a metasupervision group with their supervisees, the supervisors are modeling collegial consultation as an essential practice for professional effectiveness and sustenance. It also communicates to supervisees the high priority that supervisees place on effective supervisory practice. Participation in metasupervision further enhances an understanding of best practice for supervision and fosters a network of professional support.

An example of a metasupervision group that has existed for a number of years is one that the authors have facilitated with supervisors who are part of the APA-accredited Illinois School Psychology Internship Consortium (ISPIC). Each metasupervision group is limited to six supervisors and two facilitators. The specific goals of ISPIC metasupervision groups include: (a) increasing reflective practice as supervisors; (b) providing collegial support for professional growth as a supervisor; (c) consulting with colleagues about training and supervision issues; (d) exchanging resources for training; (e) creating a culture that supports personal professional growth of supervisors; (f) modeling collegial consultation for interns as essential for professional sustenance; (g) enhancing an understanding for best practice for supervision; and (h) fostering a network for professional support that might carry over to other issues or challenges the supervisors might face.

The ISPIC metasupervision groups employ a consistent structure and methodology. Sessions are an hour long, convened through phone or video conferencing. Individual groups may choose to meet more frequently concerning specific issues, strategies, or topics. Prior to the group session, facilitators share reflection questions that are germane to the developmental stage of the training year (early, middle, or late). This advance organizer may also include reflection questions relevant to personal or ISPIC goals for supervisory skill development (e.g., self-care monitoring, frequency of feedback, and so forth). Appendix 10A provides examples. The group utilizes an open group process format facilitated by an experienced university trainer and a field supervisor. Responses to these questions are discussed followed by a general sharing by the participants of the status of their supervisory relationships. As the groups become more cohesive, participants will frequently share supervisory challenges with a request for problem-solving feedback from colleagues. Participants are also prompted by the facilitators to share successful supervision strategies and resources related to supervision or other professional competencies.

There is also specific attention during group discussion to supervisor progress on personal professional development goals for their roles as supervisors. At the annual fall ISPIC orientation session, supervisors set personal goals for their own professional development as supervisors. These personal goals may focus on applying specific supervision methods, improving documentation, increasing the frequency of feedback and evaluation, or other issues defined by each supervisor.

Participant feedback on these metasupervision groups has been extremely positive and has highlighted the value of the feedback they receive from participants and the time set aside to focus on this specific professional competency. Participants have noted the particular benefit of having a mix of experienced and novice supervisors which suggests that metasupervision groups should be mixed rather than divided into more advanced and beginning supervisors.

University Training Supervisors

Communicating with university educators about supervisees can prove a very valuable but unfortunately rarely used resource when supervising practicum students and interns. University training supervisors can acquaint field supervisors with the training background, strengths, needs, potential areas of difficulty, and goals of their supervisees. Faculty trainers can provide input on the preferred learning styles of supervisees within field-based contexts. We recommend that supervisors routinely reach out to introduce themselves, discuss the training site, and inquire about supervisee needs within the first weeks of any preprofessional training experience. Letters of recommendation are generally designed to support attainment of an internship position. An early contact with a university liaison might provide an opportunity for a more balanced description of supervisee strengths and needs and helps the supervised field experience get off to a solid start. The recently developed APPIC standard letter of reference form for doctoral candidates has attempted to address this issue by specifically asking for recommendations for growth (APPIC, 2015). Even if the field supervisor does not communicate with the university educator prior to the start of the practicum or internship, university educators, specifically the director of the student's graduate program in school psychology, should be involved early in the process when significant problems arise in supervision that may require remediation.

University educators can also be a general resource for development of supervisory skills as more extensive training, including metasupervision, is a required competency in doctoral programs. These university educators may also be able to facilitate the formation of metasupervision groups discussed above or serve in the role of an individual consultant/peer supervisor regarding the process of providing supervision. Most doctoral programs in school psychology teach courses and offer practica in supervision that supervisors may be able to attend. We have offered an orientation to effective supervision workshop for supervisors of our graduate students. University faculty may also serve as workshop instructors to offer continuing professional development training in the professional competency of supervision at state and regional conferences.

Self-study of the Supervision Literature

There exists a growing body of literature on effective supervisory practice in school psychology as well as in the other mental health fields such as clinical and counseling psychology, mental health counseling, and social work. Attendance at CPD workshops combined with planful self-study is important to further develop and refine one's supervisory skills. Supervisors have a responsibility to stay up-to-date on supervisory practices just as they do for other professional competencies such as assessment, intervention, and program development.

Related to self-study of the supervision literature, there are a number of professional journals that publish articles focusing specifically on supervision including *Professional Psychology: Research and Practice*; *Training and Education in Professional Psychology*; *Counselor Supervision*; *The Clinical Supervisor*; *Counselor Education and Supervision*; and *Supervision in Counseling: Interdisciplinary Issues and Research*. Although not focused specifically on supervision, school psychology journals such as *Psychology in the Schools*, *Journal of School Psychology*, *Journal of Applied School Psychology*, *School Psychology Quarterly*, *School Psychology International*, *Journal of Educational and Psychological Consultation*, and *School Psychology Review* all publish articles relevant for school psychology supervisors including addressing the topic of supervision in school psychology. These are all useful journals to monitor for relevant articles.

Resources for Supervisee CPD

As part of the supervision process for current supervisees, particularly interns, it is important for their current supervisors to address their CPD needs related to transitioning from the role of supervisee to a future role as supervisor. To facilitate the process of identifying resources for supervisory skills CPD, it is important to first define the parameters of the ongoing consultation between the current supervisor and supervisee regarding future consultation across all practice issues. Will the current supervisor continue to consult with the supervisee around future work as a supervisor and/or other professional issues? The supervisor should delineate potential additional resources for professional consultation relationships including suggesting methods for creating or accessing peer consultation groups related to the intern's future role as a supervisor.

In order to reach the above objectives related to assisting the supervisee in transitioning from the role of supervisee to that of supervisor, the training plan should include explicit goals for the supervisee related to training for supervision. It should be reflected as a specific competency target in the internship plan; and all interns should be required to engage in some form of supervision under close metasupervision. These activities would typically occur in the latter stages of the internship year and may involve supervision of an activity of a practicum student, paraprofessional staff, faculty involved in SEL curriculum, or other appropriate activities. The supervisor provides close metasupervision for the supervisee's practice of supervision occurring during training to ensure appropriate service delivery, to help the supervisee to prepare for an eventual role as supervisor, and to present the benefits of metasupervision for future supervisory practice.

SUPERVISOR REFLECTION ACTIVITY: CONTINUING PROFESSIONAL DEVELOPMENT

Building upon what you learned in this and previous chapters of this book, respond to the following questions:

1. What are your goals for professional development as a supervisor?
2. What supervisory skills, strategy, or activity would you like to try that you may have not engaged in before?
3. How could you arrange for participation in a metasupervision group or collegial consultation group?

Summary

The supervisory skills discussed in this text require the same level of attention for ongoing professional development and collegial consultation as all other clinical skills utilized in school psychology practice. Self-assessment represents the first stage of the process in identifying CPD needs. Identifying sources of CPD and building networks for collegial support should represent an important task for all school psychology supervisors. CPD resources targeting supervision include individual collegial consultation available in one's district or another district, if necessary, using electronic audio or video conferencing; workshops and online discussion groups sponsored by state or national school psychology organizations; formal metasupervision groups; university training supervisors; and self-study of the supervision literature. There should be planful discussions with interns about their eventual transition from the role of a supervisee to a future role as a supervisor. This planning should include defining the parameters of ongoing consultation with the current supervisor and identification of CPD resources.

11

DEP APPLIED TO SUPERVISION OF CREDENTIALED PSYCHOLOGISTS AND PSYCHOLOGICAL SERVICES

with Daniel S. Newman*

Much of the focus on clinical supervision has centered on preprofessional train-ing particularly supervision for practicum and internship field work. However, NASP's (2011a) position statement on supervision recommends that clinical supervision be available for all psychologists at every stage of their careers from internship to senior levels of practice. We noted in Chapter 1 that despite signifi-cant interest only a minority of credentialed school psychologists receive clinical supervision (Curtis et al., 2012). It is of particular concern that this is true for early career psychologists as well (Silva et al., 2016). This chapter will apply the prin-ciples and the strategies of the DEP supervision model to supervision of creden-tialed school psychologists and to supervision of psychological service programs which may be staffed by several psychologists and other educators or school-based mental health professionals.

As we have delineated throughout this text, formal clinical supervision includes evaluation and vicarious liability. While these principles may apply in some cases for early career psychologists, typically these features are not pre-sent in supervisory relationships for veteran psychologists. We interpret NASP's call for the availability of clinical supervision for all school psychologists as aspirational and involving formal consultation relationships that are regularly scheduled and goal oriented. This contrasts with periodic consultation relation-ships that may be single case specific and involve various consultants. For the purposes of this chapter, we will apply the DEP principles and strategies to for-mal consultation relationships and clinical supervision without the expectation that they would include evaluation and vicarious liability responsibilities. We believe the DEP approach can benefit mentoring, consultation, and supervisory relationships.

Lifelong Professional Development

The NASP (2010a) Practice Model requires school psychologists to participate in annual continuing education activities and directs school systems to ensure sufficient opportunities for professional development relevant to service delivery priorities. Both the APA (2010a) and NASP (2010d) ethics codes state the requirement that psychologists must practice within the boundaries of their competence and seek out training and consultation as necessary for appropriate and competent service to the public. The APA (2010b) *Model Act for State Licensure of Psychologists* recommends that state licensing boards set up procedures to ensure maintenance of professional competency.

Most state licensing and credentialing boards in psychology and education require documentation of minimum levels of continuing professional education credits to maintain licensure. NASP requires 75 hours of CPD credit, with 10 of these hours from NASP/APA approved CPD programs, for renewal of the NCSP national credential which occurs every 3 years. NASP promotes the utilization of its *Self-assessment for School Psychologists Survey* (available at www.nasponline. org/standards/survey/self-assessment-intro.aspx). This online self-assessment tool assists school psychologists in evaluating their own practices within the framework of the complete NASP Practice Model domains. The survey helps practicing school psychologists systematically reflect upon and define their own professional development needs. Unfortunately, it does not include assessment of supervision competencies. APA, NASP, and state school psychology associations have organized and promote an extensive array of professional development opportunities that are designed to both maintain professional competence and support practitioners in staying abreast of the latest empirically supported developments within the field. All of these credentialing and professional development requirements underscore the importance the field places on continuing education. These efforts are designed to enhance the professional capacity of psychologists and to protect the public by ensuring that practitioners remain current in best practice service delivery. The profession has the responsibility to the communities it serves to be competent; up-to-date in terms of assessment, consultation, and intervention protocols; and constantly striving to improve the quality of service delivery.

Multiple Paths for Professional Development

Professional development occurs in multiple ways. Attending workshops, pursuing continuing education credits through formal programs or self-study, and staying abreast of contemporary research and best practice literature are only some of the ways to enhance professional development. Improvements in practice and skills can involve consultation with colleagues or other professionals with specialized expertise, mentoring, collegial consultation groups, and formal clinical supervision.

Consultation

Solicitation of consultation is often case specific. Practitioners typically seek consultation when they encounter a particularly challenging or complex case, a unique client issue, a clinical problem they have less experience addressing, or uncommon levels of resistance or other barriers to intervention. Most school psychologists are general practitioners serving a wide and diverse range of student, faculty, and school needs. They are generally motivated to seek consultation from specialists in their own field who have a practice emphasis with either particular populations or certain kinds of program development or system change initiatives. Depending on the expertise required, the roles of consultant and consultee may alternate between the same pair of psychologists. Consultation relationships are generally not routinely scheduled and place no requirement on the consultee to implement suggestions from the consultant. Frequent utilization of consultation resources demonstrates a commitment to best practice, extra care in service to clients, and consistency with ethical requirements regarding practice within one's professional competencies.

Mentoring

Mentoring involves structured support from a senior staff psychologist to a junior colleague who is early in his or her career or new to a particular assignment or setting. It is becoming an increasingly common practice for school districts to assign mentors for all new faculty during their first year of employment within the district. The character of this form of mentorship can vary greatly. While it may include aspects similar to consultation or supervision, it also is likely to involve support in acculturation into a new faculty and school system and practical orientation to procedural nuts and bolts specific to a particular school setting.

NASP's requirements for first time renewal of the NCSP credential now requires successful completion of at least one academic year of professional support from either a mentor or a supervisor (NASP, 2015). For practice within a school setting, the mentor or supervisor should have a minimum of 3 years of experience. NASP recommends that this supervision or mentoring occur either individually or within a group at least an hour per week. Although mentoring can occur through the use of technology such as audio or video conferencing, supervision must be face-to-face. School psychologists not practicing within a school setting should engage a mentor or supervisor who is credentialed for practice in that setting. This requirement ensures that NCSP renewal candidates access structured support relationships. However, mentorship relationships are not evaluative; and a mentor does not have vicarious liability for the cases of the mentee. The only NCSP requirement is that the occurrence of supervision or mentorship is documented with the renewal application along with the requisite CPD credits. The importance of mentorship and the optimal structure of this relationship will be addressed further later in this chapter as a support option of particular importance when the administrative supervisor is not a school psychologist.

Collegial Consultation Groups

Collegial consultation groups are regularly scheduled peer consultation sessions. They often take the form of case presentations to colleagues. In school settings these groups may include school psychologists, social workers, and counselors. Sometimes these sessions may include presentation and discussion of new assessment or intervention strategies or new research findings. In some school districts, only a section of a discipline-specific program meeting is devoted to case consultation while the rest of the meeting focuses on general school or departmental business. By definition collegial groups are nonhierarchical and all members are expected to contribute their expertise.

Clinical Supervision

Clinical supervision is the most structured approach for professional development. As has been delineated throughout this text, clinical supervision involves a structured hierarchical relationship in which the supervisor has specific responsibilities for professional development of the psychologist, shares responsibility for client outcomes, and evaluates supervisee performance. Best practice in clinical supervision of already credentialed school psychologists should include a supervision contract specifying the structure, frequency, and character of supervision. It is particularly important to delineate methods and parameters for feedback and, if it is applicable, for evaluation.

Clinical supervision is particularly helpful in new areas of practice that require additional skill sets or serve a population less familiar to the credentialed school psychologist. Sometimes school psychologists require acquisition of skills in areas where they had not received significant training in either graduate school or during their internship year. For example, a supervisee might benefit from family intervention training or supervision for applying dialectical behavior therapy skills for working with chronically self-harming or suicidal adolescents within a high school assignment. Another experienced psychologist may have been recently assigned to work in a specialized program for students with severe autism but has never worked with this population previously. In each of these cases, structured clinical supervision is an appropriate approach to support the supervisee in a new practice area, foster professional development, and ensure competent service to youth, families, and other educators.

In most states, successful completion of one year of full time postdoctoral experience under clinical supervision is a prerequisite for psychology licensure for independent practice. Some doctoral-level school psychologists trained in APA-accredited graduate and internship programs seek "dual licensure" in the practice of clinical and school psychology. To achieve this status, candidates require more extensive supervised field work, generally a full 12 months predoctoral and an equivalent length postdoctoral supervised experience. This is in addition to passing relevant competency tests and other licensure eligibility requirements.

The NASP (2010c) *Standards for Credentialing of School Psychologists* requires that graduates of programs in related fields (i.e., clinical or counseling psychology) who strive for credentialing as school psychologists must meet NASP (2010b) *Standards for the Graduate Preparation of School Psychologists* in terms of course work, field experiences, and professional competencies. Graduate school psychology programs that provide opportunities for respecialization will generally require field experience in a school setting under clinical supervision. In these cases, supervision may focus on the school psychology-specific skills that may not have been addressed in related training. The assessment and goal setting activities described in the developmental component of the DEP model serve to individualize training targets for the professional development of respecialization candidates.

Consistent with NASP (2011a) standards, clinical supervisors should hold a valid license or appropriate state credential for the setting in which they practice and have a minimum of 3 years of full-time experience. Training in supervision skills is strongly recommended. As supervision is recognized as a distinct professional competency, like all other competencies it is an ethical and best practice imperative that supervisors practice within the bounds of their competencies and training. Admittedly, the profession is only recently providing the resources to address the need for specific training in supervisory skills; however, it is important that the field accelerate its efforts for training experienced psychologists in identified competencies for clinical supervision as delineated within the DEP model, other supervision models, and the growing literature on clinical supervision. We will address this issue in greater depth in Chapter 12.

Administrative and Clinical Supervision within School Psychology

Administrative supervision is a related but distinct practice compared to clinical supervision. Administrative supervisors typically serve in roles such as program directors, department chairpersons, or other school administrators. Their tasks may involve hiring, work assignments, legal compliance with educational mandates and other regulations related to service delivery, compliance with personnel matters including contractual requirements and performance evaluation, and coordination of multidisciplinary staff. Administrative supervisors oversee organizational structures, logistics, and the overall functioning of the service unit. They monitor outcomes of the service unit's activities and the satisfaction of all consumers of professional service delivery and relevant stakeholders. They ignore or focus less on the discipline-specific professional skills of practitioners. Their focus is on supervisees as employees rather than on the development of their professional skills. Administrative supervisors are usually trained and credentialed in educational administration but not necessarily in school psychology.

In contrast clinical supervision focuses on school psychology professional practice and thus requires training, knowledge, and credentialing in this discipline and competency in supervision of school psychologists. Clinical supervisors monitor and support practice consistent with professional standards. They promote ongoing professional development in school psychology competencies. Clinical supervisors work to ensure that systems of personnel evaluation are consistent with professional standards. In this regard, clinical supervisors may also serve as advocates for supervisees to support their engagement in activities delineated by the profession as best practices in psychological service delivery.

Unfortunately, administrative supervision for school psychologists is generally not provided by a psychologist. This supervision is typically provided by a special education director, assistant principal, or student services coordinator who may or may not be a credentialed psychologist. The NASP 2010 membership survey reported that 56.2% of responding school psychologists received administrative supervision from an administrator who was not a school psychologist. In the same survey, only 28.5% reported that they had received "systematic professional support, mentoring, and/or peer supervision for your professional practice as a school psychologist through an organized program provided by your district" (Curtis et al., 2012, p. 30).

When they are not the same person, it is important for clinical supervisors to collaborate with administrative supervisors to ensure appropriate service delivery and support for school psychologists. When both administrative and clinical supervision are provided by the same person who is a school psychologist, it is necessary to balance monitoring, evaluation, and support elements of supervision. Administrative responsibilities such as personnel evaluation which can impact employment retention and salary compensation may negatively impact the comfort and trust required for supervisees to share challenges and vulnerabilities in clinical supervision. However, this is not substantially different than the character of clinical supervision that supervisees experienced during their internship training when clinical supervisors were required to certify readiness for graduation and professional credentialing as part of their gatekeeper role.

Despite this potential limitation, Harvey and Struzziero (2008) suggest that there are overall advantages for school psychologists to receive both administrative and clinical supervision from a single professional who is a school psychologist. They cite Tromski-Klingshirn and Davis's (2007) study of counselors whose supervisors held both roles to support the benefits of the single role. In this study over 82% of supervisors reported no problems with the combined role in a single person arrangement and 72.5% judged it as beneficial. School psychologists play a unique role and bring a distinct skill set to their work in schools.

Some school psychologists struggle when administrative supervisors have an inadequate grasp of their work requirements, the skill sets required for effective practice, contemporary best practices, and new roles required to implement Multitier Systems of Support (MTSS). In these cases, it is clearly better for performance reviews and work assignments to be managed by an administrator who is a school psychologist. Harvey and Struzziero (2008) emphasize that competent clinical supervisors are effective systemic change leaders. Since contemporary role changes and progressive initiatives by school psychologists can be compromised by lack of administrative support, it is important for clinical supervisors to be able to advocate for school improvements that may change the focus of activities of school psychologists based on the overall needs of the school system. If the administrative supervisor and clinical supervisor have contrary views of effective practice, the supervisee would be placed in a compromised position.

We too have underlined the importance of program development and systemic change activities in training and clinical supervision under both the ecological and problem-solving components of the DEP framework. We perceive substantial advantages to the combined role of administrative and clinical supervisor in a single supervising psychologist. The practice of school psychology always remains in the broad context of the multidisciplinary framework of education and is subject to administrative oversight by school and district administrators who may have various educational backgrounds. However, support for daily clinical practice, ongoing professional development, and performance evaluation would be best managed by a supervisor with a comprehensive understanding of the requirements of best practice in school psychology and with competencies in supervision to support development of the skills necessary to be an effective school psychologist. In this arrangement it is important for administrative and clinical supervision role responsibilities to be clearly delineated and frequently processed as we have advocated for all clinical supervision relationships. Realistically data from both administrative and clinical oriented conferences will impact professional evaluation. The administrative/clinical supervisor can ensure opportunities for additional case consultation beyond this evaluative relationship by organizing and supporting collegial consultation through formats such as peer group supervision which will be highlighted later in this chapter (Newman, 2013).

When the clinical supervisor does not also share the administrative supervisory responsibility, it still remains important for administrative issues to be discussed in supervision. Holloway's (1995) SAS model describes the institution as a critical contextual factor to address in supervision. This is consistent with the DEP ecological perspective. Reviews of agency or district policies are relevant to supervision. A key supervisory task entails preparing supervisees to navigate the politics within systems to support efforts to influence best practice on behalf of students. This knowledge base and skill set is essential not only for program development activities but for implementation of diverse daily practice activities.

Clinical Supervision for Early Career Psychologists

Clinical supervision is relevant throughout the professional lifespan, with the early career being one of the most critical junctures for its application. The early career spans the first 5 (NASP) to 10 years (APA) practicing as a credentialed psychologist. In the counseling/therapy supervision literature, Rønnestad and Skovholt (2012) described the first 5 years of a psychologist's career as the novice professional phase. During this phase individuals are challenged with establishing a clearer sense of professional identity, gaining independence in their practice, overcoming disillusionment with their preparation/training, and exploring their professional roles. Succeeding in the face of these challenges results in professional growth; faltering may result in developmental stagnation. Clinical supervision accounting for these and other developmental needs can act as a protective factor for early career school psychologists (ECSPs; Silva et al., 2014).

Indeed, a number of rationales speak to the importance of clinical supervision in the early career. To begin with, let us state explicitly that graduate education does *not* conclude with a trainee's achievement of *terminal*-level competence for school psychology practice. Consistent with the developmental framework of the DEP model, competence at the end of graduate training may be thought of as an *entry-level* benchmark indicating readiness to enter the field (Fouad et al., 2009). The broad practice role advocated by the NASP (2010a) practice model, and concurrent expectations for applied practice across multiple tiers of service delivery (Ysseldyke & Reschly, 2014), makes it likely that ECSPs encounter novel situations and concerns not addressed during training (Silva et al., 2014). In schools, the wide-ranging variety of: (a) populations (e.g., levels of intensity of student needs; range of cultural and linguistic diversity of students and families; levels of experience of school faculty); (b) contexts/settings (e.g., grade levels; school culture; school size; urbanicity); and (c) problems (e.g., students' academic, behavioral, and social-emotional concerns across multiple tiers) presents a complex matrix requiring a lifetime of professional learning (Harvey & Pearrow, 2010).

Clinical supervisors may provide immediate support to ECSPs regarding gaps in knowledge or skills, or tensions related to personal and/or professional values (Falender & Shafranske, 2012). In other words, clinical supervisors work with early career supervisees to prioritize ongoing professional learning. A supervisory dyad or group can: (a) engage in a process of competency assessment (by self and others); (b) set goals regarding knowledge, skills, and values; (c) develop an individualized professional learning plan for selected domains; and (d) monitor progress towards goals (Williams & Monahon, 2014). Although the need for supervisory support in the early career seems self-evident, the reality remains that ECSPs are not always able to access the supervision they desire (Silva et al., 2016). In such instances alternative methods of support may be made available to ECSPs, as well as psychologists at other levels of development, as is described elsewhere in this chapter.

Becoming a Competent Supervisor

Even though ECSPs are presumably in a critical stage of their own development, they are often charged with becoming supervisors for practicum or internship trainees, sometimes as early as the fourth year of practice (NASP, 2010a). Despite the increasing recognition of supervision as a clinical competency area in health service psychology (APA, 2015a), some studies have demonstrated that school psychologist supervisors lack prior training and ongoing professional development on professional supervision (Cochrane, Salyers, & Ding, 2010; Ward, 2001).

One reason for a lack of supervision training may be because school psychology is the only health service psychology subfield in which the terminal degree for many (approximately two thirds) is nondoctoral. Although supervision training is now required for APA-accredited doctoral training programs, it is not required for NASP accreditation at the nondoctoral level. Within a limited time window for professional training in school psychology (i.e., 3 years), it is unlikely that sufficient course credits or time will be devoted to supervision training. However, since (a) many school psychologists go on to supervise, and (b) supervision is in fact a clinical competency domain, training programs at *all* (i.e., nondoctoral in addition to doctoral) levels may wish to consider how to provide some amount of supervision training. In short, if supervision is to be viewed as a core competency for school psychologists, trainees must learn and practice supervision just as they do other clinical skills such as assessment, consultation, and counseling.

Recent guidelines for clinical supervision in health service psychology by APA (2015a) outline seven domains of supervision that are integrated in the consideration of supervision competence, which are discussed elsewhere throughout this book: supervisor competence; diversity; supervisory relationship; professionalism; assessment/evaluation/feedback; professional competence problems; and ethics, legal, and regulatory considerations. Should an ESCP be faced with supervising a practicum student, intern, or professional psychologist without having supervision training, these domains provide a helpful starting point to target professional learning.

Clinical Supervision for Senior Psychologists

Veteran psychologists are frequently tabbed to provide supervision or mentorship for less experienced psychologists. However, these practitioners can benefit from career-long supervision as well. Supervisory support can foster new professional development ensuring that senior psychologists remain current with new research and contemporary guidelines for best practice. Not only can clinical supervision increase exposure to practice activities throughout the field, but this collaboration can counter professional isolation, diminish risks for burnout, and stimulate professional vibrancy. Supervision may particularly be helpful when a veteran school psychologist is the lone psychologist in the school. Psychologists who serve an entire district by themselves would benefit from a structured supervision or consultation relationship with a psychologist beyond their district. While many of the features of clinical supervision might be appropriate, vicarious liability and formal evaluation would not apply.

Senior psychologists can draw from their extensive experience base to address novel and complex problems. However, they may require training in new state-of-the-art strategies and exposure to current evidence-based literature. Even senior psychologists may encounter novel situations in crisis intervention or be required at some point in their careers to serve an unfamiliar population or grade level. Their integration of new strategies into their clinical repertoire enhances effectiveness and keeps them on the cutting edge of service delivery. Veteran practitioners are often formal or informal leaders in practice settings. Specific training in skills for supervision, leadership, and program development enhances their leadership skills and benefits younger colleagues.

Application of the DEP Model to Career Lifespan Supervision

NASP and APA documents on supervision place a particular emphasis on practicum and internship training. Throughout this text, many of our examples have centered on these critical training experiences as well. However, the principles and strategies of the DEP approach apply to already credentialed school psychologists as well. Consistent with NASP's (2011a) call for career-long clinical supervision, we will discuss the application of the DEP components to credentialed psychologists.

Developmental Component

Supervision has a role from the earliest days of training through the twilight of one's career. Of course, supervision considerations differ from one career stage to the next (Rønnestad & Skovholt, 2012). However, number of years practicing is not the only factor that determines a supervisee's professional supervision needs. Regardless of career stage, the development of *competency*, *proficiency*, and eventually *expertise* is determined by a combination of professional learning of content, opportunities for applied practice, and the diversity of those opportunities (e.g., across a variety of contexts/settings, populations, and problems) over time (Newman, 2013). What is more, professional learning in school psychology is a moving target, with the half-life of professional knowledge continuously shrinking (Neimeyer, Taylor, Rozensky, & Cox, 2014). Ongoing self-assessment, and assessment by others (e.g., supervisors, consumers of services such as teachers or students) helps practitioners (a) measure their current level of performance, and (b) prioritize professional learning needs.

We have previously discussed the applicability of supervision during training and the early career. Midcareer and veteran school psychologists may also benefit from accessing supervision. The following case example illustrates this point and suggests various avenues for this senior practitioner to receive supervisory support.

CASE EXAMPLE: SUPERVISION FOR A SKILLED SENIOR PRACTITIONER

Mary is a knowledgeable/skilled senior practitioner who works in a school district that is in the early stages of adopting an MTSS framework for service delivery and resource allocation, including an RtI approach to special education decision-making for students suspected of having specific learning disabilities. District leaders assume that school psychologists will be thought and action leaders in implementing this initiative. Although she is philosophically aligned with the district's changes, Mary lacks confidence that she has sufficient knowledge and skills to lead implementation efforts in her school. For example, curriculum-based measurement was only a minor focus in her graduate-level training 20 years ago, but will be central to the district's implementation of MTSS/RtI.

Mary is also currently supervising a school psychology intern that comes from a training program with an MTSS/RtI training emphasis. The intern presumably knows more than Mary about these topics, and although Mary is glad to learn from the intern, she feels self-conscious about her perceived knowledge and skill gaps. Through clinical supervision, Mary may learn, with scaffolding, how to apply new content (e.g., CBM procedures) and processes (e.g., how to facilitate systems-level change) that support her professional growth, and help her to successfully facilitate implementation of MTSS and RtI. Supervision can be developmentally tailored for Mary, building on her extensive prior knowledge and experiences. Supervision of supervision (i.e., metasupervision) may also be beneficial to Mary. Consistent with the developmental component of the DEP model, the roles of metasupervisor and mentor are well suited to senior practitioners with well-developed expertise. Metasupervision may help Mary consider approaches to bidirectional learning that feel safe and beneficial to her and her supervisee. As described later in this chapter, supervision and metasupervision need not occur one-on-one; other supervision formats such as peer group supervision with other district psychologists may be beneficial.

Professional Supports When Administrative Supervisor Is Not a School Psychologist

When employers do not provide professional supervision for school psychologists, the practitioners themselves become responsible for seeking mentorship and collegial consultation relationships. Examples of postgraduate professional support

TABLE 11.1 Examples of Postgraduate Professional Support Relationships

Psychologists in the same school district (varying career stages)
Senior psychologist in or out of district
Psychologists from a nearby district
Paid supervisor providing supervision of postdoctoral supervision requirements
Peers/fellow alumni from graduate training program
Former faculty from graduate training program
Former field supervisors from practica and internship experiences
Mentor met at professional conference coordinated via a professional organization, such as NASP or APA
Peers that are co-leaders in a professional organization
Mentor met at professional conference through informal networking

relationships are provided in Table 11.1. Such supports may be organized within schools, districts, or regions, and with differing levels of formality. The amount of structure in these relationships is variable, including expectations regarding pre-scheduling/coordination, incorporation of tools such as a contract to clarify relational expectations, and systematic processes such as structured peer group supervision (Newman et al., 2013).

Generally speaking, postgraduate support relationships differ from supervision in that they are nonevaluative (with the exception of postdoctoral supervision) and do not involve vicarious liability on behalf of the mentor or other source of support (NASP, 2016). Postgraduate support relationships may or may not be hierarchical. For example, a peer support group extending from one's training program cohort-mates would be nonhierarchical, but when an early career school psychologist is supported by a senior practitioner, a hierarchy may inevitably be present.

Structured Peer Group Supervision

A peer group supervision format may provide school psychologists at the inservice level one avenue to access supports for professional learning (Zins & Murphy, 1996). Similar to collegial consultation, peer group supervision is nonhierarchical and does not include a formal evaluation process (Bernard & Goodyear, 2014). No research yet exists supporting the application of structured peer group supervision (SPGS) in school psychology training or practice; but a modest research base in the counseling literature supports the effectiveness of the SPGS process for trainees at the preservice level (e.g., Borders, 1991; Borders, Brown, & Purgason, 2015; Lassiter, Napolitano, Culbreth, & Ng, 2008; Wilbur, Roberts-Wilbur, Hart, & Morris, 1994).

Although extant descriptions of SPGS in the literature differ in some ways, the basic stages include: a supervisee's initial request for help; a period of systematic inquiry by peer supervisors; presentation of systematic feedback by peer supervisors while the supervisee is silent; a pause or break in time for the supervisee to reflect; a response statement by the supervisee regarding the feedback, and proposed next action steps; and a time for debriefing or group discussion. The supervisee requesting assistance may bring data (e.g., a video recording of a consultation session secured with teacher permission; data related to a student's academic or behavioral performance) to the supervision table. Peer supervisors may take on roles such as observing process dynamics or providing feedback from a particular point of view (e.g., a parent of a particular culture).

The SPGS process seems to hold promise for psychologists who desire supervision but do not otherwise have access to supervision. A district with many psychologists could have several small SPGS groups; or psychologists from a smaller school district or districts might come together to meet. SPGS may even be possible via videoconference. Through SPGS, resources can be streamlined; and professional learning and collaboration can be proliferated. In turn, SPGS may act as a protective factor against issues such as practicing outside of boundaries of professional competence and professional burnout. Since the SPGS research base is lacking, it would be useful for practitioners who apply this process to document its effectiveness, including challenges and successes, and share those with other interested professionals. Peer supervision, whether the process is structured or not, may be a key way to close the gap between practitioners' desire for supervision and their limited access of supervision.

Ecological Component

The ecological domain of the DEP model focuses on psychology's emphasis on environmental and systemic change to support individual students and to promote the academic and psychological welfare of all students. The ecological perspective's emphasis on incorporating contextual factors into intervention and program development activities requires that interventions for students are coordinated with supports and adaptive changes within the classroom, school, peer group, family, and community. The field's focus on systemic interventions has emerged over time; but key documents defining current best practice postdate the graduate training of many practitioners: the *Model for Comprehensive and Integrated School Psychological Services* (NASP Practice Model, 2010a), *School Psychology: A Blueprint for training and practice III* (Ysseldyke et al., 2006), and the APA Competency Benchmarks (2011).

Most veteran credentialed psychologists were not trained in systemic interventions; and thus this is a critical area of focus for professional development and clinical supervision. Shifting practices related to assessment and intervention and the evolution toward MTSS models to address the needs of all students require seasoned practitioners to adapt present skill sets to new paradigms and to learn additional skill sets. These areas can become focal points for ongoing professional development, collegial consultation, and/or formal clinical supervision.

School psychology's understanding of the effective adaptation of services to account for all manner of diversity is rapidly evolving and is certainly an essential focus for clinical supervision for psychologists at all levels of experience. Achieving diversity competency is a journey rather than an endpoint. Changing patterns and attitudes toward immigration have created new challenges in understanding and serving families from many cultures. Literature on multicultural competency has greatly expanded over the last decade in relation to both intervention and supervision practices (e.g., Falender et al., 2014; Falicov, 2014b; McGoldrick et al., 2005). Changes in our understanding of sexual minority issues has been rapid, at times revolutionary. As schools grapple with how to support LGBT students, school psychologists play an important role. This area is a critical target for consultation or clinical supervision for all school psychologists.

Problem-solving Component

Problem-solving activity remains the central function of psychological practice. For the benefit of the children, families, and school staff served, it is essential that all school psychologists have the ready availability of consultation regarding all aspects of assessment and intervention practice. The problem-solving domain is the practice area that all psychologists are most concerned to address in clinical supervision at all levels of professional experience.

Clinical supervision for veteran psychologists has several key functions; and we highlight three central purposes. First of all, it provides quality control for services to clients by engaging the supervisor and supervisee in collaborative case conceptualization and intervention planning. Second, it supports the professional development of the supervisee in application of state-of-the art empirically supported practices. Additionally, it supports supervisees in adapting to and mastering the changing roles and service delivery systems that continue to emerge within the field of school psychology.

Evidence-based Practice

Problem-solving is rooted in sound assessment and intervention practices. Best practice in these areas continues to be refined by new research and the development of new assessment instruments and methods. Data-based decision-making applied to clinical practice activities has changed significantly in recent years; and for many veteran credentialed psychologists, these approaches may be different than their own graduate training. New assessment instruments; data collection, analysis, and reporting methods; novel approaches to linking assessment to intervention; contemporary evidence-based intervention protocols; universal screening tools; school-wide behavior supports; and advances in systematic social, coping, and problem-solving curricula all provide critical content for clinical supervision. The focus of supervision will vary greatly depending upon the competencies of the credentialed supervisee and the character of the continuing professional development activities attended.

The link between assessment and intervention in both academic and mental health arenas requires diagnostic formulations that point to the implementation of specific empirically supported intervention strategies. The academic curricular emphasis on scientifically supported instructional methods parallels innovations in school-centered mental health intervention. In the social-emotional-behavioral domain, research is defining differential intervention protocols related to specific symptom profiles and psychological disorders (Kendall, 2012b; Simon, 2016; Weisz & Kazdin, 2010). Evidence-based school-centered intervention work requires school psychologists to understand clinical diagnostic profiles, develop competencies in implementation of contemporary empirically supported intervention protocols, and master adaptations to the unique characteristics of clients and the school setting (Simon, 2016). The complex challenges involved in this contemporary framework for intervention planning, implementation fidelity monitoring, and outcome assessment are fruitful targets for clinical supervision with a heightened emphasis on evidence-based strategies.

Integrated Individual and Systemic Interventions

Contemporary best practice is not merely focused on the individual student and his or her characteristics and concerns but addresses the student in context. Instructional variables, classroom and school-wide culture and practices, family system characteristics, peer cultures, and community factors all must be taken into account when defining student problems and designing interventions. Current best practice intervenes with the individual student and the various environmental and systemic influences simultaneously (Doll & Cummings, 2008; Simon, 2016). School psychologists are expected to demonstrate competency in program development and systems change (Castillo & Curtis, 2014; Forman, 2015; NASP, 2010a). Family-school collaboration in problem-solving is incorporated into every level of multitiered service delivery (G. Miller, Lines, & Fleming, 2014; Sheridan & Kratochwill, 2010).

Problem-solving strategies require interventions targeting individual skills and behaviors, family interactions and parenting practices, classroom management and instructional practices, school climate and culture, and community challenges and supports (Simon, 2016). Interventions are more powerful and effective when complementary strategies address both individual student development and these other contextual or systemic domains as necessary in an integrated fashion.

Academic and instructional assessment and intervention has shifted from an exclusive focus on the individual learner to also examine instructional methodologies, appropriateness of curriculum levels of content, needs and strategies to adapt curriculum, and classroom and other environmental factors (Christ, 2008; Rosenfield, 2008). Contemporary assessment strategies examine these multiple factors in the process of establishing a link between assessment and intervention. Best practices for assessment continue to be multisource and multimethod but specifically incorporate contextual and systemic variables into problem analysis and thus intervention. For example, the Review, Interview, Observe, Test—Instruction, Curriculum, Environment, Learner Matrix (RIOT-ICEL) is an organizational framework employed to structure assessment practices that are multidimensional and comprehensive and consistent with an MTSS/RtI paradigm (Christ, 2008; Hosp, 2008). RIOT addresses multiple measures and sources. ICEL addresses the domains that may affect student learning.

These paradigm shifts that require integration of individual and systemic variables require not only new ways of thinking about problem-solving but additional skill sets that many veteran school psychologists would only have been first exposed to in professional development after graduate training. Incorporation of these diverse variables requires extensive experience and practice with consultation, coaching, or supervision supports even for recently credentialed psychologists who may have been extensively trained in these frameworks in preprofessional training. This complexity of individual, contextual, and systemic variables addressed in problem-solving for academic or social-emotional-behavioral concerns requires new case conceptualization practices that require support from training, consultation, and supervision.

Population-based Services and MTSS

The emerging commitment in school psychology to population-based services executed through MTSS also requires additional skillsets for practitioners. Universal screening and school-wide social-emotional learning curricula require expanded skills. Mental health wellness initiatives, prevention work, and early intervention programming have changed role expectations for school psychologists and require training, consultation, and supervision to increase practitioner competencies and to ensure effective programming. Introduction of these innovative practices not only requires robust competencies in assessment and intervention but capabilities for program development and system change activities. The breadth of expectations and the diverse competencies required for effective design and implementation of population-based approaches and MTSS underlines the needs and potential benefits of routine clinical supervision for credentialed psychologists.

The Problem-solving Component and Supervision

Most school psychologists are general practitioners working in consultation, prevention, assessment, intervention, and program development activities addressing both standard and special needs populations. Clinical supervision can be tailored to address strengths and support needs in the problem-solving domain for each practitioner. Supervisors can tap specialists to assist in supervision of activities that are beyond their core competencies. Many credentialed supervisees are providing clinical supervision to practicum and intern students. It is essential that they are well-versed and proficient with the contemporary focus on evidence-based practice, intervention planning that integrates individual and systemic variables, and MTSS. Their own professional-level clinical supervision can include metasupervision focused on supervisory competencies. Effective clinical supervision for credentialed psychologists supports their professional development, ensures that clients are receiving state-of-the-art services, and protects against professional burnout.

A Comprehensive Support Plan for Psychologists and Psychological Service Delivery

We have articulated the principal features of the application of the DEP supervision model to credentialed psychologists. School psychologists who serve in the combined role of administrative and clinical supervisors are often also responsible for administration and supervision of the complete program of psychological service delivery for their school district. Service delivery is often coordinated with social workers, counselors, special educators, lead teachers, speech therapists, and other specialists. Program design including the supports for capacity building of staff should involve a collaborative effort. We recommend the following as essential elements for a comprehensive support plan for psychologists and psychological service delivery.

- Best practice requires all school psychologists to have access to clinical supervision from an experienced and competent school psychologist (NASP, 2011a).
- Early career psychologists should receive a minimum of 1–2 years of weekly clinical supervision individualized to address their professional development needs. The goal is to solidify their professional competencies specific to their employment setting requirements and all domains of the NASP Practice Model that are relevant in that setting. NASP *Blueprint III* suggests that expert-level competencies can only be achieved after significant postgraduate experience and generally only in some areas of practice that are the focus of daily practice (Ysseldyke et al., 2006).
- All school psychologists new to the school district or other practice setting should be assigned a mentor who is a veteran psychologist to not only address procedural orientation but to provide information on the culture of the school and its community and to provide consultation regarding professional activities.
- Collegial consultation groups should be organized either within district or across districts where psychologists can present cases and program dilemmas and receive feedback and suggestions from colleagues.

- Staff psychologists should be encouraged to develop a subspecialty that not only enhances their own professional development but benefits the psychological service team as a whole. Presentations regarding this specialty area to colleagues during collegial consultation sessions can cement their expertise and prepare them to be in-house consultants for this area of practice.
- Not every psychologist will be a primary clinical supervisor of either an intern or an early career psychologist; but every psychologist should participate in at least some individual case consultation or supervision. Thus core universal training in supervision skills should be available to all psychologists. Metasupervision groups can be assembled at the district or regional level to support clinical supervisors.
- Each psychologist's personal professional growth plan developed as part of the school district's performance review procedures should define specific areas of professional development, training and supervision requirements, planned activities, and outcome criteria. If the psychologist is learning a new skill set or intervention protocol, he or she can share learnings and new information with the collegial consultation group to benefit the team's overall practice effectiveness.
- Whenever possible, clinical supervision, particularly when it includes performance evaluation, should employ multiple methods.
- The entire psychologist team should participate in periodic reviews of psychological service delivery. Accountability and systematic collection of outcome data are important elements of program practice for all psychological services units.
  - The framework for excellence is defined by the NASP Practice Model (2010a), literature on best practices, summaries of evidence-based practice, sufficient attention to all multitiered levels of support and intervention, assessment of needs for systemic change, and evaluation of the status of collaboration with all key stakeholders, i.e., parents, teachers, school administrators, collaborating community practitioners, and relevant community agencies.
  - Assessment of the status of current psychological service delivery based on a review of elements just noted above should define needs for service improvement and identify service gaps. Feedback from key stakeholders should be a routine component of program reviews.
  - Pilot projects to introduce new programs can be developed in response to this review process. It is important to note that it is essential that all new programming include substantial education for all stakeholders regarding its relevance and importance; and sufficient capacity building and assignment of resources is required for initial success and sustenance of new state-of-the-art initiatives.
  - Leadership within school psychology teams should clearly articulate and attempt to gain the support of administrators for a vision and plan

for the best practice of school psychology consistent with the NASP Practice Model. The identification of professional activities and the essential resources to support them, including personnel, funding, and space, is required to make psychological service delivery effective for the benefit of all students.

- Leadership of psychology service units requires competencies in core clinical skills, in program development, and in clinical supervision. Leadership provides a blend of management, innovation, accountability, and advocacy to support school psychologists and the youth, families, and faculty they serve.

SUPERVISOR REFLECTION ACTIVITY: SELF-ASSESSMENT AND PROFESSIONAL DEVELOPMENT

Take a moment to complete the online *Self-assessment for School Psychologists Survey* (http://apps.nasponline.org/standards-and-certification/survey/survey_launch.aspx). Upon completion, define three professional development goals for yourself. If you are or soon will be a clinical supervisor, add an additional goal related to supervisory competencies.

Summary

NASP recommends that clinical supervision be available for all psychologists at every stage of their careers from internship to senior levels of practice. Professional learning in school psychology is a moving target, with the half-life of professional knowledge continuously shrinking. DEP provides a comprehensive framework for mentoring, consultation, and supervisory relationships that is applicable to credentialed psychologists at all levels of experience. These supports are particularly important during early career and when veteran psychologists transition to serve different populations or must apply new research and service delivery models. DEP principles guide supervision of psychological services defining staff professional development needs and ensuring that service delivery is ecologically sensitive and empirically sound.

Note

* Daniel S. Newman, Ph.D., University of Cincinnati and Routledge Series Editor for Consultation, Supervision, and Professional Learning in School Psychology.

PART IV

Preparing for the Future of Supervision within School Psychology

12

TOUCHING THE FUTURE

Teaching Supervision to Future Supervisors

The American Psychological Association (APA, 2011, 2015b) has called for explicit training and supervised practice in supervision skills to be a required component of graduate training for all doctoral-level psychologists who are preparing to be health service providers. NASP (2011a) has also highlighted the need for training in supervision skills for all those who supervise school psychologists at both the preservice and credentialed levels but does not yet include it as a required component of preservice training.

Preparation for being an effective supervisor requires a multistage developmental process. The training begins very early in the school psychology graduate student's professional training with the first exposure to clinical supervision in fieldwork or practica. The training continues with graduate coursework in supervision and extends though internship and supervision received as an early career school psychologist. Other veteran school psychologists interested in assuming the role of a clinical supervisor or who have already been assigned this role by their administrator will gain this training through continuing professional development activities. The purpose of this chapter is to review the various methods by which training in effective supervisory practices can be provided to preservice, early career, and veteran school psychologists.

Supervision Training for Preservice and Early Career School Psychologists

Initial Fieldwork and Practica

Coursework in supervision is more easily built into doctoral-level training where the number of courses is expanded. However, graduate programs need to build in initial training in supervision for specialist-level students as well since most field supervisors of school psychology graduate students function at the specialist level. Appropriate preparation for field experiences should include a review of effective supervisory process and the benefits of being a proactive supervisee (Newman, 2013).

For both doctoral- and specialist-level trainees, it is during the initial fieldwork or practicum experience that the supervisee is first learning the meaning of clinical supervision including what to expect from a supervisor and qualities of an effective supervisee. This can be supported through readings on effective supervision (e.g., Berger & Bucholtz, 1993; Corey et al., 2010; Joyce-Beaulieu & Rossen, 2016; Newman, 2013) and direct attention to the supervisee characteristics necessary for productive field experiences beginning with the practicum. In addition, it is beginning with these initial supervisory experiences that the supervisory process should be explicit and transparent with sufficient opportunities to process the supervisory relationship and its methods. This transparency and opportunities to process the supervisory relationship should occur throughout the trainees' supervised practicum and internship experiences.

Readings and practicum experiences can be supplemented with meetings and seminars that prepare students for field training and should include information on what to expect from supervision and what behaviors and attitudes enhance the learning experience for the supervisee. University programs should also require a written supervision contract that delineates roles, responsibilities, and expectations for field-based training. The topic of contracting was discussed in greater depth in Chapter 7. Routine formative feedback and summative evaluation throughout graduate education prepares the supervisee for this dynamic process in supervision and assists in delineation of individualized training goals for field experiences. Finally, coursework that accompanies initial field experiences such as an introduction to school psychology seminar can introduce supervisory best practices.

Graduate Coursework in Clinical Supervision

Due to the number of required courses based on NASP program approval standards, there is little room for additional courses at the specialist level of school psychology training. Therefore, it is typically the case that only doctoral trainees receive graduate coursework and supervised practice in clinical supervision. At the specialist level of training, it would be beneficial for graduate programs to incorporate sufficient training in effective supervision into the courses that support practica and to offer a workshop on clinical supervision to all students in advance of their internship.

We will describe recommended elements of graduate courses which can be condensed as necessary into a workshop format. Typically, this coursework and supervised practice would occur preinternship in the later course requirements in the doctoral program. The typical graduate course in supervision follows a sequence of topics similar to what was presented in this text including: (a) iden-tification of roles and responsibilities; (b) review of literature on characteristics of effective supervisory relationships; (c) presentation of a comprehensive model of supervision consistent with best practice in the field; (d) techniques of mul-timethod supervision; (e) skills for effective feedback and evaluation; (f) essential tools for recordkeeping, accountability, and risk management; (g) legal and ethical issues relevant to supervision; (h) competency in diversity and multicultural fac-tors relevant to supervision; and (i) delineation of a developmental framework for mastering core problem-solving with supervisory input. See Appendix 12A for a sample doctoral-level supervision course syllabus.

Within graduate programs in school psychology there can be a ladder of expe-rience levels (referred to as hierarchical supervision) wherein more experienced students have some opportunity to supervise aspects of the field experience of less experienced students under close metasupervision. This can be built into a graduate course in supervision (see syllabus in Appendix 12A) or be offered as an advanced practicum.

Capstone Internship

During the later stages of the capstone internship, supervisees should be afforded opportunities to engage in supervision under vigilant metasupervision. During internship, interns may supervise some activities of practicum students, moni-tor implementation of programming by paraprofessionals, or supervise teaching faculty in implementation of new programming (e.g., SEL curriculum). Routine processing of the supervisory relationship during internship also helps to prepare the intern for an eventual role as a supervisor.

Early Career

Early career psychologists should continue to receive weekly clinical supervision for the first two years of professional employment. This was discussed in more depth in Chapter 11. One component of this supervision should be focused on preparation for eventual assumption of supervisory roles. Sample activities can include collaborating with a primary supervisor on specific cases of his or her preservice supervisees. When early career psychologists become primary supervi-sors, they can be supported through collegial metasupervision support groups as described in Chapter 10.

Supervision Training for Veteran School Psychologists

In the sections above we have discussed a vision for training new supervisors beginning with a structured sequence from beginning of graduate school through early career; however, this does *not* address the reality that most practitioners and active supervisors have received little to minimal training in effective supervision (and may not even think they require it). In this section we address training veteran school psychologists and active supervisors to be effective clinical supervisors as part of their continuing professional development. To illustrate a broad range of potential training initiatives, we will share examples from within our home state of Illinois and then suggest some additional training and support activities to address this critical need. These various approaches were designed to address three areas: (a) the need for a clear description of supervisory activities that matched contemporary best practice; (b) the availability of multifaceted opportunities to engage veteran supervisors in training; and (c) creation of substantive supports to entice and then recognize participation in professional development.

In Illinois a group of university school psychology educators recognized the need to provide a comprehensive model for professional development for veteran school psychologists who were either interested in assuming a supervisory role or were already active supervisors. These school psychology faculty teamed with our state school psychology organization, the Illinois School Psychologists Association (ISPA), to initiate a state-wide professional development program in supervision. In addition, some individual universities conducted training sessions for fieldwork supervisors of their students. Our state's most comprehensive program for professional development in supervision has been conducted by the Illinois School Psychology Internship Consortium (ISPIC), a state-wide APA-accredited doctoral-level internship program. We feel that elements of many of these strategies can be generalized to other states that wish to either increase the pool of trained supervisors and/or improve the effectiveness of those currently providing supervision. We will now describe the specifics of these initiatives.

Adoption of a Single Supervision Model for Professional Development

For purposes of our state-wide initiative for providing continuing professional development in effective supervisory practices, we have adopted the Developmental, Ecological, Problem-solving model (DEP) explicated in previous chapters. We adopted this supervision model as it is school psychology-specific, defines a common core of effective supervisory practices that is task-specific, and identifies supervisory competencies with behavioral markers consistent with competency-based training initiatives. The DEP model emphasizes the need to provide transparency to demystify the supervisory process, articulates content that can serve as a basis for a supervision contract, and facilitates routine processing of the supervisory relationship. The adoption of the DEP school psychology-specific supervision model also provides a common language and framework for our regional and state-wide supervisor education initiatives, can serve as content for university coursework for graduate students for their future roles in supervision, and emphasizes training in supervision competency as a last stage goal of internship training.

The adoption of the DEP model allows for a common set of effective supervisory practices or standards throughout the state. To monitor implementation integrity, the DEP Self-reflection and Supervisor Feedback Survey (DEP-SSFS) (discussed in more detail in Chapter 10) can be completed from both the supervisor and supervisee perspectives. This survey assesses the DEP behavior markers for best practice in supervision. It is understood that best practices will continue to evolve over time and must be revised as necessary.

Supervision Manual

A manual outlining best practices in supervision that is endorsed by the state board of education, field sites represented by the state school psychology professional organization, and in-state university programs can help promote effective supervisory practices. This manual can outline the practices consistent with the state-wide supervision model and summarize best practices. The manual would include a sample supervision contract and sample forms for planning and recordkeeping. It would address the timing, character, and format for feedback and evaluation including outlining preferred practices for university and field site collaboration to address supervisee problems of professional competency. The requirement for multimethod supervision would be delineated. Any state-specific requirements regarding internship and postdoctoral training would be specified.

State-wide and University-based Workshops on Supervision

Training workshops that foster implementation of best practices and reflective supervision can be designed specifically for school psychologists who are supervising interns and/or practicum students for the first time and for experienced supervisors. In Illinois we offer beginning and advanced supervision seminars at state-wide intern/intern supervisor conferences and at a regularly scheduled annual state-wide school psychology conference.

The state-wide intern/intern supervisor annual conference is the result of a collaborative effort of the Directors of (Illinois) School Psychology Programs (DUSPP) and the Illinois School Psychologists Association (ISPA). Interns are required to attend this annual conference by their university programs and this requirement is written into the internship contract signed by both the district and university. Intern supervisors are strongly encouraged to attend this annual conference with their intern.

Programming includes a keynote and hour-long sessions for interns only (e.g., *Making the Most of Supervision*), supervisors only (e.g., *Navigating the First Year of Supervision*), and joint sessions (e.g., *Giving and Receiving Feedback*). Over the past 17 years over 2,000 interns and close to 1,000 supervisors have participated (see Kelly, Wise, Cruise, & Swerdlik, 2002 for a full description of this conference including outcome data).

Also as part of this annual intern/intern supervisor workshop, a day-long supervision training using the DEP supervision model is provided for those field supervisors who want to receive more concentrated study in effective supervisory practices. In alternating years, a more intensive 2-day workshop is offered with the second day occurring at the annual winter state-wide ISPA conference. The 1-day workshop allows for a more sequenced and intensive treatment of supervision using the DEP model. The expanded 2-day trainings include participation in a metasupervision group as described in Chapter 10. A listing of the topics included as part of the 1- and 2-day intensive trainings are provided in Appendices 12B and 12C. Since they have been offered more than 200 supervisors have participated in these more intensive trainings in effective supervisory practices.

University faculty have also offered training for practicum and intern supervisors of their graduate students. Since face-to-face meetings are a challenge to schedule for busy school-based practitioners, online webinars can also be offered to ensure that those who are not able to attend state or regional workshops can have access to this training.

The breakout sessions provided as part of the annual intern/intern supervisor conference, the onsite or online webinars provided by university faculty for supervisors of their own students, as well as the 1- and 2-day more intensive trainings provide supervisors with NASP and state-level approved Continuing Education Units. Supervisors enrolled in the 2-day more intensive course can also register for 1 hour of optional university credit. Some states (e.g., Montana) provide stipends for participating supervisors in such intensive trainings (Machek & Kelly, 2016).

ISPIC's Model Program for Supervisor Training and Support

The Illinois School Psychology Internship Consortium (ISPIC) is an APA-accredited school psychology doctoral-level internship consortium program. We discuss ISPIC in this chapter in detail as it has served as an important laboratory for development of the DEP model. ISPIC has adopted the DEP supervision model for all of its supervisors, prioritized fostering a dialogue on effective supervision as well as on supervisor professional development, incorporated training in supervisor competencies into the internship year, and has been successful in preparing the next generation of doctoral-level field supervisors.

ISPIC has made a commitment to provide a quality supervisory experience for each of its interns. Consistent with this commitment, ISPIC has focused on: (a) fostering productive supervisory relationships; (b) the development and application of a supervision model and training activities that address the multidimensional service requirements specific to school psychology; (c) the development of competencies for interns *and* for supervisors; (d) training for empirically supported practice impacting individuals and systems; and (e) preparing interns to become leaders and supervisors.

The primary intern supervisors represent those licensed for independent practice or dually licensed for independent practice and school-based practice. Collaborating supervisors include specialist-level school psychologists supervising interns in school-based sites. The comprehensive training and support program developed for ISPIC supervisors includes several components. The training for all new and experienced ISPIC primary and collaborating supervisors includes an annual August orientation. Interns participate in the morning session along with their supervisors.

The agenda for the annual August training includes a review of the ISPIC mission and fundamental principles of effective supervision including the DEP framework and behavioral markers. Structured training activities to engage supervisors and interns in directed conversations about their supervisory relationship also occur. These directed conversations center around such topics as expectations, various structural and organizational methods to support training such as the supervision contract and supervisory session planners, intern goals, cultural factors relevant to the site and the supervisory relationship, evaluation experiences, methods of supervision, and targeted training activities. At the end of each August training session, supervisors identify annual personal professional development goals for themselves as supervisors. Opportunities for supervisors to monitor their progress toward achieving these goals occurs during follow-up group metasupervision conferences.

As part of the ongoing support component of the program quarterly metasupervision meetings are held each year. As discussed in Chapter 10, metasupervision groups are collegial support groups for sharing experiences (both successes and challenges), discussing issues, and engaging in supportive and collaborative problem-solving. In keeping with the developmental perspective of the DEP model, facilitators promote reflection on key issues that emerge at each stage of the internship.

In addition to the metasupervision groups that are offered quarterly, a variety of consultation resources are available to ISPIC supervisors and the ISPIC director. These consultation resources include year-long availability of problem-solving consultation for individual ISPIC supervisors, and the offering of periodic special topic metasupervision sessions such as interviewing intern candidates and dealing with problematic intern behaviors. Consultation is also available to the ISPIC director related to the development of trainee remediation plans and managing professional competence problems.

ISPIC includes supervision competence as a training goal. All interns are required to engage in some form of supervision under close metasupervision to begin to prepare them for their future role as supervisors. This is consistent with the doctoral-level consortium's broader goal of leadership training.

The outcomes of these various training and ongoing support efforts related to supervision have been very gratifying. To date over 225 interns have graduated from ISPIC with more than 40 supervisors participating in this comprehensive training and support program. Many ISPIC graduates are now clinical supervisors applying the DEP model. Many of these new supervisors have settled in less populated areas of Illinois that now have an influx of dually licensed practitioners. A number of ISPIC graduates have also accepted positons in higher education as university educators; and they enter these positions with advanced supervisory competencies to facilitate the learning of preservice school psychology students.

For the past 15 years, ISPIC has systematically collected data from a variety of sources including intern narratives, summative supervisor evaluation forms, intern exit interviews, and the DEP-SSFS. Summarizing these data, the overall ratings of supervisors by supervisees is consistently overwhelmingly positive. Particularly noteworthy are the higher ratings in areas related to accountability, establishing trust, fostering developmentally appropriate autonomy, and encouragement of intern self-awareness and self-reflection skills. All critical aspects of supervisory practice that are consistent with current understandings of best practice are rated uniformly high across all practices. It is noteworthy that over a 7-year span there has been a continuing rise in positive ratings. This data collection has been designed for self-monitoring and quality control purposes; but it would be beneficial to be formalized into a research protocol regarding supervision practices.

Create an Endorsement Process at the State Level

An endorsement process could be developed for which supervisors can earn an endorsement on their school psychology licenses for completion of a core course on effective school psychology supervision. Best practice would suggest that participating in metasupervision should also be required for this endorsement. Although a number of states have supervisory endorsements on their school psychology credential, many do not require a specific course in clinical supervision of school psychologists; but rather the required course focuses on supervising student teachers. This precedent can be a foundation for specifying endorsements for clinical supervision within school psychology. An alternative to a state-level endorsement through the state board of education is development of a certificate program that could be earned through NASP or the state school psychology organization. As a dual incentive for veteran supervisors to obtain this credential, it would be desirable to offer continuing professional development (CPD) credits for completing the coursework and metasupervision hours necessary for obtaining this credential.

Although an honor and not a credential or certificate, NASP and its Graduate Education Committee have created a program for recognizing field-based internship supervisors who consistently demonstrate best practices in supervision and mentoring consistent with NASP's (2014c) *Best Practice Guidelines for School Psychology Internships*. Each professional selected for the recognition is designated as a NASP-Recognized Model School Psychology Intern Supervisor. Intern supervisors are nominated by university programs and require endorsements from two recent interns who have received supervision from the nominee and from a colleague at their place of employment. Selected supervisors receive a certificate which has no expiration date; and the recognition is publicized on the NASP website and in the *Communiqué*. More information about this recognition system for providing effective intern supervision can be found at www.nasponline.org/resources-and-publications/graduate-educators/model-school-psychology-intern-supervisor-recognition.

Metasupervision Groups

Metasupervision groups conducted through audio and/or video conferencing can be offered throughout the state facilitated by trained veteran supervisors or organized by university faculty. As referenced as part of the comprehensive training and ongoing support program available for ISPIC supervisors, metasupervision groups are collegial support groups for sharing supervisory experiences, issues, and concerns, and engaging in supportive and collaborative problem-solving. In keeping with a developmental perspective, facilitators promote reflection on key issues that emerge at each stage of the practicum, internship, or supervisory relationship. Outcomes of these metasupervision groups include: creating a culture that supports personal professional growth of supervisors, modeling collegial consultation for supervisees as essential for professional sustenance, enhancing an understanding of best practice for supervision, and fostering a network of professional support. Participation in these metasupervision groups can earn continuing education credits. Creating metasupervision groups and other forms of collegial support was discussed in more detail in Chapter 10.

Other Initiatives/Strategies to Enhance the Effectiveness of School Psychology Supervision

A number of other initiatives or strategies can be offered to enhance the effectiveness of school psychology supervision at all levels of practice. State school psychology organizations should lobby for increased administrative supervision for psychologists by psychologists, particularly in relation to personnel evaluation, and for formal clinical supervision and mentoring programs for early career psychologists. Efforts should be initiated to further identify specific school psychology supervision competencies and necessary training supports to facilitate implementation of best practice standards for supervision including delineating and operationalizing structures and process procedures (i.e., written contracts, frequency of one-on-one supervision, multimethod supervision and so forth) that are considered best practice for clinical supervision. Delineating and operationalizing supervisor competencies, including skills, practices, and so forth, similar to the competency benchmarks being developed for other areas of school psychology practice can also enhance the effectiveness of supervision for school psychologists. In this effort, attention should be focused to ensure that "value-added" school psychology supervisory competencies are clearly described in behavioral terms.

Summary

This chapter focused on training supervisors at the preservice, early career, and veteran stages. Although APA requires supervision as a required doctoral competency and domain of training, NASP does not yet at the specialist degree level, but only highlights the need for supervision for all those who supervise school psychologists at any level. Coursework in supervision is more easily built into doctoral-level training where the years of training are expanded; but graduate programs need to incorporate some initial training in supervision for specialist-level students as well since most supervisors of school psychology graduate students function at the specialist level. There are various junctures in the sequence of graduate preparation that supervision training can occur including initial fieldwork and practicum placements, specific graduate coursework, during the capstone internship experience, and during the first 2 years of professional employment. Training in effective supervisory practices for veteran school psychologists can be through continuing professional development (CPD). These efforts should begin with adopting a common school psychology-specific supervision model to drive all state-wide professional development activities. Various methods of delivering this training can include: (a) creating a supervision manual; (b) offering introductory and more advanced workshops at professional conferences; (c) affiliating with an established internship consortium or state-wide network offering a comprehensive training and support program for their supervisors; (d) hosting state-wide metasupervision groups; (e) creating a supervisory credential and/or recognition for effective supervisors; and (f) identifying, operationalizing, and publicizing supervisory competencies, effective structures, methods, supports; and (g) promoting the need for school psychologists to receive clinical and administrative supervision from someone trained in school psychology.

13

FUTURE DEVELOPMENT

Research to Refine School Psychology Supervision

Chapter 12 outlined a vision for the future focusing on training new supervisors. We delineated a structured sequence from graduate school through early career and for veteran school psychologists. This chapter will also have a future orientation focusing on articulating a school psychology-specific supervision research agenda to move the study of supervision in school psychology forward. The chapter will conclude with some final thoughts about supervision in the specialty of school psychology.

Consistent with our discussion in Chapter 6 regarding a need for a school psychology-specific supervision model, so too there is a need to articulate a school psychology-specific supervision research agenda for the field, one that establishes an empirical foundation for clinical supervision within the context of school service delivery. Even though it has been called upon for decades (e.g., Knoff, 1986; McIntosh & Phelps, 2000), supervision research in school psychology remains embryonic. The related disciplines of counseling and clinical psychology and social work provide some data for studying supervision, but Bernard and Goodyear (2014) note that their output of research on the impact of supervision remains relatively small. Falender (2014) highlights the field's urgent need to evaluate supervision outcomes, but cautions that the entire process of supervision and its individual components still require empirical examination.

We will examine various research targets for supervision in school psychology including: evaluation of supervisee development, assessment of client outcomes as a variable to examine both supervisee progress and the effectiveness of supervision, influence of supervisory practices on supervisee development and client outcomes, investigation of whether theoretically determined best practices are truly effective and thus whether DEP can be established as an evidence-based approach, assessment of implementation integrity of DEP, examination of training in supervision both during preservice preparation and for credentialed psychologists, and the need for multimethod research protocols.

Evaluation of Supervisee Development

Supervisee development should be evaluated within the context of the NASP Domains of Practice (2010a) that should be reflected in written internship or other training plans. APA's (2011) competency benchmarks can contribute content to evaluation of supervisee development if additional behavior anchors are added specific to the extra competencies required of school psychologists. CDSPP has done this for the practicum competencies (Caterino et al., 2010). Fenning et al. (2015) have expanded this effort by assessing the perceptions of university educators and practitioners as to the importance of competencies and foundational knowledge as delineated by APA, NASP, Council for the Accreditation of Educator Preparation, state boards of education, and best practices in the field. More sophisticated operationalization of professional skills and behaviors with clearly defined rubrics that can identify developmental markers indicating progress toward skill development is required. Multirater evaluation of supervisee progress that goes beyond reports from supervisors and supervisees themselves needs to augment primary supervisor performance reviews. School psychology is a discipline requiring effective teamwork and collaboration. Feedback from secondary clinical supervisors, collaborating educators, administrators, consultees, and direct service clients can all contribute to a complete picture of supervisee development.

Preservice training programs should incorporate pre and posttraining work samples into university portfolio requirements that reflect internship activity. These work samples should include assessment reports, intervention samples, consultation work, program development and systems change activities, and supervision activities (at the doctoral level). Grading rubrics can help to define future professional development needs requiring focus beyond the internship year, including training in supervision. In recent years, many NASP-approved school psychology graduate programs have incorporated these portfolio requirements as a required assessment to meet NASP Program Approval requirements.

For internship training, the internship plan should reflect core required competencies and be sufficiently behaviorally anchored to contribute to progress monitoring. A baseline assessment of intern competencies can involve an integration of university faculty, self-report, and supervisor interview data.

Client Outcomes to Evaluate Supervisee Progress and Supervisor Effectiveness

As noted throughout this text, the feedback, evaluation, and gatekeeping roles represent primary responsibilities of a supervisor. A focus on client outcomes should be part of all intervention work; thus adding client outcomes as an additional variable to evaluate supervisee progress supports best practice and prepares the supervisee to maintain an outcome focus throughout all professional activities. Measurement of client improvement must take into account the severity, duration, and complexity of problem manifestation (whether an individual, group, class, or system is the target). Client outcomes should be evaluated with multisource and multimethod approaches that are anchored in behavioral data from direct observation; include formal assessment instruments where appropriate (e.g., rating scales); and incorporate data from client, parent, and teacher reports. Including client progress in evaluation of supervisee progress and the effectiveness of supervision is a complex but essential task.

An outcome focus with routine collection of progress monitoring data is part of best practice for all school psychology service delivery. Many practitioners and supervisees work extensively within special education programs. This provides an additional opportunity and responsibility for monitoring client outcomes. Appropriate benchmarking of IEP goals requires behavioral specificity, reliable and valid measuring tools, and direct connection to meaningful performance. IEP benchmarks are evaluated quarterly and provide a ready mechanism for evaluating student progress and the impact of supervisee interventions. Properly designed IEP goals should account for the severity of student concerns so that benchmarks are attainable yet meaningful. It is important to note that an effective team of educators is generally required to achieve progress on IEP goals. In cases where progress is hampered by dysfunction within the education team, this must be taken into account when using IEP benchmark progress as an outcome evaluation for a supervisee's work.

Applications of evidence-based practices, implementation integrity of these intervention activities, and unique adaptations to setting and population should be noted as part of any evaluation of supervisee skills and their impact on client outcomes. Supervisor input into the selection and character of intervention activity requires monitoring as well. The quality of supervision should affect supervisee skills development and client outcomes. The interaction between demonstrated supervisee competencies and supervisory practices is important to evaluate. Whenever there is consideration of a remediation plan for a supervisee's professional competence problems, it is essential to review the fit of current supervisory strategies. This examination ensures that appropriate support strategies are implemented. Monitoring client outcomes helps to monitor both supervisee progress and the effectiveness of supervisory practices.

The Influence of Supervision on Supervisee and Client Outcomes

If clients are achieving documented positive outcomes, these data support that the two primary responsibilities of supervision are met: client welfare and supervisee development. However, this does not specify which supervisory practices are effective or even guarantee that another supervisee will achieve the same results with this supervisor. It is a complex task to assess the influence of supervision and specific supervisory strategies on supervisee and client outcomes. Clear identification of the supervisory strategies employed by supervisors with successful outcomes across multiple supervisees is a starting point. When multiple supervisors employ a similar set of strategies successfully, support builds that this package of strategies can be effective. When the implementation of these strategies is organized within a theoretically sound supervision model that also delineates best practices for the timing and process of supervision, it is possible to evaluate whether the model of supervision can prove effective across various supervisors and supervisees. Validating the effectiveness of a clearly operationalized supervision model would be a significant contribution to the field.

This sequence is similar to research on psychotherapy outcomes. Treatment efficacy is often assessed after administration of a multidimensional intervention protocol. It is only after the entire intervention package has proven beneficial that further research attempts to identify the key mediating variables that are most essential for successful outcomes. Regarding supervision, qualitative data systematically gathered from supervisees, supervisors, and collaterals may point to the relative influence of different supervision strategies and principles of the overarching supervision model. Once identified, these strategies can be studied in more depth in terms of the manner, frequency, and timing of their implementation. As with all intervention research, it is important to assess whether prescribed protocols are implemented with integrity.

Monitoring Implementation Integrity

As the field defines supervisor competencies and effective supervisory practices, it becomes essential to monitor implementation integrity to be able to test out whether those best practices are truly effective. Throughout this text, we have made the case that DEP reflects the current understanding of best practice in the field of supervision with specific application to the discipline of school psychology. The *DEP Self-reflection and Supervisor Feedback Survey* (DEP-SSFS) discussed in Chapters 4 and 10 systematically reviews behavioral markers for implementation of the DEP model. This instrument can be used as a self-reflection or self-monitoring tool by supervisors and a supervisee feedback instrument regarding supervisory practices. Research needs to be conducted investigating the reliability of this instrument as well as its validity in terms of tying the results from a feedback and self-reflection instrument to supervisory outcomes. Research using this instrument can also contribute to supporting the validity of the overall DEP supervision model. Demonstration of implementation integrity is necessary to ensure that other assessments of effectiveness of the DEP supervision approach validly reflect DEP implementation.

As part of its quality monitoring regarding supervision, the Illinois School Psychology Internship Consortium (ISPIC), which uses DEP, collects annual survey data from supervisees regarding their supervisory experiences near the conclusion of their internship. Since the integrity instrument's development, ISPIC interns also complete the DEP-SSFS. While important, limited conclusions can be drawn from supervisee surveys alone. We incorporate DEP-SSFS data into our planning for ongoing professional development opportunities for ISPIC supervisors. The long-term need is to combine varied approaches to examine supervision outcomes for supervisees and clients with implementation integrity measures that ensure DEP has been properly implemented. The next step for ISPIC would be to establish a formal research agenda that incorporates elements suggested in this chapter.

Implementation integrity of DEP is defined by the behavioral markers and specific supervisory activities delineated for each of its components. This specificity ensures that DEP is an applied practice model that informs daily supervision practice. These markers and prescribed activities can also be used to evaluate which supervisor activities demonstrate the strongest direct positive impact on supervisee and client outcomes and thus should receive particular emphasis in supervision training activities.

Supervision Training

There is also a need to study supervisor training. Central questions include the following: (a) what is the essential content of training; (b) which training methods are most effective in ensuring implementation of prescribed supervisory practices; (c) what duration of training combined with what kinds of follow-up activities and supports is required to ensure quality supervision practice; and (d) what formats and incentives recruit credentialed school psychologists to voluntarily participate in professional development focused on supervision? Since it is likely that training formats and needs may vary depending upon supervision experience and career stage, research efforts should study preservice training, training of first time supervisors, and professional development for experienced supervisors.

While supervision is now defined as a core professional competency, it currently remains as one of the few practice areas where primary training is postgraduate and dependent on workshop formats. It is critical that professional development be substantive, practical, and of sufficient duration and intensity to affect practice in the field. Study of effective professional development activities for teachers suggests that training is most effective when it targets and practices specific instructional practices directly applicable to classroom instruction, when it is active and experiential, and when it is consistent with personal goals and professional standards (Desimone, Porter, Garet, Yoon, & Birman, 2002). In our view, these characteristics are essential for professional development regarding supervision as well.

In the previous three chapters, we shared our curriculum and methods for both preservice and continuing professional development training in supervision.

We believe that even within shorter workshop formats, it is necessary to provide a theoretically sound supervision model, emphasize practical strategies, engage participants in exercises that practice application (when possible with their supervisees present), and, whenever feasible, provide follow-up support through engagement in metasupervision. The efficacy of this approach requires empirical study. When the parameters and characteristics of effective professional development training have been established, it will be possible to define minimum requirements for credentialing, certification, or formal recognition in clinical supervision.

Research Methods

Mapping Supervisor Activities by Coding Supervisory Interactions

No reliable and valid observational system for recording supervisory interactions for research purposes currently exists. Development of a coding system would support operationalization of supervisor competencies and contribute to research methodologies. Although Holloway (1995) developed a coding system based on her SAS supervision model, no reliability or validity evidence exists to support its use as a research methodology. Newman (2012) analyzed and coded university-based supervision of consultants-in-training who were involved in a consultation practicum experience. Application of similar approaches to general field-based clinical supervision could be beneficial. There is a need to develop coding systems for observing and describing supervisory interactions within supervision sessions. This observational coding system should capture a supervision session in terms of content and process as well as supervisee reactions to the supervisor's input with interactions systematically recorded. The observational system could resemble the coding of therapist responses or the systematic behavioral observation systems for the use of recording teacher, student, and peer interactions in a classroom setting. A reliable coding system could be used in research to test the impact of specific supervisory strategies and to validate the effectiveness of supervisory models.

Similar to what was outlined in Chapter 7 for observing either a live or a recorded counseling session, a coding system can be developed to record supervisor actions. Some codes could specify the type of supervisory method employed: modeling (Mod), didactic (Did), cotherapy/consultation (Co), observation (Obs), and intern self-report (Sr), or case consultation (Cc). Other codes could address the process of supervisory intervention: empathy (AL), clarifying and probing questions (Q), Socratic Questions (SQ), formative feedback (Fdbk), prompts for self-assessment (Self), intervention directives (Dir), or collaborative problem-solving (PS). Some codes could focus on the content addressed in supervision: assessment (Asmt), intervention (Int), program development (Pdev), program evaluation (Pev), professional disposition (Pdis), self-care (Sc), or future professional development (Fpd).

Coding could capture a picture of the method, process, and content occurring in supervision sessions. It would permit studying the utility of various supervisory approaches at different developmental stages of supervision. The Developmental component of DEP matches supervisory methods to developmental skill levels of supervisees. Coding supervisory transactions can indicate whether the character of supervisory strategies does indeed change over time and in relation to supervisee competencies. Mapping supervisory practice is a complex task but an important step toward understanding and eventually defining competent practice.

Qualitative and Mixed Methods

Because supervision is required for supervisee development, client welfare, and gatekeeping for the profession, it would be unethical to not provide supervision when required. This limits the possibilities for utilizing random control designs to study effective supervision. It is possible to compare supervision that emphasizes particular strategies or to compare differences in supervisee and client outcomes from supervisors who have participated in a supervision training program like DEP compared to those who have not received formal training in supervision. Studies of supervision and evaluations of supervisors have relied heavily on supervisee feedback. It is clearly important to continue to incorporate this perspective into future research. However, supervisee surveys by themselves have limitations and must be interpreted cautiously. Transparency of supervisee feedback can be compromised by the power differential between supervisor and supervisee. For example, even in final stages of an internship, the supervisee may be concerned about getting a passing grade for the field experience and will likely still require letters of recommendations from the supervisor. In a challenging supervisory experience, the supervisor may be required to frequently provide feedback regarding performance deficiencies and might need to exercise the gatekeeping role. In this case, the supervisor may be demonstrating competent skills but a feedback survey from the supervisee might be negatively biased.

Quantitative, qualitative, and mixed methods research approaches will be required for examination of supervision practices (see Yin, 2011). Survey data from multiple sources, analysis of structured or semi-structured interviews of supervisors and supervisees, observational methods, strategy logs, data collection regarding supervisee development and client outcomes, assessment of implementation integrity, supervisee portfolio and work product reviews, and client progress data are examples of varied research sources that might contribute to our understanding of effective practices of clinical supervision. Single and multiple case study designs can involve qualitative and quantitative data as well (see Yin, 2014). Case study approaches are consistent with the necessary focus on progress monitoring and client outcomes. Integrating qualitative and quantitative data can set the foundation for empirical study of supervision practices.

Summary: Research Agenda

To refine the practice of supervision in school psychology, it is necessary to establish a multifaceted research agenda. It must examine the practice of clinical supervision in the context of best practices in school psychology. The overarching goal is to define effective supervisory competencies and practices and establish best practices for training supervisors. It must take into account supervisee development, client outcomes, the impact of a theoretically sound yet pragmatic supervision model, the influence of specific methods and supervisory processes, and fidelity to current empirically supported practices. Research will be needed to operationalize and map supervisory strategies and processes. Qualitative and mixed method research tools will be required to incorporate diverse data sources into an initial research foundation for supervision within school psychology.

Final Thoughts

We began this text by making the case for a school psychology-specific supervision model. The attention to supervision and supervisory practices and competencies is long overdue. Supervision represents one of the primary mechanisms to move our field forward (Harvey & Struzziero, 2008; Knoff, 1986; McIntosh & Phelps, 2000). It should be elevated to a core competency for school psychologists at both the specialist and doctoral levels of training. Competent supervision supports the professional development of school psychologists and enhances the quality of services to clients. The field is in the midst of a significant reconceptualization of the role of school psychologists in education and mental health services. Competent clinical supervision is essential for professional preparation but can also support the professional development of school psychologists throughout their careers. The dialogue that occurs in a supervisory relationship helps to further refine our perspectives on best practice for the service of children, adolescents, families, and educators.

It is necessary to incorporate training in effective supervisory practices into professional preparation at the preservice level *and* to initiate broad efforts for supervision training at the early career and veteran career phases. Since few veteran psychologists received training in supervisory competencies in their own graduate preparation, updated professional development in the area of supervision is a critical need for experienced supervisors. Like all other professional competencies, supervision skills require continuous development.

The DEP model provides the first comprehensive framework specifically designed to guide supervisory practice within school psychology. It serves as an initial foundation for the practice and examination of best supervisory and clinical practices within our field. The DEP framework matches the complex practice requirements of school psychology. Core elements of this model are appropriate for clinical and counseling psychology and clinical and school social work as well. These fields are also experiencing dramatic shifts in service delivery systems. They remain key collaborators with school psychologists in services to children and families.

The DEP model and its components require empirical study to further refine supervisory practice and determine its impact on supervisee and client outcomes. Development of an initial model is only a starting point. It will need to be refined by feedback from supervisory practice and a commitment to research activity regarding effective supervision that has historically received insufficient attention. These investigations go hand-in-hand with the study of best practices in graduate preparation and effective service delivery.

The field of school psychology's heightened focus and dialogue about supervisory practice can be a springboard to refining best practice in supervision, ensuring quality preparation for the next generation of school psychologists, and enhancing clinical support for psychologists at every level of experience. Commitment to quality supervision is a commitment to quality services for the children, adolescents, families, and educators served by school psychologists.

APPENDICES

Select appendices items can be downloaded by practitioners from the eResource tab on the Routledge web page for this text: www.routledge.com/9781138121539.

Appendix 3A: Healthy Lifestyle Assessment

Sometimes our work becomes too important in our lives and our clients/patients or our students become our main source of social contact. Without our knowing it, we can find ourselves in a "closed system" contributing to diminished self awareness, susceptibility to boundary violations with our clients and feelings of "burnout."

The following are some statements you can use to analyze your level of self-awareness and balance of work and life. If you come across a question that gives you an uneasy feeling, note it as something for further exploration. Develop an action plan as you would for a client/patient. Then make a commitment to revisit the item, say in 30 days to measure your progress. The greater number of low scores you indicate, the greater the need for concern.

	Please rate the following 1 = Strongly Disagree thru 5 = Strongly Agree	Rating	Action Steps	Fol-Up Date
1.	I have mostly healthy relationships with family, friends, and colleagues.	1 2 3 4 5		
2.	I exercise regularly (at least 30 minutes/day, 5+ days/week).	1 2 3 4 5		
3.	I do not smoke or use other substances as coping mechanisms.	1 2 3 4 5		
4.	I eat 4-5 servings of fruits and vegetables per day.	1 2 3 4 5		
5.	I maintain a healthy weight (below 24 BMI).	1 2 3 4 5		
6.	I have adequate time for leisure and participating in activities I enjoy outside of work.	1 2 3 4 5		
7.	I am comfortable with my religion/spirituality.	1 2 3 4 5		
8.	I feel that I have of control over the future of my career.	1 2 3 4 5		
9.	I stay current on the latest data and trends in my field.	1 2 3 4 5		
10.	I feel in control of my behavior and emotions.	1 2 3 4 5		
11.	I have sufficient support through a network of my peers.	1 2 3 4 5		
12.	I believe that I maintain healthy boundaries with my clients/patients/students/professors/supervisors/peers.	1 2 3 4 5		
13.	I feel adequately prepared to manage work challenges.	1 2 3 4 5		
14.	I am comfortable in crisis situations.	1 2 3 4 5		
15.	I have adequate support to deal with my own or a close family members' chronic illness.	1 2 3 4 5		
16.	I have ample help with child/elder care.	1 2 3 4 5		
17.	I am engaged in an appropriate amount and level of professional activities (so that I am not over/under-whelmed).	1 2 3 4 5		
18.	I receive adequate rest (6–9 hours per night).	1 2 3 4 5		
19.	I am able to maintain my presence in my daily work rather than planning what I'll do after work or over the weekend.	1 2 3 4 5		
20.	My schedule is well-balanced.	1 2 3 4 5		
21.	I hold myself to an adequate amount of breaks.	1 2 3 4 5		
22.	I recently said "no" to adding something to my plate.	1 2 3 4 5		
23.	I plan less critical tasks (paperwork, returning phone calls) during the times of the day when I don't feel I work at my best.	1 2 3 4 5		
24.	I am free of habits such as gambling, pornography, video games, or other compulsive distractions.	1 2 3 4 5		
25.	I enjoy my work more than I am burdened by my career path.	1 2 3 4 5		
26.	I have been able to take one or more days off from work to relax in the past 6 months.	1 2 3 4 5		
27.	I am unbothered by my professional behavior. For example: I act ethically and in ways that I am proud of; I do not behave in any way that I feel I have to hide, cover up, or explain.	1 2 3 4 5		
28.	I call in when I am sick.	1 2 3 4 5		
29.	I have a trusted peer or mentor to provide me with honest feedback in case my personal life begins to interfere or affect my work (e.g., financial problems, conflict at home, love, personal or family illness).	1 2 3 4 5		
30.	I self-disclose appropriately. That is, I disclose only the type and degree of information that is in the best interests of clients/patients/students/professors/supervisors/peers.	1 2 3 4 5		

31.	I am able to let go of my work and not allow related concerns to interfere in social or personal activities.	1 2 3 4 5		
32.	I stop to eat lunch and not work while eating.	1 2 3 4 5		
33.	I engage in regular positive experiences (e.g., reading the paper, taking a bubble bath, going for a walk, or spending time outdoors).	1 2 3 4 5		
34.	I don't suffer from headaches, stomachaches-muscle aches, or problems sleeping that have no medical explanation.	1 2 3 4 5		
35.	I do not participate in excessive use of alcohol or illicit substances.	1 2 3 4 5		
36.	I seek nurturance from friends, family and loved ones outside of the school or office in order to minimize locking myself into a "closed system."	1 2 3 4 5		

Scoring:

160–200   Congratulations, you may be a good role model for your peers! Maybe you wish to offer a seminar on balance and self-care for the rest of us?

120–159   O.K. you're doing pretty well in most areas. You may want to take a look back over the questionnaire and identify some items that may need some attention.

80–119   Thank you for being honest. You are probably feeling pretty distressed and possibly overwhelmed. Would talking with a supervisor or other professional colleague be of help to set some self-care goals?

79 or below   Take care of yourself, there are quite a number of items that need addressing. Self-care is not an option but a requirement in order to be successful in helping others as well as yourself.

Page, L. (2008). *Healthy Lifestyle Assessment.* Unpublished manuscript, Arlington Heights, IL. Reprinted with permission.

Appendix 4A

The DEP Supervisor Self-reflection and Supervisor Feedback Survey (DEP-SSFS)

The Supervisory Relationship: Interpersonal Process

The professional literature has identified the main characteristics of an effective supervisor and supervisory relationship and the supervisory process that fosters a positive relationship.
    Rating Scale: (4) Strongly Agree, (3) Agree, (2) Disagree, (1) Strongly Disagree, (DNA) Does not Apply

My Supervisor:

1. _____ Spends time in rapport building to establish a personal foundation for our relationship
2. _____ Is empathetic
3. _____ Is genuine/nonjudgmental
4. _____ Is respectful towards me
5. _____ Creates a safe learning environment
6. _____ Is flexible
7. _____ Is accessible
8. _____ Sets high goals
9. _____ Notes and integrates my strengths into supervision
10. _____ Is open to feedback
11. _____ Maintains professional boundaries
12. _____ Demonstrates awareness of what else is occurring in my life and supports self-care
13. _____ Only addresses personal issues that are relevant to clinical and professional development and does so in a respectful and emotionally supportive manner
14. _____ Appropriately utilizes self-disclosure during supervision
15. _____ Is attuned to diversity issues in the supervisory relationship, open, supportive, and respectful in acknowledging the potential impact of differences
16. _____ Models respect and professionalism toward me and others
17. _____ Advocates for my needs
18. _____ Maintains regular "protected" time for supervision
19. _____ Specifies how to handle requests for additional supervision
20. _____ If I had more than one supervisor, my primary supervisor communicates with other supervisors for purposes of evaluation, monitoring my progress, and managing workload

Developmental Domain

Supervision requires attention to the Developmental stages of intern growth, providing as much structure as necessary, assessing training goals and needs, providing effective formative feedback and summative evaluation, deploying multiple methods of supervision, and guiding the supervisee toward independent practice.

Rating Scale: (4) Strongly Agree, (3) Agree, (2) Disagree, (1) Strongly Disagree, (DNA) Does not Apply

My Supervisor:

21. _____ Employs a Socratic approach consistent with my developmental level (does not just tell me the answers)

22. _____ Clearly defined roles, responsibilities, and expectations at the outset of supervision through utilization of a written contract and/or focused discussion of the nature of our supervisory relationship
    a. (indicate if a written contract was utilized as part of your supervisory relationship: *yes or no*)

23. _____ Requires and models appropriate planning for supervision including advance agenda planning
    a. (indicate if the *"Intern's Supervision Session Planner"* was utilized: *yes or no*)

24. _____ Requires and models appropriate planning for psychological consultation, problem- solving, and intervention activities including review and recommendations prior to engaging in these activities.
    a. (indicate if *"Intern's Client/Activity Session Planner"* was utilized: *yes or no*)

25. _____ Models and requires appropriate documentation of professional activities
    a. (indicate if a planning form is used to prepare for activities, i.e., *"Intern's Client/Activity Session Planner"*: yes or no)
    b. (indicate if a form is used for documenting activities, i.e., *"Intern's Client Summary/Progress Notes*: yes or no)

26. _____ Engages me in a developmental assessment of my entry skill levels across Internship Plan domains, delineating areas where I have some mastery and where I need additional experience and closer supervision

27. _____ Engages me in goal setting and identification of my perspective of needs for training and supervision

28. _____ Provides fair, understandable, and timely formative feedback throughout the internship recognizing my competencies and suggesting areas of growth and improvement

29. _____ Provides formal comprehensive summative feedback as required by the internship consortium, university, or site

30. _____ Provides summative feedback that is unsurprising (all issues of concern were previously noted in ongoing formative feedback)

31. _____ Notes both strengths and areas requiring further development during feedback and evaluation

32. _____ Provides a balance of dependence and independence appropriate to the various stages of the internship

33. _____ Uses multiple supervision methods during supervision (indicate methods utilized below)
    a. Modeling and Demonstration: *yes or no*
    b. Intern self-report: *yes or no*
    c. Cotherapy and consultation: *yes or no*
    d. Live observation: *yes or no*
    e. Video recording: *yes or no*
    f. Audio recording: *yes or no*
    g. Coaching: *yes or no*

Ecological Domain

Supervision requires attention to ecological, systemic, multicultural, and diversity elements of professional practice. It is impossible to understand individual students, classrooms, or school communities without understanding their interaction with larger environments.

Rating Scale: (4) Strongly Agree, (3) Agree, (2) Disagree, (1) Strongly Disagree, (DNA) Does not Apply

My Supervisor:

34. _____ Oriented me to the school culture and, as appropriate, to the representative ethnic cultures present in the school community
35. _____ Provides sufficient opportunities for training and involvement in "universal" interventions such as PBIS, social-emotional learning curriculum, and/or psychoeducational activities to promote healthy psychological development across the school community (Tier 1)
36. _____ Provides sufficient opportunities for training and involvement in parent conferencing and consultation and/or parent training programs
37. _____ Provides sufficient training and opportunities for teacher consultation centered around classroom management
38. _____ Engages me in case conceptualization, problem-solving, and intervention planning that addresses both individual and contextual factors (i.e., family, peer, classroom, school, cultural, community...)
39. _____ Fosters my acquisition of evidence-based academic and mental health intervention strategies that are "multi-tiered" (Tiers 2 & 3) and "multi-systemic"
40. _____ Provides sufficient training and involvement appropriate for an intern in program development and leadership skills
41. _____ Specifically addresses and provides sufficient training in multicultural and diversity competency
42. _____ Addresses multicultural and diversity contextual factors as part of problem-solving
43. _____ Teaches me how to manage dysfunctional elements of the system and protects my intern status (focus on training not less expensive employee)

Problem-solving Domain

Problem-solving is the core activity of school psychology. It is rooted in data-based decision-making that links assessment to intervention, addresses both individual and contextual factors, applies empirically supported intervention strategies, monitors outcomes to revise strategies as necessary, and fosters reasonable innovation to treat complex problems while continuing to monitor intervention effectiveness. Supervision activity centers on these activities and strives to teach the intern effective case conceptualization and intervention strategies to apply to the full range of psychological issues.

Rating Scale: *(4) Strongly Agree, (3) Agree, (2) Disagree, (1) Strongly Disagree,* (DNA) Does not Apply

My Supervisor:

44. _____ Engages effectively in collaborative problem-solving
45. _____ Uses a systematic approach to problem-solving (problem identification, problem analysis, etc.)
46. _____ Thinks out loud (shares his/her internal process while engaged in problem-solving)
47. _____ Encourages emotional awareness: encourages me to think more about how I'm feeling and how that impacts my client
48. _____ Specifically addresses multicultural and diversity contextual factors as part of problem-solving
49. _____ Teaches me a framework for systematic case conceptualization that addresses both individual and contextual factors
50. _____ Provides opportunities for me to be involved across multiple tiers of service delivery (preventive/universal, targeted, and intensive)
51. _____ Develops my skills in data-based decision-making across intervention domains
52. _____ Develops my skills in linking assessment to intervention
53. _____ Perceives complexity but is still able to suggest or direct concrete paths of action
54. _____ Supports consistent use of evidence-based practices
55. _____ Develops my skills in facilitating and measuring intervention integrity
56. _____ Assists me in integrating theory and research into practice
57. _____ Directs me to appropriate resources

Additional comments:

Appendix 5A

Ethics Case Examples

D. *Mary, SP Intern, is assigned to teach anger management skills to Charlie. Charlie is known as an angry and temperamental 7th grader. He has a history of suspensions for fighting in school and arrests for a variety of delinquency issues in the community. He appears to be at the entry point of street gang involvement. Charlie hotly describes the conflict he is experiencing with Nate after a public verbal confrontation in the school cafeteria that same afternoon. Despite strenuous attempts from Mary to calm his emotional intensity and to correct his "thinking errors," Charlie vows that he will confront Nate in the park tonight armed with a knife. Frustrated with Mary's attempts to suggest alternative courses of action, he bolts from her office. Mary immediately seeks out you, her supervisor, to discuss how to follow up with this situation.*

E. *SP Intern, Bertha, is a close friend of the sister of the mother of a child, Alex, who is struggling in school known to exhibit serious behavioral problems. Bertha has attended events with Alex's mother and has even babysat Alex on one occasion. When Alex is placed on the agenda for a problem-solving team agenda, Bertha asks you, her supervisor if she can be included. Bertha feels that her "inside information" and "rapport with the parent" will really assist the problem-solving process. How do you respond to Bertha's request?*

F. *Steve, SP Intern, discovers that Teresa, a high school student he is evaluating relating to concerns about crippling anxiety, is distraught because she has had a consensual sexual encounter with another female student and is having second thoughts about her actions and is confused regarding her sexual orientation. Steve tries to support Teresa as she experiences overwhelming anxiety, but is simultaneously struggling with his strong religious belief that lesbian relationships are sinful. Conflicted and confused, Steve puts his concerns on the agenda for his next supervision session with you. How do you respond?*

G. *Your intern, Phil, has an extensive Facebook page. He has begun to "friend" students at his internship site and communicate with them through social media. While he describes it as "fun and another way to build rapport with students," he does note that he had one student share a suggestive photo of another student with him. His response was to simply "unfriend" this student. What concerns do you have with Phil's establishing social media links with students? As you respond to him, delineate reasonable guidelines regarding this issue for school psychologists.*

H. *You have been working for a Special Education Cooperative for many years but primarily with an elementary aged developmentally disabled population. Due to staff cuts, you are now also assigned to work 1 day a week in the high school ED program. Your intern, Karen, mirrors your professional rotation in her activities. She is working with a high school senior who is exhibiting symptoms of a complicated "borderline personality disorder" including engaging in frequent self-abusive "cutting" behaviors. The student frequently talks of suicide, hides her wounds, and is prone to histrionic behaviors. Karen is feeling overwhelmed by the case and is looking to you for advice. What steps must you take to ensure that both your intern's and the student's needs are met?*

I. *Elvis, your SP intern, carries a counseling caseload of 10 students as part of his training assignment. He has access to tickets to the circus and is making plans to choose two of the students to take by himself to enjoy the circus as a reward for good progress. What do you say to him when he discusses this planned activity?*

J. *Stan, your SP intern, goes to observe one of the students he is working with at a football team practice after school. He witnesses one of the coaches (a legendary winner in the community) belittle his student including using a "homosexual putdown." He asks you in your supervisory session how he should respond. (Also address response if instead he witnessed the coach hit the student in anger for messing up a play.)*

K. *Socializing with trainees: The literature provides a variety of viewpoints regarding "social boundary issues" between a supervisor and supervisee. Summarize the different considerations that should be given to the following circumstances: a) group of staff members going out drinking after work; b) going out to lunch with supervisee; c) going with a group of staff members to a dinner and play on the weekend; d) going with just the trainee to a dinner and play over the weekend; e) going with your spouse and your intern to a dinner and play over the weekend. Feel free to add other gradations.*

L. *You have been part of a tight knit team of school psychologists in the district who like and support each other (sometimes socializing after school). You have just been promoted to Chairperson of the district's special services department. Now you will be responsible for evaluating your friends and colleagues. How do you go about establishing boundaries and preparing for your function as an evaluator? If one of the psychologists is your spouse, how does that differ, if at all, from the other relationships?*

Appendix 7A

Practicum Supervision Contract

Psychology 436.04, Practicum in Psychoeducational Assessment and Intervention: Psychological Services Center (PSC) Component

Your clinical supervisor is an experienced person with advanced training who is an over-seer of your clinical work and who is responsible, with you, for the quality of your clinical work. Clinical supervision focuses on the services you provide to clients and includes such areas as client welfare, the therapeutic relationship, assessment, diagnosis, mental health/educational interventions, prognosis, appropriate referral techniques, and advocating for your client with other agencies in the community. This is accomplished through a set of supervisory activities that include consultation, training and instruction, and evaluation.

I. Purpose, Goals, and Objectives of Clinical Supervision

a. To monitor and ensure welfare of clients seen by supervisee.
b. To structure the activities of the supervisee to ensure they provide competent services.
c. To ensure that the unlicensed provider functions within his or her level of competence.
d. To facilitate the provider's personal and professional development.
e. To promote accountability.
f. To fulfill academic requirement for supervisee's practicum.

II. Context of Services

1. Supervision will revolve around clients seen in the Child and Adolescent Psychoeducational Assessment and Multidisciplinary Psychoeducational Assessment Services of the Psychological Services Center (PSC).
2. One hour of individual supervision will be provided weekly; supervisor will also be available on an as-needed basis.
3. Individual supervision will be conducted in the PSC on a mutually determined day/time.

The supervisor follows the Developmental, Ecological, Problem-solving (DEP) model of supervision (Simon et al., 2014). DEP addresses the Developmental process of supervision that matches supervisory methods and supports to the skill levels and needs of supervisees. Multiple methods of supervision will be employed including live and recorded observations. Frequent formative feedback will guide activity with clients and foster supervisee professional development. The Ecological component incorporates consideration of systemic and contextual factors that impact practice. Particular attention will be paid to development of diversity and multicultural competence and to interventions that address systemic factors. The Problem-solving component of the model focuses on data-based decision-making, case conceptualization that links assessment to intervention, and the application of evidenced-based strategies that integrate interventions across individual and systemic domains. The DEP framework requires the supervisee to be proactive in asserting training needs and requires specific preparation for supervisory sessions and activities. If the supervisee wishes, the supervisor is pleased to discuss any aspect of his supervision model with her or him.

III. Duties and Responsibilities of Supervisor and Supervisee

Your clinical supervisor is legally and ethically responsible, with you, for the services you provide and the manner in which you conduct yourself. It is therefore *your* responsibility to keep your supervisor well informed as to your activities. Openness with and trust in your supervisor will enhance your experience of supervision and your professional growth. A supervisor has *full responsibility* for the supervised work of the supervisee, including assessment, diagnosis, and educational/treatment planning.

It is your *supervisor's role* to do the following:

1. Provide a location and atmosphere for supervision that is safe enough for supervisees to lay out practice issues in their own way.
2. Provide formative and summative evaluation/assessment of progress. The supervisor will view video recordings of your assessment sessions with you and provide feedback. The supervisor will also provide written and/or oral feedback (including strengths) on all aspects of your clinical work. This will culminate in the final grade for the PSC Psychoeducational Assessment and Intervention Practicum. If the supervisee desires additional feedback, it is his or her responsibility to request it from the supervisor. The supervisee is referred to the University Handbook regarding due process rights and procedures for objecting to the content and recommendations of a summative evaluation.
3. Help the supervisee explore and clarify thoughts and feelings, which underlie their practice.
4. Assist supervisee in anchoring assessment planning, diagnosis, and interventions in a theoretical approach.
5. Identify supervisee's personal and/or professional blind spots.
6. Bring to the supervisee's attention those personal difficulties of the supervisee that directly affect the supervisee's clinical work and recommend a course of action to address these difficulties.

7. Protect the confidentiality of the supervisory relationship. The nature of clinical competencies will be shared with other program faculty; but the specific content of supervisory sessions will remain confidential unless there is evidence of ethical breaches or personal problems that interfere with the supervisee's ability to work effectively with clients.
8. Present and model appropriate directives.
9. Intervene if client welfare is at risk.
10. Ensure that ethical guidelines of both the American Psychological Association (APA, 2010a) and the National Association of School Psychologists (NASP, 2010d) are upheld.
11. Conduct activities in accordance with the ISU-PSC Policies and Procedures Manual/Handbook.
12. Sign off on all client documentation including psychological reports.
13. Maintain weekly supervision notes. These notes will be kept for 7 years and then destroyed.

The supervisor will discuss any concerns regarding the supervisees' performance in a timely fashion and will develop, in collaboration with the practicum student, a remediation plan if deficits/problems are identified.

Always remember: your clinical supervisor is legally and ethically responsible, with you, for the services you provide and the manner in which you conduct yourself. It is therefore your responsibility to keep your supervisor well informed as to your activities. Openness with and trust in your supervisor will enhance your experience of supervision and your professional growth.

It is your *role as supervisee* to do the following:

1. Be punctual, both at sessions with clients as well as at supervision. In the event that you are delayed for or unable to attend a supervision session, it is your responsibility to notify your supervisor and make alternate arrangements. If the individual appointment cannot be kept due to scheduling conflicts, an effort will be made to reschedule an alternate date/time and will only be canceled upon the mutual agreement of the both the supervisee and supervisor.
2. Be prepared, both for sessions with clients as well as for supervision. A Supervision Session Planner should be submitted to your supervisor in advance of each supervision session. You are expected to: (a) have viewed assessment session video/audio recordings in advance of weekly supervision and follow any specific instructions from the supervisor; (b) have client notes, protocols, and video recordings ready to review; and (c) have an agenda of issues that you need to have addressed, together with the files of the clients involved. As part of this advanced preparation, the supervisee will have completed a Client/Activity Session Planner for each session with the client,

parent, teacher, etc. to discuss in supervision and have "scored" all formal psychological tests administered.

3. The supervisee will video or audio record all assessment sessions with the child and interviews with the parent. These video/audio recordings will be reviewed/critiqued by the practicum student and brought to the next supervisory session (keyed to a section that supervisee would like to review with the supervisor). The supervisee will also provide a written summary or transcription of all parent, teacher, and student (client) interviews and intervention activities for the supervisor and the client's folder.

4. If the supervisee believes that client issues/concerns have not been adequately addressed during the regularly scheduled supervisory session, the supervisee will bring this to the attention of the supervisor and another session will be scheduled.

5. Share with the supervisor your learning goals for the practicum experience. This will require self-reflection and self-evaluation regarding your current level of clinical skill.

6. Be receptive to guidance and instruction from your supervisor, that is, be attentive to feedback and suggestions from your supervisor and follow through on such instruction promptly. It may be necessary to take notes during supervision in order to execute all instructions identified by your supervisor.

7. Inform your supervisor of any difficulties you are having in the areas of delivering services to clients, completing paperwork, or coordinating with other agencies or providers such as schools or independent practitioners.

8. As you establish a working relationship with your supervisor, it is hoped that you will become increasingly able to share issues and concerns you may have that impact your clinical work, be open to feedback from others, and monitor any tendency you may have toward defensiveness.

9. Select a theoretical model(s) from which you will work. Formulate client case conceptualizations from this approach. Be ready to discuss the theoretical reasons for your assessment approaches, interventions, and techniques.

10. You will not engage in dual relationships with clients, that is, student clinicians will not socialize with clients or their families, nor will they provide services to individuals they know from other contexts, such as friends or acquaintances. In the event that someone you know is being seen at the PSC, you are expected to remove yourself from situations where that client's assessment, treatment, and progress are being reviewed. It is your responsibility to alert your supervisor to such situations.

11. You are responsible for insuring that the parents/guardians of all clients are informed of the supervised nature of your work as a supervisee, and of the ultimate professional responsibility of the supervisor.

12. You are responsible for insuring that all evaluative letters and reports concerning clients are co-signed by your clinical supervisor before they are

sent out from the PSC. It is also your responsibility to determine that an active Authorization for Release of Confidential Information form is present in the client's file before presenting the letter/report to the supervisor for signature.

13. Supervisees must advise their clinical supervisor of all important changes related to a case, i.e., client starting a new school, suspensions and other disciplinary actions, school progress, and/or client becoming involved in a legal case. The results of intake parent interviews must be reviewed with your supervisor to determine an assessment plan. Any changes to the assessment plan must be reviewed with and approved by your supervisor before they are presented to the client.

14. Keep your supervisor informed about clients who are suicidal, homicidal, or threatening to harm others. Notify your supervisor about clients who are involved in child custody disputes, Disability Determination assessments, or any other matter that affects the client's legal status. Notify your supervisor immediately if you receive any summons to testify or you are told that you will be subpoenaed to testify. Do not under any circumstances release client information to an attorney or court or anyone else without a proper Authorization for Release of Confidential Information signed by the client and with your supervisor's signature on the document being released.

15. Seek supervision whenever you are uncertain about a situation. Make every attempt to reach your clinical supervisor before taking action with that client. If your supervisor cannot be reached, contact another clinical supervisor (Mary in the PSC has a list of supervisors and their phone numbers). You may also consult informally with more experienced clinicians in the PSC, but your clinical supervisor must be kept abreast of any and all emergencies. In the event of emergency, the supervisee is to contact Dr. Swerdlik at his office at xxx.xxx.xxxx, at home at xxx.xxx.xxxx, or by cell at xxx.xxx.xxxx. Follow the guidelines in the PSC Policy and Procedure Manual for emergency situations.

16. Implement supervisory directives in subsequent assessment sessions.

17. Uphold ethical APA and NASP principles in all client-related activities.

18. Be familiar with and follow the PSC Policy and Procedure Manual/ Handbook. The supervisee agrees to complete all required PSC forms, including billing, termination summaries, and parent interpretive summary reports, in a timely fashion for all cases. The final written psychological report will also be completed in a timely fashion according to the agreed upon date.

19. Complete professional tasks (clinical documentation, reports, contacting clients) within time frames specified by the PSC Policy and Procedure Manual and Quality Assurance guidelines.

IV. Terms of the Contract

This contract serves as verification and a description of the clinical supervision provided by Mark E. Swerdlik, Ph.D., ABPP to _____ ("Supervisee"), enrolled in the Psychoeducational Assessment and Intervention Practicum in the School Psychology program at Illinois State University for _____ semester 20_____.

    Supervisee: _____   Date: _____

    Supervisor: _____   Date: _____

    This contract is effective from _____ (start date) to _____ (finish date).

Appendix 7B
School Psychology Internship In Illinois
School Psychology Internship Supervision Contract

Your clinical supervisor is an experienced professional with advanced training who is an over-seer of your school psychology internship activities and who is responsible, with you, for the quality of all of your clinical work and internship activities. Clinical supervision focuses on the services you provide to all clients including students, parents, and educators. Supervision responsibilities cover all aspects of client welfare as impacted by assessment, intervention, training, diagnostic, consultation, problem-solving, program development, and community referral activities. Supervision involves a broad array of training activities that include monitoring, consultation, training, direct instruction, and performance evaluation.

I. Purpose, Goals, and Objectives of Clinical Supervision

a. To monitor and ensure welfare of clients seen by supervisee.
b. To structure the activities of the supervisee to ensure she or he provides competent services.
c. To ensure that the unlicensed provider functions within her or his level of competence.
d. To facilitate the intern's personal and professional development.
e. To promote accountability.
f. To fulfill academic requirement for supervisee's internship.

II. Context of Services

a. Supervision will revolve around clients seen at the primary school site, associated elementary or secondary school experience rotation sites, and all community venues linking with student services.
b. A minimum of 2 hours of individual supervision will be provided weekly; the supervisor will also be available on an as-needed basis.
c. Individual supervision will be conducted in the supervisor's office on a mutually determined day/time.
d. The supervisor works within the framework of the *Developmental, Ecological, Problem-solving (DEP) model* of supervision (Simon et al., 2014). The *Developmental* focus tailors supervision activity to the intern's experience and skill level at each stage of training. This approach is committed to supporting the trainee's growth from intensely monitored and supported practice to relatively independent functioning characteristic of an entry-level professional. Multiple methods of supervision will be employed including live and recorded observations. Frequent formative feedback will guide

activity with clients and foster supervisee professional development. The *Ecological* focus accounts for contextual and systemic factors impacting clients and the professional development of the intern. It recognizes that multiple systemic contexts must be considered when supporting students and faculty. Training will develop competency in understanding and supporting the full range of student diversity including multicultural factors. A variety of supervisor and supervisee tasks (e.g., skills in assessment and intervention planning, professional role and function, self-evaluation) and functions (e.g., monitoring, advising, consulting, and evaluation) are addressed within a developmental framework, which is impacted by client, supervisee, supervisor and systemic/organizational contextual factors. The *Problem-solving* focus applies systematic analysis and data-based decision-making skills to all aspects of psychological assessment and intervention. It sets the foundation for choosing and implementing evidence-based practices for promotion of healthy psychological development and problem prevention, assessment, early intervention, crisis intervention, and therapeutic strategies. The DEP framework requires the supervisee to be proactive in asserting training needs and requires specific preparation for supervisory sessions and activities. If the supervisee wishes, the supervisor is pleased to discuss any aspect of this supervision model with her/him.

III. Duties and Responsibilities of Supervisor and Supervisee

Your clinical supervisor is legally and ethically responsible, with you, for the services you provide and the manner in which you conduct yourself. It is therefore *your* responsibility to keep your supervisor well informed as to your activities. Openness with and trust in your supervisor will enhance your experience of supervision and your professional growth. A supervisor has *full responsibility* for the supervised work of the supervisee, including assessment, diagnosis, intervention, consultation, problem-solving, professional development, and community referral activities. It is particularly important that any intern activity that uncovers potential risk for harm to a client be immediately reported to the supervisor for consultation.

It is the *supervisor's role* to do the following:

1. Provide a location and atmosphere for supervision that is safe enough for supervisees to lay out practice issues in their own way.
2. Conduct formative and summative evaluation/assessment of intern progress. To enhance intern growth and legitimize accuracy of intern progress evaluation, the supervisor will engage in direct observation of intern activities, review recordings of work, provide consultation and training in response to trainee questions and activity reviews, model and demonstrate appropriate school psychology skills, and review all reports, IEPs, and recordkeeping. The

supervisor will also provide written and/or oral feedback on all aspects of your school psychology work highlighting strengths and making specific recommendations for professional growth. Formal written summative reviews will minimally occur on a quarterly basis. Throughout this process, the intern will be guided in developing self-monitoring skills. If the supervisee desires additional feedback at any time, it is his or her responsibility to request it from the supervisor. The supervisee is referred to the Internship Program Handbook regarding due process rights and procedures for objecting to the content and recommendations of a summative evaluation.

3. Help the supervisee explore and clarify thoughts and feelings, which underlie psychological practice.
4. Assist supervisee in anchoring assessment planning, diagnosis, interventions, consultation, and problem-solving in a theoretical approach.
5. Identify supervisee's personal and/or professional blind spots.
6. Bring to the supervisee's attention those personal difficulties of the supervisee that directly affect the supervisee's clinical work and recommend a course of action to address these difficulties.
7. Protect the confidentiality of the supervisory relationship. The nature of clinical competencies will be shared with other program faculty; but the specific content of supervisory sessions will remain confidential unless there is evidence of ethical breaches or personal problems that interfere with the supervisee's ability to work effectively with clients.
8. Present and model appropriate directives.
9. Intervene if client welfare is at risk.
10. Ensure that ethical guidelines of both the American Psychological Association (APA, 2010a) and the National Association of School Psychologists (NASP, 2010d) are upheld.
11. Conduct activities in accordance with the School District and University policies.
12. Sign off on all client documentation including psychological reports.
13. Maintain weekly supervision notes. These notes will be kept for 7 years and then destroyed.

The supervisor will discuss any concerns regarding the supervisee's performance in a timely fashion and will develop, in collaboration with the intern, a remediation plan if deficits/problems are identified.

It is the *intern's role* as supervisee to do the following:

1. Be punctual, both at sessions with clients as well as at supervision. In the event that you are delayed for or unable to attend a supervision session, it is your responsibility to notify your supervisor and make alternate arrangements. If the individual appointment cannot be kept due to scheduling conflicts, an

effort will be made to reschedule an alternate date/time; and a supervision session will only be canceled upon the mutual agreement of the both the supervisee and supervisor.

2. Be prepared, both for sessions with clients as well as for supervision. You are expected to have client notes, protocols, and recordings ready to review, to have "scored" all formal psychological instruments administered, and to have prepared an agenda of issues that you need to have addressed, together with the files of the clients involved. As part of this advanced preparation, the supervisee will have completed an *"Intern's Supervision Session Planner"* and shared this document with your supervisor *prior* to each supervisory session.

3. Provide summaries of all student, parent, educator, and other client contacts, interviews, and intervention activities for the supervisor. If a recording is required, it will be reviewed/critiqued by the intern and brought to the next supervisory session (keyed to a section that supervisee would like to review with the supervisor). The supervisee is responsible for planning and documenting work with clients as required by the school district. The *Intern's Client/Activity Session Planner* and the *Intern's Client/Summary Progress Notes* can be helpful tools to share with supervisors.

4. If the supervisee believes that client issues/concerns have not been adequately addressed during the regularly scheduled supervisory session, the supervisee will bring this to the attention of the supervisor and another session will be scheduled.

5. Share with the supervisor your learning goals for the training experience. This will require self-reflection and self-evaluation regarding your current level of clinical skill.

6. Be receptive to guidance and instruction from your supervisor, that is, be attentive to feedback and suggestions from your supervisor and follow through on such instruction promptly. It may be necessary to take notes during supervision in order to execute all instructions identified by your supervisor.

7. Inform your supervisor of any difficulties you are having in the areas of delivering services to clients, completing paperwork, or coordinating with other agencies or providers such as schools or independent practitioners.

8. As you establish a working relationship with your supervisor, it is hoped that you will become increasingly able to share issues and concerns you may have that impact your clinical work. Be open to feedback from others and monitor any tendency you may have toward defensiveness.

9. In consultation with your supervisor and after review of evidence-based literature, select a framework for integrating theory, research, and practice; formulate client case conceptualizations from this approach; and be ready to discuss the theoretical reasons and empirical supports for your assessment approaches, interventions, consultation, and problem-solving techniques.

10. The supervisee cannot engage in dual relationships with clients; that is, interns will not socialize with clients or their families, nor will they provide services to individuals they know from other contexts, such as friends or acquaintances. It is the intern's responsibility to alert the supervisor of any instances where the intern has prior knowledge of a client or his/her family from beyond the school setting. Appropriate measures to protect confidentiality will be employed in these circumstances.

11. The intern is responsible for insuring that the parents/guardians of all clients are informed of the supervised nature of your work as a supervisee, and of the ultimate professional responsibility of the supervisor.

12. You are responsible for insuring that all evaluative letters and reports concerning clients are co-signed by your clinical supervisor *before* they are sent out to parents, educators, or other approved third parties, i.e., private practitioners, governmental agencies, etc. When required, it is also your responsibility to determine that an active *Authorization for Release of Confidential Information* form is present in the client's file before presenting the letter/report to the supervisor for signature.

13. Assessment and intervention plans must be reviewed prior to implementation with the supervisor to determine appropriateness and monitored for effectiveness and potential revision on an ongoing basis. Supervisees must advise their clinical supervisor of all important changes related to a case, i.e., significant family events, disciplinary actions, legal issues, medical concerns, etc.

14. The intern must keep the supervisor informed about clients who are suicidal, homicidal, threatening to harm others, or engaged in any self-harm activities such as "cutting," substance abuse, eating disorders, or other dangerous risk taking behaviors. Any disclosure by a student or collateral informant of potential child abuse must be reported to the supervisor *immediately*. Notify your supervisor about clients who are involved in child custody disputes, Disability Determination assessments, or any other matter that affects the client's legal status. Notify your supervisor *immediately* if you receive any summons to testify or you are told that you will be subpoenaed to testify. Do *not* under any circumstances release client information to an attorney or court or anyone else without a proper *Authorization for Release of Confidential Information* form signed by the client, legal guardian, and the supervisor as prescribed by regulation. *In all circumstances, legal and ethical guidelines for the protection of client confidentiality must be followed.* Do not communicate confidential information or identify clients in email communications.

15. Seek supervision whenever you are uncertain about a situation. Make every attempt to reach your clinical supervisor before taking action with that client. If your supervisor cannot be reached, contact another staff school psychologist. You may also consult informally with more experienced clinicians on staff, but your clinical supervisor *must* be kept abreast of any and all emergencies.

In the event of emergency, the supervisee is to contact _____ at his/her office at _____, at home at _____, or by cell at _____. If unable to reach your supervisor, contact another psychology staff member. Follow the guidelines and procedures in the District and School Manuals for emergency situations.

16. Implement supervisory directives in subsequent psychological activities.
17. Uphold ethical APA and NASP principles in all client-related activities.
18. Be familiar with and follow the policies and procedures delineated in the District, School, and University manuals and documents. The supervisee agrees to complete all required reports and recordkeeping in a timely fashion for all cases and within guidelines specified in school and special education regulations. Drafts of psychological assessment reports and IEP paperwork should be submitted to the supervisor for review with enough time for review and editing prior to meetings.
19. Complete all professional tasks within time frames that address legitimate client needs and meet the requirements of all team participations.

IV. Terms of the Contract

This contract serves as verification and a description of the clinical supervision provided by _____ to _____ ("Supervisee"), engaged in a formal school psychology internship at _____ under the auspices of _____ (Internship Site) (University) for the 20_____ school year.

Supervisee: _____ Date: _____
Supervisor: _____ Date: _____
This contract is effective from _____ (start date) to _____ (finish date).

Appendix 7C

Supervision Session Planner

Date: Supervisor: Supervisee:

Last supervisory session follow-up:

Activity summary since last supervision:
(How time spent)

Cases/Activities to review:

Questions/Concerns/Feedback requested of Supervisor:

Self-assessment of Progress:
([Not completed every time] Include strengths and areas of need)

Appendix 7D

Client/Activity Session Planner

Client initials: Clinician: Date of Session/Activity:

Referral Questions/Activity Goals:

Session Objectives:

Plan of Activities:

Preparation Requirements:

Questions/Concerns:

Supervisor Notes:

Appendix 7E

Client Summary/Progress Notes

Date: Counselor: Client:

Session content:
(Topics, themes)

Session process:

(Therapeutic techniques, skills training)

Assessment of Progress:

Plans for Next Session:

Needs for Supervision:

Appendix 7F

Supervisor's Supervision Notes

Date:　　　　Supervisee:　　　　Supervisor:

1. **Content Summary:**
   (Follow-up from last session, critical case/activity reviews, and supervisor initiated agenda/feedback/concerns, professional development domain)

2. **Process Summary:**
   (Supervisee presentation, session dynamics, supervisory strategies employed)

3. **Feedback/Recommendations Summary:**
   (Skill/work feedback, intervention/activity recommendations)

4. **Next Steps/Future Action:**
   (Intervention homework/research, skill practice, case follow-up, activity prescription)

5. **Developmental Status Summary:**
   ([Not completed for each entry] Overall progress, key goals for improvement/professional development, formative feedback)

Appendix 7G

Illinois School Psychology Internship Consortium Internship Plan

ILLINOIS SCHOOL PSYCHOLOGY INTERNSHIP CONSORTIUM
INTERNSHIP PLAN

School Year: _____   Supervising Psychologist: _____

School Psychology Intern _____

	Prescribed Activities	Time Frame — Expectancy for STANDARD Level of Accomplishment (Indicate Month & Yr)	INTERN SELF-RATING Pre-Internship (Date:)			INTERIM MID YEAR EVALUATION SUPERVISING PSYCHOLOGIST (Date:)						SUMMATIVE END OF YEAR EVALUATION SUPERVISING PSYCHOLOGIST (Date:)					
			New Skill Level	Developing Skill Level	Competent Skill Level	Not Applicable	Not able to perform activity satisfactorily	Can perform activity but requires supervision	Acceptable and typical level of performance	More than acceptable and typical level performance	Outstanding ability, initiative and adaptability	Not Applicable	Not able to perform activity satisfactorily	Can perform activity but requires supervision	Acceptable and typical level of performance	More than acceptable and typical level performance	Outstanding ability, initiative and adaptability
PWC 1: Research	❖ Presents workshop, in-service, or course ❖ Completes research project																
❖ Applies research design and data analysis techniques when conducting research/program evaluation.																	
❖ Evaluates psychometric properties when selecting assessment methods.																	
❖ Applies knowledge of professional literature and research findings to all aspects of professional practice.																	
❖ Accesses and critically evaluates current research.																	
❖ Provides information about relevant research findings to school personnel, parents, and the public.																	

Prescribed Activities	Time Frame — Expectancy for STANDARD Level of Accomplishment (Indicate Month & Yr)	INTERN SELF-RATING Pre-Internship			INTERIM MID YEAR EVALUATION SUPERVISING PSYCHOLOGIST							SUMMATIVE END OF YEAR EVALUATION SUPERVISING PSYCHOLOGIST						
		New Skill Level	Developing Skill Level	Competent Skill Level	Not Applicable	Not able to perform activity satisfactorily	Can perform activity but requires supervision	Acceptable and typical level of performance	More than acceptable and typical level performance	Outstanding ability, initiative and adaptability		Not Applicable	Not able to perform activity satisfactorily	Can perform activity but requires supervision	Acceptable and typical level of performance	More than acceptable and typical level performance	Outstanding ability, initiative and adaptability
Date:		Date:			Date:							Date:					
❖ Charts student progress on measures sensitive to incremental change.																	
❖ Routinely follows up with implementers to ensure treatment integrity.																	
❖ Uses data to evaluate outcomes of services and to facilitate accountability.																	
❖ Uses data to identify factors that influence functioning at the individual, classroom, or building levels.																	
❖ Designs, implements, monitors, and evaluates programs that promote school, family, and/or community partnerships and enhance outcomes for students.																	
❖ Assists school personnel and other agency administrators with the interpretation of data to evaluate classroom, and/or building level programs.																	

Prescribed Activities	Time Frame: Expectancy for STANDARD Level of Accomplishment (Indicate Month & Yr)	INTERN SELF-RATING Pre-Internship Date:			INTERIM MID YEAR EVALUATION SUPERVISING PSYCHOLOGIST Date:						SUMMATIVE END OF YEAR EVALUATION SUPERVISING PSYCHOLOGIST Date:					
		New Skill Level	Developing Skill Level	Competent Skill Level	Not Applicable	Not able to perform activity satisfactorily	Can perform activity but requires supervision	Acceptable and typical level of performance	More than acceptable and typical level performance	Outstanding ability, initiative and adaptability	Not Applicable	Not able to perform activity satisfactorily	Can perform activity but requires supervision	Acceptable and typical level of performance	More than acceptable and typical level performance	Outstanding ability, initiative and adaptability
PWC 2: Ethical & Legal Standards																
❖ Completes Ethics Assignment																
❖ Practices in full accordance with APA Ethical Principles and Code of Conduct & NASP Principles for Professional Ethics.																
❖ Identifies complex ethical and legal issues, analyzes them, & proactively addresses them.																
❖ Follows legal, regulatory, and ethical parameters in record keeping and communicates information responsibly to others in compliance with confidentiality/privacy requirements.																
❖ Develops strategies to seek consultation regarding complex ethical & legal dilemmas.																
❖ Proactively addresses concerns regarding professional behavior of others.																
PWC 3: Individual & Cultural Diversity																
❖ Engages in two immersion experiences ❖ Presents case to cohort highlighting diversity																

Provides services to families

Prescribed Activities	Time Frame — Expectancy for STANDARD Level of Accomplishment (Indicate Month & Yr)	INTERN SELF-RATING Pre-Internship			INTERIM MID YEAR EVALUATION SUPERVISING PSYCHOLOGIST							SUMMATIVE END OF YEAR EVALUATION SUPERVISING PSYCHOLOGIST						
		New Skill Level	Developing Skill Level	Competent Skill Level	Not Applicable	Not able to perform activity satisfactorily	Can perform activity but requires supervision	Acceptable and typical level of performance	More than acceptable and typical level performance	Outstanding ability, initiative and adaptability		Not Applicable	Not able to perform activity satisfactorily	Can perform activity but requires supervision	Acceptable and typical level of performance	More than acceptable and typical level performance	Outstanding ability, initiative and adaptability	
❖ Recognizes the subtle racial, class, gender, cultural, and other biases and the ways in which these biases influence decision making, instruction, behavior, and long-term outcomes for students.																		
❖ Demonstrates sensitivity and other skills needed to work with families, students, and staff with diverse characteristics.																		
❖ Uses nondiscriminatory evaluation procedures.																		
❖ Incorporates information about students, families, cultures, and communities in assessments, interventions, and evaluations of progress.																		
❖ Promotes practices that help students and families of all backgrounds feel welcome and appreciated in the school.																		
❖ Works effectively with school personnel to promote supportive learning environments (e.g., anti-bullying programs).																		

Date: _____   Date: _____   Date: _____

	Prescribed Activities	Time Frame — Expectancy for STANDARD Level of Accomplishment (Indicate Month & Yr)	INTERN SELF-RATING Pre-Internship Date:			INTERIM MID YEAR EVALUATION SUPERVISING PSYCHOLOGIST Date:							SUMMATIVE END OF YEAR EVALUATION SUPERVISING PSYCHOLOGIST Date:						
			New Skill Level	Developing Skill Level	Competent Skill Level	Not Applicable	Not able to perform activity satisfactorily	Can perform activity but requires supervision	Acceptable and typical level of performance	More than acceptable and typical level performance	Outstanding ability, initiative and adaptability		Not Applicable	Not able to perform activity satisfactorily	Can perform activity but requires supervision	Acceptable and typical level of performance	More than acceptable and typical level performance	Outstanding ability, initiative and adaptability
Considers students' abilities in their primary and secondary languages and the effects of second language learning when designing assessments and planning interventions.																		
PWC 4: Professional values, attitudes, & behaviors	❖ Completes Cultural Self-Awareness Project ❖ Complete Leadership Project																	
❖ Prepares for & utilizes supervision to become increasingly independent.																		
❖ Consistently conducts self in a professional manner across settings & situations.																		
❖ Anticipates and self-identifies disruptions in professional functioning and intervenes early.																		
❖ Regulates affect during unexpectedly intense circumstances; seeks supervision and uses available resources to effectively manage the situation.																		
❖ Routinely engages in self-care.																		

Prescribed Activities	Time Frame Expectancy for STANDARD Level of Accomplishment (Indicate Month & Yr)	INTERN SELF-RATING Pre-Internship Date:			INTERIM MID YEAR EVALUATION SUPERVISING PSYCHOLOGIST Date:							SUMMATIVE END OF YEAR EVALUATION SUPERVISING PSYCHOLOGIST Date:						
		New Skill Level	Developing Skill Level	Competent Skill Level	Not Applicable	Not able to perform activity satisfactorily	Can perform activity but requires supervision	Acceptable and typical level of performance	More than acceptable and typical level performance	Outstanding ability, initiative and adaptability		Not Applicable	Not able to perform activity satisfactorily	Can perform activity but requires supervision	Acceptable and typical level of performance	More than acceptable and typical level performance	Outstanding ability, initiative and adaptability
❖ Elicits and incorporates constructive feedback.																	
❖ Reflects on performance, accurately assesses own strengths and weaknesses.																	
❖ Develops mutually supportive relationships with professional colleagues.																	
❖ Participates in personal continuing professional development/Takes initiative in learning new strategies/techniques.																	
❖ Completes ≥ 600 hours in the school and ≥2000 total internship hours.																	
❖ Attends ISPIC training seminars & completes assigned readings/projects.																	
❖ Promptly completes ISPIC forms and logs.																	
❖ Develops one's identity as a doctoral-level school, & health service psychologist.																	
❖ Maintains useful and accurate records of services provided.																	
❖ Demonstrates knowledge of current public policy issues																	

	Prescribed Activities	Time Frame Expectancy for STANDARD Level of Accomplishment (Indicate Month & Yr)	INTERN SELF-RATING Pre-Internship Date:			INTERIM MID YEAR EVALUATION SUPERVISING PSYCHOLOGIST Date:							SUMMATIVE END OF YEAR EVALUATION SUPERVISING PSYCHOLOGIST Date:						
			New Skill Level	Developing Skill Level	Competent Skill Level	Not Applicable	Not able to perform activity satisfactorily	Can perform activity but requires supervision	Acceptable and typical level of performance	More than acceptable and typical level performance	Outstanding ability, Initiative and adaptability		Not Applicable	Not able to perform activity satisfactorily	Can perform activity but requires supervision	Acceptable and typical level of performance	More than acceptable and typical level performance	Outstanding ability, Initiative and adaptability
impacting educational and mental health service delivery systems.																		
PWC: 5 Communication & Interpersonal Skills	❖ Leads a problem-solving team																	
❖ Articulates assessment findings in a manner that is understandable for the intended audience.																		
❖ Demonstrates appropriately assertive/direct verbal and non-verbal communications within the professional context.																		
❖ Participates in collaborative decision-making and problem solving with other professionals to achieve student success.																		
❖ Demonstrates positive interpersonal skills and shows patience in difficult situations through use of active listening, conflict resolution, and group facilitation skills.																		
❖ Communicates clearly with diverse audiences (e.g., parents, teachers, school																		

Prescribed Activities	Time Frame Expectancy for STANDARD Level of Accomplishment (Indicate Month & Yr)	INTERN SELF-RATING Pre-Internship Date:			INTERIM MID YEAR EVALUATION SUPERVISING PSYCHOLOGIST Date:							SUMMATIVE END OF YEAR EVALUATION SUPERVISING PSYCHOLOGIST Date:						
		New Skill Level	Developing Skill Level	Competent Skill Level	Not Applicable	Not able to perform activity satisfactorily	Can perform activity but requires supervision	Acceptable and typical level of performance	More than acceptable and typical level performance	Outstanding ability, Initiative and adaptability		Not Applicable	Not able to perform activity satisfactorily	Can perform activity but requires supervision	Acceptable and typical level of performance	More than acceptable and typical level performance	Outstanding ability, Initiative and adaptability
boards, policy makers, community leaders, colleagues). ❖ Effectively leads problem-solving teams with attention to positive tone, time-management, and accountability.																	
PWC: 6 Assessment ❖ Completes Traditional Initial Evaluations and/or Reevaluations ❖ Completes "Response to Intervention" Evaluations ❖ Completes personality assessment involving differential diagnosis (DSM5)																	
❖ Collects assessment results and other environmental data to identify student needs, establish goals, and design intervention strategies.																	
❖ Accurately administers, scores, and interprets standardized measures of cognition, achievement, and social-emotional functioning.																	

		INTERN SELF-RATING Pre-Internship			INTERIM MID YEAR EVALUATION SUPERVISING PSYCHOLOGIST						SUMMATIVE END OF YEAR EVALUATION SUPERVISING PSYCHOLOGIST					
Prescribed Activities	**Time Frame** Expectancy for STANDARD Level of Accomplishment (Indicate Month & Yr)	New Skill Level	Developing Skill Level	Competent Skill Level	Not Applicable	Not able to perform activity satisfactorily	Can perform activity but requires supervision	Acceptable and typical level of performance	More than acceptable and typical level performance	Outstanding ability, initiative and adaptability	Not Applicable	Not able to perform activity satisfactorily	Can perform activity but requires supervision	Acceptable and typical level of performance	More than acceptable and typical level performance	Outstanding ability, initiative and adaptability
	Date:				Date:						Date:					
❖ Prepares clearly written reports that address referral questions appropriately, report data accurately, and provide guidance for interventions.																
❖ Selects, implements, and integrates multiple methods of assessment reflecting an awareness of student characteristics.																
❖ Provides meaningful, useful feedback tied to the selection of evidence-based interventions.																
❖ Incorporates relevant developmental and ecological factors in diagnosis and intervention planning.																
❖ Reports include discussion of strength and limitations of measures and/or interpretation as appropriate.																
PWC: 7 Intervention ❖ Utilizes empirically supported mental health interventions ❖ Completes "Risk of Harm" Assessment ❖ Conducts individual, group, &																

Prescribed Activities	Time Frame — Expectancy for STANDARD Level of Accomplishment (Indicate Month & Yr)	INTERN SELF-RATING Pre-Internship — New Skill Level	Developing Skill Level	Competent Skill Level	INTERIM MID YEAR EVALUATION SUPERVISING PSYCHOLOGIST — Not Applicable	Not able to perform activity satisfactorily	Can perform activity but requires supervision	Acceptable and typical level of performance	More than acceptable and typical level performance	Outstanding ability, initiative and adaptability	SUMMATIVE END OF YEAR EVALUATION SUPERVISING PSYCHOLOGIST — Not Applicable	Not able to perform activity satisfactorily	Can perform activity but requires supervision	Acceptable and typical level of performance	More than acceptable and typical level performance	Outstanding ability, initiative and adaptability
		Date:			Date:						Date:					
family therapy																
❖ Participates in prevention or early intervention program																
❖ Utilizes empirically supported academic interventions																
❖ Utilizes empirically supported behavioral treatments																
❖ Conducts a skill-building group																
❖ Assists parents and other caregivers with the development and implementation of behavior change programs in the home.																
❖ Develops methods to assist teachers and families in teaching pro-social behavior to students.																
❖ Demonstrates ability to establish rapport and maintain appropriate boundaries.																
❖ Demonstrates knowledge of psychopathology and psychopharmacology.																
❖ Conceptualizes cases using various theoretical orientations.																
❖ Provides empirically supported interventions to individuals/ groups, addressing social-																

Prescribed Activities	Time Frame: Expectancy for STANDARD Level of Accomplishment (Indicate Month & Yr)	INTERN SELF-RATING Pre-Internship Date:			INTERIM MID YEAR EVALUATION SUPERVISING PSYCHOLOGIST Date:						SUMMATIVE END OF YEAR EVALUATION SUPERVISING PSYCHOLOGIST Date:					
		New Skill Level	Developing Skill Level	Competent Skill Level	Not Applicable	Not able to perform activity satisfactorily	Can perform activity but requires supervision	Acceptable and typical level of performance	More than acceptable and typical level performance	Outstanding ability, initiative and adaptability	Not Applicable	Not able to perform activity satisfactorily	Can perform activity but requires supervision	Acceptable and typical level of performance	More than acceptable and typical level performance	Outstanding ability, initiative and adaptability
emotional factors.																
❖ Provides empirically supported interventions to individuals/ groups, addressing academic factors.																
❖ Participates in the development and implementation of instructional strategies for students at different stages of development, including those who do not meet academic expectations.																
❖ Evaluate individuals' risk of harm to self and others and engage in appropriate safety planning and follow-up.																
❖ Applies the principles of behavior change to enhance student behavior/performance at the individual/classroom level.																
❖ Applies the principles of generalization and transfer of training to the development of interventions.																
❖ Effectively adapts intervention to address student needs.																

	Prescribed Activities	Time Frame — Expectancy for STANDARD Level of Accomplishment (Indicate Month & Yr)	INTERN SELF-RATING Pre-Internship — New Skill Level	Developing Skill Level	Competent Skill Level	INTERIM MID YEAR EVALUATION SUPERVISING PSYCHOLOGIST — Not Applicable	Not able to perform activity satisfactorily	Can perform activity but requires supervision	Acceptable and typical level of performance	More than acceptable and typical level performance	Outstanding ability, initiative and adaptability	SUMMATIVE END OF YEAR EVALUATION SUPERVISING PSYCHOLOGIST — Not Applicable	Not able to perform activity satisfactorily	Can perform activity but requires supervision	Acceptable and typical level of performance	More than acceptable and typical level performance	Outstanding ability, initiative and adaptability
			Date:			Date:						Date:					
PWC 8: Supervision	❖ Completes Supervision Project																
❖ Articulates a philosophy or model of supervision and reflects on how the model is applied in practice.																	
❖ Integrates and encourages self-care practices within supervision philosophy.																	
❖ Integrates and encourages culturally competent practices with supervisory philosophy.																	
❖ Reflects on one's effective use of supervision as supervisee and supervisor.																	
❖ Provides supervision to less advanced trainees, peers, or others.																	
PWC: 9 Consultation & Interprofessional/interdisciplinary skills	❖ Completes Systems-Level Consultation Project ❖ Actively participates on committee or administrative project																
❖ Uses knowledge and skills in consultation/collaboration to promote change at the																	

Prescribed Activities	Time Frame: Expectancy for STANDARD Level of Accomplishment (Indicate Month & Yr)	INTERN SELF-RATING Pre-Internship Date:			INTERIM MID YEAR EVALUATION SUPERVISING PSYCHOLOGIST Date:						SUMMATIVE END OF YEAR EVALUATION SUPERVISING PSYCHOLOGIST Date:					
		New Skill Level	Developing Skill Level	Competent Skill Level	Not Applicable	Not able to perform activity satisfactorily	Can perform activity but requires supervision	Acceptable and typical level of performance	More than acceptable and typical level performance	Outstanding ability, initiative and adaptability	Not Applicable	Not able to perform activity satisfactorily	Can perform activity but requires supervision	Acceptable and typical level of performance	More than acceptable and typical level performance	Outstanding ability, initiative and adaptability
individual, classroom, building, district, and/or other agency levels.																
❖ Analyzes group performance and assists school personnel in developing and monitoring goals.																
❖ Demonstrates knowledge of and skills involved in systems-change process.																
❖ Empowers students, their families/guardians, educators, and others to gain access to and effectively use school and community resources.																
❖ Collaborates with parents/guardians/teachers when designing interventions.																
❖ With properly signed releases, coordinates with other professionals in mental health, legal, medical, social service, and recreational programs involved with identified student.																

Supervisor's Signature _____ Date: _____

Supervisor's Signature _____ Date: _____

Intern's Signature _____ Date: _____

Appendix 7H

Sample Remediation Plan

Supervisee: Trainee
Primary Clinical Supervisor: CS
University Supervisor: US

This remediation plan is initiated in response to specific concerns in two domains of core professional competency noted in the recent summative evaluation completed by CS, the primary clinical supervisor, dated xxxx. This plan will target improvement in these two domains. The goal of this remediation plan is to intensify training focus on these areas of concern and provide additional supports so that Trainee can improve performance to expected levels of competency by xxxx. This plan will be implemented and supported by the Internship Clinical Supervisor (CS) and the University Supervisor (US) and discussed with the Supervisee (Trainee) on xxxxx. The clinical supervisor, CS, will complete another summative evaluation by _____ across all required practice domains but with particular attention to the domains requiring remediation.

I. Competency Domains Targeted: Intervention and Consultation Skills

The following competencies from Domain 2 of the Internship Plan:

Interns will acquire skills in culturally responsive <u>intervention</u> to address mental health and learning problems in children, adolescents, and their families.

Competencies components:

1. Understand the strengths and limitations of available evidence-based interventions consistent with best practice.
2. Select, administer, and provide evidence-based interventions consistent with assessment data.
3. Develop and evaluate evidence-based direct interventions.
4. Communicate (orally and in writing) results effectively to concerned parties, such as children, parents, and teachers.

The following competencies from Domain 4 of the Internship Plan:

Interns will acquire skills in culturally responsive <u>consultation</u> to address mental health and learning problems in children, adolescents, and their families.

Competencies components:

1. Establish effective, collaborative relationships with consultees including teachers, parents, and administrators consistent with best practice.

2. Plan and evaluate evidence-based indirect-service interventions based on the consultation plan developed with teachers, administrators, parents, or systems.
3. Communicate (orally and in writing) results effectively to concerned parties, such as children, parents, and teachers.

II. Professional Competence Problem Behaviors

The specific behaviors outlined below have been identified by CS and US as problematic:

1. Appropriately responding to unexpected answers and questions by child clients.
2. Effectively making and following through on in-the-moment decisions when working with a client.
3. Effectively interviewing clients, parents and teachers.
4. Communicating clearly and effectively with parents, school staff, and children (both written and orally).
5. Effectively integrating feedback from supervisors.

III. Expectations for Acceptable Performance

Intern must meet internship requirements as outlined in the University Internship Plan and in the internship competency summary delineated in the University Program Handbook. The requirement is to achieve benchmarks required for satisfactory completion of internship and readiness for entry-level professional practice.

IV. Trainee's Responsibilities and Actions

In addition to meeting all internship requirements specified in the Internship Handbook, the trainee will complete the following activities.
Trainee will:

1. Bring audio/visual recordings of client/group sessions to supervision sessions as agreed upon by the assigned supervisor(s).
2. Complete self-ratings of her clinical effectiveness and emotional awareness during client sessions and bring to supervision sessions as agreed upon by her assigned supervisor(s).
3. Be prepared to increase time engaged in individual supervision as needed.
Trainee is encouraged but not required to:

4. Review the textbook utilized in the course Theories and Techniques of Counseling Children and Adolescents, *School-Centered Interventions* (Simon, 2016), with particular attention to the case examples.
5. Consider initiating personal counseling to deal with stress-related issues that could be negatively impacting her clinical work.

V. Supervisors and Faculty Responsibilities and Actions

Clinical supervisors will provide more intensive supervision, increased time in individualized supervision as needed, additional observations of her clinical work, and frequent reviews of video and audio recordings of her client sessions. The University Supervisor will be available for consultation from the Trainee and Clinical Supervisor.

VI. Time Frame for Acceptable Performance

Trainee has until the end of this Spring semester (xxxx) to demonstrate her competence in all areas described above and meet all responsibilities/requirements associated with her internship and those outlined in this Remediation Plan.

VII. Assessment Methods

Trainee's performance will be assessed through review of self-administered checklists, supervisors' direct observations, reviews of audio and video recordings of her sessions, and feedback from all collaborating supervisors. These data will be integrated into a final summative evaluation of professional competencies within all domains included in the Internship Plan. Performance ratings will utilize the benchmark rubrics and criteria outlined in the Plan.

VIII. Evaluation Dates

Trainee must demonstrate competency by the end of the Spring xxxx. The primary clinical supervisor will share the written evaluation with Trainee by that date and then forward it to the University's School Psychology Coordinating Committee for final review and determination of status. Trainee can prepare a written response to this final summative evaluation to accompany its submission to the Committee. The Due Process rights delineated in the Program Handbook and discussed at the beginning of the internship year continue to be a resource for Trainee throughout this process.

IX. Consequences for Unsuccessful Remediation

If the remediation plan is unsuccessful as determined by the School Psychology Coordinating committee (with input from all supervisors), Trainee will be immediately terminated from the school psychology doctoral program.

The supervisors and faculty with responsibilities or actions described above agree to participate in this Remediation Plan.

Primary Clinical Supervisor: Date:
University Program Supervisor: Date:

I, _____, have reviewed the above remediation plan with my primary clinical supervisor and university supervisor. My signature below indicates that I fully understand the above plan. I agree disagree (check one) with the decision to initiate a remediation plan. My comments, if any are below.

Note: If Trainee disagrees, comments with a detailed description of the trainee's rationale for such disagreement are REQUIRED. Additional pages for comments and rationale are acceptable.

Trainee   Date

Appendix 7I

Feedback and Evaluation Case Examples

Three case examples are provided in this chapter with commentary. The following case examples are presented without authors' notes. They are provided for additional practice in feedback and evaluation skills and can be helpful in graduate or professional development training programs.

CASE EXAMPLE D: CHECKING OUT AND LOSING FOCUS

It is late February, you note that your intern who had been working very diligently has begun to lose focus, is less "on top of things," increasingly late with assigned tasks, and showing less energy and initiative. He seems much more stressed; and you wonder if there are personal issues affecting his performance. He also talks a lot about job hunting recently; and you wonder if he is shifting his focus prematurely to the next steps in his career.

How do you provide feedback about the drop in performance? Would you explore potential personal stressors? If so, how? What feedback would you give about the shift in focus to next year's job search?

CASE EXAMPLE E: AN ANXIOUS SUPERVISEE

Your intern, Danny, has gone straight through school and had no professional experience prior to entering graduate school. He is a young, intelligent, highly motivated, and enthusiastic intern. However, he is very anxious about performing everything correctly and wants very much to please you as his supervisor. You have just conducted a live counseling session observation with him working with a male adolescent client. It is very apparent that your intern's need for his client to like him is impacting his counseling. Your intern often asks the client if he thinks talking with him as a counselor is helping him and asks how much he likes working with him in these meetings. He ended the session by asking the client to rate how good a job he is doing counseling him.

How would you address Danny's high level of anxiety in supervision?
What strategies would you suggest to him to deal with his need for perfection?

CASE EXAMPLE F: CONCERNS ABOUT PERSONAL SAFETY

Your student, who grew up in a small farming community, is completing her practicum at an urban elementary school which is highly diverse and is in the center of an economically challenged neighborhood. She is asked to complete a home visit with you (her supervisor) in order to secure parent permission to conduct a full individual evaluation to determine a student's needs and possibly consider eligibility for special education placement. You have made many home visits to families in this neighborhood without any incidents. Margaret refuses to accompany you on this home visit explaining that it is too dangerous.
How would you address this issue in supervision?

CASE EXAMPLE G: BOUNDARY ISSUES

You are supervising a male intern in his high school placement. Bill is a young and enthusiastic intern. He is working with a group of adolescent boys in a social skills group. In the group are some boys who have no social skill difficulties who serve as positive role models for the others in the group. During a supervision session Bill was excited to share with you that he invited all of the boys over to his apartment last weekend; and all attended. As part of the discussion, you asked what he viewed as the purpose and benefits of this encounter. You asked about food and beverages, specifically if any alcohol was present. Bill responded that although none of the boys (all underage) drank, he did drink some beer in front of the boys.
What are the issues that need to be addressed in supervision? How would you address each?

CASE EXAMPLE H: STAFF RELATIONSHIPS

You are supervising A'Shadieeyah, in her elementary school placement. She is a bright, young, and highly motivated Muslim-American school psychology intern. This suburban community is relatively homogenous and primarily Caucasian. She routinely wears a Hijab; and, on occasion, she has been

(Continued)

(Continued)
asked by students to explain the meaning of this custom. You have observed that she connects very well with students and is doing effective work. She is working with a group of parents providing parent training. You participated in early sessions, discuss them routinely with her, and are pleased with how they are going. As a follow-up to a recent intervention team meeting, A'Shadieeyah is assigned to consult with a particular teacher. After inquiring whether A'Shadieeyah followed up with the teacher, your supervisee reports that the teacher refused to work with her because she was a Muslim and she does not like "those people."

What are the issues that need to be addressed in supervision? What would you do?

CASE EXAMPLE I: HIGHLY NERVOUS PRACTICUM STUDENT

You are providing the practicum supervision for Angie, a young second year (pre-internship) graduate student. You have observed her with several students completing activities such as administering cognitive ability and achievement tests. Angie is highly nervous to the point that she struggles to maintain her composure and to complete her tasks (e.g., dropping test materials, losing her place, voice cracking and so forth). You wonder if she can successfully complete this assessment practicum, and worry that you might need to take over these assessment assignments to protect the welfare of the child.

How would you share these observations in supervision? What strategies would you suggest to assist Angie in dealing with her nervousness? What supervisory strategies would you use to support her yet ensure appropriate client service? What communication would you provide to the university liaison?

CASE EXAMPLE J: PERCEPTIONS OF STAFF RELATIONS

Jenny is a very bright intern who is highly motivated to assist her clients to succeed. As part of her internship plan, Jenny is working with a number of general education classroom teachers on inclusion strategies for a number of students on her caseload with IEPs, who are also African American. During supervision, your intern is very critical of a couple of these teachers related to their willingness to work with these special education students in their classrooms and her sense that they are prejudiced against these minority students. They have shared with Jenny that they do not believe the students can be successful "as those are just not bright enough." Jenny is very upset and asks to no longer work with these teachers and wonders if there is any way to transfer these students to other classes for inclusion in general education.

How would you address this in supervision?

Appendix 7J

Counseling Skills Identification for Purposeful and Reflective Therapeutic Interventions

Core Foundation Counseling Skills

Attending (A) [nonverbal presence]
Active Listing/Accurate Empathy (AL)
    [Includes "paraphrasing," "reflection"]
Checking for Understanding (CU)
    [Includes "Clarification"—AL as a question]
Questioning and Information Gathering (Q & IG)
- Open ended [leading to description, elaboration, clarification]
  - How (H?)
  - What (W?)
- Probing (PQ)
  - Statements about counselor confusion
  - Requests for more information
  - Questions to explore other aspects of the problem
  - Repeating key word of client's to achieve focus or emphasis

Direct Communication (DC) ["I-Messages"]
- Immediacy (IM)
- [Process comments about the "here and now" interaction within the counseling session]
- Positive Similarity Self-disclosure (SD)

Summarizing (S)
- Tying together or *integrating* content often with additional insight
- *Reviewing* understanding of experiences, problem definition, progress, goals…

Challenging (C)
- Perceptions (CP), attributions (CA) (Cognitive Restructuring [CR] in CBT)
- Behavior (CB)
- Underutilized strengths (CS)

Problem-solving (PS)
- Solution generating (PS-SG)
- Pros and cons evaluation (PS-PC)
- Behavior planning (PS-BP)

Self-awareness Linkage

*(Case Conceptualization using Self-Understanding Model (SUM))**

- Exploration of individual domains of Self-Understanding Model
  - Experiences
  - Bodily reactions
  - Feelings
  - Thoughts (including self-talk)
  - Behaviors
- Action planning in SUM domains
- Recognition of contextual variables, i.e., family, peers… (SUM-CXT)

*Integrative interventions that connect these various aspects of functioning (Simon, 2016).

Cognitive-Behavioral Strategies

Collaborative Empiricism (CE)
- Therapist and client as co-investigators to together see if empirical evidence supports client's cognitions and thought patterns.

Socratic Dialogue (SD)
- Using Socratic questioning method to
  - clarify and define problems;
  - identify thoughts, images, and assumptions;
  - examine meanings of events;
  - assess consequences of maintaining maladaptive thoughts and behaviors.

Guided Discovery (GD)
- Explore weaknesses in behavioral stances and faulty thinking through creating experiences and experiments and thus create new thought patterns and remove constraints to implementation of adaptive.

Self-instruction Training (SI)
- Identifying self-defeating or negative self-talk patterns;
- Creating and rehearsing self-instruction scripts for adaptive coping and problem-solving.

Appendix 7K

Problem-solving Team Observation Checklist

Instructions: While reviewing the live observation or video recording, rate the teams on the following components of effective teaming.

Quality Scale:

1 = Yes, Present/Occurred
2 = No, Not Present, Did not Occur

Expectation	Rating	Evidence/ Comments
Problem-solving Teams		
Area 1: Pre-/Early meeting Set-Up/Structure and Use of Effective Communication		
1. Team met in a setting that was conducive for participation	1 2	
2. Various roles (e.g., facilitator, note taker, time keeper, etc.) were assigned to team members	1 2	
3. Data (e.g., preliminary baseline data) were collected prior to the meeting	1 2	
4. Notetaker took notes	1 2	
5. A parent was present and seemed to understand the process	1 2	
6. Parent and teacher were prompted to participate	1 2	
7. Facilitator encouraged participation of all team members	1 2	
8. Facilitator noted the purpose of the meeting	1 2	
9. Facilitator noted the Steps of Problem Solving before and during the meeting	1 2	
10. Facilitator used effective communication (more open-ended questions, reflective listening, clarification)	1 2	
11. Facilitator used summarization and validation to obtain consensus	1 2	
12. The next meeting date is set	1 2	
13. Did all team members participate?	1 2	
14. Brainstorming was used effectively	1 2	
15. Facilitator or group member used refocusing or limit setting effectively	1 2	
16. Consensus was reached effectively	1 2	

Expectation	Rating	Evidence/ Comments
Problem-solving Teams		
Area 2: Problem Identification		
1. Are problems operationally defined (i.e., observable and measurable?	1 2	

2. When multiple problems are identified, does the team prioritize them?   1 2

3. Are replacement behaviors identified during the problem identification stage?   1 2

4. Did a team member review records, conduct an interview(s), conduct observations, and/or conduct assessment to determine the presence of discrepancies between expectations and what is occurring?   1 2

5. Are the data collected during the problem identification stage displayed in a graphic or summary format?   1 2

6. Are there procedures for addressing the needs of severe problems in a timely manner?   1 2

Expectation	Rating	Evidence/ Comments

Problem-solving Teams

Area 3: Problem Analysis

1. Does the team have a systematic approach to analyzing problems?   1 2

2. Does the team use survey-level assessment to analyze academic problems?   1 2

3. Does the team use functional behavioral assessment techniques to analyze behavior problems?   1 2

4. Does the team assess whether the identified problem is a skill-based or a performance-based problem?   1 2

5. Does the team develop hypotheses for why a problem is occurring?   1 2

6. Are the hypotheses focused on relevant and alterable variables?   1 2

7. Are hypotheses specific, observable, measurable, and testable?   1 2

8. Do the hypotheses generated during problem analysis consider all potential factors that influence behavior/ academics (e.g., child, curriculum/instructional, peer, teachers, school, and community factors)?   1 2

9. Are problem analysis data useful in designing and implementing interventions?   1 2

10. Does the team obtain baseline data before a plan is developed?   1 2

11. Is there a system for communicating problem analysis results to parents and teachers?   1 2

12. Is there a commitment to collecting problem analysis data within 10 days of an initial referral?   1 2

Expectation	Rating	Evidence/Comments
Problem-solving Teams		
Area 4: Plan Development		
1. Is the intervention plan supported by research?	1 2	
2. Is the plan a result of the problem identification and analysis processes (i.e., is the intervention linked to the assessment)?	1 2	
3. Is the intervention plan realistic to implement?	1 2	
4. Is the plan focused on factors that are alterable (i.e., instructional, curriculum)?	1 2	
5. Does the team identify the goal of an intervention plan in observable terms?	1 2	
6. Does the team identify the goal of an intervention plan (who, what, where, when) and is it provided to all team members?	1 2	
7. Does the intervention plan have predetermined criteria to evaluate its efficacy and rules for making decisions?	1 2	
8. Are the criteria for effectiveness attainable and realistic?	1 2	
9. Is there a system in place to collect frequent ongoing data to determine if the plan is working?	1 2	
10. Can data collected to evaluate the plan be displayed in a graphic format?	1 2	
11. Is there a commitment to continue an intervention, as prescribed in the plan, until a team decision is made to discontinue it?	1 2	
12. Are parents involved in the development of an intervention plan, when applicable?	1 2	
13. Is the student involved in the development of an intervention plan, when applicable?	1 2	
14. Is there a system in place to communicate the ongoing results of the intervention plan with teachers and parents?	1 2	

Expectation	Rating	Evidence/Comments
Problem-solving Teams		
Area 5: Plan Implementation		
1. Does a member of the team commit to evaluating whether the intervention is being implemented as planned?	1 2	
2. Is there a procedure for providing the teacher with support if the plan is not being implemented as described?	1 2	
3. Is student progress towards the identified goal being evaluated on a regular basis, as described?	1 2	

4. Are the data being displayed in a graph for decision-making purposes?   1 2

5. Is the student progress communicated with teachers and parents?   1 2

6. Is there sufficient support provided to implement intervention plans?   1 2

7. Are parents involved in implementing intervention plans?   1 2

Expectation	Rating	Evidence/ Comments
Problem-solving Teams		
Area 6: Plan Evaluation		
1. Does the team follow decision-making rules when evaluating plans?	1 2	
2. Are the baseline and progress monitoring data displayed in a graph for the purpose of evaluating the plan effectiveness?	1 2	
3. Is there an agreed upon timeline for plan evaluation?	1 2	
4. When a plan has not been successful, does the team recycle through the problem-solving process?	1 2	
5. When a plan is effective, are decisions made about fading the intervention?	1 2	
6. Are there criteria for determining when a child's needs exceed the resources of the problem-solving team and special education eligibility is considered?	1 2	

Source: Cates, G.L., & Swerdlik, M.E. (2005). Problem-solving team observation checklist. Unpublished manuscript, Department of Psychology, Illinois State University, Normal, IL.

Appendix 9A

Case Conceptualization Flow Chart

The Self-Understanding Model (SUM)

1. Assessment

a. Baseline data available through PBIS, RtI problem-solving data collection…
b. Functional Behavioral Assessment
c. Assessment of cognitive variables
    i. Self-talk patterns
    ii. Attributional style
    iii. Locus of control
d. Assessment of dominant mood states
    i. Stress management style
    ii. Capacity for self-awareness
e. Systemic/ecological/contextual analysis
    i. Family
    ii. Peers
    iii. Culture/Diversity
    iv. SES factors
f. Biological, neurological, medical factors
    i. Learning issues
    ii. Health concerns and medications
    iii. Relevant genetic history
g. Diagnostic considerations (EBIs are symptom specific)
    i. Psychological testing (as necessary)
    ii. Co-morbidities

2. Intervention Planning

a. Chart current functioning and potential intervention strategies within each SUM Domain
    i. Experiences
    ii. Bodily reactions
    iii. Feelings
    iv. Thoughts
    v. Behaviors
b. Define social, coping, problem-solving skill needs
c. Delineate systemic/contextual factors
    i. Family
    ii. Peers
    iii. School

    d.   Investigate EBI for symptom profile

    e.   Prioritize concerns and set initial intervention targets

    f.   Design and implement intervention plan

3. Progress Monitoring and Outcome Assessment

    a.   Establish behavioral markers consistent with baseline and pre-intervention assessment data

    b.   Utilize progress monitoring data to modify intervention planning

    c.   Within special education build into IEP benchmarks

Essential Domains for Comprehensive Treatment Planning

- Symptom/diagnostic profile examined
- Developmental considerations (assessment and treatment)
- Empirically supported therapeutic intervention strategies
- Classroom instructional and behavior management strategies
- Crisis intervention (differentiated)
- Parent/family intervention considerations

Self-Understanding Model (SUM) Case-Conceptualization Flow Chart from Simon, D.J. (2016). *School-centered interventions: Evidenced-based strategies for social, emotional, and academic success.* Washington, DC: American Psychological Association Press. Copyright 2016 American Psychological Association Press. Reprinted with permission.

Appendix 10A

Sample Metasupervision Group Reflection Questions for Early, Middle, and Late Stages in the School Year

Reflection Questions for First Quarter

Reflective Practice of Supervision: Setting the Correct Tone and Structure from the Beginning

Starting the Supervisory Relationship

- How did you structure the beginning of supervision?
  - Did you use a written contract?
  - Did you directly talk about the anxiety of starting the relationship?
  - Did you share your "model" of supervision?
  - Did you discuss the evaluation aspects of supervision?
  - How did you assess the current skill set, goals, and needs of this specific intern?
  - Were any of the above strategies particularly helpful?
  - What else did you do that helped to get the internship and your supervisory relationship off to a positive start?

First Quarter Progression

- How has the intern's training and the supervisory relationship progressed during this first quarter of the school year?
  - Did you encounter any difficulties or challenges in the beginning of the relationship?
  - Did you do anything new or different as a supervisor that you found particularly helpful?
  - From the perspective of the Developmental component of DEP, has your intern progressed to more independent functioning at an appropriate or expected level?
  - Are there any special moments, great successes, concerns, issues, or questions that would be worth sharing with your colleagues?
  - Are there unique challenges you are encountering in training this supervisee that would be worth discussing with colleagues?

Personal Professional Growth as a Supervisor

- Are you feeling positive about your supervisory relationship and feeling like it is enhancing your own professional growth?

- Did you delineate personal growth goals in your role as a supervisor for this training cycle?
    - What were they?
    - How has this been progressing?
- Have you tried anything new or different as a supervisor this year?
    - What did you try?
    - Was it effective?
    - What other follow-up regarding this would you like to try?
- Is there any specific skill you want to develop or enhance as this training year progresses?
- (If you are a first time supervisor: has the supervisory experience matched your hopes and expectations? Are there areas of development of your supervisory skills you would like to focus on?)

Key **Behavioral Markers** *for Start of Year within DEP* *Supervision Model*

- *Written contract*
- *Collaborative assessment of strengths, weaknesses, training needs and goals*
- *System for advance planning for supervision—Supervision Session Planner*
- *Frequent provision of formative feedback*
- *Multiple methods of supervision*

Reflection Questions for Supervisors at Half Way Point of the School Year

- Intern progress
    - Has my intern progressed to expected levels of performance?
    - Has his/her functioning appropriately grown in independence?
    - Is he/she being viewed more as a "staff" member or an "intern" at this stage?
    - Has he/she sufficiently worked on targeted areas of development or new experience (i.e., supervisor-supervisee agreed upon areas of limited experience designated to receive special focus during training)?
    - Is intern being sufficiently exposed to the varied roles and responsibilities of a school psychologist?
    - Are there specific skill areas that should be the focus of more training, practice, and supervision?
- Supervisory relationship
    - Is the intern sufficiently prepared for supervisory sessions and demonstrating appropriate initiative in bringing concerns to sessions?
    - Are supervisory session times being kept sacred, rescheduled if canceled?

- Have supervisor and supervisee been able to comfortably discuss concerns, challenges, problems, and areas requiring focus for development?
  - Are there any concerns about performance and professional development that should be addressed but have either been insufficiently focused upon or avoided?
- Supervisor development
  - Are you feeling positive about your supervisory relationship and feeling like it is enhancing your own professional growth?
  - What should be the focus of your intern's growth in the half school year remaining so that you will feel comfortable that he/she is ready for an entry-level position in our profession?
  - Is there a different approach or strategy that you would like to employ in supervision but have delayed implementing?
  - Have you insisted on consistency with the written contract between you and your intern delineated in August?
  - Are there unique challenges you are encountering in training this supervisee that would be worth discussing with colleagues?

Key Behavioral Markers *for Midpoint of Year within DEP* Supervision Model

- *Was my halfway point summative evaluation complete and did it point to training goals for this semester?*
- *Has my intern been involved in the full range of professional activities delineated in the NASP Practice Model?*
- *Have we routinely processed the effectiveness of our supervisory relationship?*
- *Have I ensured that diversity and multicultural factors have been addressed as appropriate in all assessment and intervention activities?*
- *Have I successfully taught my intern a case conceptualization model for all problem-solving activities that is evidence-based and addresses individual and systemic variables?*

Reflection Questions for the Final Quarter of the School Year

Based on the stage of training we are in as we begin the last quarter of the school year, the following reflections can help us focus our discussion.

Developmental Status

- Supervision is a developmental process. The character of sessions changes over time.
  - Does the intern now take primary responsibility for supervisory session content?

- Is the nature of supervisor feedback becoming more consultative and less directive?
- Are there skills or behaviors that you need to focus on developing in your intern in the last quarter for either of the following reasons:
  - important area of training that has just not yet been addressed;
  - area of need that should be emphasized or challenged.

Feedback and Evaluation and Goal Setting

- Are you comfortable that you have given sufficient direct formative and summative feedback?
- If your intern is doing extremely well, is there a new activity or responsibility he/she could be given to challenge growth to the next level (e.g., an opportunity to provide supervision, an observed lead role in facilitating an Annual Review or a difficult parent conference, experience with a different disabling condition)?

Professional Growth as a Supervisor

- Do you feel you have grown professionally as a supervisor this year?
- Is there any area of your own development in the supervisory process that would be worth brainstorming with colleagues?
- Have you been able to work on the personal professional goals you set for yourself in August?
- Are there other strategies that you would like to employ in supervision but have delayed implementing?

Additional Questions for Administrators of School Psychological Services who Conduct Clinical Supervision

Supervision of Psychologists

- Which of the principles of supervision delineated in the Fall workshop have proven applicable to the supervision of certified staff? How?
- Have I assessed the scope and level of skills of professional staff in terms of my vision of psychological services?
  - How have I focused my individual supervision and in-service training agendas to address the skill needs identified in my assessment of staff skills?
  - How does the Developmental component of the DEP model of Supervision apply to my supervisory and mentoring interactions with staff based on factors such as years of experience, contemporary skill set demands, and my vision of a state-of-the-art psychological services delivery system?

- Holloway's Systems Approach to Supervision Model delineated five functions of supervision (Monitoring/evaluating, Instructing/advising, Modeling, Consulting, Supporting/sharing):
  - In which functions have I spent most of my time?
  - Is there a function I would like to engage in more frequently (and if so, how can I accomplish that)?

Supervision of Psychological Services

- Have I clearly articulated a vision for the character of psychological services delivery in my school or district?
  - What is this vision and how have I communicated it?
  - How do I manage resistance to change either by those in administration, the classroom teaching faculty, or my own staff of psychologists?
  - Can I place our program development within the "developmental model" framework?
    - What stage of development have we reached?
    - Are some programs, teams, or staff at more advanced levels than others?
      - How does that affect how I supervise and support them?
    - What steps have I taken or do I need to take to "build capacity" (i.e., in-service training, removal of time-consuming barriers to engaging in new roles and activities, etc.)?
- What goals do I have for staff and for program development for the remainder of this school year and looking ahead to next school year?
  - What steps do I need to take in "capacity building" of staff to make progress on these goals?

Appendix 12A

Sample Syllabus for a Seminar and Practicum in Supervision of School Psychological Services

Illinois State University
Seminar and Practicum in Supervision of School Psychological Services
Psychology 536
Spring 2016

Instructor: Dr. Mark E. Swerdlik
Office: 422 Degarmo Hall
Office Phone: XXX
Cell Phone: XXX
Email: meswerd@ilstu.edu
Office hours: When available in Degarmo Hall 422 or anytime by appointment
Class Meeting Day/Time: Tuesdays, 2:00–4:50
DeGarmo Hall 504

Any student in need of a special accommodation should contact 438–5853 (voice) or 438–8620 (TDD).

Description of Course and Instructional Strategies:

The goal of this course is to prepare school psychologists, as competent scientist-practitioners, to supervise colleagues at various stages of their professional development. The course will also address issues related to administering school psychological services (creating a mission/vision for a school psychological services unit, selecting staff, accountability, staff development, etc.). After completing this course, students will be able to articulate research questions to investigate the supervisory process. During this seminar, theoretical, empirical, and practical aspects of the supervision process and administration of school psychological services will be considered.

This doctoral-level class is taught as a seminar. In other words, the primary instructional approach will not be lecture; but rather our seminar will be discussion oriented and participative. It is, therefore, imperative that you prepare for and participate in class. Class activities will be structured; and evaluation methods will be consistent with this instructional approach. I want to hear your reactions to course content and the small class size coupled with your advanced standing should accommodate all students feeling comfortable sharing their reactions. Attendance at all class sessions is expected.

A number of experienced supervisors will be invited to class as guest speakers. They will be asked to share the following: 1) the work settings in which they have provided supervision, 2) what they enjoy most and find most challenging about supervision, 3) their philosophy of supervision, 4) what model(s) of supervision they have adopted and how they arrived at this model, 5) how they apply this model with their supervisees, 6) what they have found to be the most pressing ethical issue(s) in the supervisory relationship, and 7) if any crisis situations occurred in supervision and how they have handled them.

It is also expected that class members will prepare questions for guest speakers to further explore our guest speakers' supervision philosophies and how they would handle particular situations/issues based on class readings and class members' own experiences as supervisors in the practicum component of this course. When scheduled, discussions with guest speakers will typically last for 30–45 minutes beginning at 3:30 (or in some cases at the beginning or end of class).

As a further effort to address both clinical supervision and administration of school psychological services issues and provide you with different models/experiences of supervisory/administrative practices and the challenges of the role, you will be assigned a cyber mentor (see #8 below for more detailed information).

Discussion of legal-ethical issues impacting supervision will be discussed throughout the course through readings, the use of vignettes, and discussions with guest supervisors.

Doctoral Program Course Objectives/Competencies Addressed In Psychology 536:

Students will:

Objective II.6: Doctoral students will acquire skills in culturally responsive clinical and administrative *supervision*.

Competency II.6.1: Establish effective culturally responsive supervisory relationships.

Competency II.6.2: Develop a personal philosophy and model of supervision that can guide future administrative and clinical supervision activities.

Competency II.6.3: Implement effective supervisory methods.

Competency II.6.4: Implement effective methods of evaluating supervisee growth.

Competency II.6.5: Implement legal-ethical practice related to the administration of school psychological services and clinical supervision.

Competency II.6.6: Implement self-evaluation (of the supervisor) in the supervisory process.

Competency III.2.5: Demonstrate knowledge of current professional issues and roles in the field (e.g., supervision).

Specific Course Objectives

1. Each student will acquire a working knowledge of the Developmental/ Ecological/Problem-solving (DEP) model of Supervision (Simon & Swerdlik, 2017) as well as other topics related to clinical supervision of school psychologists.
2. Each student will acquire knowledge of issues and effective strategies related to the administration of school psychological services.
3. Each student will be able to articulate aspects of the DEP supervision model that they would find most useful in the supervision process of school psychologists at various stages of their professional development.
4. Each student will become familiar with legal-ethical issues related to the administration of school psychological services and clinical supervision.
5. Each student will become familiar with diversity and multicultural issues impacting the supervision process.
6. Each student will be able to articulate their own philosophy of clinical supervision and school psychological services.
7. Each student will develop an awareness of the importance of accountability/ evaluation procedures and of a continuing professional development plan for an administrative unit of school psychological services.
8. Through the practicum component of this course, each student will demonstrate an understanding of and the ability to effectively participate in the clinical supervision of first year school psychology practicum students.
9. Although a practicum component related exclusively to the administration of school psychological services is not possible to arrange as part of this course, class projects will allow students to demonstrate their ability to integrate and apply relevant literature to effectively administer a school psychological services unit.

Texts/Readings:

Primary Text: Simon, D.J. & Swerdlik, M.E. (2017). *Supervision in school psychology: The Developmental, Ecological, Problem-solving Model.* New York, NY: Routledge Publishing.

Selected Chapters From:

Harvey, V.S., & Struzziero, J. (2008). *Professional development and supervision of school psychologists: From intern to expert.* Thousand Oaks, CA: Corwin Press.
Holloway, E. (2016). *Supervision essentials for a Systems Approach to Supervision.* Washington, DC: American Psychological Association Press.

Requirements:

1. *Class participation*: regular attendance, completion of all assigned readings and class exercises, and participation in seminar discussions is expected. (100 points)

2. *Reaction papers*: As noted above, it is imperative for all students to prepare for and participate in class. Consistent with this expectation, students will prepare reaction papers on assigned readings and append other weekly assignments. The reaction papers are also used to guide your participation in our structured discussion groups, which will occur each week and will be based on the assigned readings and assignments for the week. If you are absent for the discussion, you can receive up to 12 of the points allotted for completion of the reaction paper. The format of the reaction papers will be discussed in class (25 points each/12 points if you do not attend the discussion). Papers should be a *maximum of 3–4 pages and will be graded according to the degree to which you identify common themes in the readings, integrate the readings with prior readings from your graduate (and/or undergraduate) coursework, your personal experiences as a supervisor or supervisee, and application of the content specifically to your supervision work.*

3. *Self-reflection journal:* A self-reflection journal of your weekly supervisory activities and development as a supervisor will be required. The weekly journal should document your supervision activities (i.e., the number of hours of your supervision activities per week and the nature of those activities), and include a discussion of issues, strengths, and problems related to your work as a supervisor of first year graduate students this semester, and *should serve as a vehicle for you to reflect on your own development as a supervisor.* The weekly self-reflection entry log should be appended to your weekly reaction paper but as noted above is not included as part of your 3–4 page weekly reaction paper page guideline.

4. *Clinical supervision form/instrument:* You will develop *a form/instrument* for your clinical supervision (50 points) reflecting characteristics of effective supervision you have learned in this course and *your own supervision philosophy. You should also include a section appended to your form/instrument that addresses how this instrument reflects your personal supervision philosophy.* This task is meant to be completed individually and is not part of any group project. *Due: April 26th as part of your portfolio.*

5. *Practicum experience:* Each doctoral student will be required to supervise up to three first year school psychology fieldwork students (exact day and time of supervision meeting will be mutually agreed upon between you and your supervisee(s). In addition to supervising their field placement work, these students are all enrolled in Psychology 473, Theories and Techniques of

Counseling for Children and Adolescents. As part of the course requirements you will be engaging in a series of role plays (you as the child or parent and the first year student the school psychologist) and providing corrective feedback related to the development of their active listening/counseling skills. You will be completing evaluation forms of each of your supervisees (and providing your supervisee a copy (as well as Dr. Tobin, the course instructor) related to their performance during these weekly role plays as an assessment of the development of their active listening/counseling skills. Dr. Tobin, the course instructor, will be visiting our seminar class to receive an update on her students' progress and to respond to any questions/concerns you may have related to this component of your supervision.

You must meet weekly with each of your school psychology supervisees for approximately 1 hour. You are responsible, in consultation with the instructor, for monitoring your supervisees' progress in their field placements and progress in conducting the role plays through your individual meetings and collecting, reading, and approving your supervisees' weekly logs, both EXCEL (for SSP students) /MY PSYCHTRACK (for doctoral students) log and *observation logs*. Observation logs should be submitted to you in advance of your individual meetings and you should provide your comments/questions either using "MSWord track changes" or by hand directly on the hard copy of the submitted observation log. You are also responsible for preparing *weekly supervision progress notes* (which will be discussed in class), which are to be typed and attached to your weekly reaction paper (also not part of the 3–4 page reaction paper guideline) to be reviewed by the instructor. You will also complete a final evaluation of each of your supervisees and provide input into their final grade in Psychology 498.05, First Year Fieldwork in School Psychology.

Your grade for this practicum component of the course will be determined by the instructor based on evaluations of your supervision by your supervisees and audio recordings/transcripts of your supervisory sessions (to be discussed further in class). You will be required to audio-record your supervision sessions each week and bring the CD or audio-file on your computer to class each week to discuss during metasupervision. PLEASE TEST OUT THE PLACEMENT OF THE MICROPHONE TO BE SURE IT IS ADEQUATELY RECORDING BOTH YOU AND YOUR SUPERVISEE. The instructor will be providing weekly group and individual (as needed) metasupervision. (150 points)

You will also each be asked to serve as a supervisor for up to three first year school psychology graduate students during fall semester 2017 by enrolling in 1 hour of Psychology 590.03, Advanced Practicum in Supervision. This will allow you to further develop your supervisory skills building upon your initial practicum experiences as part of this current course. Your supervisory efforts also benefit the program by providing increased supervision/support for first year school psychology graduate students to facilitate their entry into their elementary, Head Start, and TAP placements, and their initial adjustment to graduate school. Planning for this experience will be discussed further in class.

6. *Cyber mentors:* Each student will be assigned a school psychology supervisor/administrator who will be your mentor for the semester and with whom you will communicate weekly via email (see list of assigned cyber mentors later in this syllabus). You are expected to communicate with your mentor weekly related to questions/issues raised in your assigned readings, class discussion including any group-determined common questions that we want all of our cyber mentors to respond to, and issues/questions related to your own supervisees. Embed your email correspondence (including your mentors' responses if available) to your weekly reaction papers (this cyber mentor correspondence also does not count toward the 3–4 page reaction paper page limit). Class discussion will incorporate reactions of your cyber mentor to the issues/questions you have raised. You are asked to formally set goals for the semester with your cyber mentor so that we may have a measure of the effectiveness of this particular type of support system. This would also allow our mentors to give both formative and summative feedback to you as well. Please inform the instructor if your cyber mentor does not respond to two of your emails so that he can determine, after consultation with the cyber mentor, if an alternate should be assigned for the rest of the semester. We do have a list of alternates if your cyber mentor is not able to respond to you consistently and in a timely fashion.

7. *Tasks related to assuming the role of a Director of Psychological Services*: In lieu of a final exam in this course, the following tasks represent additional opportunities for you to demonstrate mastery of the course readings/discussions. These tasks require integration and application of course material.

    Assume you are now promoted to Director of Psychological Services for a Psychological Services Unit. In this role complete the following five tasks which are due April 26th (the last day of class) and are to be included as part of your portfolio:

    a. *Provide a description of your unit.* This should include the demographics of your district – rural, urban, or suburban; student enrollment, numbers of schools, type of school district-unit, elementary, or high school district; percentage of diverse students, type of organizational structure of your unit (i.e., who is included in the unit in addition to school psychologists), and the organizational structure of your unit (provide an organizational chart reflecting lines of authority). (25 points)

    b. *Develop a Vision, Mission, and Goals* of your School Psychological Services Unit. (25 points)

    c. *Develop an evaluation system (process)*, including an evaluation form, for the evaluation of an individual school psychologist. This evaluation process/system should be related to your Mission, Vision, and Goals of your unit and is focused on a practicing school psychologist. (25 points)

d. *Develop an Accountability System/Plan* for your Unit. This Accountability System/Plan should also be related to your Mission, Vision, and Goals for your unit. (25 points)

e. *Develop a Staff Development Plan* for your Unit. This Staff Development Plan should also be related to your Mission, Vision, and Goals of your unit. (25 points)

8. *Portfolio:* Create a portfolio of materials, to include the following:
   I. Your weekly logs/self-reflection journals, supervisory notes/memos.
   II. A discussion (2–4 typed pages) of your philosophy (i.e., key beliefs underlying your practice, your personal supervision model) of supervision.
   III. Your supervision contract (revised from first draft based on your philosophy developed/knowledge gained through completing this supervision course. Please include your first draft of the contract signed by your supervisees in your portfolio for comparison purposes). *Please highlight the revised sections of your contract.*
   IV. Your supervisor evaluation form (developed on your own based on your supervision philosophy, *not part of any group project*) including a description of how this form reflects your philosophy of supervision.
   V. Your individual or group project that includes the Description of your Psychological Services Unit, Vision, Mission, and Unit Goals; proposed evaluation process, including form, of individual school psychologist; unit accountability plan, and unit staff development plan.
   VI. *The last section of the portfolio must include a review of your "self-reflection logs" and a final discussion of your growth as a supervisor including strengths, weaknesses, how your supervision has changed over the course of the semester, and a listing of your <u>own</u> individualized goals for the advanced supervision 590.03 practicum in the fall.*

   The portfolio is due *April 26th (the last day of class)* and will be returned to you. (100 points for organization of portfolio, philosophy statement and revised supervisory contract, and for the reflection paper on your growth as a supervisor. Other components of the portfolio have assigned points specified elsewhere in this syllabus)

9. *Analysis of one supervision session using the DEP model.* You are to provide a transcription of the complete session, including time markers on your transcription, DEP Behavioral Markers, and how they are impacting your supervisee/supervisor relationship/supervisory session. *Be sure to include a critique of your session* (considering your supervision philosophy and goals and objectives of the session, what went well, what you would improve upon based on your DEP analysis). To help you prepare your analysis refer to the *DEP Supervisor Self-reflection and Supervisor Feedback Form (DEP-SSFS),* and SAS chapters related to task, functions, and contextual factors. Due *March 15th.*

Course Grading Scale:

90% of total points = A; 80% of total points = B; 70% of total points = C; 60% of total points = D and less than 60% of total points = F

Reading Schedule/Assignment Due Dates

January 12th

Activities/Class Content

Review of Syllabus including discussion of Practicum Component of Course and Cyber Mentorship and your personal goals for the course (please review syllabus prior to first class period and come prepared with questions).

Creating a Supervisory Alliance—questions completed (handout provided, consider duplicating for your supervisees)

Initial Discussion of Roles and Responsibilities and Characteristics of an Effective Supervisor

Discussion of first supervision session with your supervisee

(4:15), PSY 473 instructor, will come to class to discuss role plays with first year students enrolled in 473 (tentatively scheduled).

Assignment

Development of Practicum Contract: Develop your contract based on the readings under January 19th, your own personal supervisory experience to-date, and current philosophy. In your contract include that you will not ask about personal life unless it impacts their professional development/work behavior. Turn-in (Contract) to instructor by Tuesday, January 19th for approval (send as an email attachment).

January 19th

Readings

Developmental, Ecological, Problem-solving (DEP) Model: Chapters 1 (The Status of School Psychology Supervision and 2 (Clinical Supervision: Roles and Responsibilities)

NASP Position Statement on Supervision www.nasponline.org/about_nasp/position_paper.aspx *(then scroll down to supervision)*

APA Position on School-based school psychological services www.apa.org/about/policy/chapter-10.aspx

Search: *Supervisors for psychological services in schools*

Readings about Supervision Notes: DEP Chapter 7, pp. 13–18.

Assignments

Supervisory Contract. Final signatures on your contract should occur after the instructor approves your contract.

Review NASP Supervision Interest Group (Join Supervision Group by accessing NASP Web Page: www.nasponline.org/membership-and-community/get-involved/interest-groups and scroll down to the NASP Supervision group).

Audio-record First Supervision Session. Related to negotiating your contract provide a one-page critique (attached to your first reaction paper or your negotiated supervision contract). You may not have your final supervision contract for your supervisee to sign until your third session. Bring recorded session to class to discuss during metasupervision. This should occur each week.

January 26th

Activities/Class Content

Guest Speaker: XXX (3:30)

Readings

Developmental, Ecological, Problem–solving (DEP): Chapters 3 (Characteristics of Effective Supervisory Relationships) and 4 (Processing the Supervisory Relationship).

Holloway: Chapter 1 (Essential Dimensions of Systems Approach to Supervision).

Inadequate and Harmful Clinical Supervision: Testing Revised Framework and Assessing Occurrence (Ellis, Berger, Hanus, Ayala, Swords, & Siembor, 2014) (instructor provided reading).

Handouts on Characteristics of Effective Feedback and Supervisee Feedback form on Effective Feedback (provided by instructor).

Read Falender et al. (2004) on Defining Competencies in Psychology Supervision (provided by instructor).

Assignments

Administer Feedback Form to each of your supervisees over the next few weeks to gain input on how you provide feedback on role plays (record what you learned in your weekly reaction paper under integration).

Audio-record supervision session.

February 2nd

Activities/Class Content

Guest Speaker: XXX (3:30)

Readings

Developmental, Ecological, Problem-solving (DEP): Chapter 6 (Introduction to the DEP Model)
Holloway Chapter 2 (Case Illustration of Process in Supervision)

Assignments

What model(s) of supervision seems to fit best with your interpersonal style and how you view your supervisory role? Which models seem furthest from your style? Sketch out your own model of supervision (25 points). Attach as a separate assignment from your weekly reaction paper self-reflection log, and supervision progress notes.
Audio-record supervision session.

February 9th

No Class—NASP

February 16th

Readings

Holloway: Chapter 3 (Handling Common Supervisory Issues).
Developmental, Ecological, Problem-solving (DEP): Chapter 7 (The Developmental Component of the DEP Model).
Newman (2013) Structured Peer Group Supervision Format (we will begin using in class during metasupervision; instructor provided reading).
Smith, Riva, and Cornish (2014) The Ethical Practice of Group Supervision: A National Study (instructor provided reading).
Triantafillou (1997) A Solution-Focused Approach to Mental Health Supervision (instructor provided reading). Note in your reaction paper (application section) any aspects of this model you might incorporate into your own supervision model.

Assignments

Review (as examples) websites for Clark County Schools Psychological Services Units (Nevada) http://ccsd.net/divisions/student-support-services-division/psychological-services and Cypress-Fairbanks (TX) www.cfisd.net/en/about/know-your-district/departments/psychological-services/ school districts and include what you find in integration section related to mission/vision/philosophy statements and unit organization.

Audio-record supervision session.

February 23rd

Activities/Class Content

Guest Supervisor: XXX (3:30).

Readings

Developmental, Ecological, Problem-solving (DEP): Chapter 8 (The Ecological Component: Incorporating Contextual Factors).

Holloway: Chapter 3 (Handling Common Supervisory Issues).

Harvey & Struzziero: Chapter 3 (Multicultural Competencies).

Christiansen et al. (2011) Multicultural Supervision: Lessons Learned about an Ongoing Struggle (instructor provided reading).

Assignments

Complete Multicultural Competency Supervisor Rating Scale (provided by instructor) and be prepared to discuss in class.

Audio-record supervision session.

March 1st

Activity/Class Content

Guest Supervisor: XXX (3:30).

Readings

Developmental, Ecological, Problem-solving (DEP): Chapter 9 (The Problem Solving Component: Core Activity of Psychological Practice).

Grant, Crawford & Schofield (2012). Managing Difficulties in Supervision: Supervisors' Perspectives (instructor provided reading).

Harvey & Struzziero: Chapter 8 (Computer Assisted Supervision).

Assignment

Audio-record supervision session

March 8th

No Class—Enjoy your Spring Break.

March 15th

Readings

Developmental, Ecological, Problem-solving (DEP): Chapter 5 (Ethical and Legal Issues in School Psychology).

Barnett et al. (2007) Commentaries on Ethical and Effective Practice of Clinical Supervision (instructor provided reading).

Olley, R. I. (2004) Communicating Effectively to Resolve Ethical Concerns: The Role of School Psychology Supervisors (instructor provided reading).

Assignments

Look up Clinical Psychology Licensing Act (On State of Illinois Department of Professional Regulation website). Then find link for Section 1400.80 Unethical, Unauthorized, or Unprofessional Conduct www.ilga.gov/commission/jcar/admincode/068/068014000000800R.html and comment on what you found.

Analysis Due – Turn in Recording, Transcription (with time markers) Analyses, and Critique.

Audio-record supervision session.

March 22nd

Activity/Class Content

Guest Supervisor: XXX 3:30.

Readings

Developmental, Ecological, Problem-solving (DEP): Chapter 10 (Professional Development and Collegial Support Networks).

Harvey & Struzziero: Chapter 4 (Data-Based Decision Making and Accountability).

Assignment

Audio-record supervision session.

March 29th

Doctoral-level internships

Activity/Class Content

Guest Speakers on the Internship Application Process—Current class of doctoral students going on internship for 2015–16 school year 3:30

Readings

Harvey & Struzziero: Chapter 5 (Systems-Based Service Delivery).

Crespi & Lopez (1998) Practicum and Internship Supervision in the Schools: Standards and Considerations for School Psychology Supervisors (instructor provided reading).

Prus, J. (2009) Best Practice Guidelines for School Psychology Internships (instructor provided reading).

Phelps & Swerdlik (2011) Evolving Internship Issues in School Psychology Preparation (instructor provided reading).

Making Supervision Work for You www.apa.org/gradpsych/2003/05/supervision.aspx

Assignments

Review APPIC (Association of Professional Psychology Internships Centers) website www.appic.org (review and summarize various links in Integration section of reaction paper including online application if available).

Audio-record supervision session.

April 5th

Readings

Developmental, Ecological, Problem-solving (DEP): Chapter 11 (DEP Applied to Supervision of Credentialed Psychologists and Psychological Services).

Developmental, Ecological, Problem-solving (DEP): Chapter 7 (Review Section on Evaluation).

The DEP Supervisor Self-reflection and Supervisor Feedback Form (see DEP text Appendix 4A).

Cruise, T. & Swerdlik, M.E. (2010) Problematic Behaviors: Mediating Differences and Negotiating Change (instructor provided reading).

Karpenko and Gidycz (2013) The Supervisory Relationship and the Process of Evaluation Recommendations for Supervisors (instructor provided reading).

Assignment

Audio-record supervision session.

April 12th

Activity/Class Content

Guest Supervisors—Field Based School Psychology Administrators (3:30 pm)

Readings

Harvey & Struzziero: Chapters 13 (Leading and Managing), 14 (Recruiting and Orienting), and 15 (Performance Evaluations and Professional Development).

Assignments

★Review the *NASP Model for Comprehensive and Integrated School Psychological Services*. This resource is also important to review as you complete your tasks for the Director of Psychological Services project. www.nasponline. org/standards-and-certification/nasp-practice-model. Complete a search on supervision and note in your reaction paper how supervision is integrated into this model.

Based on the readings above, prepare five questions for our guest speakers (all administrators/supervisors of school psychological services) and include with reaction paper.

Audio-record supervision session.

April 19th

Readings

Developmental, Ecological, Problem-solving (DEP): Chapter 12 (Touching the Future: Teaching Supervision to Future Supervisors).

Harvey & Struzziero Chapters 10 (Supervising Consultation) and 11 (Supervising Services That Enhance Cognitive and Academic Skills).

Assignment

Audio-record supervision session.

April 26th

Readings

Developmental, Ecological, Problem-solving (DEP): Chapter 13 (Future Development: Research to Refine School Psychology Supervision).

Harvey & Struzziero Chapter 12 (Supervising Services That Enhance Wellness, Social Skills, Mental Health, and Life Competencies).

Harvey, V.S. & Pearrow, M. (2010). Identifying challenges in supervising school psychologists (instructor provided reading).

Association of State and Provincial Psychology Boards (ASPPB) Access at http://c.ymcdn.com/sites/www.asppb.net/resource/resmgr/Guidelines/Final_Supervision_Guidelines.pdf.

Assignments

Complete all Evaluation Letters.
Audio-record supervision session.

Portfolios Due – Clinical Supervision Evaluation Questionnaire Due as Part of Portfolio

May 3rd

Activities/Class Content

Wrap Up

Discuss your growth as a supervisor this past semester and goals for Fall for advanced practicum in supervision.

Evaluations of Cybermentors.

Appendix 12B

List of Topics for 1 Day (6 Hour) Supervision Workshop

I.   Building an Effective Supervisory Relationship
II. Definitions and Goals of Supervision
III. Roles and Responsibilities of Supervisors
IV. The DEP Model of Supervision
    a. Developmental
       • Structure: Contracting & Supervision
       • Session Planners, Supervision Notes
       • Multimethod Supervision
       • Evaluation and Feedback
    b. Ecological
       • Multicultural & diversity competency
       • Systems change & program development
    c. Problem-solving
       • Evidence-based practice
       • Case Conceptualization
V.   Ethics and Legal Practice
VI. Professional Development as a Supervisor
    a. DEP Self-reflection Instrument
    b. Collegial Supports
    c. Working with Universities
VII. Wrap up: Feedback and Next Steps

Appendix 12C

List of Topics for 2 Day (15 Hour) Intensive Supervision Workshop

Day 1 (September)

Defining Supervision and Clarifying Supervisor and Supervisee Roles
The Character of Effective Supervisory Relationships
Developmental, Ecological, Problem-solving Supervision Model
>   Developmental Component
> - Getting Started/Contracting
> - Structure and Organization to Support Training (Accountability, Session Planning, Recordkeeping)
> - Multiple Methods of Supervision
> - Evaluation and Feedback Part 1

Day 2 (January)

Reflections on Supervision Practice and Review
- Reflection Exercise
- Warm-Up Quiz
- Brief Review of September Session
- Metasupervision Themes: Review and Discussion

Ecological Component
- Systemic contexts for supervision
- Diversity and multicultural competency
- Incorporation of contextual and systemic factors into practice

Problem-Solving Component
- Case Conceptualization in the Context of Evidence-based Interventions
- Multimethod Supervision for Problem-solving
- Crisis Intervention Supervision

Applications of DEP Model: Case Examples
Evaluation and Feedback Part 2: Challenging Cases
- Problematic Professional Behaviors: Mediating Differences and Negotiating Change

Supporting Transitions
- Termination and Closure in Supervisory Relationships
- Letters of Recommendation and Other Considerations

Legal and Ethical Considerations in Supervision
Continuing Your Professional Development as a Supervisor

Three 1-hour group Metasupervision Sessions are scheduled with participants facilitated by course instructors.

REFERENCES

Alessi, G.J., Lascurettes–Alessi, K.J., & Leys, W.L. (1981). Internships in school psychology: Supervision issues. *School Psychology Review*, 10, 461–469.

Alexander, J.F., Waldron, H.B., Robbins, M.S., & Neeb, A.A. (2013). *Functional family therapy for adolescent behavior problems.* Washington, DC: American Psychological Association Press.

American Counseling Association (ACA). (2014). *ACA Code of Ethics.* Retrieved from www.counseling.org/resources/aca-code-of-ethics.pdf.

American Psychological Association (APA). (2000). Guidelines for psychotherapy with lesbian, gay, and bisexual clients. *American Psychologist*, 55, 1440–1451.

American Psychological Association (APA). (2002). Ethical principles of psychologists and code of conduct. *American Psychologist*, 57(12), 1060–1073.

American Psychological Association (APA). (2003). *Guidelines on multicultural education, training, research, practice, and organizational change for psychologists.* Retrieved from www. apapracticecentral.org/ce/guildelines/multicultural.pdf.

American Psychological Association (APA). (2007). Record keeping guidelines. *American Psychologist*, 62, 993–1004.

American Psychological Association (APA). (2008). *Report of the APA Task Force on the implementation of the Multicultural Guidelines.* Retrieved from www.apa.org/about/policy/multicultural-report.pdf.

American Psychological Association (APA). (2009). *Resolution on appropriate affirmative responses to sexual orientation distress and change efforts.* Retrieved from www.apa.org/pi/lgbc/publications/resolution-resp.html.

American Psychological Association (APA). (2010a). *Ethical principles of psychologists and code of conduct including 2010 Amendments.* Retrieved from www.apa.org/ethics/code/.

American Psychological Association (APA). (2010b). *Model Act for State Licensure.* Retrieved from www.apa.org/about/policy/model-act-2010.pdf.

American Psychological Association (APA). (2011). *Revised competency benchmarks for professional psychology.* Retrieved from www.apa.org/ed/graduate/revised-competency-benchmarks.doc.

American Psychological Association (APA). (2012a). *A practical guidebook for the competency benchmarks*. Retrieved from www.apa.org/ed/graduate/guide-benchmarks.pdf.

American Psychological Association (APA). (2012b). Guidelines for psychological practice with lesbian, gay, and bisexual clients. *American Psychologist, 67*(1), 10–42.

American Psychological Association (APA). (2013). *Guidelines for the practice of telepsychology*. Retrieved from www.apapracticecentral.org/ce/guidelines/telepsychology-guidelines.pdf.

American Psychological Association (APA). (2015a). Guidelines for clinical supervision in health service psychology. *American Psychologist, 70*(1), 33–46.

American Psychological Association (APA). (2015b). *Standards of accreditation for health service psychology*. Retrieved from www.apa.org/ed/accreditation/about/policies/standards-of-accreditation.pdf.

American Psychological Association, APA Task Force on the Assessment of Competence in Professional Psychology. (2006). *Report of the APA Task Force on the assessment of competence in professional psychology*. Washington, DC: Author.

American Psychological Association (APA) & National Association of School Psychologists (NASP). (2015). *Resolution on gender and sexual orientation diversity in children and adolescents in schools*. Retrieved from www.nasponline.org/about_nasp/resolution/gender_sexual_orientation_diversity.pdf.

American Psychological Association (APA) Board of Professional Affairs' Advisory Committee on Colleague Assistance. (2016). *Professional health and well-being for psychologists*. Retrieved from APA Practice Central: www.apapracticecentral.org/ce/self-care/well-being.aspx.

Americans with Disabilities Act of 1990, 42 U.S.C.A. §§12101 *et seq.*

Amerikaner, M., & Rose, T. (2012). Direct observation of psychology supervisees' clinical work: A snapshot of current practice. *The Clinical Supervisor, 31*, 61–80.

Angus, L., & Kagan, F. (2007). Empathic relational bonds and personal agency in psychotherapy: Implications for psychotherapy supervision, practice, and research. *Psychotherapy: Theory, Research, Practice, Training, 44*(4), 371–377.

Armistead, L.D. (2014). Best practices in continuing professional development for school psychologists. In P.L. Harrison & A. Thomas (Eds.), *Best practices in school psychology: Foundations* (pp. 611–626). Bethseda, MD: National Association of School Psychologists.

Association of Psychology Postdoctoral and Internship Centers (APPIC). (2011). *APPIC membership criteria: Doctoral psychology internship programs*. Retrieved from www.appic.org/Joining-APPIC/Members/Internship-Membership-Criteria.

Association of Psychology Postdoctoral and Internship Centers (APPIC). (2015). *Standard Reference Form*. Retrieved from www.appic.org/AAPI-APPA.

Association of State and Provincial Psychology Boards (ASPPB). (2013a). *The ASPPB Code of Conduct*. Retrieved from http://c.ymcdn.com/sites/www.asppb.net/resource/resmgr/Guidelines/Code_of_Conduct_Updated_2013.pdf.

Association of State and Provincial Psychology Boards (ASPPB). (2015). *Supervision guidelines for education and training leading to licensure as a health service provider*. Retrieved from http://c.ymcdn.com/sites/www.asppb.net/resource/resmgr/Guidelines/Final_Supervision_Guidelines.pdf.

Baird, B.N. (2008). *Internship, practicum, and field placement handbook: A guide for the helping professions* (5th ed.). Upper Saddle River, NJ: Pearson.

Barkley, R.A. (2013). *Defiant children: A clinician's manual for assessment and parent training* (3rd ed.). New York, NY: Guilford Press.

Barnett, J.E. (2008). Impaired professionals: Distress, professional impairment, self-care, and psychological wellness. In M. Hersen & A.M. Gross (Eds.), *Handbook of clinical psychology* (pp. 857–884). New York, NY: John Wiley and Sons.

Barnett, J.E., Erickson Cornish, J.A., Goodyear, R.K., & Lichtenberg, J.W. (2007). Commentaries on the ethical and effective practice of clinical supervision. *Professional Psychology: Research and Practice*, 38(3), 268–275.

Berger, S.S., & Bucholtz, E.S. (1993). On becoming a supervisee: Preparation for learning in a supervisory relationship. *Psychotherapy*, 30(1), 86–92.

Bernard, J.M. (1979). Supervisor training: A discrimination model. *Counselor Education & Supervision*, 19, 60–68.

Bernard, J.M., & Goodyear, R.K. (2014). *Fundamentals of clinical supervision* (5th ed.). Upper Saddle River, NJ: Pearson.

Bersoff, D.N., & Koeppl, P.M. (1993). The relation between ethical codes and moral principles. *Ethics & Behavior*, 3(3–4), 345–357.

Bieschke, K.J., Blasko, K.A., & Woodhouse, S.S. (2014). A comprehensive approach to competently addressing sexual minority issues in clinical supervision. In C.A. Falender, E.P. Shafranske, & C.J. Falicov (Eds.), *Multiculturalism and diversity in clinical supervision: A competency-based approach* (pp. 209–230). Washington, DC: American Psychological Association Press.

Bieschke, K.J., & Mintz, L.B. (2012). Counseling psychology model training values statement addressing diversity: History, current use, and future directions. *Training and Education in Professional Psychology*, 6, 196–203.

Borders, L.D. (1991). A systematic approach to peer group supervision. *Journal of Counseling and Development*, 69, 248–252.

Borders, L.D., & Brown, L.L. (2005). *The new handbook of counseling supervision*. New York, NY: Erlbaum.

Borders, L.D., Brown, J.B., & Purgason, L.L. (2015). Triadic supervision with practicum and internship counseling students: A peer supervision approach. *The Clinical Supervisor*, 34, 232–248.

Brock, S.E., Reeves, M.A., & Nickerson, A.B. (2014). Best practices in school crisis intervention. In P.L. Harrison & A. Thomas (Eds.), *Best practices in school psychology: Systems-level services* (pp. 211–230). Bethesda, MD: National Association of School Psychologists.

Bronfenbrenner, U. (1977). Towards an experimental ecology of human development. *American Psychologist*, 32(7), 513–531.

Bronfenbrenner, U. (1979). *The ecology of human development: Experiments by nature and design*. Cambridge, MA: Harvard University Press.

Burian, B., & Slimp, A. (2000). Social dual-role relationships during internship: A decision-making model. *Professional Psychology: Research and Practice*, 31(3), 332–338.

Canadian Psychological Association (CPA). (2000). *The Canadian code of ethics for psychologists* (3rd ed.). Retrieved from www.cpa.ca/cpasite/UserFiles/Documents/Canadian%20 Code%20of%20Ethics%20for%20Psycho.pdf.

Canadian Psychological Association (CPA). (2009). *The Canadian Psychological Association ethical guidelines for supervision in psychology: Teaching, research, practice, and administration*. Retrieved from www.cpa.ca/docs/File/Ethics/EthicalGuidelinesSupervisionPsychologyMar2012. pdf.

Cantillon, P., & Sargeant, J. (2008). Giving feedback in clinical settings. *British Medical Journal (International Edition)*, 337(a1961), 1292–1294.

Carifio, M.S., & Hess, A.K. (1987). Who is the ideal supervisor?. *Professional Psychology: Research and Practice*, 18(3), 244–250.

Castillo, J.M., & Curtis, M.J. (2014). Best practices in systems-level change. In P.L. Harrison & A. Thomas (Eds.), *Best practices in school psychology: Systems-level services* (pp. 11–28). Bethesda, MD: National Association of School Psychologists.

Caterino, L., Li, C., Hansen, A., Forman, S., Harris, A., Miller, G., & CDSPP Practice Taskforce. (2010). *Practice competencies outline: A reference for school psychology doctoral programs.* Retrieved from https://sites.google.com/site/cdspphome/system/app/pages/search?scope=search-site&q=task+force+on+competencies.

Cates, G.L., Blum, C.H., & Swerdlik, M.E. (2011). *Effective RTI training and practices: Helping school and district teams improve academic performance and social behavior.* Champaign, IL: Research Press.

Cates, G.L., & Swerdlik, M.E. (2005). *Problem-solving team observation checklist.* Unpublished manuscript, Department of Psychology, Illinois State University, Normal, IL.

Chorpita, B.F. (2007). *Modular cognitive-behavioral therapy for childhood anxiety disorders.* New York, NY: Guilford Press.

Christ, T.J. (2008). Best practices in aligning academic assessment with instruction. In A. Thomas & J. Grimes (Eds.), *Best practices in school psychology V* (pp. 159–176). Bethesda, MD: National Association of School Psychologists.

Christiansen, A.T., Thomas, V., Kafescioglu, N., Karakurt, G., Lowe, W., Smith, W., & Wittenborn, A. (2011). Multicultural supervision: Lessons learned about an ongoing struggle. *Journal of Marital and Family Therapy,* 37(1), 109–119.

Cochrane, W.S., Salyers, K., & Ding, Y. (2010). An examination of the preparation, supervisor's theoretical model, and university support for supervisors of school psychology interns. *Trainers' Forum: Journal of the Trainers of School Psychologists,* 29(1), 6–23.

Collins, C., Falender, C.A., & Shafranske, E.P. (2011). Commentary on Rebecca Schwartz-Mette's 2009 Article, "Challenges in Addressing Graduate Student Impairment in Academic Professional Psychology Programs." *Ethics & Behavior,* 21(5), 428–430.

Corey, G., Haynes, R., Moulton, P., & Muratori, M. (2010). *Clinical supervision in the helping professions* (2nd ed.). Alexandria, VA: American Counseling Association.

Council of Directors of School Psychology Programs (CDSPP). (2012). *Doctoral level internship guidelines.* Retrieved from https://sites.google.com/site/cdspphome/2012guidelines.

Cramer, R.J., Johnson, S.M., McLaughlin, J., Rausch, E.M., & Conroy, M.A. (2013). Suicide risk assessment training for psychology doctoral programs: Core competencies and a framework for training. *Training and Education in Professional Psychology,* 7, 1–11.

Cruise, T.K., Kelly, R.M., Swerdlik, M.E., Newman, D.S., & Simon, D.J. (2012, February). *School psychology intern supervision training: A state-wide universal system—the Illinois model.* Poster session presented at the annual conference of Trainers of School Psychologists. Philadelphia, PA.

Cruise, T.K., & Swerdlik, M.E. (2010). Problematic behaviors: Mediating differences and negotiating change. In J. Kaufman & T. Hughes (Eds.), *Handbook of education, training and supervision of school psychologists in school and community, Vol. II: Bridging the training and practice gap: Building collaborative university/field practices* (pp. 129–152). New York, NY: Taylor & Francis, Inc.

Curtis, M.J., Castillo, J.M., & Gelley, C. (2012). School psychology 2010: Demographics, employment, and the context of professional practices—Part 1. *Communique,* 40(7), 1, 28–30.

Daly, E.J., Doll, B., Schulte, A.C., & Fenning, P. (2011). The competencies initiative in American professional psychology: Implications for school psychology preparation. *Psychology in the Schools,* 48(9), 872–886.

Daniels, A.C. (2009). *Oops! 13 management practices that waste time and money (and what to do instead)*. Atlanta, GA: Performance Management Publications.

Desimone, L.M., Porter, A.C., Garet, M.S. Yoon, K.S., & Birman, B.F. (2002). Effects of professional development on teachers' instruction: Results from a three-year longitudinal study. *Educational Evaluation and Policy Analysis*, 24(2), 81–112.

Doll, B., & Cummings, J.A. (2008). *Transforming school mental health services: Population-based approaches to promoting the competency and wellness of children*. Bethesda, MD: National Association of School Psychologists.

Durlak, J.A., Domitrovich, C.E., Weissberg, R.P., & Gullotta, T.P. (Eds.). (2015). *Handbook of social and emotional learning: Research and practice*. New York, NY: Guilford Press.

Eber, L., Breen, K., Rose, J., Unizycki, R.M., & London, T.H. (2008). Wraparound as a tertiary level intervention for students with emotional/behavioral needs. *Teaching Exceptional Children*, 40, 16–22.

Egan, G. (2016). *The skilled helper: A problem-management and opportunity-development approach to helping* (10th ed.). Belmont, CA: Brooks/Cole Cengage Learning.

Ekstein, R., & Wallerstein, R.S. (1972). *The teaching and learning of psychotherapy* (2nd ed.). New York, NY: International University Press.

Elman, N.S., & Forrest, L. (2007). From trainee impairment to professional competence problems: Seeking new terminology that facilitates effective action. *Professional Psychology: Research and Practice*, 38(5), 501–509.

Falender, C.A. (2014). Supervision outcomes: Beginning the journey beyond emperor's new clothes. *Training and Education in Professional Psychology*, 8(3), 143–148.

Falender, C.A., Cornish, J., Goodyear, R., Hatcher, R., Kaslow, N.J., Leventhal, G., Shafranske, E., & Sigmon, S.T. (2004). Defining competencies in psychology supervision: A consensus statement. *Journal of Clinical Psychology*, 60(7), 771–785.

Falender, C.A., & Shafranske, E.P. (2004). *Clinical supervision: A competency-based approach*. Washington, DC: American Psychological Association Press.

Falender, C.A., & Shafranske, E.P. (2007). Competence in competency-based supervision practice: Construct and application. *Professional Psychology: Research and Practice*, 38(3), 232–240.

Falender, C.A., & Shafranske, E.P. (2012). *Getting the most out of clinical training and supervision*. Washington, DC: American Psychological Association Press.

Falender, C.A., Shafranske, E.P., & Falicov, C.J. (2014). Reflective practice: Culture in self and other. In C.A. Falender, E.P. Shafranske, & C.J. Falicov (Eds.), *Multiculturalism and diversity in clinical supervision: A competency-based approach* (pp. 273–281). Washington, DC: American Psychological Association Press.

Falicov, C.J. (2014a). Psychotherapy and supervision as cultural encounters: The multidimensional ecological comparative approach framework. In C.A. Falender, E.P. Shafranske, & Falicov, C.J. (2014a). *Multiculturalism and diversity in clinical supervision: A competency-based approach* (pp. 29–58). Washington, DC: American Psychological Association Press.

Falicov, C.J. (2014b). *Latino families in therapy* (2nd ed.). New York, NY: Guilford Press.

Family Educational Rights and Privacy Act of 1974. 20 U.S.C. 1232g; 34 C.F.R. Part 99.

Farber, E.E. (2010). Humanistic-existential psychotherapy competencies and the supervisory process. *Psychotherapy Theory, Research, Practice, Training*, 47, 28–34.

Fenning, P.A., Diaz, Y., Valley-Gray, S., Cash, R., Spearman, C., Hazel, C.E., … & Harris, A. (2015). Perceptions of competencies among school psychology trainers and practitioners: What matters? *Psychology in the Schools*, 52(10), 1032–1041.

Forgatch, M.S., & Patterson, G.R. (2010). Parent management training—Oregon Model: An intervention for antisocial behavior in children and adolescents. In J.R. Weisz & A.E. Kazdin (Eds.), *Evidence-based psychotherapies for children and adolescents* (2nd ed., pp 159–178). New York, NY: Guilford Press.

Forman, S.G. (2015). *Implementation of mental health programs in schools: A change agent's guide.* Washington, DC: American Psychological Association Press.

Forman, S.G., Shapiro, E.S., Codding, R.S., Gonzales, J.E., Reddy, L.A., Rosenfield, S.A., ... & Stoiber, K.C. (2013). Implementation science and school psychology. *School Psychology Quarterly*, 28(2), 77–100.

Fouad, N.A., Grus, C.L., Hatcher, R.L., Kaslow, N.J., Hutchings, P.S., Madson, M.B., Collins, F.L., & Crossman, R.E. (2009). Competency benchmarks: A model for understanding and measuring competence in professional psychology across training levels. *Training and Education in Professional Psychology*, 3, S5–S26.

Friedberg, R.D., & McClure, J.M. (2015). *Clinical practice of cognitive therapy with children and adolescents: The nuts and bolts* (2nd ed.). New York, NY: Guilford Press.

Fristad, M.A., Goldberg-Arnold, J.S., & Gavazzi, S.M. (2002). Multi-family psychoeducation groups (MFPG) for families of children with bipolar disorder. *Bipolar Disorders*, 4, 254–262.

Goodyear, R.K., & Rodolfa, E. (2012). Negotiating the complex ethical terrain of clinical supervision. In S. Knapp, M. Gottlieb, M. Handelsman, & L. VandeCreek (Eds.), *APA handbook of ethics in psychology, Vol 2: Practice, teaching and research* (pp. 261–275). Washington, DC: American Psychological Association.

Gottlieb, M.C., Robinson, K., & Younggren, J.N. (2007). Multiple relations in supervision: Guidance for administrators, supervisors, and students. *Professional Psychology: Research and Practice*, 38, 241–247.

Haley, J. (1976). *Problem-solving therapy*. San Francisco, CA: Jossey-Bass.

Harvey, V.S., & Pearrow, M. (2010). Identifying challenges in supervising school psychologists. *Psychology in the Schools*, 47, 567–581.

Harvey, V., Stoiber, K.C., & Krejci, R. (2014, February). *A comparison of supervisor and supervisee ratings during internship.* Paper presented at the annual conference of the National Association of School Psychologists, Washington, DC.

Harvey, V.S., & Struzziero, J.A. (2008). *Professional development and supervision of school psychologists: From intern to expert* (2nd ed.). Thousand Oaks, CA: Corwin Press.

Harvey, V.S., Struzziero, J.A., & Desai, S. (2014). Best practices in supervision and mentoring of school psychologists. In P. Harrison & A. Thomas (Eds.), *Best practices in school psychology: Foundations* (pp. 567–580). Bethesda, MD: National Association of School Psychologists.

Henggeler, S.W., Cunningham, P.B., Rowland, M.D., & Schoenwald, S.K. (2012). *Contingency management for adolescent substance abuse: A practitioner's guide.* New York, NY: Guilford Press.

Henggeler, S.W., Schoenwald, S.K., Borduin, C.M., Rowland, M.D., & Cunningham, P.B. (2009). *Multisystemic therapy for antisocial behavior in children and adolescents* (2nd ed.). New York, NY: Guilford Press.

Hoffman, M.A., Hill, C.E., Holmes, S.E., & Freitas, G.F. (2005). Supervisor perspective on the process and outcome of giving easy, difficult, or no feedback to supervisees. *Journal of Counseling Psychology*, 52(1), 3–13.

Holloway, E.L. (1995). *Clinical supervision: A systems approach.* Thousand Oaks, CA: Sage.

Holloway, E.L. (2016). *Supervision essentials for a systems approach to supervision.* Washington, DC: American Psychological Association Press.

Hosp, J.L. (2008). Best practices in aligning academic assessment with instruction. In A. Thomas & J. Grimes (Eds.), *Best practices in school psychology V* (pp. 363–376). Bethesda, MD: National Association of School Psychologists.

Hsu, W. (2009). The components of solution-focused supervision. *Bulletin of Education Psychology*, 41, 475–496.

Huebner, E.S. (1992). Burnout in school psychology: An exploratory investigation into its nature, extent, and correlates. *School Psychology Quarterly* 7(2), 129–136.

Huebner, E.S., Gilligan, T.D., & Cobb, H. (2002). Best practices in managing stress and burnout. In A. Thomas & J. Grimes (Eds.), *Best practices in school psychology IV* (pp. 173–182). Bethesda, MD: National Association of School Psychologists.

Huey, S.J., Jr., & Polo, A.J. (2010). Assessing the effects of evidence-based psychotherapies with ethnic youth minorities. In J.R. Weisz & A.E. Kazdin (Eds.), *Evidence-based psychotherapies for children and adolescents* (2nd ed., pp. 451–465). New York, NY: Guilford Press.

Illinois State Board of Education (ISBE). (2007). *Social work manual.* Retrieved from www.isbe.state.il.us/spec-ed/pdfs/social_work_manual.pdf.

Individuals with Disabilities Education Improvement Act of 2004. Pub. L No. 108–446, 20 U.S.C.1400 *et seq.* 34 C.R.R. Part 300.

Jacob, S., Decker, D., & Hartshorne, T. (2011). *Ethics and law for school psychologists* (6th ed.). Hoboken, NJ: John Wiley & Sons.

Jaycox, L. (2004). *Cognitive behavioral intervention for trauma in schools (CBITS).* Longmont, CO: Sopris West.

Joyce-Beaulieu, D., & Rossen, E. (2016). *The school psychology practicum and internship handbook.* New York, NY: Springer.

Juarez, J.A., Marvel, K., Brezinski, K.L., Glazner, C., Towbin, M.M., & Lawton, S. (2006). Bridging the gap: A curriculum to teach residents cultural humility. *Family Medicine*, 38, 97–102.

Kapp-Simon, K.A., & Simon, D.J. (1991). *Meeting the challenge: Social skills training for adolescents with special needs.* Chicago: University of Illinois Press.

Karpenko, V., & Gidycz, C.A. (2012). The supervisory relationship and the process of evaluation: Recommendations for supervisors. *The Clinical Supervisor*, 31(2), 138–158.

Kaslow, N.J. (2004). Competencies in professional psychology. *American Psychologist*, 59, 774–781.

Kaslow, N.J., Borden, K.A., Collins, F.L., Forrest, L., Illfelder-Kaye, J., Nelson, P.D., … & Rallo, J.S. (2004). Competencies Conference: Future directions in education and credentialing in professional psychology. *Journal of Clinical Psychology*, 60, 699–712.

Kaslow, N.J., Grus, C.L., Campbell, L., Fouad, N.A., Hatcher, R.L., & Rodolfa, E.R. (2009). Competency Assessment toolkit for professional psychology. *Training and Education in Professional Psychology*, 3, S27–S45.

Kaslow, N.J., Rubin, N.J., Bebeau, M.J., Leigh, I.W., Lichtenberg, J.W., Nelson, P.D., … & Smith, I.L. (2007). Guiding principles and recommendations for the assessment of competence. *Professional Psychology: Research and Practice*, 38(5), 441–451.

Kaufman, J. (2015). Introduction: The future is now—challenges in the new age of psychological practice. In R. Flanagan, C. Allen, & E. Levine (Eds.), *Cognitive and behavioral interventions in the schools: Integrating theory and research into practice* (pp. 3–14). New York, NY: Springer.

Kelly, R.M., Wise, P.S., Cruise, T.C., & Swerdlik, M. (2002). A state-wide collaborative approach to intern supervision. *Trainer's Forum*, 22(2), 5–8.

Kendall, P.C. (2012a). Anxiety disorders in youth. In P.C. Kendall (Ed.), *Child and adolescent therapy: Cognitive-behavioral procedures* (pp. 143–189). New York, NY: Guilford Press.

Kendall, P.C. (Ed.). (2012b). *Child and adolescent therapy: Cognitive-behavioral procedures* (4th ed.). New York, NY: Guilford Press.

Kendall, P.C. (2012c). Guiding theory for therapy for children and adolescents. In P.C. Kendall (Ed.), *Child and adolescent therapy: Cognitive-behavioral procedures* (pp. 3–24). New York, NY: Guilford Press.

Kendall, P.C., & Hedtke, K.A. (2006). *Cognitive-behavioral therapy for anxious children: Therapist manual* (3rd ed.). Ardmore, PA: Workbook Publishing.

Knoff, H.M. (1986). Supervision in school psychology: The forgotten or future path to effective services? *School Psychology Review*, 15, 529–545.

Koocher, G.P., & Keith-Spiegel, P. (2008). *Ethics in psychology: Professional standards and cases.* New York, NY: Oxford University Press.

Kosciw, J.G., Greytak, E.A., Diaz, E.M., & Barkiewicz, M.J. (2010). *The 2009 National School Climate Survey: The experiences of lesbian, gay, bisexual, and transgender youth in our nation's schools.* New York, NY: GLSEN.

Kratochwill, T.R., & Bergan, J.R. (1990). *Behavioral consultation in applied settings: An individual guide.* New York, NY: Plenum Press.

Kratochwill, T.R., & Shernoff, E.S. (2004). Evidence-based practice: Promoting evidence-based interventions in school psychology. *School Psychology Review*, 33(1), 34–48.

Ladany, N., Lehrman-Waterman, D., Molinaro, M., & Wolgast, B. (1999). Psychotherapy supervisor ethical practices adherence to guidelines, the supervisory working alliance, and supervisee satisfaction. *The Counseling Psychologist*, 27(3), 443–475.

Ladany, N., Mori, Y., & Mehr, K.E. (2013). Effective and ineffective supervision. *The Counseling Psychologist*, 41(1), 28–47.

Lamb, D.H., & Swerdlik, M.E. (2003). Identifying and responding to problematic school psychology supervisees. *The Clinical Supervisor*, 22(1), 87–110.

Lambers, E. (2007). A person-centered perspective on supervision. In M. Cooper, M. O'Hara, P.R. Schmid, & G. Wyatt (Eds.), *The handbook of person-centered psychotherapy and counseling* (pp. 366–378). New York, NY: Palgrave Macmillan.

Larson, J. (2005). *Think first: Addressing aggressive behavior in secondary schools.* New York, NY: Guilford Press.

Larson, J., & Lochman, J.E. (2011). *Helping schoolchildren cope with anger: A cognitive-behavioral intervention* (2nd ed.). New York, NY: Guilford Press.

Lassiter, P.S., Napolitano, L., Culbreth, J.R., & Ng, K. (2008). Developing multicultural competence using the structured peer group supervision model. *Counselor Education and Supervision*, 47, 164–178.

Liddle, H.A., Breunlin, D.C., Schwartz, R.C., & Constantine, J.A. (1984). Training family therapy supervisors: Issues of content, form, and context. *Journal of Marital and Family Therapy*, 10, 139–150.

Loganbill, C., Hardy, E., & Delworth, U. (1982). Supervision: A conceptual model. *The Counseling Psychologist*, 10, 3–42.

Lowry, J.L. (2001, August). Successful supervision: Supervisor and supervisee characteristics. In J. Barnett (Chair), *The secrets of successful supervision.* Symposium conducted at the meeting of the American Psychological Association, San Francisco, CA.

Lynch, E.W., & Hanson, M.J. (2011). *Developing cross-cultural competence: A guide to working with children and their families* (4th ed.). Baltimore, MD: Paul H. Brookes Publishing.

McCabe, P.C., & Rubinson, F. (2008). The behavioral intention of school psychology and education trainees to advocate for lesbian, gay, bisexual, and transgendered youth. *School Psychology Review*, 17(4), 469–486.

McGoldrick, M., Giordano, J., & Garcia-Petro, N. (Eds.). (2005). *Ethnicity and family therapy*. New York, NY: Guilford Press.

Machek, G.R., & Kelly, S.R. (2016, February). *Building systems for training and support of clinical supervisors: Local and regional initiatives*. Presentation at the meeting of Trainers of School Psychologists, New Orleans, LA.

McIntosh, D.E., & Phelps, L. (2000). Supervision in school psychology: Where will the future take us? *Psychology in the Schools*, 73(1), 33–38.

McKevitt, B.C. (2012). School psychologists' knowledge and use of evidence-based, social-emotional learning interventions. *Contemporary School Psychology*, 16, 33–45.

McNeil, B.W., & Worthen, V. (1989). The parallel process in psychotherapy supervision. *Professional Psychology: Research and Practice*, 20, 320–333.

McNeill, B.W., & Stoltenberg, C.D. (2016). *Supervision essentials for the integrative developmental model*. Washington, DC: American Psychological Association Press.

Mash, E.J., & Barkley, R.A. (Eds.). (2006). *Treatment of childhood disorders* (3rd ed.). New York, NY: Guilford Press.

Miller, G., Lines, C., & Fleming, M. (2014). Best practices in family-school collaboration for multitiered service delivery. In P.L. Harrison & A. Thomas (Eds.), *Best practices in school psychology: Systems-level services* (pp. 491–504). Bethesda, MD: National Association of School Psychologists.

Miller, G.A. (1969). Psychology as a means for promoting human welfare. *American Psychologist*, 24, 1063–1075.

Miller, W.R., & Rollnick, S. (2012). *Motivational interviewing: Helping people change* (3rd ed.). New York, NY: Guilford Press.

Milne, D.L., Sheikh, A.I., Pattison, S., & Wilkinson, A. (2011). Evidence-based training for clinical supervisors: A systematic review of 11 controlled studies. *The Clinical Supervisor*, 30(1), 53–71.

Minuchin, S. (1974). *Families and family therapy*. Cambridge, MA: Harvard University Press.

Mychailyszyn, M.P., Brodman, D.M., Read, K.L., & Kendall, P.C. (2012). Cognitive- behavioral school-based interventions for anxious and depressed youth: A meta-analysis of outcomes. *Clinical Psychology: Science and Practice*, 19, 129–153.

Naar-King, S., & Suarez, M. (2011). *Motivational interviewing with adolescents and young adults*. New York, NY: Guilford Press.

National Association of School Psychologists (NASP). (2010a). *Model for comprehensive and integrated school psychological services*. Bethesda, MD: Author.

National Association of School Psychologists (NASP). (2010b). *Standards for the graduate preparation of school psychologists*. Bethesda, MD: Author.

National Association of School Psychologists (NASP). (2010c). *Standards for credentialing of school psychologists*. Bethesda, MD: Author.

National Association of School Psychologists (NASP). (2010d). *Principles for professional ethics*. Bethesda, MD: Author.

National Association of School Psychologists (NASP). (2011a). *Supervision in school psychology* (Position Statement). Bethesda, MD: Author.

National Association of School Psychologists (NASP). (2011b). *Lesbian, gay, bisexual, transgender, and questioning (LGBTQ) youth* (Position Statement). Bethesda, MD: Author.

National Association of School Psychologists (NASP). (2014a). *Position statement on sexual minority youth.* Bethesda, MD: Author.

National Association of School Psychologists (NASP). (2014b). *Safe schools for transgender and gender diverse students* (Position Statement). Bethesda, MD: Author.

National Association of School Psychologists (NASP). (2014c). *Best Practice Guidelines for School Psychology Intern Field Supervision and Mentoring.* Retrieved from www.nasponline.org/Documents/Best_Practice_Guidelines_for_Intern_Supervision.pdf.

National Association of School Psychologists (NASP). (2015). *National Certified School Psychologist eligibility.* Retrieved from www.nasponline.org/standards-and-certification/national-certification.

National Association of School Psychologists (NASP). (2016). *Guidance for postgraduate mentorship and professional support.* Bethesda, MD: Author.

National Reading Panel (US), National Institute of Child Health, & Human Development (US). (2000). *Report of the national reading panel: Teaching children to read: An evidence-based assessment of the scientific research literature on reading and its implications for reading instruction: Reports of the subgroups.* National Institute of Child Health and Human Development, National Institutes of Health.

Neimeyer, G.J., Taylor, J.M., Rozensky, R.H., & Cox, D.R. (2014). The diminishing durability of knowledge in professional psychology: A second look at specializations. *Professional Psychology: Research and Practice,* 45, 92–98.

Nelson, J.R., Benner, G.J., & Mooney, P. (2008). *Instructional practices for students with behavioral disorders: Strategies for reading, writing, and math.* New York, NY: Guilford Press.

Newman, D.S. (2012). A grounded theory study of supervision of preservice consultation training. *Journal of Educational and Psychological Consultation,* 22, 247–279.

Newman, D.S. (2013). *Demystifying the school psychology internship: A dynamic guide for interns and supervisors.* New York, NY: Routledge.

Newman, D.S., Nebbergall, A.J., & Salmon, D. (2013). Structured peer group supervision for novice consultants: procedures, pitfalls, and potential. *Journal of Educational and Psychological Consultation,* 23(3), 200–216.

Noguera, P.A. (2009). Preparing for a new majority: How schools can respond to immigration and demographic change. In A. Hargreaves and M. Fullan (Eds.), *Change wars.* Bloomington, IN: Solution Tree.

Norcross, J.C., & Guy, J.D. (2007). *Leaving it at the office: A guide to psychotherapist self-care.* New York, NY: Guilford Press.

Olweus, D., Limber, S., & Mihalic, S.F. (1999). *Blueprints for violence prevention, book nine: Bullying prevention program.* Boulder, CO: Center for the Study and Prevention of Violence.

Osborn, C.J., & Davis, T.E. (1996). The supervision contract: Making it perfectly clear. *Clinical Supervisor,* 14(2), 121–134.

Overholser, J.C. (1991). The Socratic method as a technique in psychotherapy supervision. *Professional Psychology: Research and Practice,* 22(1), 68.

Page, L. (2008). *Healthy Lifestyle Assessment.* Unpublished manuscript, Arlington Heights, IL.

Patterson, G.R. (1982). *Coercive family process.* Eugene, OR: Castalia.

Patterson, G.R., Reid, J.B., Jones, R.R., & Conger, R.E. (1975). *A social learning theory approach to family intervention: Volume I. Families with aggressive children.* Eugene, OR: Castalia Publishing.

Phelps, L., & Swerdlik, M.E. (2011). Evolving internship issues in school psychology preparation. *Psychology in the Schools,* 48(9), 911–921.

Pluymert, K. (2014). Problem-solving foundations for school psychological services. In P.L.1 Harrison & A. Thomas (Eds.), *Best practices in school psychology: Data-based and collaborative decision making* (pp. 25–39). Bethesda, MD: National School Psychologists Association.

Reinke, W.M., Hermann, K.C., & Sprick, R. (2011). *Motivational interviewing for effective classroom management: The classroom check-up.* New York, NY: Guilford Press.

Reiser, R.P., & Milne, D. (2012). Supervising cognitive-behavioral psychotherapy: Pressing needs, impressing possibility. *Journal of Contemporary Psychotherapy*, 42, 161–171.

Remley, T.P., & Herlihy, B. (2010). *Ethical, legal, and professional issues in counselling* (3rd ed.). Upper Saddle River, NJ: Merrill/Prentice Hall.

Reschly, D.J. (2008). School psychology paradigm shift and beyond. In A. Thomas & J. Grimes (Eds.), *Best practices in school psychology V* (pp. 17–36). Bethesda, MD: National Association of School Psychologists.

Rønnestad, M.H., & Skovholt, T.M. (2003). The journey of the counselor and therapist: Research findings and perspectives on professional development. *Journal of Career Development*, 30, 5–44.

Rønnestad, M.H., & Skovholt, T.M. (2012). *The developing practitioner: Growth and stagnation of therapists and counselors.* New York, NY: Routledge.

Rosenfield, S. (2008). Best practice in instructional consultation and instructional consultation teams. In A. Thomas & J. Grimes (Eds.), *Best practices in school psychology V* (pp. 1645–1660). Bethesda, MD: National Association of School Psychologists.

Rosenfield, S. (2014). Best practice in instructional consultation and instructional consultation teams. In P. Harrison & A. Thomas (Eds.), *Best practices in school psychology: Data-based and collaborative decision making* (pp. 509–524). Bethesda, MD: National Association of School Psychologists.

Rosenfield, S., Levinsohn-Klyap, M., & Cramer, K. (2010). Educating consultants for practice in schools. In E. Garcia Vazquez, T. Crespi, & C. Riccio (Eds.), *Handbook in education, training, and supervision of school psychologists in school and community* (Vol. 1, pp. 337–347). New York, NY: Routledge.

Sarnat, J.E. (2010). Key competencies of the psychodynamic psychotherapist and how to teach them in supervision. *Psychotherapy, Research, Practice, Training*, 47, 20–27.

Schwartz-Mette, R.A. (2011). Out with impairment, in with professional competence problems: Response to commentary by Collins, Falender, and Shafranske. *Ethics & Behavior*, 21(5), 431–434.

Searles, H.F. (1955). The informational value of the supervisor's emotional experience. *Psychiatry*, 18, 135–146.

Section 504 of the Rehabilitation Act of 1973. Pub. L No.93–112), 29 U.S.C. 794, 34 C.R.R. Part 104.

Sergiovanni, T.J. & Starratt, R.J. (2002). *Supervision: A redefinition* (7th ed.). New York, NY: McGraw-Hill.

Sheridan, S.M., & Gutkin, T.B. (2000). The ecology of school psychology: Examining and changing our paradigm for the 21st century. *School Psychology Review*, 29, 485–502.

Sheridan, S.M., & Kratochwill, T. (2010). *Conjoint behavioral consultation: Promoting family-school connections and interventions* (2nd ed.). New York, NY: Springer.

Shriberg, D., Bonner, M., Sarr, B., Walker, A., Hyland, M., & Chester, C. (2008). Social justice through a school psychology lens: Definitions and applications. *School Psychology Review*, 37, 453–468.

Shulman, L. (2006). The clinical supervisor-practitioner working alliance. *The Clinical Supervisor*, 24(1–2), 23–47.

Silva, A.E., Newman, D.S., & Guiney, M.C. (2014). Best practices in early career school psychology transitions. In P. Harrison & A. Thomas (Eds.), *Best practices in school psychology: Foundations* (pp. 553–566). Bethesda, MD: National Association of School Psychologists.

Silva, A.E., Newman, D.S., Guiney, M.C., Valley-Gray, S., & Barrett, C.A. (2016). Supervision and mentoring for early career school psychologists: Availability, access, structure, and implications. *Psychology in the Schools*, 53, 502–516.

Simon, D.J. (2012). Organizational tools for social emotional learning: Linking self-understanding and problem-solving models. *School Psychology in Illinois*, 33(3), 11–13.

Simon, D.J. (2013). Understanding school-based groups: Applications of evidence-based treatments. *School Psychology in Illinois,* 35(1), 7–11.

Simon, D.J. (2015a). *Counseling skills identification for purposeful and reflective therapeutic interventions.* Unpublished manuscript, School Psychology Program, Loyola University of Chicago.

Simon, D.J. (2015b). *A systematic approach to program development and systems change.* Unpublished manuscript, School Psychology Program, Loyola University of Chicago.

Simon, D.J. (2016). *School-centered interventions: Evidence-based strategies for social, emotional, and academic success.* Washington, DC: American Psychological Association Press.

Simon, D.J., Cruise, T.K., Huber, B.J., Newman, D.S., & Swerdlik, M.E. (2014). Supervision in school psychology: The developmental/ecological/problem-solving model. *Psychology in the Schools*, 51(6), 636–646.

Spence, S.H., Wilson, J., Kavanagh, D., Strong, J., & Worrall, L. (2001). Clinical supervision in four mental health professions: A review of the evidence. *Behaviour Change*, 18(03), 135–155.

Stark, K.D., Schnoebelen, S., Simpson, J., Hargrave, J., Molnar, J., & Glenn, R. (2006). *Children's workbook for ACTION.* Ardmore, PA: Workbook Publishing.

Stoiber, K.C. (2014). A comprehensive framework for multitiered systems of support in school psychology. In A. Thomas & P. Harrison (Eds.), *Best practices in school psychology: Data-based and collaborative decision making* (pp. 41–70). Bethesda, MD: National Association of School Psychologists.

Stoltenberg, C.D., & Delworth, U. (1987). *Supervising counseling and therapists: A developmental approach.* San Francisco, CA: Jossey-Bass.

Stoltenberg, C.D., & McNeill, B.W. (2010). *IDM Supervision: An integrative developmental model for supervising counselors and therapists* (3rd ed.). New York, NY: Routledge.

Stoltenberg, C.D., McNeill, B.W. & Delworth, U. (1998). *IDM: An Integrated Developmental Model for supervising counselors and therapists.* San Francisco, CA: Jossey-Bass.

Storm, C.L., Todd, T.C., Sprenkle, D.H., & Morgan, M.M. (2001). Gaps between MFT supervision assumptions and common practice: Suggested best practices. *Journal of Marital and Family Therapy*, 27(2), 227–239.

Sugai, G., Horner, R.H., & McIntosh, K. (2008). Best practices in developing a broad-scale system of support for school-wide positive behavior support. In A. Thomas & J. Grimes (Eds.), *Best practices in school psychology V* (pp. 1487–1504). Bethesda, MD: National Association of School Psychologists.

Sullivan, J.R., & Conoley, J.C. (2008). Best practice in the supervision of interns. In A. Thomas & J. Grimes (Eds.), *Best practices in school psychology V* (pp. 1957–1974). Bethesda, MD: National Association of School Psychologists.

Swenson, C.C., Henggeler, S.W., Taylor, I.S., & Addison, O.W. (2009). *Multisystemic therapy and neighborhood partnerships: Reducing adolescent violence and substance abuse.* New York, NY: Guilford Press.

Tarasoff v. *Regents of California*, 118 Cal. Rptr. 129, 529, P.2d 533 (Cal.1974). (Tarasoff I).

Tarasoff v. *Regents of California*, 131 Cal. Rptr. 14, 551, P.2d 344 (Cal. 1976) (Tarasoff II).

Texas Board of Examiners of Psychologists (2015). *Proposed Rules for Psychologist Licensure.* Retrieved from www.sos.state.tx.us/texreg/archive/October22015/Proposed%20 Rules/22.EXAMINING%20BOARDS.html#27.

Tilly, W.D., III. (2008). The evolution of school psychology to science-based practice: Problem solving and the three-tiered model. In A. Thomas & J. Grimes (Eds.), *Best practices in school psychology V* (pp. 17–36). Bethesda, MD: National Association of School Psychologists.

Tromski-Klingshirn, D.M., & Davis, T.E. (2007). Supervisees' perceptions of their clinical supervision: A study of the dual role of clinical and administrative supervisor. *Counselor Education and Supervision, 46,* 294–304.

Ward, S.B. (1999). Field-based intern supervision: A study of practices. *Communiqué, 28*(3), 32–33.

Ward, S.B. (2001). Intern supervision in school psychology: Practice and process of field-based and university supervisors. *School Psychology International, 22*(3), 269–284.

Watzlawak, P., & Weakland, J.H. (Eds.). (1977). *The interactional view: Studies at the Mental Research Institute.* New York, NY: W.W. Norton.

Webster-Stratton, C., Rinaldi, J., & Reid, J.M. (2011). Long-term outcomes of Incredible Years Parenting Program: Predictors of adolescent adjustment. *Child and Adolescent Mental Health, 16,* 38–46.

Weisz, J.R., & Kazdin, A.E. (Eds.). (2010). *Evidence-based psychotherapies for children and adolescents* (2nd ed.). New York, NY: Guilford Press.

White, S.W. (2011). *Social skills training for children with Asperger syndrome and high-functioning autism.* New York, NY: Guilford Press.

Wilbur, M.P., Roberts-Wilbur, J., Hart, G.M., & Morris, J.R. (1994). Structured group supervision (SGS): A pilot study. *Counselor Education and Supervision, 33,* 262–279.

Williams, B.B., & Monahon, L.W. (2014). Best practices in school psychologists' self-evaluation and documenting effectiveness. In A. Thomas & P. Harrison (Eds.), *Best practices in school psychology: Foundations* (pp. 581–598). Bethesda, MD: National Association of School Psychologists.

Wise, E.H., Sturm, C.A., Nutt, R.L., Rodolfa, E., Schaffer, J.B., & Webb, C. (2010). Life-long learning for psychologists: Current status and a vision for the future. *Professional Psychology: Research and Practice, 41*(4), 288–292.

Yin, R.K. (2011). *Qualitative research from start to finish.* New York, NY: Guilford Press.

Yin, R.K. (2014). *Case study research: Design and methods* (5th ed.). Thousand Oaks, CA: Sage.

Ysseldyke, J., Burns, M.K., Dawson, M., Kelly, B., Morrison, D., Ortiz, S., & Telzrow, C. (2006). *School psychology: A blueprint for training and practice III.* Bethesda, MD: National Association of School Psychologists.

Ysseldyke, J.E., & Reschly, D.J. (2014). The evolution of school psychology: Origins, contemporary status, and future directions. In P. L. Harrison and A. Thomas (Eds.), *Best practices in school psychology data-based and collaborative decision making* (pp. 71–84). Bethesda, MD: National Association of School Psychologists.

Zins, J.E., & Murphy, J.J. (1996). Consultation with professional peers: A national survey of the practices of school psychologists. *Journal of Educational and Psychological Consultation, 17,* 175–184.

INDEX

Note: **bold** page numbers denote a table, *italics* an illustration, and the suffix 'a' an Appendix.

Systemic 25–6, 157, 160, 183, 214–15; Targeted 168–9
ISBE (Illinois State Board of Education) 74
ISPA (Illinois School Psychologists Association) 13, 224, 225, 226
ISPIC (Illinois School Psychology Internship Consortium) 12, 13, 48, 104, 195–6, 224, 226–8, 229, 234–5, **265a–77a**

Jacob, S. 58, 66, 68
justice 58, 59, 60, 67; interactional 146; social 145–6, 150–1

Karpenko, V. 115
Keith-Speigel, P. 68
Kendall, P.C. 165
Knoff, H.M. 4
Koocher, G.P. 68
Kratochwill, T.R. 143

Ladany, N. 35, 65
Lamb, D.H. 118–19
Larson, J. 135
Latino Families in Therapy 148
law and ethics 24, 33, 57–78, 98, 110, 191; Family Rights and Privacy Act (1974) (FERPA) 62–3, 66, 70, 74; *see also* vicarious liability
leadership 111, 130, 166, 168, 169, 180, 209, 217–18, 226, 227, 244a
learning styles 107
Lerhman-Waterman, D. 65
LGBT issues 152–4, 212, 247a
liability 67; *see also* vicarious liability
limits to confidentiality 61, 62, 63, 65; case examples 70–6
live (direct) observation 9, 93, 115, 125, 126, 127, 128–30, 131, 134, 169, 170, 248a, 253a, 254a; *see also* observation
Lochman, J.E. 135

McClure, J.M. 129
McIntosh, D.E. 4, 19
macrosystem 26, 141
MECA (Multidimensional Ecosystemic Comparative Approach) 150
Mehr, K.E. 35
mentoring 23–4, 202–3, **211**, 216, 229, 304a
metacognitive skills 40–1

metasupervision 9, 12, 93, 136, 139, 197, 198, 210, 223, 227, 236, 294a–8a, 303a; for supervisors 120, 134, 193, 194–6, 216, 217, 223, 226, 227, 228, 229, 230
microsystems 26, 141
minors 41, 62, 65, 70, 73–6
Mintz, L.B. 154
Minuchin, S. 142
Model Act for State Licensure of School Psychologists (APA) 10, 201
Model for Comprehensive and Integrated School Psychological Services (NASP) 4, 212, 232, 312a; *see also* Practice Model (NASP)
modeling 8, 25, 29, 33, 37, 41–2, 44, 66, 67, 126–7, 137, 154, 169, 193; case examples 135, 183, 184, 185, 283a
Model Program for Supervisor Training (ISPIC) 226–8
Molinaro, M. 65
Montana 226
Mori, Y. 35
MTSS (Multitiered Systems of Support) 44–5, 143, 167–70, 171, 173, 206, 210, 212, 215, 216
multicultural competence *see* diversity and multicultural competency
multidisciplinary problem-solving 14, 166–7
multimethod supervision 49, 68, 91, 97–8, 125–35, 139, 140, 184, *186*; case examples 134–5, 183–4
multiple relationships 44–5, 61, 64; dual relationships 44, 251a, 259a
multirater feedback 115–16
multisystemic interventions 142, 160–1, 170

NASP (National Association of School Psychologists): career-long supervision 200, 209, 218; CPD 201; early years 5, 207; effective supervision 9, 47; endorsements 228–9; ethical standards 33, 34, 76, 201; Graduate Education Workgroup 47; LGBT issues 153; mentoring 202; peer consultation 194; practice domains 4, 104, 117, 138, 181, 232; requirements 9, **11**; supervision training 8, 221, 230; survey (2010) 205; *see also* Practice Model (NASP); *individual publications*
NCSP (Nationally Certified School Psychologist) 5, 10, 191, 201, 202